D1084347

THE MUSICAL HUMAN

THE MUSICAL HUMAN

A History of Life on Earth

MICHAEL SPITZER

BLOOMSBURY PUBLISHING
NEW YORK · LONDON · OXFORD · NEW DELHI · SYDNEY

BLOOMSBURY PUBLISHING
Bloomsbury Publishing Inc.
1385 Broadway, New York, NY 10018, USA
29 Earlsfort Terrace, Dublin 2, Ireland

BLOOMSBURY, BLOOMSBURY PUBLISHING, and the Diana logo
are trademarks of Bloomsbury Publishing Plc

First published in 2021 in Great Britain
First published in the United States 2021

Copyright © Michael Spitzer, 2021

All rights reserved. No part of this publication may be reproduced or
transmitted in any form or by any means, electronic or mechanical,
including photocopying, recording, or any information storage or retrieval
system, without prior permission in writing from the publishers.

Bloomsbury Publishing Plc does not have any control over, or responsibility for,
any third-party websites referred to or in this book. All internet addresses given
in this book were correct at the time of going to press. The author and publisher
regret any inconvenience caused if addresses have changed or sites have
ceased to exist, but can accept no responsibility for any such changes.

ISBN: HB: 978-1-63557-624-5; EBOOK: 978-1-63557-625-2

Library of Congress Cataloging-in-Publication Data is available.

2 4 6 8 10 9 7 5 3 1

Typeset by Newgen KnowledgeWorks Pvt. Ltd., Chennai, India
Printed and bound in the U.S.A. by Berryville Graphics Inc., Berryville, Virginia

To find out more about our authors and books visit
www.bloomsbury.com and sign up for our newsletters.

Bloomsbury books may be purchased for business or promotional use.
For information on bulk purchases please contact Macmillan Corporate and
Premium Sales Department at specialmarkets@macmillan.com.

For Karen, Emily and Kiera

My Three Graces

CONTENTS

PART ONE

LIFE

CHAPTER 1
VOYAGER

Imagine that several billion years from now, possibly long after Earth has been consumed by the Sun, aliens open the *Voyager 1* space probe launched forty years ago by NASA and listen to the Golden Record, packed with twenty-seven samples of Earth's music, as well as greetings in fifty-one languages (see **Figure 1.1**).[1] Assuming our aliens could decipher the hieroglyphic operating instructions etched on the metal disc, they could choose from a mind-boggling array of sounds: Bach's *Brandenburg* Concerto No. 2, court gamelan from Java, percussion from Senegal, 'Johnny B. Goode' by Chuck Berry, Beethoven's Fifth Symphony, pan pipes from the Solomon Islands and much more. What might these aliens say? The comedian Steve Martin quipped that an extraterrestrial message had been intercepted and decoded: 'Send more Chuck Berry!'[2] It is rather more likely that we will never know. But the sobering lesson of this thought experiment is that it knocks musical heads together and puts into perspective music's petty territorial squabbles. Viewed from an interstellar distance, Earth may not have a

Figure 1.1 Voyager 1 and the Golden Record

single musical language – just as it is unlikely that there is a single alien language. But we can discern that there very well might be something irreducibly *human* about all the music of the Earth. Imagining human culture from the perspective of a non-human species can be salutary. The philosopher Thomas Nagel did that for our theory of consciousness with a famous essay called 'What is it like to be a bat?'[3] What can aliens tell us about what it is like to be a musical human?

Put Beethoven, Duke Ellington and Nusrat Fateh Ali Khan, the king of Qawwali (see **Figure 1.2**), in a bar, buy them a drink, and ask them where music came from. Their answers would not be as far apart as you might think. It doesn't mean anything if it doesn't swing, says Ellington. 'From the heart, may it go to the heart,' answers Beethoven. According to Khan, 'One must be willing to release one's mind and soul from one's body to achieve ecstasy through music.'[4] They are saying that music is about life, emotion and the spirit. That what pours out of music can't

be pinned down to the notes. That music is essentially human, and that it makes us human.

Music is linked to our origins as a species. So it is irresistible to write a big and bold account, a 'big history'. Such a history would go deeper than the usual story of who wrote what and when (Bach, 1685–1750; wrote the *St Matthew Passion* in 1730). It would be a party to which all are invited: King David with his lyre and the composers of the psalms; Pythagoras; Lucy the australopithecine; singing apes and dancing parrots. It would begin with the cosmic music of the spheres and how simple organisms flinch to sounds. It would take in the protomusical languages of early *Homo sapiens*, and ask what marks them apart from birdsong or the calls of gibbons. It would track the dissemination and parallel development of musics around the planet, and focus on how and why Western music splintered off as a law unto itself, not as an inevitable triumph, but with consequences both good and bad. One consequence, for instance, is that Western music operated within the vehicle of white supremacy.

An evolution of music is an exciting prospect. But it hits one roadblock after another. There is no recorded music before 1877, when Edison invented his phonograph. Musical works exist, at a stretch, no earlier than AD 800. The earliest Greek music notation is 500 BC. Before then, nothing and silence. Music historians can only look with envy at the archaeologists working with relics and fossils. Music doesn't have any fossils, other than the odd bone flute discovered in ancient caves. A description of the evolution of music from physical objects would be *Hamlet* without the Prince, times ten. The rest is silence indeed.

Some Preliminaries

Luckily, the prospect is actually a lot more promising than it seems. But first, let's consider some preliminary limitations. It feels self-evident that there has been music for as long as there have been people, so writing its evolution might seem straightforward. The elephant – or woolly mammoth – in the room is that, for nearly the entirety of its existence, we have no idea what music sounded like. The first ever sound

Figure 1.2 Nusrat Fateh Ali Khan

recording of a piece of music was a scratchy and unidentified twenty-three-second cornet solo, made on a phonograph in 1878 at St Louis in the US.[5] Before then, we have to make do with signs on paper called scores. We like to pretend that we agree how to reproduce these signs into sounds. But the reality is that performance practice is built on a rickety edifice of conventions. The institutions that are Radio 3's *Record Review* or *Building a Library* are founded on the assumptions that no two versions of a work sound alike. Performance practice is always changing. The liberties opera singers took in the early twentieth century, such as *portamento*, make us laugh today (*portamento* is when the singer slides from note to note like a trombone).[6] If you line up recordings of Tchaikovsky's *Pathétique* Symphony from Serge Koussevitzky in 1930 to Sir Simon Rattle today, then they are getting faster.[7] Tchaikovsky is getting faster. The choirs at St John's and King's College in Cambridge pride themselves on having unique sounds, shaped in part by the distinctive acoustics of the two chapels. If you walk across Cambridge from one evensong to another, you will get a different experience, even when the choirs are singing the same pieces.

The situation gets more desperate once you consider how much, or how little, the musical score tells you. Let's begin our timeline in 1786, when Mozart composed a wonderful piano concerto in A major, K. 488. And for the sake of argument, let's pretend that the score handed down to us is a more or less accurate representation of the sounds the audience heard in Vienna during one of the subscription concerts Mozart himself performed during the spring of that year (overlooking the fact that Mozart doubtless would have 'jazzed up' his piano part, like a modern improviser).[8] Now, let's reverse-engineer music history, going back as far as we can. We'll do this by watching the signs of musical scores melt away one by one until there is nothing left.

300 years ago

Robinson Crusoe is published in 1719. Jean-Antoine Watteau paints *The Pleasures of Love* the same year. Bach completes book one of the *Well-Tempered Clavier* in 1722. The score shows us melody, harmony and rhythm. But we don't know how loudly or how fast the music was played. The C-major prelude that begins the set is nowadays performed either softly, piano, or more confidently, forte, at all manner of speeds. The signs of tempo and dynamics have fallen off the map.

500 years ago

Michelangelo begins painting the Sistine Chapel ceiling in 1508. He writes a sequence of sonnets to his lover, Tommaso dei Cavalieri, in 1509. During his sojourn in Ferrara in 1505, the great Flemish composer, Josquin des Prez, writes a mass in honour of its ruler, Duke Ercole d'Este I, his *Missa Hercules dux Ferrariae*. Not only are there no indications of loudness or speed, Josquin doesn't notate legato or staccato expression – how smoothly or sharply notes are to be sung. Expression has fallen off the map.

800 years ago

The first Gothic cathedrals. Cimabue's crucifix, 1287. In 1250, Hildegard of Bingen, abbess of a nunnery at Rupertsberg, theologian, composer, poet and inventor of German botany, writes both the words and the music of her liturgical drama, the *Ordo Virtutum*. These chants have no harmony, no rhythm, no tempo, no dynamics, no expression, just pitches. We don't even know whether the nuns sang these chants solo or together as a group. Nearly everything has fallen off the map.

1,700 years ago

Saint Augustine completes his *Confessions* in AD 400. A champion of music, Augustine writes: 'Do not seek for words, as though you could explain what God delights in. Sing in jubilation.'⁹ We have no idea what music Augustine heard, and need to wait until the ninth century AD for the earliest chant notation. Written as wavy lines above the text, this 'neumatic' notation indicates the contour of a note, not the exact pitch. It is a descendant of the Masoretic accents (*ta'amim*) of Jewish biblical cantillation in the reciting of the Torah. It is really a mnemonic, jogging the memory of readers who would already have known the melody. Pitch, the last parameter left on music's map, is gone. Also dead is the idea of individual authorship. We are used to crediting music to human beings with a name. But this music is an orphan. It is fitting that the idea of the composer goes down with the ship of music.

2,000 years ago

We are not finished yet, for music has a ghostly proto-life. The ancient Greeks devised an elaborate theory of music, and invented types of musical scale we still use today, such as the Dorian, Aeolian and Lydian modes. We can be sure that their world was full of music. Yet very little of this music survives in a notation that can be deciphered. The contrast with the temples, statues and tragic drama of the ancient world is stark. Where is the musical equivalent of the Parthenon? Of Sophocles' *Theban Trilogy*? A poignant counterexample is the great Alexander Mosaic, preserved in the Naples National Archaeological Museum. A copy of an early third-century BC Hellenistic painting, this vital, vivid depiction of the battle between Alexander the Great and Darius gives the lie to the myth that realism in art had to wait until the Italian Renaissance. Painters and poets could represent the human long before that. So why not in music? Or, if the musical human *was* around in ancient times, why has the proof vanished? An ancient world flooded with sculptures, temples, poems and plays would presumably have resounded with music too. But from where we stand today, there is a deafening silence.

Pushing right back, the endgames of recorded human art are the period 4,000 years ago, the time of *The Epic of Gilgamesh*, the earliest known narrative poem, and then a ten-fold leap back of 40,000 years or more to the first cave paintings, such as in the Lubang Jeriji Saléh cave in Borneo (which contains, at time of writing, the oldest known figurative painting we have, a picture of a bull). We have literature, we have painting, but no music. It is relatively easy for a modern reader to identify with the adventures of the 4,000-year-old Sumerian demigod described in *The Epic of Gilgamesh*. Yet we know that the epic was originally sung, and although there is an imaginative reconstruction of the music by Peter Pringle, the Canadian singer-songwriter, who accompanies himself singing in ancient Sumerian on a three-string 'gishgudi' lute, there is no way of evaluating its accuracy.[10] Similarly, it is probable that the ancient caves were sites of music-making because of their acoustic properties. A French archaeologist called Igor Reznikoff proposed that the paintings clustered at points of maximum resonance in the caves. Next to the paintings were discovered shards of bone flutes.[11]

The lack of a material record should not be mistaken for a lack of music; pessimism is unwarranted. We can be almost certain that the ancient world had music. The curvature of caves amplified sound on similar acoustic principles to the vaulted ceilings of churches and cathedrals, which are essentially modern caves for praising a god through music. And while music may not have fossils, it wrapped itself around the bones of ancient technologies and rituals. Most promisingly, half of the musical human lies in us, in the structure of cognition and in the musical practices it supports. We haven't changed that much since, to most intents and purposes, *Homo sapiens* became fully evolved 40,000 years ago, at the same time as recorded art. The idea that evolutionary modernity happened forty millennia ago is bracing; it relegates modern history to footnotes. If we can hear through the surface differences, we can extrapolate a great deal from where we are today.

The Big Idea

The present book moves progressively back in time, reverse-engineering music from the musical human in the early twenty-first century, through the several thousand years of recorded human history, fanning out more speculatively to prehistory and the prehuman music of animals. It is in three parts, counterpointing three timelines a little like Christopher Nolan's film *Dunkirk*, which tells its story simultaneously as a week, a day and a single hour. The first timeline is a human lifespan. I explore the many ways music is interwoven with life from the sounds in the womb to old age. The second timeline is music in world history. The third and broadest timeline is evolutionary.

We expect histories to move from left to right, from past to future, so why have I chosen to do the opposite? We have no choice, given that virtually everything we can know about music's deep history is an extrapolation from the present. This is the first strand of my argument. The second strand is that everything happens three times, in a recurrent act of rejecting music's nature. The musical human's original sin is turning away from animal music. This is re-enacted, aeons of time later, in the peculiar fate of European music, in its turn towards abstraction. And the rejection of nature is performed in the microcosm of a Western lifespan, in the betrayal of our musical birthright in favour of passive listening. We are all born with the capacity to be active musicians. Very few of us end up actively participating in music-making. Why is that?

The hoary idea that life repeats history, or that 'ontogeny recapitulates phylogeny', according to the nineteenth-century biologist Ernst Haeckel, was once consigned to the dustbin of history.[12] Psychologists of musical emotion have gingerly picked this idea out of the dustbin. For instance, it is now believed that the human embryo acquires emotional sensitivity in the same order as animal evolution. It develops brainstem reflex first, a crude reaction to extreme or rapidly changing acoustic signals. This is something that simple organisms do. The embryo next learns to associate sounds with negative or positive outcomes. Such 'evaluative conditioning' is achieved by reptiles. Mammalian understanding of basic emotions (such as fear, anger or happiness) is acquired by a newborn baby in its first year. Children outstrip other mammals when they learn more sophisticated emotions, such as jealousy or pride, in their pre-school years.[13] These degrees of emotional sensitivity are associated with brain regions: from brainstem (the brain's deepest part, extending from the spinal cord) through the amygdala (located in the basal ganglia, and part of the brain's reward system) to the neocortex (part of the cerebrum's outer layer, and responsible for higher-order brain functions such as thought). It is hard to resist associating the layering of the human brain with archaeology. Freud couldn't:

> Suppose that Rome is not a human habitation but a psychical entity with a similarly long and copious past – an entity, that is to say, in which nothing that has once come into existence will have passed away and all the earlier phases of development continue to exist alongside the latest one.[14]

There is a well-known bit in Haydn's so-called *Surprise* Symphony that makes even knowledgeable listeners flinch every time. The loud orchestral bang, after a patch of murmuring string figures, trips our brainstem reflex. Familiarity doesn't lessen the shock, because the brainstem is stupid (it never learns from experience: it will flinch to Haydn's surprise no matter how many times it hears it). Many levels above that, Haydn crafts a musical surface of exquisite complexity. This speaks to the listener's neocortex, because this is the part of the brain that processes the patterns, expectations and memories of musical syntax. Music, like the human brain itself, embodies its own evolution.

The First Timeline: Life

The musical world is a blooming, buzzing confusion of sounds. The music on your iPhone may carry different harmonies, scales and rhythms from the gamelans of Bali or the chants of the Brazilian rainforest. As the linguist Noam Chomsky taught us, we find universality not on the surface of spoken utterances but in the deep mental structures that generate them – in the rules of the game. It is the same with music. People across the planet may speak different musical languages. However, the musical mind displays surprising consistency. Nearly everyone in the world can follow a rhythmic pattern, clap or dance in time, sing a song (however accurately or inaccurately), remember a melody, and identify an emotion associated with some music they like. One particular capacity is akin to the 'cocktail party' trick of picking out a conversation among a hubbub of voices. The psychologist Albert Bregman called this 'auditory scene analysis', and we do something similar when we discern an ominous noise in the jungle or follow one strand of a musical conversation in a Bach fugue or a jazz ensemble.[15] Although such abilities are second nature to most people, the neurological architecture that makes it possible is massively complex, and well beyond the capacity of animals. For instance, no animal can consciously move in time to a regular beat, with the interesting exception of parrots.[16] Our musicality is related to the sheer size of our brains, but also to our bipedalism. Much of our sense of bodily rhythm stems from the fact that we walk upright on two feet in a regular gait. It is odd that humans associate music with motion, given that tones are invisible and, strictly speaking, don't really 'move' in any space.[17]

The cognitive represents one side of musical universality. Another is the world of musical behaviours. Every aspect of our lives is interwoven with music, and a key element of this is emotion. Consider these three examples. A few years ago, when my daughter was two years old, we took her to a London Symphony Orchestra children's concert at the Barbican. At some point in the programme, the orchestra struck up with Rossini's *William Tell* Overture, which readers of a certain age might associate with the theme tune of *The Lone Ranger*. Within seconds several thousand toddlers instinctively began delightedly bouncing up and down on their parents' knees in time with the orchestra. They had probably never heard the music before, and if they had, I doubt they would have linked it to memories of galloping cowboys. Music psychologists term such intuitive and immediate responses to music 'emotional contagion', as if one 'caught' an emotion , as in an epidemic.[18] The lessons of this episode are manifold. Despite their varying cultural and educational backgrounds, the children responded to the music in the same way, and instantly. Their reaction made clear the connections between music and emotion – an overwhelming joy – and between emotion and *motion* – in this case, a gallop. They never saw Clayton Moore riding Silver in the 1950s TV show. But the children instinctively 'felt' these motions in the music.

The links between motion, emotion and universality are apparent in my second example. When my daughter was a little older and at primary school, she and her friends were caught up in the 'Gangnam Style' dance craze that swept the world. We all know the song and the moves; we've all danced it ourselves. How strange, though, that a Korean pop song broke through all language barriers, to the extent that British schoolchildren even learned the words (my younger daughter now knows the Korean lyrics of songs by the band BTS)? Scholars of K-Pop tell us two interesting things.[19] First, that 'Gangnam Style' spread from the schoolyard up: long before it penetrated the national consciousness, it was being incubated in the playgrounds of primary schools. Second, that the vehicle for this contagion was the dance move itself, which children loved to copy. The physical action was the 'meme', to borrow Richard Dawkins's term for a cultural gene spread through mass imitation.[20]

The third example is my own adult reaction to watching the tragic denouement of Akira Kurosawa's 1985 film *Ran*, a Japanese adaptation of *King Lear*. As the film ends with the blinded fool Tsurumaru feeling his way on a cliff-edge, the score plays a haunting Japanese flute lament. Toru Takemitsu, the contemporary composer who wrote the music, based it on ancient Japanese scales. And yet the pathos contained in the flute lament effortlessly communicates to Western audiences. When I first saw the film, although I had very little exposure to Japanese music, I found the emotions communicated by Takemitsu's score instantly comprehensible and devastating. The psychologist of emotion, Paul Ekman, demonstrated that we are able to recognise the meaning of facial expressions in photographs of people from other cultures.[21] Takemitsu's lament taught me that music was also like that. As with the downturned lines of a sad face, the descending contours and exhaustion of sad music travels across vast cultural distances.

Emotion, a fundamental aspect of musical experience, is an important theme for this book. Charles Darwin taught us that emotion is something we share with animals.[22] It is an inter-species umbilical cord back to Mother Nature. This will emerge at the end of the book when I turn to animal music. But the role of musical emotion will hover over my first chapters, where I consider how music brings together cognition, feeling and behaviour at every stage of a human life.

Before she is born, a baby will have heard sounds *in utero* gurgling through her amniotic fluid.[23] On arrival, the child's musical skills will be surprisingly developed. They will be able to recognise irregularities in beats, discriminate the contour of vocal intonations, and participate in the 'motherese', or infant-directed speech exchanged with their caregiver, their first musical game. Newborn infants are predisposed to learn a vast array of musical materials, and the West's preoccupation with consonance and symmetry (epitomised in nursery tunes such as 'Twinkle, Twinkle Little Star', a melody that spawned Mozart's piano variations, *Ah, vous dirais-je maman*, K. 265) represents a narrowing of possibilities. Had the child been born, say, in Java or Ghana, then they would have been exposed to – and internalised as second nature – complex tuning systems and metrical patterns that sound irregular, or even 'unnatural', to Western ears. This narrowing of scope represents one of the key markers of the musical human in the West. Another marker, perhaps the very signature trait of Western music compared to the rest of the world, is a trajectory from active musical participation to passive listening. Even in the West, childhood is saturated with music-making, from games and nursery songs with mother, to glockenspiel fun at kindergarten, to the delight kids take in the music on children's TV. Most children will have some level of performing experience at school, from singing in a choir to playing in the orchestra or a band. By adulthood, Western people's experience of music is usually entirely passive. The propensity to perform has been taught out of them and an iron curtain has come down. On the one side of this barrier there are the creative composers and musicians. On the other side sits the audience. One symptom of this divide is the idea of creativity as God-given genius, rather than as a universal birthright, like language acquisition. The contrast with the rest of the world is stark. In the 1960s and 1970s, the British anthropologist John Blacking wrote a series of ground-breaking books on the Venda people of the Northern Transvaal region of South Africa, including *Venda Children's Songs* and *How Musical is Man?*[24] Blacking showed that, for the Venda, music-making – or 'musicking' as many scholars now call music as an activity – was communal, participatory and seemingly as natural as breathing. The philosopher Kathleen Higgins's book *The Music Between Us* has claimed Blacking's participatory vision as an ideal for Western music too.[25] But this sounds like special pleading, given how far the Western apple seems to have fallen from the tree.

The gap between listening and doing widens in adult musical life. Our passive consumption of music in the West goes beyond sitting and listening (alone or in a concert), although that is the model for how we attend to music. In practice, music soundtracks nearly every walk of life, from driving our car, to cooking an evening meal, to shopping in the aisles of a supermarket, to pounding a treadmill in the gym. There is music in lifts, in airports, on television, in films and accompanying video games, and, thanks to earbud culture, literally everywhere we walk or sit. Music can regulate mood (cheer us up or calm us down), influence shopping decisions (should I buy a German or a French bottle of wine?), and reflect or express actions in a movie (here comes the shark!). Music has attained a climax of ubiquity, thanks to the easy and limitless availability of seemingly everything on digital streaming media such as Spotify. *Everything now*, to quote the title of the Canadian indie band Arcade Fire's most recent album. Why have we become so dependent on ubiquitous music, while being at the same time almost completely disengaged from actually *making* it?

Things aren't quite so bleak, however. Popping through the looking glass to the other side of this barrier, we find that there is life *within* the music itself. A beneficiary of the West's disengagement from performance is that music itself has become more performative. Music has a magical capacity to imitate our gestures, intonations and emotions.[26] Its expressivity is obvious in a vast spectrum of styles, genres and historical periods: the string instruments seemingly 'talking' to each other in a Haydn string quartet, as do the jazz musicians in Miles Davis's *Kind of Blue*; the orchestra in Stravinsky's *The Rite of Spring* appearing to 'murder' its sacrificial victim; the sexual energy in 'Great Balls of Fire' leaping out of Jerry Lee Lewis's manic piano playing. How does music do that? The anthropologist Michael Taussig has revived Darwin's idea that mimesis – the capacity of art to imitate human nature – is due to the primal human gift of mimicking or miming.[27] Is Western music's hyper-developed mimesis a compensation for its abstraction?

Mimesis informs the many social practices with which music is involved, practices that I will later show are common worldwide. As we shall see, nearly every culture, at every epoch, has versions of these musical activities, and this opens a door into a global music history. Darwin saw the origin of music in animal courtship rituals, where singing prowess could be as attractive to a possible mate as colourful plumage. We now think there is much more to music's evolutionary origin than that. But love, desire and sex are certainly well represented in romantic lieder, opera and popular music. And the dynamics of yearning and climax are also wired into our musical language, when a chromatic chord strives to resolve to a fulfilling consonant harmony.

Music also fights. It can energise soldiers or sportsmen, or be weaponised as noise to extract a Central American drug baron from his lair or teenagers from a shopping mall. It can embody aggression in music, from Verdi's 'Dies Irae', to the posturing MCs in hip-hop, to rival football anthems in a stadium. We use music to party. What happens, I ask, when you move your body to dance music; how does dance bring people's bodies together? When you listen to music without moving, as in a concert hall or your armchair at home, does your brain 'dance'? We use music to worship, and to fill up the God-shaped gaps in our secular world with a sense of the numinous. Going to a concert, or indeed a rave, is an act of collective spiritual contemplation. The anthropologist Judith Becker's notions of musical 'trancing' and 'deep listening' help build useful bridges with world music.[28] I ask whether the musical 'genius' is really divine, and wonder why only the West has this concept. We use music for travelling. I'll reflect on how the spread of music gives us news from elsewhere; and how we use music to map our places and spaces. Piped world music, such as we might imbibe with our cup of coffee at Starbucks, affords an instant ear-shot of cultural tourism.

The Second Timeline: Music in World History

A Western child's gradual shift from musical participation to passive listening is emblematic of what happened to Western music as a whole as it broke away from music's continental shelf. How does one show this, in the light of all the challenges I have identified? How can one even imagine a world history of music? We can begin by ruling out the obvious, which is to piggyback simply on established frameworks, such as John Roberts's *History of the World*, or indeed his later *The Triumph of the West*.[29] Some timelines are compelling, such as the idea that, in the first centuries AD, the world was dominated by two empires, the Roman and the Chinese, and that the Roman empire fractured into religious warfare while the Chinese more or less held together. Such a perspective picks out something essential about the perplexing variety of European music, while the arresting feature of the Chinese musical tradition is its continuity. Yet what breaks the back of this framework is that the vast majority of world music was never written down because its musical cultures were oral, not literate. Africa, traditionally the cradle of civilisation, epitomises that. Take the case of the fourteenth-century empire of Mali, sub-Saharan Africa's most formidable kingdom. It is refreshing to be reminded that there was more to ancient African culture than Egypt; and that there is life beyond the usual story of music's development from Egypt and Mesopotamia through to Greece, Rome and Western Europe. Under the rule of Mali's colourful King Mansa Musa, allegedly the richest man in history, Timbuktu became the cultural centre of the medieval world. The 60,000 people Mansa took with him on his pilgrimage to Mecca included many musicians, who sang and played while they marched.[30] Sitting on his throne, next to the court executioner, Mansa liked to surround himself with trumpeters and drummers. None of this music survives, although some of ancient Mali's instruments, such as the lute-like kora and the djembe drum can still be heard on the streets of Mali today. The situation in highly literate China is not much better. One of the most famous figures of the Tang Dynasty (618–907), the golden age of Chinese civilisation, was the poet, painter and musician Wang Wei (701–761).[31] Much of Wang Wei's poetry is anthologised, and some, in translation, was set by Gustav Mahler in his orchestral song cycle, *Das Lied von der Erde*. Yet of Wang Wei's music itself we have nothing.

There is also the broader question of what 'history' actually is. History as 'one damn thing after another', in the historian Arnold Toynbee's choice phrase, stubs its evolutionary toe against the proposition that nothing has *really* changed since human modernity was achieved 40,000 years ago. Within the rolling chronicle of kings, empires and wars, this hyperbole can be enjoyed with a very large dose of salt. The dose is smaller in the relatively hermetic world of music, especially when the means of production – to borrow a Marxist perspective – does not appear to have changed very much over the millennia, as is the case, for instance, with the many hunter-gatherer societies across the world. The American ethnomusicologist Anthony Seeger, relative of the folk singer Pete, wrote his book *Why Suyá Sing* based on his fieldwork with the Kisedje Indians of the Mato Grosso, Brazil.[32] One of his encounters with the Kisedje opened up a wonderful crack of insight into how they conceive of time. Answering their curiosity about his own musical culture, Seeger played them some songs on an old tape machine. The Kisedje told him that the music sounded very old, and Seeger realised that this was because the machine was playing too slowly, so that the pitches were unusually low. The Indians associated low pitch with the sound of their ancestors, and they heard Seeger's tape as the voice of something ancient. Moving north, an encounter between the ethnomusicologist David Samuels and a San Carlos Apache musician illuminates Native American attitudes to history.[33] During a band rehearsal, the musician explained to Samuels the Apache concept of *bee nagodit'ah*:

[H]e told me he liked it when I turned the fuzz box on in the middle of the guitar solo. He said it added something to it. He called it 'bee nagodit'ah', 'inagodit'ah'. I asked him what that meant, and he said it means 'something being put on top of something else'.

Native Americans view history not like a linear succession of events but as a simultaneous layering of past, present and future. The Navajo word for 'the tribes' past' is *atk'idaa*, which means 'on top of each other'. This does suggest ways of remembering the past beyond linear written records. For instance, the songs of the First Nations record genealogies, events, tribal migrations, even travel pathways through dangerous landscapes such as glaciers. Not only are these sung 'histories' non-linear and circular (stressing renewal through adaptation rather than change), they also mix up tenses of past, present and future, primal myth leaking into the memory of individuals while also sliding into prophecy. Their way of doing history makes our fixation with dry succession look a bit mundane; instead, they are more interested in the layering of attitudes and emotional relationships. It certainly tells us that non-Western culture is not 'timeless' in the stereotypical sense that used to be fashionable in academic circles, where historians charted the West, and anthropologists studied the rest.[34]

One way of resolving this quarrel between history and anthropology is to look at the ways music can perform history. The 'songlines' of contemporary Australian Aboriginal people, in which they record clan histories and mythologies, suggest how this might have been done in the ancient past long before writing.[35] There is a gathering scholarly fashion to extrapolate modern African American music back to Mother Africa, as in the songs of the griots of Mali and Senegal.[36] A griot is a kind of troubadour, a strolling poet, who tells the history of their ethnic group or nation in song. Again, there is no reason to disbelieve that a griot plying his trade in contemporary Mali, on principles not dissimilar to a Detroit rap artist, would be so different from one of those musicians accompanying King Mansa Musa on his pilgrimage in 1324.

By contrast to the walking music historians of the Australian Northern Territory, Mali or North America, another window into music in world history is peoples' own origin myths, the stories cultures themselves tell about where music comes from. Although each culture has its own musical origin myth, one aspect is very common. It is extraordinary how much of the world imagines that music emanates from the resonance of the cosmos, that musical harmony comes out of *universal harmony*, the music of the spheres. One of the earliest such myths is inscribed on a set of Bronze Age chime-bells discovered in China in 1978. The so-called 'Marquis Yi of Zeng' bells, dated around 400 BC, are engraved with a system of music notation. This is one of the first examples of a music theory that hears in the harmoniousness of music an echo of the harmoniousness of the universe as well as a model for good government, a way of thinking that stamps Chinese thought for thousands of years. This philosophy was put into the eloquent words of the *Yue Ji*, dating from the same period:

> Music has its being in the harmony between Heaven and Earth. Ceremonies have their being in the hierarchical gradations between Heaven and Earth. Music-making starts from Heaven, and the ceremonies are fixed by means of the Earth.[37]

Fast-forward to the English mystic Robert Fludd, in his 1617 treatise *Utriusque Cosmi* (*The Origin and Structure of the Cosmos*), or to the astronomer Johannes Kepler's 1619 *Harmonices Mundi* (*The Harmony of the World*), and nothing much has changed.[38] A cutting-edge example of universal harmony is the Quantum Music Project being conducted even now by a group of scientists and music theorists based in Oxford and the Serbian Academy of Sciences and Arts in Belgrade, led by Dr Ivana Medic.[39] The group investigates musical properties in the basic principles of quantum physics. There is something daunting and rather humbling in the thought that there was music long before humans came along, and in the certainty that there will be music long after we have disappeared.

All the same, something in world history does move. There is a timeline. Sometimes we know more about the musical history of other cultures than in the West. For instance, the collapse of the Han Dynasty in AD 220 instigated a comparable period of change and instability in music.[40] The arrival of Buddhism in China made melodies more flowing (or 'melismatic', meaning several notes would be sung per syllable), whereas earlier Chinese tunes were as monosyllabic as its words. By comparison, music history of the European 'Dark Ages' is much murkier.[41] The problem for a 'timeline' model of history is that the river of time has many bends. A dramatic example is the staggered arrival of the Bronze Age since, obviously, cultures discovered bronze at different times. While the Bronze Age was established through most of the world 4,000 years ago, it reached the islands of Java and Bali somewhat belatedly around A D 500.⁴² This was the bronze that was fashioned into the gongs of Bali's and Java's fabulous gamelan ensembles. This little vignette reminds us that world history is shaped by geography as well as climate, and so seldom marches in single file. The physical materials of music history become available to various parts of the world at different times.

World history, then, is not straightforwardly 'linear', progressing episode by episode like a story told by a narrator. If one reason for that is geography, another is because enduring musical practices may cut across the timeline. For instance, a rock painting in Tassili n'Ajjer, part of the Sahara desert, dated 6000 B C, depicts five women and three men dancing together. The anthropologist Gerhard Kubik thinks that it prefigures a contemporary Zulu stamping dance called *indlamu*.⁴³ It is as if time has stood still for 8,000 years. Yet another reason why history doesn't 'progress' in a line is that musical practices associated with so-called 'primitive' social and cultural conditions are still alive in corners of the world today. See for example the music of contemporary hunter-gatherer societies, such as the Inuit and African Pygmies. It is precisely the survival of such music that opens a door to the past, however. The archaeologist Iain Morley extrapolates from Eskimos, Pygmies and other hunter-gatherers to imagine what prehistoric music might have sounded like. In short: if music is shaped by cultural conditions, and if these conditions are similar to prehistoric conditions, then we really do have an insight into music 40,000 years ago.⁴⁴

As a taster of that, let's consider how music might have reflected the three stages of human civilisation: hunting and gathering, farming and town life.

The story begins with nature and the musical human's relationship primarily with animals. This is the case in contemporary Papua New Guinea, where communion with animals or animal spirits is the basis of music for the Kaluli tribe.⁴⁵ They are obsessed with the songs of the *muni* bird, which they hear as the weeping of their ancestral spirits.

The invention of farming and agriculture heralds both a cyclical and longer-term conception of time, and a grounding of music in a sense of space. As well as adopting repetitive, cyclical rhythmic patterns, music can now draw a line between culture and nature. In the music of the

African Nyau, masked figures representing animals emerge from the forest to take over the village and then retreat.[46]

The coming of towns is sporadic across world civilisation. In the Fertile Crescent, the advent of early town life is reflected in the music of the Bible. One striking consequence of the shift into towns and cities is that music needed to become louder so as to carry across larger groups of listeners. The Caananite lute would have had to have been played more virtuosically and in a more dance-like way than earlier lutes so as to be audible within a busy urban community.[47] We can speculate that the shepherd boy David would have played his lyre (or 'harp') more gently before he ascended the throne, or perhaps played a different instrument altogether. The psalms contain no less than 117 superscriptions about how their music is to be played, although Hebrew scholars can't agree how to decipher them. For instance, some scholars interpret the superscription *mizmôr* as meaning 'song'; others, that the psalm is to be accompanied by plucked-string instruments.[48]

Music reflected evolving social and then courtly relationships in many ways. Scholars have mapped the distribution of kingship systems in Africa according to the texture of their songs.[49] Thus tribes organised loosely around a strong king tend to sing by alternating snatches of melody between a leader and a chorus, and with multiple rhythms at the same time – 'polyrhythms'. It is as if the leader symbolises the king, the chorus, his people. The structure of music tends to reflect the structure of society in many of the world's musical cultures – Chinese, Balinese, Indian and the courts of medieval and Renaissance Europe. The stratified polyphony resounding in Queen Elizabeth's Chapel Royal in Hampton Court, perhaps a motet by Thomas Tallis or William Byrd, is a sonic symbol of a feudal hierarchy, with the God-Queen sitting on top. The soaring boy trebles are airy analogues of those cherubs painted on the ceiling.

While historical epochs do march on, if not in single file, some do so more slowly, or not at all. This takes us back to the beguiling problem of cultural universals. Though universalising has fallen out of fashion in anthropology, there is a case to be made that how we use music today in the West has lots in common with the rest of the world, and that it probably hasn't changed very much historically. One striking example of a cross-cultural universal is the lullaby. In a study ranging from the rainforests of Gabon to rural Vietnam, the psychologists Sandra Trehub and Laurel Trainor found clear similarities between lullabies and play songs. Across the world, lullabies tend to be gentle, fairly slow and highly repetitive, with descending melodies, rocking rhythm and a lot of onomatopoeia ('hush!'). Play songs are more animated because they are meant to amuse the child. It is also striking how many lullabies contain an element of threat, as if to make the safety of the cradle all the more comforting. In a standard lullaby, Japanese mothers terrify their infant with scary night birds: 'Owls, owls, big owls and little/ Staring, glaring, eyeing each other.'[50] In the West, terrified babies dream of breaking boughs and falling cradles. Similar analogies abound across the spectrum of music. Among the Inuit of Canada, an aggrieved man has the right to challenge his opponent to a contest in which they sing taunts and gibes at each other.[51] Song contests go back to the duelling shepherds in Virgil's pastoral *Eclogues*.[52] And the film *8-Mile*, in which the rapper Eminem battles rival MCs in the clubs of Detroit, vividly shows how song contests are also the basis of hip-hop. In a classic study, the great anthropologist Alan Merriam lists a plethora of songs used by the Tutsi of Rwanda:

> Songs for boasting purposes, for war and greeting, songs sung when young married women meet together and reminisce about absent friends, children's songs, songs to flatter a girl, and many more [including] boasting songs called *ibirirmbo*, in which two men sing in competition with each other, alternating musical phrases; they may vie either in praising one cow or in singing of the merits of one cow against another.[53]

Clearly, what is sauce for the cow is sauce for the gander, and the many other musics of social life: hunting, healing, war, lament, love, worship and so on. The concept that knits all these practices together is ritual, a name for a repeated pattern of activity we invest with meaning. Going to hear a classical music concert in Carnegie Hall is as much a quasi-religious ritual (sit quietly, attend reverently, applaud the leader, applaud the conductor, do not clap between movements...) as the ancient Sumerian 'sacred marriage' ceremony for the Babylonian fertility goddess, Inanna, which was performed annually for 2,000 years.[54] The West worships Beethoven as a god; behold Him scowling imperiously like Jupiter on his throne in Max Klinger's statue (see **Figure 1.3**). It

Figure 1.3 Max Klinger's *Beethoven* depicted as a Greek god

could even be argued that listening to your favourite piece on your
headphones, lovingly traversing the music's journey from start to finish,
is a kind of mental ritual, not so distant from praying or meditating.
What is so interesting about the ritual we call 'Beethoven's *Eroica*
Symphony' (No. 3 in E-flat major) is that it bundles together a lot of
mini-rituals: hunting, fighting, grieving, playing, celebrating. The hero
of the *Eroica* is a French horn, the European instrument of hunting.
The hero fights a battle against the orchestra, mourns his losses and
returns in triumph.[55] Each time and culture renders these rituals in
its own particular musical language. Beethoven's reference was the
Napoleonic wars, and his soundscape was an empire of notes. Two
things set Beethoven's symphonic ritual apart. First, the encyclopaedic
multiplicity: across the world, all these particular musical rituals
(hunting, mourning, etc.) are normally conducted separately, not
thrown together within a single work, ruled by Beethoven's empire of
the mind. Beethoven once said, after his love affair with the Corsican
general was over, that if he knew as much about fighting as he did
about musical composition, he would teach the French military a
thing or two.[56] The second difference is the rituals' abstraction from
context: there is no real hunting or fighting going on in this symphony,

not even any words or actions. Just tones floating in space. Something has changed.

What *really* exercises anthropologists and historians alike is the question of why rituals change.[57] What are the drivers of historical change? When change does leave its mark on history, it is often recorded as an encounter between one musical culture and another. These encounters can be as benign as migration or trade, or happen through warfare, colonialism and religious conversion. Bronze arrived in Java on the back of Hinduism. The reason why so much choral music in modern Africa sounds like Anglican hymn tunes couldn't be more straightforward: African music was colonised by British missionaries. The Ghanaian ethnomusicologist Kofi Agawu goes so far as to call Western tonality 'a colonising force'.[58] In pre-modern times, nearly all accounts of African music come from Muslim writers in the train of the 'Arabisation' of North Africa. Most of these reports, starting around AD 700 and culminating in the books of the first significant African historian, Ibn Khaldun (1332–1406), are appallingly racist. At his mildest, Ibn Khaldun wrote that Africans 'are found eager to dance … due to expansion and diffusion of the animal spirits'.[59] Islam also has a powerful role in the music of the Indian subcontinent, where Hindu–Muslim conflicts inflect an otherwise relatively stable and continuous tradition based on the Vedic hymns of the Sanskrit *Rigveda*.[60] Of all the world's musical cultures, India's is the closest to Western models of a linear history. The 253 ragas mentioned in the *Sangita-Ratnakara* bespeak the flowering and proliferation of an ancient tradition – a central historical stream – to encompass great diversity. The historical shift from *marga* (divine ritual music) to *desi* (secular, provincial) traditions also parallels the evolution in Western Europe from Latin Church music to more popular or folk-like vernacular styles after the Middle Ages.[61] The key difference is the Indian guru system. While India enjoyed methods of written notation and music theory every bit as sophisticated as those in the West, this wasn't the main conduit of transmitting music from one generation to the next. Music in India was handed down in an oral tradition from master to pupil in an unbroken chain.

So why is change in European music so different? Over and above the fact that Christianity was often – but not always – on the aggressive end of colonial encounters (Buddhism, Islam and Hinduism did their work too), we can throw back a number of red herrings. The first misconception is that Western music was more abstract. There is plenty of highly speculative and rarefied music in China, India and the Middle East. The equal-tempered tuning system, the basis of J. S. Bach's revolutionary *Well-Tempered Clavier*, was discovered more than a century before the Germans by Chu Tsai-yu, a prince of the Ming Dynasty, in 1584.[62] The treasure-house of ancient Greek music theory (including the ideas of Pythagoras, Aristoxenes and Aristotle) passed into the safe custody of Islamic thinkers in the Middle Ages.[63] Nor is Western music distinguished by its distanced, reflective attitude. What the anthropologist Judith Becker calls 'deep listening' is assumed also in the Indian concept of *rasa*, which literally means the 'juice' or 'taste' of an emotion.[64] Immersed in the music, the listener distils its emotion to its essence, transcending the feelings of everyday life. Indian music's transcendental quality attracted the attentions of Romantics such as Schopenhauer and Wagner. Indeed, a raga performed by a classical Carnatic singer – or, from the devotional Sufi tradition, by Nusrat Fateh Ali Khan – can soar as ecstatically as *Tristan und Isolde*.[65]

The classical explanation for the 'triumph' of Western music begins with the bureaucracy of the militant Church and the reforms of Pope Gregory VII in the eleventh century, the man who roped Christendom in a network of Gregorian chants. It then segues in the late Middle Ages to the febrile energies of the rising merchant classes on the path, after the Renaissance, to liberal democracy, climaxing with the heroic idealism of a Beethoven.[66] Guillaume de Machaut's 1365 *Messe de Notre Dame*, the first musical mass setting in history, is a useful touchstone.[67] His mass is as embedded in time, place and function as any music in Africa, India or China. Its sounds can also be savoured as objects in themselves, abstracted from these contexts. However, it is not this abstraction or distancing that is so unusual; we have encountered that elsewhere. Rather, it is Machaut's creatively destructive attitude to layers of history inscribed within a written musical language. He could do that because the norm in Western music was to write music down and disseminate it far beyond a face-to-face, oral encounter between master and pupil. The French musicologist Jacques Chailley has touched upon Western music's paradoxical fusion of continuity and destruction in a notorious 1961 book called *40,000 Years of Music*.[68] The joke was that Chailley got through the first 39,000 years in two pages. Nevertheless, Chailley's lasting insight is that Western music is at heart a violent culture in which every style kills the one before.

Although the fruits of the Western musical tradition are glorious, it is not hard to see in this cycle of destruction a reflection of the peculiarly critical cast of Western thought in general. This critical outlook really took off in the early seventeenth century with scientists and philosophers such as Galileo and Descartes. Experimental science proceeds by falsifying earlier theories. Cartesian philosophy defers not to ancient authorities such as Aristotle or Aquinas but to the operations of the mind alone ('I think, therefore I am'). However, this way of looking at the world probably originates with the ancient Greek philosophers' notion of the human as a spiritual and rational being separate from nature. By this light, the destiny of the human would be to climb ever higher out of nature's swamp, and to progressively control, if not to suppress, natural impulses such as emotion. Accordingly, the dignity and freedom of human reason inheres, in the final analysis, in its distinction from animal instinct. And by exactly the same argument, the identity of the musical human lay in its separation from the music of the animals.

The Third Timeline: The Evolution of Music

Now imagine that those aliens listening to the Golden Record on *Voyager* were octopods, like those gigantic hyper-sentient beings in the film *Arrival*. The film is more highbrow than most sci-fi cinema; *Arrival*'s heroine was a linguist struggling to penetrate an intergalactic language barrier, and Villeneuve, the director, brought in a real linguistics professor, Jessica Coon from McGill University, to advise. She could easily have been a musicologist attempting to decode the creatures' *musical* language. The fog-horn-like deep bass drones in Jóhann Jóhannsson's haunting soundtrack evoke what the aliens' music might sound like, but this remains a suggestion. Marine biologists at the Taiwan National University of Science discovered that cephalopods, including octopuses and squids, have a hearing range of between 400Hz and 2,000Hz, and hear best at 600Hz (D5), which is about an octave above middle C on a piano keyboard.[69] The human range is vastly superior, 20Hz–20,000Hz, somewhat broader than the piano's eighty-eight keys. So what the aliens would be capable of hearing on the Golden Record might be very restricted by our terms. Bach's *Brandenburg* Concerto No. 2 would sound as muffled as if it were being played underwater (this is why swimming pools don't bother with the gimmick of underwater speakers). In space no one can hear you perform.

But that is just the acoustic side of the musical species barrier. Octopuses use sound to locate prey, avoid predators and communicate with each other, so the boundaries between music and language, and between music and acoustic signal – sheer sound – are much more blurred than in what humans think of as 'music'. This goes for most of the animal kingdom on Earth. We take for granted many of the other ways that human music is adapted to our species-specific bodies and minds. Musical rhythm grew from our experience of walking on two feet, as already mentioned. When the primal ape stood up to walk, it triggered an evolutionary process through which the vocal tract gradually expanded, allowing us to speak and sing. A creature swimming with eight legs would have none of these experiences. Moreover, two thirds of an octopus's neurons are distributed across its tentacles rather than being concentrated, as with humans, in a central brain.[70] Our central processing informs our mind–body dualism and sense of balance, which in turn radiates through our conception of musical structure. The cognitive linguists George Lakoff and Mark Johnson have argued that human embodiment pervades our understanding of both language and concepts.[71] Music theorists have extended Lakoff and Johnson's idea to music.[72] Human music really is intrinsically human.

The last part of the book reviews what we know about the evolution of human music from animal communication and that of our hominin ancestors. What are the similarities and differences between animal and human music? Aspects of human music, such as melody, rhythm, synchronisation and turn-taking, were present 8 million years ago in the vocalisations of the African great apes, with which we share our lineage with modern-day gorillas, bonobos and chimpanzees.[73] These same aspects were inherited from the apes by our first human ancestors 6 million years ago. The alarm calls of vervet monkeys specify different predators, a little like words in language. Baboons seem to chatter. Male and female gibbons 'sing' duets together before and after mating. And yet these similarities with human language or music are deceptive. There are several differences:

- Ape and monkey vocalisations are holistic: unlike a sentence or a musical scale, they can't be broken down into building blocks, such as words or discrete pitches.
- Unlike language or music, they are not hierarchic, in that they don't reveal levels of complexity.
- They are not combinatorial: apes aren't able to build new calls out of pre-existent units, and have a limited repertoire.
- Finally, the calls, barks or hoots of an animal are manipulative or transactional signals designed to make something happen (for example, alerting another animal by pointing to a threat). They don't display the key human ability of 'thinking at a distance' from immediate proximity, a basic kind of abstraction.

By contrast, a hallmark of both human speech and musical composition is the ability to combine units into a limitless variety of new sentences or pieces. All musical 'languages' in human history are hierarchic and combinatorial.[74] And even if they originate in specific contexts, they can be repeated and ritualised – thus abstracted from those contexts.

This seems to draw a sharp line between animals and humans. In part, human music evolved by starkly rejecting animal music, a symbolic equivalent of our killing of animals and indeed the suspected genocide of parallel hominin species such as Neanderthals at the hand of *Homo sapiens*.[75] This book's theme of 'killing musical nature' thus threads its way from our own passive listening through the rise of European music to our deepest evolutionary past.

But there is another side to this story, represented by animal emotion. In his studies of gelada monkey vocalisation, Bruce Richman discovered that the monkeys used different kinds of calls to resolve emotional conflicts.[76] One call, a 'long series' of fast sounds in a steady rhythm and melody, expressed friendly approach and positive emotion. Another call, a 'tight series' of higher frequencies, was used to express anger and aggression. The problem, then, that gelada calls aren't really a language is more than compensated by the fact that we can identify with the emotions they express. They bear out Darwin's idea that there is an evolutionary continuity in the *emotions* between animals and humans. It is not the music that binds us and them, it is the common emotions. It is possible that our music shares a similar repertoire of basic emotions with animals from 8 million years ago. To strip away the surface of a Mahler symphony, to peel the young (in evolutionary terms) neocortex to expose the amygdala, the seat of the primal emotions, is to sing with the Neanderthals and the ancient African apes.[77]

The superstar in the hominin pantheon, and the mother of us all, is Lucy, the australopithecine discovered in Africa in 1974, and dated about 3.2 million years ago.[78] Lucy stood one metre tall, like a chimpanzee, had a brain size one third that of a modern human, was bipedal, yet probably spent half her time in trees. Her call repertoire would not have been dissimilar to that of apes. Lucy and her descendants on the long evolutionary march towards *Homo sapiens* indicate the adaptive links between habitat, brain size and social complexity. For the more recent *Homo ergaster* 1.5 million years ago, hunting out on the open savannah where he would have been much more exposed, there would have been safety in numbers. This would have led to more complex social interactions with others in the group, and we can assume that his repertoire of calls would have expanded, along with his brain size. Most importantly, he walked upright on two feet. For *Homo ergaster*, as well as later hominins such as *Homo habilis* and *Homo rudolfensis*, bipedalism would have had many musical consequences. The larynx dropped in the throat and became less rigid, further increasing the range of possible sounds. Rhythmic walking or running enhanced the hominin's sense of time-keeping, coordinating actions and group activities. Bipedalism freed the hands to make tools and perhaps bang together primitive musical instruments. But it also meant mothers would not always have been able to carry their child, and there is a theory that lullabies evolved as a surrogate for touching the baby – reassuring the set-down infant through the mother's voice. Mastery of movement, in the independence of the torso from arms and legs, would also have enabled dancing. The archaeologist Steven Mithen has proposed that rhythm had even more valuable effects.[79] The possibility of synchronised music-making (clapping, singing or dancing together) enhanced group cohesion by enabling the tribe to share the same emotional state. Emotional attunement through music would have strengthened the early human's 'theory of mind', an intuition of another person's thoughts and feelings.

According to the linguist Alison Wray, 700,000 years ago, in the Middle Pleistocene era, *Homo heidelbergensis* would have spoken or sung a 'protolanguage', a series of holistic, syllable-like utterances.[80] Most evolutionary linguists think that it would have been difficult to disentangle language from music at this period. In other words, there is a view that what later became language and music split apart from a common source.[81] For music to become an idiom of artistic expression also required a certain amount of leisure. Symmetrical stone hand-axes, discovered as early as the Acheulean bifacials (a stone tool with two faces) 1.5 million years ago, evidenced a degree of surplus display, perhaps for sexual selection, or even simply as an object of aesthetic pleasure in itself.[82] Symmetry is beautiful, but the skill to carve it would also have been attractive to a prospective mate.

Mithen, in his influential book *The Singing Neanderthals*, has portrayed the Neanderthals as both an evolutionary dead end and as a lost musical ideal of what human musicality could have been, and might still become.[83] *Homo neanderthalensis* first appeared about 250,000 years ago, and the last ones died out as recently as 30,000 years BC, either from hunger or, more likely, picked off by adaptively stronger *Homo sapiens*. Mithen persuasively speculates that the Neanderthals' musical ability was heightened in compensation for not having evolved a language as *sapiens* did, which he infers from their lack of symbolic artefacts, from their cultural stability (their tools did not evolve), and from their small communities (which required limited communication). Mithen dubs their protolanguage 'Hmmmmm', which is an acronym for 'Holistic, manipulative, multi-modal, musical and mimetic'. The eighteenth-century philosopher Jean-Jacques Rousseau would not have known about the singing Neanderthals. But perhaps they are the nearest thing to his ideal of the 'noble savage', a mythical just-so story of human origins in a musical paradise.

Our prehistoric timeline ends in Chapter 10, 100,000 to 40,000 years ago, with what Gary Tomlinson has provocatively called musical 'modernity'.[84] For *Homo sapiens* in the Upper Pleistocene, our 'modern' musician, the following pieces of the musical jigsaw fell into place: discrete pitches; a dual-system hierarchy of melodic contours and individual notes; a combinatorial system to arrange the building blocks into new music; wider diversity and greater precision; tighter control and more specific meanings. These are all aspects that music shares with symbolic systems and languages. The irony is that to achieve all this, music needed to diverge from language, something the Neanderthals never managed. How can we infer that? From the archaeology of bones and tools we can deduce the co-evolution of musical sophistication with cognitive and social complexity. Also, at a critical point, culture feeds back into human evolution to apply selective pressure. Culture is what transmits non-genetic information across generations via archival group memories. We have encountered distant descendants of Pleistocene musical memory in the walking song-historians of the African griots, Australian Aboriginal people and Native Americans.

All this refutes the cognitive scientist Steven Pinker's egregious put-down of music as 'auditory cheesecake' with no evolutionary significance.[85] The truth could not be further away. The Cambridge music scholar Ian Cross has contended that the very 'semantic indeterminacy' of music, what he terms music's 'floating intentionality' or flexibility of meaning, has been invaluable for hominins in their negotiation of social situations of uncertainty or ambiguity.[86] Far from being a derivative luxury, what the philosopher Daniel Dennett calls a 'spandrel', music always conferred evolutionary advantage.[87] But the long view does reveal a stark truth about the nature of music across the aeons, and a certain darkness. This darkness continues to shadow music's most brilliant achievements. Musical modernity seems to have drawn a line under nature twice over, epitomised in two epochal steps: the step from animal communication to hominin protolanguage; and the dead end of Neanderthal 'Hmmmmm' song. Our consolation is that the relative abstraction of music can be viewed from two angles. From one side, music mirrored the abstract 'thinking at a distance' (from immediate proximity) of mind and symbolic language. From another side, however, music has always continued to harbour the emotional immediacy and holistic, gestural nature of animal cries and early protolanguage. Musical emotion is our 'species memory'. The fact that even contemporary music carries along with it such prehistoric baggage says something incredibly central about how we experience music, the value it brings to our lives and to our civilisations. This book will argue that, as far as we can infer from performances, recordings, historical records and archaeological relics, this has always been the case for music across the world. It may be particularly true for Western music, for good or ill.

Postscript: The Musical Posthuman?

Writing this book in the Holocene, between two Ice Ages, it is difficult for me to avoid the many grounds for pessimism about music's future. Music's fate is most precarious in the West, where it came of age incredibly late in geological terms, long after the other arts, and has already slipped back behind them again. Everyone reads new novels, art galleries are thriving, yet concert halls struggle to find audiences even for the music of composers long dead. Music is certainly ubiquitous, thanks to digital media, but cheap and without human value for that very reason. In Beethoven's day, you would be lucky to hear a symphony twice in your lifetime, and would have cherished it all the more because of that. Music can now be composed by computers using algorithms, and its outputs can pass a 'Turing Test' for stylistic authenticity.[88] If it sounds like new Vivaldi, who needs a composer? This pessimism can be flipped on its head. Some would say that music's interaction with technology, through electro-acoustic composition, ubiquitous computing, distributed cognition and the general 'gamification' of sound, actually brings back the performative element of music.[89] I lamented that the fate of music across the world, and especially in the West, was a decay from participation into passive listening. Perhaps posthuman music has the potential for being more democratic, inclusive and dynamic.[90] After all, wasn't the piano, like all musical instruments that extend a body's physical capacities, a species of technology? A violin is as much a human prosthesis as the vocal Auto-Tune (a kind of audio processor software), which has become a fixture of pop singing. So, what is it to be for music: apocalypse or brave new world? The answer partly depends on whether you read this book forwards or backwards. A positive outcome is perhaps also implicit in the Navajo model of history as layered, a way of thinking that I believe grasps the essential time of music. We cannot all be Navajo, of course. But Navajo culture happens to foreground the peculiar experience of listening to music, *any* music, which is that you can dive at will through the sea of time. This book follows, then, where music wants to go. Into the past.

CHAPTER 2
CRADLE AND ALL

There is no question that learning to sing or to play a musical instrument changes the structure of your brain. If you enjoy music but have no special training, then your brain processes it mostly through its right hemisphere, the side of the brain that deals with language.[1] In the face of music, you are 'right-lateralised'. Many studies show that musical training shifts the brain's processing of music to its left hemisphere. Musicians are left-brained. There are several conjectures as to why this happens. One explanation is that they have learned to hear music more like language, discerning a level of structural complexity beyond the grasp of lay listeners. When trained musicians hear music, it activates the part of the brain associated with language comprehension called Wernicke's area (the planum temporale, a posterior part of the auditory cortex situated in the temporal lobe).

There are many other ways that practising music changes the brain. For example, one study found that professional musicians had more grey matter in the motor, auditory and visual-spatial brain regions than amateurs, and that amateurs had more than non-musicians.² From an early age, musicians learn complex motor and auditory skills, so it makes sense, given the neuroplasticity of the human brain, that it adapts.

I could go on, citing a mountain of evidence that, in effect, the musical human is biologically different from humans at large.³ But that would take this chapter in the wrong direction, for it is arguable that the musical human is born, not made. I am far more interested in what I consider to be people's universal predisposition to music than in their elite accomplishments. Or rather, given that the benefits of musical training are literally a 'no-brainer', I am much more concerned with the cultural factors that shape – and often stunt – it across the world, and across the life cycle. The crucial question is this: if the music instinct is innate, why is it so often not allowed to blossom? We can take nothing for granted, not least what we even mean by the word 'music' itself.

In Africa, where the musical human was born, there is a common assumption (explored later) that *everyone is musical*. And yet the puzzle is that hardly any indigenous group in Africa has a word for what the West calls 'music'.⁴ The Vai of Liberia have words for 'dance' (*tombo*), 'song' (*don*) and 'instrumental performance' (*sen fen*), but no all-encompassing concept of music as organised sound. For the Tswana of Botswana, singing and dancing mean the same thing (*gobina*), and the Dan in Côte d'Ivoire, while lacking a single term for music, name a variety of songs, such as dance song (*ta*), praise song (*zlöö*), and funeral laments (*gbo*). By comparison, no indigenous African language has managed without a word for song, dance or, indeed, language. Africans don't tend to separate sound from song and dance, from words and movement. The absence of a word for 'music' resonates with the Namibian philosophy of *ngoma*, which describes the interconnectedness of the arts in sub-Saharan Africa.⁵ Another aspect of *ngoma* is the inseparability of composing, performing and listening, three other activities that have split apart in the West.

Africa is the cradle of the musical human, and I shall speculate on its infancy in Chapters 5 and 10. For now, Africa can stand for the musical world outside the West. Most of Asia and South America share the African belief that musicality is a birthright. Just as importantly, their arts are similarly interconnected. Against this baseline of common and richly (not narrowly) defined musicality, the career of the Western musician, from the cradle to the retirement home, can be construed as a kind of fall. Assuming that musical human nature is the same across the world – and I shall interrogate that assumption – then the Western child falls, and fails, at two hurdles. Every child is a born performer, but most lapse into a state of artistic passivity. Every child is creative, but falls, at the second hurdle, into a misconception that only some are talented. How much of this is due to the complexities of modern urban life simply getting in the way? One study found that 90 per cent of amateur musicians in modern Germany, the home of European music, had interrupted their musical activities between the ages of twenty and sixty because of family and career.[6] Even if the modern teenager is more likely to be messing around with laptops than guitars, the forty-year hiatus in musical life is arresting.

This chapter shines a light on the arc of our musical lives from gestation and infancy through puberty, maturity and death, from amateurs to professionals. There are beguiling questions along the way, all pointing to the immense variety of music. What does bouncing a baby on your knee have to do with polygamy? Or drunkenly circling an Oxford quad anti-clockwise at midnight with an African dance? Why did the West invent teenagers, and to which devil did Beethoven sell his soul? Was Mozart *that* different from you and me, and who was the Carnatic Mozart? Lastly, I shall wonder whether the Western cult of genius is at bottom a disability culture.

It's a shame, because the story begins so promisingly. Then down comes baby, cradle and all.

Beginnings

This is how it starts. The cochlea curls into its snail-like spiral in the sixth week of gestation.[7] Two weeks later it sprouts auditory receptors, the corti. In the eighth week, the foetus acquires ossicles, those small bones in the middle ear. By week eleven, it grows a tympanic membrane with auditory cells, but the apparatus only starts to work in the twentieth week. At this point, a loud noise above 100 decibels will startle the embryo, and make its legs kick and its heart race. By week thirty-six, ear and brain are fully interconnected (via afferent and efferent nerve fibres), and the human ear is finished. On the cusp of birth, the baby can discriminate a recording of her mother's voice from the real thing. The recording agitates her. After birth, that voice will captivate her. Play the child the sound of a heart beating seventy-two times a minute and she will be soothed, sleep more soundly and gain weight faster.[8]

Scientists have spent a lot of time measuring what the infant listener can do. She can perceive a regular beat from her first day, and will move rhythmically to music, but *not in time with music* until she is four years old.[9] Synchronising to a beat is what nearly all animals can't do. Humans can, but it is interesting that we only acquire this ability slowly. Aged two to five months, babies can tell two rhythms apart; and when they reach seven to nine months, they can recognise the rhythmic pattern even when it is played faster or in a different key. Young children are more sensitive than adults to very high pitch, and to tiny changes in pitch. On the other hand, ask any three-year-old to sing a melody back to you, and they are likely to remember the broad up-down contour, not the exact notes. This propensity stays the same between five months and five years. As for hearing harmonic relationships within keys, that only settles when they are seven years old, an age when, in many ways, a person becomes musically mature.

Why is melodic contour so important for infants, rather than exact pitch? It is because the idea of contour – the up-down arc of intensity – crosses over boundaries between music, language, motion and emotion. Meaning for pre-verbal children is cross-modal because all these elements are blended together seamlessly. The connection between music and movement is especially important, and is due to the vestibular system within our inner ear, which is responsible for our sense of balance.[10] Physical motion drives our musical careers, from motor control of our vocal cords and being bounced or rocked by a parent, to learning to manipulate the keys of a piano, and swaying or beating time. The neural link of auditory and motor systems is almost unique to humans; it is present only in some (but not all) songbirds, and cetaceans such as whales and dolphins.

Contour is important because that is how we first conversed with our parents in so-called 'proto-conversations'. When our mother or caregiver talked to us, intuitively employing the exaggerated contours, slow tempo and drawn-out vowels psychologists call 'motherese' or infant-directed speech, we heard it as music, except that 'music' was yet to crystallise out from that mélange of sound, language, motion and emotion. The emotional bond between mother and child plays out as an intricate duet of mutual gazing and imitation, as each mirrors the other's smiles and vocal intonations.[11] The child psychologist Daniel Stern calls this bond 'affect attunement', because mother and child are tuning into each other's emotions.[12] Long after music and language have parted and gone their separate ways, synchronised affect attunement remains a model for how jazz musicians improvise with each other. In proto-conversations, be they in a jazz café or on a mother's knee, distinctions between composing, performing and listening are meaningless.

So the beginnings of music are not in the mother's voice by itself. Music is born from the intricate micro-drama she enacts with her infant. Music is intrinsically relational; in the philosopher Kathleen Higgins's phrase, it is 'the music between us'.[13] A good mother (or parent or caregiver) is a child's first music teacher. Long before the first words come at one or two years, the contours of motherese guide the infant's cooing towards melody and gradually broaden her repertoire of sounds, while her rhythmic repetitions draw her into games of anticipation, playful surprise and turn-taking – aspects that are absolutely central to music. Mother-infant duets can't be notated as conventional musical scores. But the Australian psychotherapist Stephen Malloch, one of the leading experts on motherese, has transcribed them using acoustic spectrograms. A particularly delightful example follows a mother singing 'di dum di dum di dum' to a four-month-old baby girl:

> In the third verse, the baby consistently vocalizes on the last beat
> of each bar, and provides the up-beat to the beginning of the verse,
> which the mother omits. This is very different to what the baby did
> during the second verse. It appears that the baby is changing her
> musical style from verse to verse. In the third bar of the third verse,
> the baby makes what can be described as a 'musical joke'. After
> vocalizing precisely on the last beat of bars 1 and 2 of verse 3, the
> baby still provides this beat in bar 3, but enters a semiquaver early
> [...] Whether or not this is a deliberate act on the part of the infant,
> that this 'early' vocalisation is sensed and appreciated by the mother
> is suggested by the mother's laughter immediately following.[14]

Utilising music for the social dynamics of humour bespeaks a complex intelligence. How fanciful is Malloch's little narrative? Is all of opera, all of the witty conversation of a Haydn string quartet, really already in place in the cooing of a four-month-old child? It is perhaps too good to be true; Malloch's notion of synchronised 'communicative musicality' doesn't square with the bulk of evidence that children can't follow a beat till the age of four. The lesson, perhaps, is that we almost *will* ourselves to believe it, such is the attraction of the ideals of natural musicality and the child genius – myths that, of course, pull in opposite directions.

How universal are these beginnings? While common sense suggests that musical behaviour diverges once culture takes hold, it is actually difficult to say. The problem is that the vast majority of scientific studies are based on Western children. Even if studies were extended to the rest of the world, it would be hard to screen out the influence of Western music – both inside and outside the womb – because it has colonised the planet. But it is not all mist and shadows: initial findings are highly suggestive, if tentative and sporadic. A study of immigrant Indian mothers living in France found that their vocal interactions with their infants kept poorer time compared with Indian mothers living in India.[15] There is wide evidence that children prefer the rhythm they are bounced to.[16] Bounce your child in groups of two beats, and they will smile more at music in 2/4 time; if you bounce them in groups of three, they will prefer a ternary waltz. Because young children's brains are more pliant than adults', they can learn to switch or adapt more quickly and easily. But over the years, a cultural preference for the local rhythms becomes ingrained, so children get used to the musical metre of their home culture. Thus Turkish children prefer complex and (to Western ears) highly irregular Balkan dance rhythms.[17]

There are also many beguiling studies on the links between local rhythms and infant-carrying practices, that is, whether mothers carry their babies on their backs or hips while they move, work or dance, as happens in much of the world; or whether babies are kept apart from their mothers in boxes and cradles, as they tend to be in the West. One study found that cultures in which babies were carried, either in the mother's arms or in a sling or shawl, had more complex rhythms: polyrhythm (the simultaneous performance of several regular patterns) is most highly developed in West and Central Africa, perhaps because those areas have the highest incidence of polygamy. Thus co-wives 'frequently cooperate in the care of children, and infants are typically carried at different times by the various wives, each of whom would presumably have a distinctive tempo and rhythm of movement'.[18] The effect of carrying practices is well known among the African-American community. Here is the New Orleans trombonist, Craig Klein:

> Uncle Lionel [Batiste], who was the bass drummer in the Treme brass band, explained to me one time why it was that we have such fantastic second-line dancers and drummers in New Orleans. 'In the black community,' he said, 'we put our babies on our knees and bounce them up and down to the rhythm of the music. More than that, the mothers are dancin' with the babies in their bellies.' So the kids feel the rhythm from their earliest experiences. It's different in that way between black families and white families. For black families the music is just more a part of the culture. My parents didn't put me on their laps and do that.[19]

A similar story can be told about why Western listeners come to like simple, consonant intervals and chords. Experiments on Western children show that infants aged four months look at a person playing consonant sounds for longer than at one playing dissonances, and are more still.[20] A preference for consonances gets locked in at age nine, while non-Western children develop a taste for (to our ears) irregular tunings and greater dissonance.[21] A centrepiece of Western harmony is octave equivalence, as when children and adult men sing the same melody an octave apart (that is, singing eight notes up the scale brings you back to the same note, but an octave higher). Playing an octave slightly out of tune creates acoustic interference beats that sound hideous to Western ears, but quite palatable to people in Bali.[22] In Bulgaria, it is common for choruses to sing in parallel minor seconds (a semitone apart): one culture's noise is another culture's spice.

Children across the world are born into a diversity of musical languages. Like gravity, the laws of physical acoustics are the same wherever you go. What is distinctive in the West is its partiality for the most simple acoustic ratios: the octave resonates twice as fast as the tonic; the ratio of the fifth is 3:2; the fourth is 4:3; the major third is 5:4. This propensity can sound literally simple-minded, even childish, to most of the world, just as the West's obsession with symmetrical rhythmic and formal patterns (from four-bar phrases in classical music to 'four-to-the-floor' grooves in rock) seems hopelessly square. Of course, Western music more than compensates for these shortcomings. Simple acoustic ratios are the scaffolding for harmonic cathedrals. Square rhythms are never performed mechanically, because a sensitive performer will shape the tempo expressively.

What, then, might we have in common? The neuroscientist Aniruddh Patel has noticed two similarities across world music.[23] First, musical scales – from Austria to India, from Turkey to New Guinea – tend to number between five and seven notes, although they are divided up differently. Why five to seven? There is a universal cognitive threshold for 'chunking' (a psychological term for grouping) categories in units of not less than five and not more than seven.[24] Seven is a particularly comfortable set. We have the seven seas; the seven colours; the seven dwarves; the seven notes of the scale. The second thing we have in common is asymmetry. The distance between notes of the scale is almost always irregular. In the West, when we do have a totally regular scale – such as the whole-tone scale, or a chain of major thirds (the octave divides symmetrically into three thirds) – it can sound mysterious or spooky. That is the sound of Paul Dukas's *Sorcerer's Apprentice*, whose motto is a symmetrical chain of thirds. Patel suggests that we use asymmetry to orient ourselves in the world. Think how disorientating it would be to move around a perfectly circular room with all the windows exactly the same distance apart: it would be as confusing as a perfectly circular scale.

Complexities

The thread between child and adult is cut when language comes along and elbows music into its niche. Yet sometimes this thread continues, as when a child *fails* to acquire language, and instead uses music as a proxy for communication. This was the case with the remarkable Romy Smith, a girl born with severe learning difficulties who was taken under the wing of the equally remarkable Professor Adam Ockelford, a foremost authority on music and autism, and Romy's piano teacher. Despite being developmentally delayed, never learning to speak, and displaying many of the characteristics of autism, the eleven-year-old Romy was exceptionally musical, had perfect pitch and used melodic fragments from the 100 pieces of music she had learned to interact emotionally with other musicians and, indeed, to control these interactions. Ockelford helps shatter the myth that children on the autism spectrum can't read or express emotions. Romy enjoys teasing Adam by playing her 'Music has Finished' motif as a joke, not really intending her music lesson to be over at all, or by playing the opening notes of one melody and veering off into another (such as the Irish song 'Cockles and Mussels', or the Christmas carol 'Away in a Manger', tunes which begin with the same motif).[25] Ockelford points out that such humour requires a sophisticated 'theory of mind': for Romy to make him believe the opposite of what she was thinking meant she had to put herself in his shoes; to imagine another person's consciousness. This is to pick up Malloch's thread several years down the line. For Ockelford, 'music provided Romy with a medium with which to explore the dynamics of social interaction in the absence of language'.[26]

Neuroscientists such as Patel have taught us that, while the brain regions responsible for music and language interact in complex ways, damage to one does not necessarily lead to a deficit in the other.[27] Pamela Heaton, another leading autism expert, has clarified that 'deficits' do not generalise from the social to the musical: that is, a child may have difficulty reading people's faces, but have no trouble identifying whether a musical theme is happy or sad. Nor is this facility affected by intellectual impairment.[28] Like most people, children on the autism spectrum can read musical emotions by the age of six, and achieve mastery when they are eight.

Children with complex needs train a powerful searchlight on the core of the musical human. What emerges from such studies, loud, clear and majestic, is the spectacular power of music. This is why Ockelford eloquently rejects the 'deficit model' that governs our top-down systems of education, by which we measure children's attainment by what they *can't* do. The once-standard term 'deficit' has begun to jar because it is so negative, and because it presupposes an idealised state of physical or cognitive 'normality'. Far more humane, surely, is to begin with what children *can* do. Ockelford's *Sounds of Intent* programme – whose website has had 9 million visits worldwide – is a practical framework for evaluating a child's growing musicality in six rising steps.[29] Young people with the profoundest learning difficulties can be at the six-month prenatal stage of just becoming aware of sound. Ockelford's later stages align with how all children develop. The key word is *pattern*. At stage 4, children can make up their own songs by cobbling together bits of other tunes, using them as raw material to improvise. At stage 6, when the brain is fully acculturated to musical patterns, children learn to perform in time and in tune, and with emotional meaning. Many people assume that musical creation happens *ex nihilo*, from nothing. But all composition begins with pattern. This is extremely important for what happens next.

Waiting patiently and ineluctably for us at the end of this road is Mozart. When we ask what bridges the gap between the normal and the talented, between the average and the genius, we might imagine a spark flashing across that gap between the fingers of Adam and God in Michelangelo's fresco. There is no more corrosive and misunderstood concept in Western music than 'genius', a notion that doesn't feature much in the rest of the world. I don't need to rehearse all the miracles of the boy Mozart, recounted by generations of awestruck historians. One example will do, recorded by the English naturalist Daines Barrington during Mozart's trip to London aged eight in 1764. Attesting to the boy's 'thorough knowledge of the fundamental principles of composition', Barrington examined Mozart's ability to sight-read a complex musical manuscript: 'The score was no sooner put upon his desk than he began to play the symphony in a most masterly manner.' Impressed, Barrington then tasks Mozart to improvise a 'Love Song' in an operatic manner: '[He] began five of six lines of a jargon recitative proper to introduce a love song.' Barrington then tells Mozart to improvise a 'Song of Rage': '[He] beat his harpsichord like a person possessed, rising sometimes in his chair.'[30]

Now, I yield to no one in my worship at Mozart's altar. But I need to footnote the Myth of Mozart with a list of caveats:

1. Eight is the normal age to achieve musical maturity.
2. Mozart lived with a personal guru, his father, also a composer. Research indicates that musical success comes from supportive parents and teachers, self-motivation and sheer hard work rather than pure 'talent'. Actually, in a self-reinforcing feedback loop, success may happen by manufacturing a perception that a child *is* talented.[31]
3. Mozart's facility lay in playing with clichés and patterns absorbed from other people's music. This was entirely normal at the time. Italian conservatoires and foundling hospitals churned out hundreds

of child keyboard-composers drilled to their fingertips in the conventions of the classical style. It was the basic training of all composers.[32]

4. His mature masterpieces are no less reliant on conventional patterns strung together. The American musicologist Robert Gjerdingen compares these 'schemata' to the stereotypes of fairy tales ('Once upon a time'; 'There was once a poor miller'; 'Just outside the forest there dwelled a poor woodcutter'), or, more strikingly, the figures strung together by a skilled ice-skater: glides, spins, jumps, salchows, axels, lutzes and camels. Mozart's best-known piano sonata, K. 545 in C major, almost synonymous with the sound of a toy piano, is a chain of *musical* figures: an 'Opening Gambit', such as a 'Romanesca', could be followed by a 'Prinner', an 'Indugio', a 'Ponte', another 'Prinner', and so on. Mozart could easily have improvised this chain of clichés, and probably did, extremely quickly.[33]

5. The crux of Barrington's tale is that Mozart could also imitate *emotional* patterns; the conventional musical expressions of love, rage and other dramatic types. He was a mimic. There is no indication that he understood these adult operatic emotions, or even felt them. It was enough that he knew which musical patterns evoked them.

This final caveat is perhaps the most telling, given the still-raging debate in autism research on the recognition of emotion. Did Mozart have Asperger syndrome?[34] Remarking on another of his students, the exceptionally gifted composer-pianist Derek Paravicini, a blind autistic savant, Ockelford makes a striking observation. Even if the twelve-year-old Paravicini didn't appreciate the emotions he was improvising, the music itself taught him to understand emotion as he grew older.[35] Before he was eighteen, Mozart had composed nothing with the emotional depth of Mendelssohn's Octet or *Midsummer Night's Dream* Overture, written when he was sixteen (although in his twenties, with a critical mass of experience, Mozart's emotions go nuclear). Mendelssohn, not Mozart, wins the prize for history's greatest, and best-adjusted music prodigy. The adult Mendelssohn keeps alive the mercurial emotional plasticity of children's music; how infants' feelings flow like quicksilver. Pieces like his Violin Concerto, completed in 1844 three years before Mendelssohn died, are evidence, should we still require it, that creativity is playfulness. The polymath Peter Pesic calls this 'deep play'.[36]

Against Mozart: The Venda Life

> Most Venda children are competent musicians: they can sing and
> dance to traditional melodies, and many can play at least one
> musical instrument. And yet they have no formal musical training.[37]

Mozart is an icon of the West. An icon of the anti-West is not a person
but a people. This is the Venda, from the Limpopo region of South
Africa. The social anthropologist, John Blacking, conducted fieldwork
with the Venda in the 1950s, which led to a series of landmark books
and a theory of universal musicality.[38] Given how much change has
occurred in South Africa since then, it is remarkable how Blacking's
findings have stood the test of time. So in what ways do the Venda
overturn all our Western assumptions about music? Here is a series
of binary oppositions, and we can imagine them sung as call and
response:

> The West: music is a rare talent, tapering into still rarer genius.
> The Venda: everyone is musical!
> The West: music is enjoyed through passive listening.
> The Venda: it is the norm to participate in music, with no
>   distinction made between performer and audience!
> The West: music is a well-defined, separate artistic activity.
> The Venda: music is inseparable from singing and dancing!
> The West: the goal of a performance is technical and artistic
>   perfection.
> The Venda: the goal is not self-display, but social harmony and
>   well-being!
> The West: music is separate from everyday life.
> The Venda: music is embedded in life!
> The West: music is taught to children by adults, originally the
>   mother.
> The Venda: we children teach music to each other, through
>   hundreds of hours' practice in the *kraal* [homestead] or
>   playground. And our music forms a distinct repertoire, not at all
>   simpler than that of our parents!

It is tempting to add yet another opposition here: Western music is historical, but the Venda's traditions are timeless. While there is evidence that the Venda brought their songs with them when they migrated from the Congo in the sixteenth century, the flux of time and change within 'tradition' is quite sophisticated, as is revealed by the fate of the iconic dance known as the *tshigombela* (see **Figure 2.1**).[39] The *tshigombela* is performed by young girls singing and dancing anticlockwise around a group of drums, with changes in pattern prompted by the lead singer and lead dancer. That the dance is open to anyone does not mean that it doesn't entail and reward skill, because its object is to synchronise as well as possible. When dance troops compete against each other in a competition, the prize goes to the most harmonious performance. The *tshigombela* epitomises the 'integrative' ethos of African culture: the coming together of the performers symbolises, and enacts, the harmony of society at large. Rather than reflecting culture, the music *performs* culture.

Figure 2.1 Venda children dancing the *Tshigombela*

After Blacking noted the *tshigombela* in the 1950s, disapproving Christian missionaries got their hands on it, took it away from the children and gave it to older women. While the *tshigombela* wasn't actually banned by the missionaries, as they did many Venda traditions and cultures, giving it to their mothers and grandmothers reflected a Western prejudice against children's music. That is, the Western dogma that music created by children was somehow inadequate, immature or without a proper identity. And then in the 1970s the political climate changed again and the women returned the *tshigombela* to the children. Rather than teaching their children this music, the mothers gave it back to them as their birthright. The next move in this cultural three-step happened when the teaching of *tshigombela* was formalised in the classroom under the supervision of a national curriculum. The dance was still 'owned' by the children, and practised in the school playground. But the Venda children were now recognised as custodians and ambassadors of a national treasure, bulwarks against the cultural drift towards the cities.

The Marxist historian Eric Hobsbawm famously argued that tradition was invented.[40] When I arrived, aged eighteen, at Merton College, Oxford, I encountered a tradition that once a year on the last Sunday in October, when the clocks go back one hour at 2 a.m. to Greenwich Mean Time, hundreds of scholars, wearing gowns, bow ties and mortarboards, linked arms and rotated backwards around the Fellows' Quadrangle for the full extra hour between 1 a.m. and the new '1 a.m.', sipping port.[41] Directed to the Gods of Greenwich, the Time Ceremony was meant to assure that the clocks did indeed go back and the sun would rise (see **Figure 2.2**). We pretended that the tradition was timeless. But it was invented in 1971 by a student called Barry Press, who annually returns to Merton to monitor the ritual in his role as Keeper of the Watch.

Figure 2.2 The Merton Time Ceremony

Unlike Merton's little anticlockwise dance, it would be more accurate to say that the Venda's *tshigombela* tradition was not invented but *managed*. In some ways, the state and its mothers steered the dance back to where it had started. Filtered through the momentous changes from apartheid to the inclusive ethos of the 'rainbow nation', *tshigombela* came into its own as more unifying than ever before.

The Invention of the Teenager

Pop and rock, modern music's most troublesome offspring, happened because bored teenagers messed about with guitars in their bedrooms. It has been said that 'unemployment brings out the guitar in everyone'.[42] Yet the teenager was invented in the leisure hours and spare cash afforded by the post-1945 economic boom. Teenage rebellion is directed against work; the music sociologist Richard Middleton expresses it formally as 'an antagonism to industrial time-discipline'.[43] Teenagers are also an intensification of the biological fact of the extended immaturity of the human species, the problem being that we are born prematurely, and then children stay longer at school because capitalism requires greater education. This wedge between childhood and maturity is very much a modern invention: no grumpy teenager intervenes in Shakespeare's 'Seven Ages of Man' speech from *As You Like It* between the 'whining schoolboy' and 'the lover, sighing like a furnace'. Technically speaking, Romeo and Juliet are adolescent, but they are not teenagers: they are dutiful towards their parents, and display none of the rebellious angst of the modern specimen.

This is not to discount all the biological changes happening inside the adolescent brain. The neuroscientist Linda Spear discovered that the adolescent amygdala, part of the brain's reward system, was more involved in processing emotions than the amygdala of adults.[44] This is why teenagers are moody. But the question is how all this emotion is managed. Across most of the world, initiation rites cluster around the threshold between child and adult, what the anthropologist Victor Turner calls 'liminality'. Turner's account of the Ndembu circumcision rites may upset Western sensibilities. Young adolescent males were kidnapped from their families, held in the forest for months, starved of food and sleep, psychologically and physically tortured, and finally circumcised by red-stained elders (called the 'killers') in a communal ceremony accompanied by incessant drumming.[45] A much milder initiation ritual is the Kisedje Indians' Ceremony of the Mouse.* Anthony Seeger, whose beautiful book *Why Suyá Sing* is one of the classic texts of ethnomusicology, attended his first Mouse Ceremony from 24 January to 7 February 1972. At puberty, a boy's ears were pierced, and the verbs 'to hear' (*mba*) and 'to behave morally' (*ani mba*) are related, because to behave well was to listen (*mba*) to the speeches of the elders.[46] The boy leaves his mother and sisters to live in the men's house. He joins the men to sing an *akia* 'shouting song' to their sisters in the women's house. As the night air resounds with song, music bridges the spatial distance between men and women across the village and also heals the boy's separation from his family. This is why Kisedje sing.

How the West treats its own apprentice singers is nothing to crow about. Western music is a secret history of their pain. The thirteenth-century adolescent girls forced into Hildegard's nunnery were also coerced to sing the excruciatingly high notes she composed for them. In her writings, Hildegard complains of the fierce resistance she met when attempting to subjugate the will of her unruly nuns.[47] Tucked into Geoffrey Chaucer's *Prioress's Tale* is the grisly Chorister's Lament, sung by a choirboy (a 'clerk') with his throat cut. While the story blames the boy's murder on the Jews, Chaucer presents it as a satire on the violence of medieval choir schools.[48] In the 1720s and 1730s in Europe, it is estimated that 4,000 boys were annually castrated to feed opera's craze for the pure, unbroken voice of the *castrato*. The procedure was sanctioned by the Church, and symbolically connected with Christ's Passion.[49]

The history of musical pain is also the ten thousand hours of practice it takes to turn a novice into a master.[50] It includes the fiendish chiroplast, a kind of straitjacket for the fingers patented by Johann Logier in 1814 in order to strengthen a child's hand, and which crippled Robert Schumann's career as a concert pianist.[51] But doesn't all music need discipline? It depends partly on attitudes to authority: whether it is to be fought or dutifully embraced. The South Indian guru system of *gurukula* offers an instructive contrast, as in the case of renowned *veena* prodigy, Ranganayaki Rajagopalan (the *veena* is a kind of lute). In 1936,

---

* The ceremony is so called (as explained in Chapter 5) because the Kisedje believe that they were taught agriculture in ancient times by a mouse.

she was sent at the tender age of four to live in the household of the great *veena* virtuoso, Karaikudi Sambasiva Iyer. Lessons would begin at 4.30 in the morning, and the friendless and lonely child would be punished for her mistakes with slaps from a bamboo rod. Ranganayaki recalled her experience as 'devil's practice'.[52] Training in the *gurukula* system is a process of handing down a tradition from master to student; by the age of twelve, Ranganayaki was accompanying Iyer in concerts, and by fifteen, she had left the nest to perform solo. Closer to home, we see a similar deference to authority and tradition in the role of the extended family in Irish trad (folk) music, where children learn from older siblings and parents.[53]

And this is where the teenage rebellion of Western rock music so strikingly takes leave of mainstream coming-of-age rituals. In the guru or Irish trad system, a parent (or parent figure) is to be imitated, and tradition is handed down. If the teenage guitarist can only play two chords, however, then so much the better: they wear their lack of proficiency as a badge of authenticity. Most times, the separation stage of liminality at an end, the teenager drifts back to the fold and possibly gainful employment. Sometimes, if the band 'makes it', then the stage of separation is indefinitely arrested, and you may get seventy-year-old teenagers playing Wembley Stadium. They can't get no satisfaction.

Beyond the West, the rest of the world manages rock rebellion in other ways, sometimes less well. 'Youth is always revolutionary; revolution always belongs to youth,' said the Chinese poet and democrat Wen Yiduo (1899–1946).[54] Since the opening up of the Chinese media and entertainment industries in the late 1990s, there has been a complex tension between state control and the inherent rebelliousness of rock music, reflecting China's unique fusion of communism and capitalism. When the Chinese rock band Miserable Faith played at the MIDI Music Festival at Beijing in 2010, the audience was permitted to shout along with its anthemic line, 'Whenever there's oppression, there's resistance'. When the concert was televised, this line was deleted.[55] The real puzzle for Western observers is how contemporary Chinese youth can espouse English-language rock music yet be so nationalistic. One argument is that the one-child policy, which ended in 2016, had tightened the apron strings between parents and offspring, intensifying traditional Confucian respect for one's elders. In urban India, a similarly mitigating role is provided by the continuing vitality of religion. A young Indian driving through Bangalore blasting pop through his car window may have an effigy of Lord Ganesha on his dashboard.[56] On the whole, however, Western pop has been co-opted by the rich, metropolitan youth of India to reject their local traditions, including traditional Indian classical music. While this is quite typical of modernity in the developing world, pop has been particularly disunifying in a nation already bristling with vibrant cultural contrasts.

The Pact

I'm going to spin you a yarn. And then I'm going to rip that yarn to shreds in order to make a point. Bear with me.

The devil comes calling. He offers you fame and riches for the sake of your immortal soul. What do you do? For Georg Solti, a Hungarian Jew who lost friends and family in the Holocaust (just like my dad), the invitation to conduct at Munich in 1946 was irresistible. In Solti's own words: 'Like Faust, I would have been prepared to make a pact with the devil and go to hell with him in order to conduct.'[57] And so he did, one of the greatest yet most controversial conductors of the post-war era, whose nickname, 'the screaming skull', was earned through his aggressive rehearsal tactics. Professor Howard Gardner, a developmental psychologist who has done more than anyone else to uncover the wellsprings of creativity across the arts and sciences, proposed that outstandingly creative individuals buy their success through a 'Faustian bargain'.[58] Through this pact with the devil of artistic mastery, individuals such as Freud, T. S. Eliot, Einstein, Stravinsky and Picasso sacrificed normal human relations, either isolating themselves or becoming combative. In some ways artists choose to become less human, which is a paradox, since their art expresses so much humanity. They buy one by selling the other.

How human is a musician? The question becomes especially pressing when the musical human hits maturity, and it is a fair one. The enormous sacrifices it takes to turn a child into a professional musician inevitably cut a person off from everyday life experiences. Not for nothing are the most interesting composer biographies – say, Wolfgang Hildesheimer's *Mozart* and Maynard Solomon's *Beethoven* – written by card-carrying psychoanalysts rather than by musicologists.[59] Anton

Ehrenzweig, whose *The Hidden Order of Art*[60] is the most sophisticated Freudian interpretation of creativity we have, goes so far as to see artworks, including music, as a form of managed schizophrenia. From this angle, it seems plausible – to pick up the teenage thread again – that the great Western composers were aggressive because they never worked out their combative attitude towards musical authority figures through a natural adolescence. Bach, Haydn, Mozart and Beethoven never enjoyed what Victor Turner would call a liminal, teenage phase. When Beethoven was eleven, he got a job as an assistant organist. When he was fourteen, he joined the Court Chapel. Denied a formal period of teenage parental rebellion, it is possible that he channelled his aggression towards authority figures during his period of maturity. John Eliot Gardiner surmises that the young Johann Sebastian Bach ran with the village toughs and was a bit of a thug himself: an image quite far from the jowly, periwigged stuffed shirt in the official oil paintings, but consistent with his future quarrels with the Leipzig town councillors.[61] Bach riled them by filling the church with secular songs and dances. Back in 1703, when he was eighteen and composing music for a church at Arnstadt, Bach dodged a provocation to fight a duel by an incompetent bassoon player called Geyersbach. Instead of fighting him, Bach sublimated his aggression into music. He embarrassed Geyersbach by composing a cruelly exposed bassoon solo in one of his cantatas, BWV 150, whose technical difficulty was well beyond the musician's abilities.[62] On 25 June 1781, Mozart was dismissed from the service of Archbishop Colloredo of Salzburg by being kicked up the backside by a functionary called Count Arco. Given the feudalism of the Salzburg class system, Mozart could never have returned the gesture in kind.[63] So he avenged himself, like Bach, in the rarefied realm of music, in his case by composing inappropriately operatic masses. See the melody of the 'Agnus Dei' in Mozart's *Coronation Mass*, K. 317, which crops up a few years later as the Countess's aria, 'Dovè sono', in *The Marriage of Figaro*. Even Joseph Haydn, a servant of Prince Esterházy of Hungary for thirty years, and outwardly the very model of an obsequious lackey, was much less conventional than he seems on the surface. In his case, he sublimated social subversion as musical buffoonery. In Haydn's music, all the hallmarks of the classical style are systematically mocked. One of his signature devices is to open a piece with a cadence, a musical full stop that is supposed to come at the end. See his String Quartet

Op. 74 in C major. It begins, absurdly, with a perfect cadence, a grand dominant-to-tonic progression, which scrambles the musical syntax. One can imagine the Viennese audience in 1793 scratching their heads, if not laughing. Was Haydn laughing at *them*?

The story fits Beethoven particularly well because he is such a poster boy for the West's idea of a creative genius. When Beethoven left Bonn in 1792 aged twenty-two, he studied for a while with his own guru, 'Papa' Joseph Haydn, whose nickname for his proud student was 'The Great Mogul' – a beguiling inversion of the Indian teacher–disciple arrangement. Here is the exchange between the young Beethoven, proud of his latest effort, the somewhat lightweight ballet *The Creatures of Prometheus*, and his former teacher, whose oratorio, *The Creation*, was sweeping all of Europe:

> Haydn: 'I heard your ballet yesterday and it pleased me very much!'
> Beethoven: 'O, dear Papa, you are very kind; but it is far from being a *Creation*!'
> Haydn (taken aback by this pun): 'That is true; it is not yet a *Creation* and I can scarcely believe that it will ever be one.'[64]

So what's wrong with this narrative? Obviously, composers often *do* manage to enjoy blamelessly ordinary lives. There is a photograph of Arnold Schoenberg and George Gershwin playing tennis in California; and Schoenberg, that austere bogeyman of European modernism, was often spotted in supermarkets near his Hollywood home shopping for his family's dinner. There are even recordings of Schoenberg reciting fairy tales he wrote for his children's bedtimes.[65] The counter-narrative is the history of women composers, many of whom didn't – or *couldn't* – sacrifice life for art; and most of whom wrote music just as uncompromising as that of their male peers nonetheless. Not many people know that one of the greatest American composers of the twentieth century (thus of *all* centuries so far) was Pete Seeger's stepmother. Ruth Crawford Seeger (1901–53) wrote an extraordinary string quartet in 1931, married the ethnomusicologist Charles Seeger in 1932, then largely gave up composition to bring up their five children and keep home for Charles, before dying of intestinal cancer in 1953.[66] The point is that Seeger's music, before and after her marriage, was the equal of Schoenberg's in dissonance, difficulty and sophistication.

Seeger is not alone in this. There is a creeping realisation that one of the outstanding composers of our time was a forgotten old lady living in poverty in a freezing St Petersburg flat. Shostakovich thought that his pupil Galina Ustvolskaya (1919–2006) was a better composer than him, and I would have to agree. Ustvolskaya didn't write much, but what she did has the weight and killer intensity of a black sun, to borrow an image from her compatriot, the poet Osip Mandelstam. To open the door into Ustvolskaya's cold flat, to listen to, say, her brutal sixth and final piano sonata, is to be pummelled with truth.[67] This is music that defiantly bears witness. Yet Ustvolskaya's fight is not with the world; it is with musical material itself. What do I mean by that?

Here is where the yarn unravels. Howard Gardner's critics complain that the 'Faustian bargain' theory of creativity fits many artists, but not all. It is certainly possible for creative artists to have normal and fulfilled lives. For composers, hell is not other people, as Sartre claimed; it is far worse than that. Their quarrel is with music itself. In particular, music notation – the sharpest tool in the composer's arsenal – is the device that most clearly splits the West from the rest. A shockingly mean-spirited letter by Beethoven, written to his girlfriend Eleanore von Breuning, says it all. At the time, Beethoven earned his bread by improvising music at the piano. The letter, dated 2 November 1793, when Beethoven was twenty-three, pinpoints his decision to have his piano variations on 'Se vuol ballare' (a theme from Mozart's *Figaro*) published; indeed, to stop messing about and begin writing music down:

> I should never have written down this kind of piece, had I not already noticed fairly often how some people in Vienna after hearing me extemporize of an evening would note down on the following day several peculiarities of my style and pass them off with pride as their own. Well, as I foresaw that their pieces would soon be published, I resolved to forestall those people. But there was yet another reason, namely, my desire to embarrass these Viennese pianists, some of whom are my sworn enemies.[68]

The medium of writing changes a composer's entire relationship with sounds. Pinned down on paper like netted butterflies, sounds are distanced from their source and moment of production, and can be considered, planned, edited and honed over a period of hours, months and years. Beethoven moved house seventy times in forty-three years, and each time he lugged his lifetime's hoard of compositional sketches up and down the stairs, sketches he never threw away.[69] They record the slow gestation and perfection of his musical ideas. Notation allows a musical mind to talk to itself, even to struggle against itself. It also enables a composer to fight other composers by deconstructing their musical language. It's one thing physically to assault a person; much easier to trample over a pattern of notes, as simple as signing someone's death sentence in the comfort of an armchair. The abstraction has a distancing effect, and renders violence dispassionate. The history of Western music is a chronicle of war without end, as one composer after another bites the hand that taught him. This idea isn't new: the American critic Harold Bloom's theory of 'the anxiety of influence', based on Freud's Oedipal complex, held that great writers symbolically killed their artistic father figures in order to carve out their personal creative space. The difference is that composers can murder their fathers much more ruthlessly and dispassionately, because notes are more abstract than words.

Beethovenian long-range planning also comes to define Western attitudes to musical mastery: compositions are to be built on a vast scale, with every detail prescribed and non-negotiable (i.e. non-interpretable) by performers. Reciprocally, this music demands masterly feats of attention in its listeners, especially in their appetite for music that may take many hours to understand or even like. We are firmly on the path of musical modernism, leading to Schoenberg, Stockhausen, Crawford Seeger and Ustvolskaya – great composers, to be sure, but geniuses without audiences. Just as composers have lost their listeners, at an individual level the ordinary and innately creative musical human has become alienated from her natural abilities.

The Other Way

In Kazuo Ishiguro's surreal novel *The Unconsoled* a fictional pianist, Ryder, gets lost during a concert tour in an imaginary Central European country. In this parallel universe, the greatest composers of the twentieth century are not Schoenberg, Bartók and Stravinsky, but Grebel, Mullery and Kazan (Ishiguro borrowed these names from World Cup footballers). These counter-factual fakes offer a neat postcolonial twist, defamiliarising our comfortable Western assumptions about tradition. The British Raj encountered a very real 'Holy Trinity' of Carnatic composers, all born at about the same time as Beethoven: Kakarla Tyagaraja (1767–1846), Muthuswami Dikshitar (1775–1835) and Syama Sastri (1762–1827). Of these the most revered is Tyagaraja, both a true master, or *dheera*, and a figure who upends and underlines many of our Western assumptions about musical 'mastery'.

This saintly and ascetic singer-songwriter spent twenty years with his guru, Sonti Venkata Ramanayya, and chose to be buried next to him at his death rather than with his wife. Tyagaraja is said to have written 24,000 *kritis*, devotional songs aimed at a particular Hindu deity, of which the 700 that survive are treasures of Carnatic classical music. The *kriti* 'Sogasuga' captures our imagination because it deals with the actual process of composing. Here are the lyrics, as translated by William Jackson:[70]

> Who is the stalwart able to melt you, arranging an ensemble of elegant drum rhythm, with truthful words full of the gist of the Panisads and with great purity of notes?
>
> Is it possible for Tyagaraja to sing bhajans with kritis full of the nine emotions, smacking with sweetness of grape nectar?
>
> Is he able to make the rhythmic pauses in songs of loving devotion, with rhythms and in line with the lyrical rules?

The poem progresses through the rudiments of the singer's craft – from elegant rhythm to truthful words and pure notes – and then rises to the higher qualities of the nine Hindu emotions, or *rasas* (love, joy, wonder, courage, calmness, anger, sadness, fear and disgust), to climax with the highest virtue of all, *bhakti*, devotion. The melody soars up from its low beginnings completely in tune with this spiritual ascent. One note, the third degree of the raga 'Sriranjani' (the particular mode of this song, which Tyagaraja is believed to have invented), is conspicuously withheld until the climactic peak of 'Sogasuga', and when it finally arrives, it makes the hairs stand on end. And yet Tyagaraja's formal mastery is interwoven with devotional humility: each line of the poem is a question, because he is unsure if the song succeeds in melting the heart of the god Rama, or the hearts of the listeners. This questioning modesty is heard in the ambivalence of the raga 'Sriranjani' itself, which can't decide whether its key-note is the first or fourth degree of the scale.

Uncertainty suffuses every aspect of this music, beginning with its transmission. Tyagaraja composed 'Sogasuga' in his head rather than on a score. As he sang and played, it was recorded on palm leaves by his circle of disciples, or committed to memory via an Indian system of oral mnemonics akin to Western solmisation – a way of remembering each note of a scale by associating it with a one-syllable word. We have our own solmisation songs, as when Julie Andrews teaches 'Do-Re-Mi' to her children (Doe is a female deer, Ray is a sunbeam, Me is a personal pronoun, and so on). Given the precariousness of this thread from master to disciple down the generations, it is a wonder that the hundreds of available recordings of 'Sogasuga' are all recognisable as essentially the same song, although performances can range in length from three minutes to more than fifteen, according to whether the musicians serve the song neat, or with lashings of rich decorations and improvised interludes. There is uncertainty also in the very notes of an Indian song. Listen to a performance of 'Sogasuga' by the most renowned Indian singer of the twentieth century, M. S. Subbulakshmi, Gandhi's favourite. Unlike the fixed and stable notes of a Western piano, a note (*svara*) sung in a Carnatic *kriti* oscillates like a constellation of pitches. Here, the difference between a note and a decoration is a matter of degree. The note is really a vanishing point in an infinite regress of fractal decoration, drawing the listener ever inwards into the secret heartwood of the music. In comparison with that, the fixed Western note is cold, mechanical and abstract.

Such was Tyagaraja's humility that he refused to sing at court for princes. His spiritual withdrawal can look deceptively like a twentieth-century Western composer's detachment from his audience. In reality, because Tyagaraja's audiences shared in his devotional values, the border between composer and listener was much more porous than for Beethoven and his listeners. This rapport is symbolised by the way Carnatic audiences are invited to sway and count to the music (counting alternates between clapping and touching the right-hand little finger on the palm of the left hand). A listener at a Western concert is expected to sit stock still.

The ethnomusicologist Bruno Nettl compares Tyagaraja to Mozart because of his prodigious facility in manipulating musical patterns.[71]

Just like Mozart in the European classical tradition, Tyagaraja was lucky to be born into a pre-existing musical language he could swim through like a fish in water. In Tyagaraja's case, the medium was the framework of ragas standardised by the seventeenth-century theorist-composer Venkatamakhi, who tidied up the bewildering variety of ragas into the seventy-two 'parent' scales called melakarta.[72] Even the greatest composers stand on the shoulders of previous masters. Still, the historical coincidence between Western and South Indian 'classical' styles in the eighteenth century points up all the dramatic contrasts:

1. Tyagaraja deferred to his guru; Beethoven rebelled against his.
2. Tyagaraja's ascetic withdrawal was religious, not egotistical.
3. Tyagaraja relied on listeners writing down his music; Beethoven wanted to stop them from doing so.
4. Although Tyagaraja was particularly skilled, the emphasis lay in the chain of tradition, not on the individual 'genius'.

And yet we have the delicious fact that the literal translation of *kriti* is 'creation'; the two words share the same root (kr) in Sanskrit, the fountainhead of Indo-European languages. Would that the English audiences of Haydn's *Creation* had known that. The common ties of European and South Asian *creativity* may be as deep as their linguistic roots.

The Beethovenian model of individual mastery is not the only one in the West. The collective model of group creativity, which is how most popular music is composed and performed, has loomed larger as audience interest in 'art-music' has waned. My colleague Sara Cohen, a founding member of Liverpool University's Institute of Popular Music (the world's very first), conducted fieldwork embedded in unsigned bands in the 1980s, and discovered that songs arose in two main ways.[73] In the more democratic model, the song crystallised slowly through a group dynamic as the musicians riffed on ideas and bounced them around each other. In the other model, a dominant artist would come along to a rehearsal with an established idea for a song, and would teach it to the other players. The Lennon and McCartney partnership is a fascinating hybrid of these two approaches. Here is Beatles producer George Martin's description of how they created together:

Now, Paul would help John musically, because I think that he had a greater understanding of the theory of music, and harmony and so on, and he would be able to make a thing more well-rounded; John tended to drive the car without a clutch rather, he'd just go from one gear to another. On the other hand again, John would have perhaps more of a mastery of imagery and words and would make Paul work harder at his lyrics.[74]

The magical 'Yesterday' began as 'Scrambled Eggs', until John prodded Paul to change his words.[75] McCartney's starting point was usually the music, Lennon's was the lyrics. Of course, Martin – the 'fifth Beatle', without whom 'Eleanor Rigby' would lack her haunting string quartet accompaniment – helped teach the world that creativity can also inhere in sound engineering and record production; in how music is 'mediatised'.

It may be, despite all our Beethovens and Tyagarajas, that group rather than individual creativity is the norm in world music. It runs the whole gamut from the exquisitely coordinated Balinese gamelan,[76] which performs fully composed traditional works and permits little or no individual expression, to the fully improvised vocal polyphonies of the Bedzan Pygmies of Cameroon, every performance of which is different, so that the concept of a 'work' is unthinkable.[77] Western jazz comes somewhere in the middle. Many people hear jazz as a wordless conversation, just as a conversation is a kind of improvisation. When Charlie Parker plays 'How High the Moon' with the Milt Jackson Quartet at Birdland in 1952, the notes are so evocative of words one could almost reach out and touch them before they disappear in a puff of thought. Echoing Stephen Malloch's transcriptions of mother–baby proto-conversations, Maya Gratier analysed jazz dialogues and came to a similar conclusion as Malloch.[78] The performance she chose was French jazz guitarist Misja Michel and drummer Christophe Lavergne's improvisation around Ornette Coleman's 'Chopin'. Visually (through videos), Gratier saw how Michel and Lavergne locked into each other through mutual gaze and the sharing of smiles, head nods and upper-body movements. Sonically, her spectrograms evidenced how the musicians synchronised by exchanging licks, riffs and beats, anticipated and reacted to each other, and miraculously even seemed to complete each other's thoughts, all on the basis of split-second, moment-to-moment decisions inhabiting an elastic 'wiggle space' between composition and performance.

The sociality of jazz sends us back in time along three orders of magnitude. According to Gratier, it recapitulates the non-verbal 'mutual understanding' of early childhood, the infant's proto-conversations with its caregiver. Much deeper still, it echoes the social roots of music in the synchronous chorusing of hominins in the Miocene period; and – even earlier, according to an evolutionary scenario sketched by Björn Merker – the pulse-based chorusing of insects, frogs and fiddler crabs.[79] This is a startling hypothesis, which rather throws the gauntlet down to Part Three of this book. But we have a long way to go before we descend that far back. First, there is a little matter of personal extinction.

Death

A prominent psychologist, raking through a stack of statistics, discovered that composers' creativity peaks at the age of fifty-six and then declines. Beethoven was lucky because he died ten months before his fifty-seventh birthday.[80] Schubert, dead at thirty-one, not so much. Musicians and music lovers actually have a lot to look forward to in old age. Many people who played or sang when younger go back to active music-making when they retire. Research shows that older people also use music differently to regulate their emotions. When teenagers are in a bad mood, they are more likely to reinforce that mood by listening to sad or angry music. Older people do the opposite, and tend to use music to improve their mood. There are two explanations for why they do that.[81] The good news is that as we age, we get better at controlling (or 'regulating') our feelings, and so experience less anger and anxiety. The bad news is that the positive bias of this late-life 'sunset glow' may be due to cognitive impairment because of the deterioration of the amygdala, the part of the brain's limbic system most closely associated with emotion. Ironically, brain decline is the source of another often-remarked virtue of the twilight years: a broadening of musical taste and a willingness to try different things. My own late father discovered the joys of Stravinsky and other modern composers only in his seventies. Psychologists call this trait 'openness',[82] and it counters the received view that older people are set in their ways. Admittedly, older people do prefer the music they enjoyed in their teens, an age when a lifetime's musical taste is 'imprinted'.[83] On the other hand, openness to the unconventional is actually just as much a feature of old age as nostalgia. Not all older people open up to new music, but many do.

Nevertheless, the overriding reality of old age is, of course, physical and mental decline. It is on this ground that music really comes into its own as a kind of panacea. Music's benefits for health and well-being are incalculable. For people living with dementia, music can trigger memories and even recall a sense of self.[84] Music outlives language, just as babies acquire music before language. When people have lost the faculty of speech, music can be a lifeline. Experiments have found that, for older people, listening to music was superior to audio books in improving or recovering verbal memory and focusing attention.[85] Music reduces loneliness and depression, and enhances physical coordination, while singing can even alleviate the effects of lung disease. This is why it is so important to support initiatives that bring professional musicians into care homes and hospitals, such as the UK charity Live Music Now. The organisation was founded in 1977 by Yehudi Menuhin and the philanthropist Sir Ian Stoutzker to promote their vision of music's power to touch lives.[86] Every year, LMN musicians deliver thousands of interactive music programmes in a range of community and healthcare settings, for older people as well as children with disabilities or special educational needs. Organisations such as Live Music Now enshrine the truth that, across the whole arc of life, music helps.

On the other hand, one mustn't over-sentimentalise the power of music; therapists have moved beyond the old rose-tinted view of music as a blanket good, and are much more discriminating in how they use it. It is important to fit the music to the symptoms. For instance, it now seems obvious that complex music can be distressing for people living with Alzheimer's or dementia because their cognitive impairment makes it harder to process it. The appropriate music needs to be carefully selected for people with depression. Music therapy is particularly effective for people with high levels of apathy. Therapists avoid playing fast music to agitated patients because it makes them more anxious.[87] Most curious is the finding that baroque music in dementia-care units increased the number of observed behavioural disturbances.[88] If and when music is ever officially medicalised and dispensed by doctors as a drug, Bach and Vivaldi might not be suitable for Alzheimer's patients.

These biological symptoms of old age – decline, nostalgia and openness to novelty – also define the fruits of the ageing composer. In other words, physical and mental degeneration can actually have creative outcomes, by analogy, perhaps, to a fermenting cheese or wine. The following are the medical challenges that some ageing great composers had to reckon with: Bach, Handel, Delius and Ockeghem (blindness), Smetana (deafness), Schumann and Ravel (mental illness), Mahler and Schoenberg (heart disease), Debussy (rectal cancer), Stravinsky (stroke), Copland (Alzheimer's), Bartók (leukaemia), Chopin (tuberculosis), Schubert (syphilis), Beethoven (deafness, dropsy and lead poisoning). Given that, to most intents and purposes, the older person can be seen as effectively disabled, it is extraordinary that the West prizes the late style of its ageing artists – the last pastorals of Shakespeare (*The Tempest, A Winter's Tale*); Van Gogh's paintings at Auvers-sur-Oise (*Wheatfield with Crows*); the late sonatas and quartets of Beethoven – as the absolute summit of its civilisation. Late style has even been called 'disability style' – an ironic bookend to my earlier reservations (following Ockelford) about the West's 'deficit' culture.[89] Medicalising genius, putting it on a material footing, makes sense of symptoms that seem to point in opposite directions. What are the symptoms of late style?

It is February 1827, and Beethoven lies on his deathbed. He has a month to live. Friends bring him delicacies such as spiced wine, which he cannot touch. The London Philharmonic Society sends £100. The publisher Diabelli gives Beethoven a lithograph he has just published of the humble cottage in which Haydn was born, in the Moravian village of Rohrah. 'Look, I got this today,' Beethoven is reported to have said. 'Just see the little house, and such a great man was born in it.'[90] Quite a turnaround in Beethoven's feelings towards his old teacher and father figure. All passion spent, this spirit of reconciliation is borne out in Beethoven's forgiveness of chords. He is content to just let chords *be*. In the little 'Arietta' finale of his last piano sonata, Op. 111, craft is stripped away to reveal the building blocks of music, simple tonics and dominants, polished till they gleam with a childlike simplicity. With one eye fixed on death, Beethoven's other eye turned back to the origins of music. The late quartets relax club membership rules so everyone can get in: fugues, variations, scherzos, cavatinas, bagatelles, mighty sonata forms. This freedom might look like chaos to outsiders (Weber thought that Beethoven was 'ripe for the madhouse'),[91] but Beethoven doesn't care. This divine madness is the spiritual flip side of physical and mental decay. The intensity of Beethoven's late style is a heroic standing firm against a battery of ailments. We like to think of our composers as a mixture of golden goose, battery hen and dying swan. Perhaps there is no mystery after all, and late style is simply a side effect of things falling apart.

Is there a late style in popular music? It shone darkly out of *Blackstar*, David Bowie's last studio album, released two days before his death, and whose title artfully half-rhymes with the name of the disease that was killing Bowie when he wrote it. Bob Dylan is still very much with us, but lateness descended on him more than twenty years ago in 'Not Dark Yet', from the 1997 *Time Out of Mind*. The cracks and whispers of Dylan's voice exude the stripped-down resilience of late Samuel Beckett. But Dylan continues to surprise. A spirit of reconciliation breathes through the circus-like variety of his minstrel voices and genres. His last three albums (*Shadow in the Night*, *Fallen Angels* and *Triplicate*) are a history lesson in the Great American Songbook, making peace with Tin Pan Alley and Frank Sinatra. It delivers the shock of the old.

Is there a late style in world music? A clue that there may not be is the perception in India, as with many developing countries, that dementia is a social rather than an individual syndrome; indeed, one that isn't even labelled.[92] In such a societal culture, cognitive impairment is often seen to be a symptom of a breakdown in a person's family support structure or even a lack of love. On the other hand, from the West's perspective, Asia is perceived to be 'late' in the sense, being literally more ancient and mysterious. The crumbling city, for centuries the West's gateway to Asia, has epitomised this poetic idea. See, for example, Thomas Mann's novella, *Death in Venice*, as well as Luchino Visconti's lugubrious film version, for ever associated with Gustav Mahler's haunting Adagietto from his Fifth Symphony. It is revealing, then, that the great Palestinian writer Edward Said made his name with two complementary texts: *Orientalism*, which virtually invented the discipline of postcolonialism; and *On Late Style*.[93] And it is equally telling that discussions of what the West styles as 'the East' are conspicuously absent from the latter book, and this makes perfect sense. Said's political agenda was to defend 'the East' from the West's condescension; thus portraying the ancient civilisations of Egypt, India or China in states of beautiful decay would have played into the West's orientalist fantasies.

Yet these fantasies still sell. So when late style *is* discovered outside the Western mainstream, it is folded into the lateness of an entire culture or a country. In 1996, Ry Cooder travelled to Havana to record an album of *son cubano* (an Afro-Spanish style originating in the highlands of Cuba) with ageing local musicians, and unleashed a perfect storm of cultural nostalgia. With sales of 7 million, *The Buena Vista Social Club* is the most successful world-music album of all time. The reviewer on Sputnikmusic nails it: 'The first thing you notice when you press play is the frailty of the instruments [...] These men have aged like wine.'[94] It's all there in the four-chord riff, or *son* (meaning 'sound' in Spanish), of the opening track, 'Chan Chan', written by the 89-year-old *trova* guitarist Compay Segundo in 1985 when he was 78, and it is the signature sound of the entire album and film. One doesn't listen to these chords so much as smell them; it is as if Cooder has unscrewed the top of a vintage bottle of rum, and released the intoxicating aromas of 1920s Havana, incubated by Cuba's long political isolation. Such music is evocative because of, not despite, the frailties of the ageing voice or instrumental technique. As with the late style of a Bach or a Beethoven, this music of old age is not a decline but a refinement. The proximity of death strips away pretension and concentrates the mind. The difference here is that the lateness of these musicians is inseparable from the life story of their entire culture.

'Here one *must* always feel fine and excellent even if dying,' complained Béla Bartók in 1941, as he languished in his American exile.[95] The Hungarian titan of twentieth-century music had done his bit in the fight against the Fascists, defending Toscanini against Mussolini's goons in 1931.[96] But Bartók fought best for racial harmony on his home turf as a professional artist, bringing together the classical, avant-garde and folk traditions of the world (from North Africa to the Balkans) in a dance of humanity. The finale of his *Concerto for Orchestra*, Bartók's American masterpiece, composed in a fifty-four-day blaze of remission from his leukaemia at a sanatorium in the Adirondack Mountains in 1944, is a head-spinningly exhilarating Transylvanian gypsy dance, a *hora nemtseasca*.[97] One can only imagine, as they listened to the work's premiere with the Boston Symphony Orchestra under Koussevitsky on 1 December, that the well-heeled American audience felt like leaping out of their seats to join the dance.

Running a high temperature, Bartók lay fully clothed on his bed in his cramped Manhattan apartment and dreamed of gypsy fiddlers on village greens. Sketched in no more than fourteen manuscript pages, his unfinished Viola Concerto includes the Scottish folksong 'Comin' Thro' the Rye', a memory of a visit he made to Glasgow in 1933. The melody charmingly sticks out because, as Bartók explained in a lecture delivered at Harvard in 1943, Scottish long-short dotted rhythms (as in 'Should auld acquaintance be forgot...') are 'anti-Hungarian': Hungarian (Magyar) words, like Hungarian melodies, emphasise their first syllable.[98] Although a proud patriot, Bartók had always embraced the diverse folk traditions of the world, both in his ethnographic research and his composition. He would have been horrified by any notion of musical purism, including the tendency of ultra-nationalist governments, then as now, to purge national folksongs of 'foreign' elements.

Bartók's death in September 1945 was marked in *Time* magazine sandwiched between adverts for an Argoflex camera and a 'Sunday Nite Cheff griddle'.[99] Various hands had a go at completing the Viola Concerto; a version by Csaba Erdély received its first performance by the Berlin Philharmonic as recently as October 2017.[100]

The concerto's posthumous births and rebirths underline the fact of Western music notation, and its saving grace. Notation cheats death, steals from the devil his due. No sketches – no music. Western music is in its bones a gesture against death. This is why, compared to the music of the rest of the world, it makes such a meal out of dissonance and pain. To what end? I shall leave that question hanging until the end of Chapter 4, and will spend most of Part Two of this book attempting to answer it.

CHAPTER 3

THE SOUNDTRACK OF OUR LIVES

On the face of it, music has never been more plentiful or accessible. But appearances can deceive and surveys mislead. In 2019, Youth Music, an organisation that invests in music-making projects across England, commissioned a comprehensive review of children's and young people's relationship with music, and the image it captured was extremely encouraging.[1] Music, it found, was young people's favourite hobby, equal to gaming and ahead of sport, drama and dance. In a given week, 97 per cent of people aged seven to seventeen in England had listened to music; 67 per cent had made music; and 30 per cent played an instrument. A staggering 85 per cent said that music made them happy, and 64 per cent of all young people considered themselves musical, up from 48 per cent in 2006. The report seems to buck the pessimism of my previous chapters, particularly in its finding that more than half of young people are actively creating music. We are witnessing, in short, a new blossoming of music. That said, there is more – or less – to the report than meets the eye, as can be gleaned from its map of the respondents' favourite music genres (see **Figure 3.1**).

Among this dizzying diversity (synth pop, grime, jazz, trap, K-Pop…) there is a classical-shaped hole. Is it really the case that young people today don't listen to much classical music? Admittedly classical music has always been a taste acquired through age and experience, as witness the typical 'blue-rinse' demographic in orchestral concerts. On the other hand, perhaps classical music is being punished for all those crimes detailed in Chapters 1–2, for being too abstract, too complex, too expensive; in a word, too *elitist*. If so, then the pessimism of Chapters 1–2 is pinned onto classical music alone, and popular music walks away scot-free. Otherwise put, the musical human is alive and well, and is a popular musician. But one could hardly accept such a one-sided interpretation, not least because it follows the money, and equates good music with popular and financial success. It turns out that Youth Music's report is more nuanced, and much less sanguine, than it first appears. The apparent death of classical music is really only the canary in the mine signalling a bigger casualty: music education as a whole.

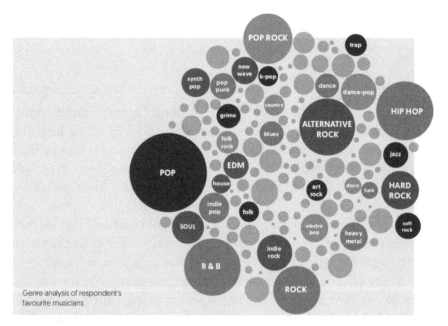

Figure 3.1 Young people's favourite music genres

It is striking that most of the creativity reported by Youth Music happens outside school, as DIY activities such as karaoke, producing beats and bars on a computer (often in bedrooms), song-writing, rapping, DJing, and recording and posting music videos on social media. And much of it has been unleashed by digital technology. For example, the Tik Tok app (aka Musically) allows the user to create short-form (lip-synched) music videos and upload them to Snapchat and Instagram, and has 200 million users worldwide. So musical creativity has blossomed without the interference of elders or teachers, a far cry from the way music was transmitted in the past, both in the West and in the rest of the world. Even half of the minority (30 per cent) of young people who play instruments have learned them from YouTube tutorials rather than from a personal teacher. Significantly, the majority of children who see themselves as musical come from lower-income backgrounds that can't afford music lessons.

It is an interesting question why music has become so misaligned with music education. School teaching is more diverse than ever, and accommodates both Stormzy and Mozart. Yet the curriculum struggles to keep up with the fluidity, ubiquity, immediacy and accessibility of digital technology, as well as with its sheer speed of change. In this brave new world, music notation has yielded to computer coding, instruments to technological interfaces, physical spaces to virtual spaces. But the deeper reason is that teaching music is expensive in time and money, and is thus out of step with the government policy of monetising education. That is, the policy that studying music at school isn't as lucrative as the subjects permitted by the EBacc system (English, maths, science, geography, history and foreign languages). The fact that the music industry annually contributes £4.4 billion to the UK economy doesn't help this argument, because to think in this way is to still consider music in terms of money instead of its countless 'softer' benefits to well-being. For instance, here is Filip, one of the respondents to Youth Music's survey:

I enjoy it because I make lots of friends, it makes me work with them all the time, never leave them, play all the time music, never give up with them, always stay with them.

How can you put a price tag on that? On the other hand, it is easy to see how the life skills afforded to children like Filip by music, abilities to empathise and bond with others and to work in teams, are attractive to future employers.

Without a solid foundation in training, much of the good news reported by Youth Music ends up evaporating as so much froth, with a dramatic drop-off in musical activity as children get older, from 79 per cent (seven- to ten-year-olds) to 53 per cent (sixteen- to seventeen-year-olds). There is no established path to success in the music industry, other than the precarious ones of independent releases, *X Factor* and YouTube. What remains after people have stopped creating is what had always been the majority activity: listening to music, alone (rather than in groups), to recordings (rather than to live performances), and nearly always (76 per cent) when listeners are doing something else, as an accompaniment. In a nutshell, if the UK data is typical, then the most common use of music in the modern West is as a *soundtrack* – a soundtrack to our lives.

One could take a dim view of this state of affairs, as music seems to have become mostly passive. Such a result appears to confirm the idea in Chapters 1–2 that it is the fate of the musical human in the West to lose her innate musicality. But the situation is more nuanced than that. This chapter will test the theory that music can be active while passive, a peculiar trademark of modern life. Young people, as Youth Music concludes, are 'DJs carefully curating the soundtracks to their lives. Just as a composer would write a musical score for a film, young people are using music to convey and reflect their feelings, to change their emotional state, and to regulate their mood.' Importantly, such 'emotional self-regulation' (as psychologists call it) tends to happen in the modern West as we go about our daily lives within cities; and cities are the natural space for a thousand and one activities to which music is an accompaniment. This chapter focuses on the city in which I live, Liverpool, a UNESCO 'world city of music'. We will explore how listening can be a kind of performance, a kind of 'work', both in the soundtracks of our lives, and in the tracks music makes when it follows us around the city.

Whistle While You Work

In some ways it was ever thus. Music was used as an accompaniment to other activities in ancient Greece, according to this report by Aristides Quintilanus written around AD 300:

> There is certainly no action among men that is carried out without music. Sacred hymns and offerings are adorned with music, specific

feasts and the festal assemblies of cities exult in it, wars and marches are both aroused and composed through music. It makes sailing and rowing and the most difficult of the handicrafts not burdensome by providing an encouragement for the work. It has even been employed by some of the barbarians in their funeral rites to break off the extreme of passion by means of melody.[2]

Festivals, religious ceremonies, funerals, wars, marches, sailing, rowing and all varieties of labour are adorned with music to this very day. Perhaps music was always a soundtrack. But there are four big differences between then and now. First, Quintilanus was writing as a leisured aristocrat within a slave society. For the vast majority of common people, music happened at work. The idea of listening to music in itself, apart from other activities, would have been laughed at as an outrageous luxury until society carved out a sphere of leisure. Second, music was by its nature something people made, and its cadences flowed out of the rhythms and emotions of work. It is not an accident that the Latin for 'piece of music', *opus* (as in Beethoven's Fifth Symphony, Opus 67) means 'work', as does, obviously, a musical *work*. If music was a soundtrack, then it was performed by the workers, not heard as something apart from the labour of producing it, as it is by modern audiences. Third, creating and listening to music was a group activity, whereas today it is mostly a solitary one. Finally, most musical work in pre-industrial societies was rural, in the fields or on the water, not in cities.

One of the earliest accounts of whistling while you work is of ploughmen in Elizabethan England in 1586:

How heartily doth the poorest swain both please himself and flatter his beast with whistling and singing. Alas, what pleasure could they take at the whip and ploughtail in so often and unsellant labours.[3]

A retired labourer called Fred Mitchell reminisced about the joy of singing while working the East Anglian fields in the mid-nineteenth century:

There was nothing in my childhood, only work. I never had pleasure … But I have forgotten one thing – the singing. There was such a lot of singing in the villages then and this was my pleasure, too. Boys sang in the fields, and at night we all met at the Forge and sang.[4]

Paramount in both reports is the idea that the joy of music alleviates the misery of work – that musical work is self-medicating. A spooky modern version of that is how the loneliness of social media is alleviated by the music created on social media. Compared to the leisured music of today, however, ancient work songs intermingled work and play. They also incorporated the sounds of work into the fabric of the song, echoes of which can be heard in many folksongs. A spinning song from Shetland begins with the sounds, 'Tim-tim-ta ra-a, tim-tim-ta-ree', evoking the spinning wheel.[5] In classical spinning songs, such as Schubert's 'Gretchen am Spinnrade', the job of imitating the wheel is taken up by spinning piano figurations. The heavy pulling work on a ship demanded by sea shanties can be heard in the stressed (italicised) syllables: 'Oh, it's hand-y high and a-way we'll go, *Hand-y*, me boys, so *hand-y*!'[6] A shanty calls on concentrated bursts of highly coordinated activity as the sailors heave a sail or an anchor. When we listen to 'Blow the Man Down', the most famous shanty, we practically mime along with the work rhythms. Cotton-field hollers sound nothing like that; they are melancholy rather than lusty, and their drooping contours resemble sustained wailing, designed to carry great distances in the wide open space, for the obvious reason that pickers worked much further apart than sailors.[7] The 'waulking songs' of the Hebridean weavers show that the relationship between song, work and product can be extremely subtle (waulking, or 'fulling', was the practice of rhythmically beating woven tweed to soften it). The women believed that if they sang the same song twice, the cloth would be damaged. Musical variety translated into the cloth's evenness of texture.

One of the key differences between folk and pop songs is that the latter hardly ever refer to work. Quite the contrary: popular music celebrates a release from work, as in John Travolta's swagger in the opening scene of *Saturday Night Fever*. The film draws a sharp line between Tony's two worlds. From his point of view, the modern world of work is grey, disciplined and largely silent; the world of leisure is colourful, free and pulsing with disco. How these two worlds drew apart is a story of the great silencing.[8]

A veil of silence fell on work music after the Industrial Revolution for the simple reason that the music was drowned out by the noise of the machines. Also, Gradgrind factory owners didn't look kindly upon voices raised in joy. The exception that proves the rule is the North/South divide in antebellum America.[9] Before the American Civil War, the industrial cities of the free North were as noisy as one might expect, but with the sounds of machinery, not music. Conversely, the soundscape of the Southern plantations was eerily quiet, yet punctuated by the sounds of slavery in such a regimented fashion that visitors compared the effect to that of an orchestra. The 'baton' of the orchestral 'conductor', in the memory of an old Southern gentleman called James Battle Avirett writing in 1901, was 'the old plantation bell which, in the hands of Uncle Jim, regulates the movements of the servants, calling them to and from labor and telling out the hours for the various duties'. And what this 'orchestra' played was 'the hum of the spinning wheel, the noise of the loom, with the stirring whiz of the weaver's shuttle, all accompanied, many times, by the melody of plantation songs'.[10] And yet the fence between worker and listener was more permeable than it seemed. In the following anecdote, consider who is listening to whom:

> We are told of a research student who took a seat on a fence to
> listen to the singing of a negro work gang on a railroad. When he
> finally detected their words he found they were singing lines that
> sounded like, 'See dat white man … sittin' on a fence … sittin' on a
> fence … wastin' his time … wastin' his time'.[11]

The cotton plantations were an anachronism, of course. Music only returned to factories in the middle of the twentieth century, during the Second World War. Managers realised that, in the context of low-skilled repetitive work, music raised productivity and lowered boredom.[12] The catch was that work music was now imposed from above, by the managers, in the form of radio music broadcast on loudspeakers, rather than sung by the workers; and it was rationed in two half-hour daily doses. The story of work music after the war is essentially one of workers gradually taking back control. First, they were allowed to choose which stations the radio played, and when.

Work music was arguably always a kind of tool. According to the great sea-shanty scholar, Stan Hugill, 'a shanty was as much a part of the equipment as a sheath-knife and a pannikin'.[13] The difference now was that work music became a tool for music sung or played or composed by *somebody else*, be they John Lennon, Ariana Grande or Vivaldi. Nevertheless, as before, the music tool did a range of jobs, only they were new jobs, thanks in large part to portable devices such as MP3 players, iPods and iPhones. In the modern work environment, earbuds can create aural privacy, sealing you off in your personal sonic bubble. A bit of personal sonic space is especially useful within an open-plan or shared workspace because it lets you cope with prolonged proximity to other people.[14] Earbud music can help you concentrate on your task by blocking distractions, masking external sounds. It can also distract you from your work, which is why people learn which kind of music works best for them (not necessarily 'easy listening'). Work music can also shrink and expand personal space according to office politics. A manager or alpha worker can take the earbuds off, raise the volume and impose *their* music on everybody else. In all these situations, what is interesting is how the two realms of work and play – so sharply demarcated in the past – are nested within each other. The Industrial Revolution had established labour and leisure as separate worlds; now we bring our own soundtracks into work, blurring the boundaries between the public and the personal, and between 'doing' and 'listening'.

Soundtracks

We have seen how music can be a tool. The sociologist Tia DeNora goes further and calls music a 'technology of the self'.[15] This happens both inside and out. Outside, music configures not just work environments – making borders and bubbles – but streets and shops, as we shall see. Inside our skulls, music manages our moods, memories and identities, enabling us to build images of ourselves we want to project to others. Music is our second skin, and it covers every surface of our body, and of the body of the city. From the moment our iPhone wakes us with a curated playlist, every moment of our day – driving to work, work itself, shopping, eating, playing, exercising – has a soundtrack. This soundtrack can be chosen by ourselves to regulate how we feel, how we appear and relate to others, how we walk, even how we think, like a self-administered drug. Or it can be chosen for us in places that we visit: cafés, airports, retail outlets, telephone on-hold music. This element of choice, enabled by the easy accessibility of music, is something new in history, and it reflects the peculiarly fluid and malleable nature of the modern subject, our sense of self, of who we are. We can be whoever we want to be, and music helps us do that, like a sonic prosthesis or a shrink-wrapped exoskeleton. The fluidity of the modern self is exactly mirrored in the vibrant chaos of the modern city of music. The two go together as naturally as pathways through urban space. Ever on the move, soundtracks are the tracks made by sound.

Let's track music's journey through the city, beginning with a place in which it appears to do nothing at all: the home. Sitting in your home listening to your favourite tracks, you are resting within a pocket of idleness carved out by centuries of social progress. Yet even in the home, music is busy. It can be a tool of interior design, setting the mood like scented candles and atmospheric lighting.[16] Music scripts the circle of love, from those first, cautious encounters in teenage bedrooms. Romantic music is slow because courtship needs to be slow: sufficiently hesitant and exploratory so that an intimate encounter can be speeded up, walked back or cooled down if it doesn't go well.[17] As to what happens next, older readers may recall the classic scene in Dudley Moore's 1979 romantic comedy, *10*, where Bo Derek teaches him how to make love to the rhythms of Ravel's *Bolero*. It turns out that Spotify knows what music you're having sex to. The most likely song to appear on its user-made 'sex' playlists is 'Intro' by the indie band XX.[18] And, tracking your search history, including the kind of songs you like, Google is likely to know you're pregnant before you do.[19] Much later, married couples can enjoy the 'Darling, they're playing our song' effect, when music in restaurants evokes special memories.[20]

It's become a truism that we decorate our homes with music, and that music's main function in everyday life seems to be to help us 'relax'. The radio station Classic FM markets itself as 'the best relaxing classical music',[21] and it retails an album called, simply, *Relax*, featuring works by Rachmaninov, Vaughan Williams, Pachelbel, Rodrigo, etc. Such objects, as much a design-intensive furnishing as strip lighting or gourmet kitchen utensils, are for background listening. Yet it is fascinating that interior design has even penetrated the inner sanctum of classical recording techniques and music that demands close, concentrated listening. The typical 'soundstage' in the most highly prized classical CDs seems to locate the listener directly in front of the instrument through close microphone placement. At the same time, the reverberant, spacious stereo imaging increases the distancing effect, so that the listener is simultaneously situated further back. We get the benefit of both exquisitely sharp detail and full-fat resonance, an ideal impossible to achieve in any live performance. It is a space unique to recent classical recordings, and takes the practice of private indoor listening to its limit. It creates what has been called an 'abstract musical soundstage'.[22]

Let's leave the home and drive into Liverpool's city centre. I park at the university, head down Mount Pleasant, turn into Hope Street (so-called because it is bounded by two cathedrals), go past the Bombed Out Church and walk through Bold Street, named after the noted slaver Jonas Bold, who became Mayor of Liverpool in 1802. Lonely Planet hailed Bold Street as a shopper's paradise, one of the best in Britain.[23] And I am walking in step with the beats of my prized Bose QuietComfort 35 wireless and noise-cancelling headphones. It feels natural to walk to music, because music originates in the rhythm of walking. But strolling in the privacy of a personal stereo – be it a Walkman, an MP3 or an iPhone – feels special: an inner space equal and opposite to the pleasures of the collective. This is the delicious core of twenty-first-century individualism and freedom. And also, perhaps, the peculiar selfishness of an atomised society – each of us alone, savouring the intensity of being ourselves.

Walking with a personal soundtrack 'musicalises' the city.[24] The flow of the music bestows a narrative logic on the fragmentary environment, exactly like music in a film, except that this is my film. Look at Tony Manero strutting his way through the Bee Gees' 'Staying Alive'. Travolta's confident gait triangulates between the music, the city and the human body.[25] If I put this song on my iPhone, would any passer-by be able to tell by the way I walk what I'm listening to? The music does even more than that. It affects my mood. It colours the scene, inflecting the city with the stylised, lurid camp of disco.[26] And it works as a shield, cocooning me against the cacophony of car horns, police sirens, shouts and laughter, the rival beats leaking out of shop fronts and the press of other people. Songs can also map a vision of a city. The 'Downtown' in Petula Clark's 1964 smash hit is an exciting place of pleasure and adventure. In the rapper 50 Cent's 'In My Hood', from his 2005 album, *The Massacre*, it is a nightmarish urban dystopia.[27] Bold Street falls somewhere in the middle.

As soon as I take off my headphones, I fall in with the music of the street. Each café, shop and restaurant has a sonic welcome-mat, the Muzak it pipes out to lure me in.[28] It's a Saturday afternoon, so the music is clubby, funky and up-tempo, in tune with the hordes of young people hunting for evening outfits. On weekdays, shops intentionally start with laid-back or ambient easy listening: drum 'n' bass; club music; definitely nothing classical or tacky. The music is fastest and loudest at lunchtime, and then begins its slow descent into the early evening. A global chain like Canyon, specialising in casual sportswear, receives its music from central office in the US, distributed by the Muzak Corporation, and ensures that shoppers in the same time zone hear the same music at the same instant.[29] Each retail space uses music to create a sonic environment to sell us a self-image. When we try on a garment, we imagine ourselves wearing it in a place as glamorous as the music. Music also sets the tempo for shopping. If business is slow, slow music makes the shoppers linger. If it is brisk, fast music speeds shoppers along. For impulse purchases such as wine or perfume, music can tilt you in one direction or another. Experiments show that classical music makes you buy more expensive wine, and that piping French or German music can influence you to choose bottles from those countries, as I said in Chapter 1.[30] The more uncertain we are, the more we latch on to external cues.

In Bold Street the music both draws you in and draws you *down*: downhill and downtown towards the vast shopping and leisure complex known as Liverpool One, just behind the Liver Building by the river. Scooped out of forty-two acres of post-industrial wasteland, this £1 billion development was the epicentre of Liverpool's regeneration in 2008, the year it became a Capital of Culture. It typifies inner-city transformations across the First World, from Baltimore to Bilbao, and is quite cleverly designed. The mall is open to the sky and feels connected to the surrounding streets, with terraces planted with ornamental trees meandering down to the Old Dock. As with all retail complexes, piped music divides up the spaces and manages the flow between them as you walk, browse and purchase.[31] The gentle music masks and relieves the claustrophobia of being in a huge crowd of people trapped in a semi-enclosed space; it is something to cling on to, an inverted mirror image of how earbud music blocks out the street. And the stupefied, distracted shopper is kept in motion by the ambiguity of music just beyond earshot, its details just below the threshold of discernment. This is the soundtrack of desire, the never-sated yearning for materialist acquisitions. It is a distorted echo of how Liverpool's river has come to

embody a yearning for distant places. Struggling to identify a specific
Liverpool 'sound', people claim to hear it in the watery, 'riverine'
sonorities of albums such as Echo and the Bunnymen's *Ocean Rain*,
with its reverberant blend of synths, strings and lugubrious vocals.[32]
In a port city, water, commerce and music are inextricably mixed.
Soundtracks melt into the wakes left by ships.

The central point about Liverpool is that it is a *port*. When Thomas
Steers pooled the Mersey's tidal basin into the world's first enclosed wet
dock – the Old Dock – in 1715, he set in motion a powerful triangular
flow of trade. Manufactured goods from all over England were sent
through Liverpool to West Africa. African slaves were transported to the
New World. The ships brought back cotton, rum, sugar and tobacco.
They also carried music. In the nineteenth century, songs crisscrossed
the North Atlantic. After the Second World War, the 'Cunard Yanks',
the waiters and catering staff on the Cunard shipping line between
Liverpool and New York, carried home rock 'n' roll, rhythm 'n' blues,
country 'n' western and the music of Motown and the girl groups.[33] The
1964 Beatles invasion of the US would return the compliment.

But the first musical cargo was sea shanties, one of which became
Liverpool's unofficial anthem.[34] Given the city's troubled debt to slavery,
it is fitting that 'Maggie May' was adapted from an American Civil War
abolitionist song called 'Darling Nelly Gray' (or 'Nelly Ray'), written
by Benjamin Hanby in 1856.[35] The notes and rhythms are more or less
the same, as is the scenario: Nelly is sold downriver to a plantation
in Georgia; Maggie is transported from Liverpool to the Australian
penal colony of Van Diemen's Land. The biggest difference is in their
setting. Both are work songs, designed to accompany heavy labour,
yet there is all the distance in the world between the rhythms of a ship
and those of a cotton field. We can hear the wailing typical of hollers
online in J. W. Myers's rendition of 'Nelly Gray', recorded in 1904.[36]
Despite Nelly and Maggie's outward family resemblance, their DNA
sends them in different directions. Nelly becomes a blues standard, as
in Louis Armstrong's recording of 1937. Maggie's destiny was in the
more upbeat world of pop and rock, including a 1957 version by the
Liverpool skiffle band, The Vipers.

When the iron ship *Dawpool* landed at Liverpool in 1891, returning
from San Francisco via Cape Horn, the singing of the seamen
resonated across the whole waterside, and 'people said that they

heard the capstan chanties [*sic*] on St James Mount, where Liverpool Cathedral now stands', according to the sea writer Basil Lubbock.[37] For Lubbock, the ship was a maritime church choir; on that Sunday morning, the choir was chanting in memory of the sailors who had died on that difficult crossing. Lubbock's analogy is far from fanciful. The nave of a church comes from the Latin *navis*, meaning ship, and its vaulted roof echoes that of a ship's keel turned upside-down. For St Augustine, Noah's ark was a 'symbol of the City of God on pilgrimage in this world'.[38] And whatever one might think of Paul McCartney's *Liverpool Oratorio*, his first venture into classical music, performed in the cathedral, it is no accident that the name of its hero was 'Shanty'. Now that shanties are no longer sung by sailors, their monuments are the multi-ethnic churches that dot the city – Scandinavian, German and Greek Orthodox churches; a mosque; one of the finest synagogues in the world – all with their own flavours of music. The first wave of Chinese migration – sailors who married local girls in the 1860s – is marked not by a temple but by a Chinese Arch, entry to Europe's earliest Chinatown. Today, it is the site of the Pagoda Chinese Children's Orchestra.

Liverpool's Cotton Line was as much a path of musical migration as the old Silk Road of Central Asia, a topic for a later chapter (as it happens, those 1860s Chinese seamen were bearing silk from Shanghai). The city brings an ancient principle to vivid life: it shows the way music travels. Once on dry land, the musics of the world, carried by migrants, settle, mix and disperse through the city, then throughout the land. Music is always on the move, not only because tunes spread virally from singer to listener, but because professional musicians need to be peripatetic to find their next gig, audience and meal.

World City of Music

The proper unit of soundtracks is not the individual, not the workplace, home or other setting, but the modern city as a whole, a living, breathing entity bursting with music. This vitality is what so impressed the young Herman Melville when he visited Liverpool in 1839, twelve years before he completed *Moby-Dick*:

In the evening, especially when the sailors are gathered in great
numbers, these streets present a most singular spectacle, the entire
population of the vicinity being seemingly turned into them. Hand-
organs, fiddles and cymbals, plied by strolling musicians, mix with
the songs of the seamen, the babble of women and children and
the whining of beggars. From the various boarding houses [...]
proceeds the noise of revelry and dancing.[39]

A United Nations data report found that in 2016 more than half of
us (54 per cent) lived in cities, and estimates that this figure will rise
to nearly two thirds of the planet by 2030.[40] In 2015 Liverpool was
designated a UNESCO World City of Music. However, Liverpool
can stand for musical cities the world over, for the modern experience
of music as essentially *urban*. As Ruth Finnegan demonstrated in her
seminal book *The Hidden Musicians*, English cities are hives of grass-
roots music-making.[41] A mid-sized southern town such as Milton
Keynes, the subject of Finnegan's study, is crisscrossed by thousands
of musical pathways trodden by members of amateur choirs, jazz,
blues, folk and classical groups, brass bands, rock bands and school
orchestras. That said, by Finnegan's reckoning, no more than 6 per
cent of the population was actively engaged in musical performance.
This is not just a tiny minority; it is much, much lower than the 67
per cent of children between the age of seven and seventeen who are
actively involved with music, according to the Youth Music report.
How much can this collapse be pinned down to the changing fortunes
of a world city of music, between Melville and now? The best guide to
Liverpool's historical, seemingly precipitous, soundtrack turns out to
be, surprisingly, a humble music shop.

The magnificent buildings in Liverpool's Cultural Quarter include
St George's Hall, the Walker Gallery and the stunning rotunda of the
Picton Reading Room. Just outside the quarter, a patch of land was
cleared for a flyover between the County Court Session and the TUC
trade union building, part of the new inner ring-road system. This bit of
land used to have the most important musical institution in Liverpool's
history, Rushworths Music House.[42] Five generations of Rushworths ran
Liverpool music from 1840 to 2002, when the shop closed. Rushworths
sold pianos to New York, Europe and West Africa, and its instruments
cruised the seven seas on the *QE2* and *Queen Mary*. It built organs and

supplied Liverpool's 440 churches with organ pipes. Paul McCartney bought his first guitar there, a Zenith. Over two centuries the shop was a hub of social life, where tradesmen, dockers, doctors and judges could freely consort, so long as they didn't talk politics or religion. John Lennon leant over the counter there one morning in 1962 bragging about an upcoming photo-shoot, worried that his coat wouldn't cover a hole in the backside of his jeans. Like many other city musicians, the Beatles hung out in the shop for gossip and contacts, availing themselves of Rushworths' 'try before you buy' policy in the listening booths. One sales assistant recalls Lennon repeatedly playing a Coasters record, sketching its chords and lyrics, before nipping off to the Cavern for a lunchtime concert.

If you walked past no. 13 Islington, Liverpool, on any weekday morning in the 1850s, you might have been lured into the original shop by the sound of music being played by William Rushworth, the founder (flute) and his three sons (piano, violin, cello). The building doubled as a family home; fortuitously, the establishment next door at no. 11 was a victualler and purveyor of alcoholic drink. Music and drink always helped each other out, and not just in the city's 2,000 pubs (a ratio of 5:1 to Liverpool's churches). In the early nineteenth century street musicians sang for a drink. In the 1840s, when dazzlingly bright gas lighting chased away the pubs' shadows, drinkers were baited with music and dancing, and singing saloons became hubs of working-class leisure. Rushworths targeted cheap, second-hand pianos at the culturally ambitious middle class, and the piano – a desirable item of furniture – became as much a centre of bourgeois family life as, in successive generations, the gramophone, the radio and the modern plasma screen.

This evolution of music technology – from piano to CD to digital media – happened in sync with Liverpool's economic fortunes, and inevitably also with those of a shop. A music shop can't sell if customers have no money. In 1850 the port of Liverpool enjoyed twice the export business of London, £35 million. By 1985, Liverpool's unemployment rate was 27 per cent, nearly four times the national rate of 7.5 per cent. The presence of 1,000 Liverpool bands in the 1980s seems to buck that trend. But unemployed musicians don't buy new instruments.[43] Because of this symbiosis of music and economics, Rushworths' business model provoked demand by developing audiences. They built a 200-seater concert hall behind their premises; to get to their seats, audiences had to file past the 300 pianos on permanent display. And there followed a long list of philanthropic activities: support of local festivals, brass bands, music competitions and city institutions such as the Bluecoat Arts Society, the Rodewald Concert Society and the Philharmonic Orchestra. A Rushworth Concert Bureau even took charge of organising concerts. And when the shop sold LPs, it made sure that Rushworths became the headquarters of the Liverpool Gramophone Society. Today, long after the shop's demise, a Rushworth Trust (directed by the fifth-generation Jonathan Rushworth) continues to support a wide range of musical causes. In the words of third-generation William: 'The concerts should not represent a financial proposition, but the loss will prove to be an investment for the future in creating a music-loving public.'[44]

It is an interesting question whether the enemy of music retail is economic decline or technological progress. The rot is always said to start with Edison's invention of the phonograph in 1877. It seemed to fire the starting gun on the emerging battle between playing and listening to music; or, in Nick Wong's nice phrase, the 'disengagement between the practical musician and the consumer'.[45] But the thriving health of music in Liverpool is evidence that history can be read in two directions. John Philip Sousa, the composer of cheery marches, took the high ground and hated the phonograph:

> The time is coming when no one will be ready to submit himself to the ennobling discipline of learning music. Everyone will have their ready made or ready pirated music in their cupboards.[46]

Adopting a much more pragmatic standpoint, Sir Henry Wood, founder of the Proms, champions the gramophone as a 'musical instrument capable of highly artistic performance … The gramophone more than any other single influence I know has brought good music to the ears and understanding of the ordinary man.'[47]

Authenticity is a movable feast. I have already heard people lament the passing of wired earphones (in favour of wireless earbuds), because friends or couples can no longer enjoy the intimacy of sharing them, a single bud in each ear. Rushworths never got to that stage. At its height in the 1960s, when it was literally the largest music house in the whole of Europe, it stacked all the available music technologies over five sales floors: from sheet music in the basement to pianos and guitars, record players and LPs, radios and televisions. A vertical timeline of music. Might it have diversified up to a sixth, digital, floor? The business closed in 2002, ultimately because the world no longer buys music from shops, or buys music at all. Most of the music being played up above, in the sound systems of the vehicles barrelling along the New Churchill Way flyover, is probably free.

Some kinds of music can't be sold. A city experiences its communal identity most powerfully when 20,000 people chant together in a football stadium. The sea of sound – an exhilarating cross between the roar of a jet engine and the tug of an ocean rip tide – voices collective emotion and defines a sense of place. This is why Anfield, or the 'Kop', as it is known, is sacred ground for Liverpool, a theatre of locality. It gives credence to those who believe that the ultimate aim of music is the expression of group solidarity, and that an individual's keenest musical pleasure is to dissolve into a crowd. This is nothing new: there is a distant echo in the terraces of how the Greek city state, or *polis*, regarded itself in the amphitheatre, and listened to the mass performance of wild, ecstatic hymns – dithyrambs – by rival tribes.[48]

The Greek precedent also shows how naturally a celebration of identity slips into being a case for war; there is nothing like an enemy to bring people together. One of my favourite cartoons shows a jubilant football fan leaving the stadium, waving his flag and singing 'You'll Never Walk Alone', Liverpool's football anthem, borrowed from Gerry and the Pacemakers (who took it from Rodgers and Hammerstein's *Carousel*).[49] And he really isn't alone, because he is being pursued by a snarling pack of defeated rival supporters (see **Figure 3.2**). Football is a continuation of war by other means. In the 1970s and 1980s, British stadium terraces were segregated to stop rival fans killing each other. Then and now, they simply insult each other by trading chants. In these post-hooligan and post-racial times, the chants can be humorous. One chant mocks Manchester United player Cristiano Ronaldo for his habit of falling over: 'Ronny, he's on his arse again, he's on his arse again' to the melody of Rodgers and Hart's 'Blue Moon'.[50] In 2018 the *Liverpool Echo* carried the heartening story that fans were greeting the new Egyptian signing, Mohamed Salah, with this chant, to a tune by the Britpop band Dodgy:

Figure 3.2 A cartoon from *Punch*

If he's good enough for you, he's good enough for me.
If he scores another few, then I'll be Muslim too.
If he's good enough for you, he's good enough for me.
Sitting in the mosque, that's where I wanna be!
Mo Salah-la-la-la, la-la-la-la-la-la-la.[51]

It was not always like this. Vince Hilaire, one of Crystal Palace's first black players, shares this recollection of playing at Anfield in the late 1970s: 'I've run out the tunnel and all of a sudden … I heard this lone voice in the Kop go: "Dayo – we say dayo, we say dayo", and then the rest of the Kop started.'[52] The chant was sung as a Calypso parody, with overtones of black minstrelsy.

Actually, Liverpool is only one of many Kops: it is a generic name for British football stadiums shared by many other clubs (including Wigan, Derby, Blackpool and Leeds), and is short for Spion Kop, the site of the bloodiest battle in the South African Boer War. To what extent does the multiculturalism of football chants begin to make amends for the slavery at the root of Liverpool's wealth?

All Together Now

We can imagine various sources for the origin of music. A popular idea is that music arose from the coordinated activity of a group of people, and there was probably no distinction between performers and audience. Both these aspects were inherent to ancient work music when hominins first banged rocks together, an idea I will explore in Chapter 10. They were also present when music broke apart from work and was practised as an activity in itself, in festivals or over an evening drink. The anthropologist Thomas Turino calls this type of music – where the performers and the listeners are the same people – *participatory*.[53] In their funny way, the chants of football stadiums, when an entire city comes together, are a perfect example of participatory music. So the historical evolution from participating in music to simply listening to it is another flavour of the decline of musical engagement from active to passive. As before, however, the story is more interesting than that. For a start, there are examples of participatory music all around us today, from football chants to the music of the unpretentious village fête. And the evolution away from participatory music need not unfold over aeons; it can happen in an abbreviated time period, and within the journey of a single band.

Maggie May next washes up on dry land in an imposing Victorian Gothic church in Woolton on 6 July 1957, the day John met Paul.[54] She shared the Quarrymen's (Lennon's first band) set list with other skiffle staples ('Railroad Bill', 'Cumberland Gap', 'Be Bop A Lula') and – always the bridesmaid, never the bride – would become the Beatles' favourite warm-up song, but not recorded until the throwaway forty-two-second fragment in their final album, 1970's *Let It Be*. Great writers bury what is most significant to them in their footnotes, and so it is with musicians.

A meeting as mythical as when Marty McFly's parents danced in the 'Enchantment Under the Sea' ball in *Back to the Future*, Lennon and McCartney's mutual audition is tinged with the idyllic glow of English pastoral. Even today, Woolton Village, the leafiest and wealthiest suburb of Liverpool, still exudes George Orwell's fantasy of 'old maids biking to Holy Communion through the mists of the autumn mornings'.[55] Saturday 6 July 1957 was the day of the Woolton garden fête, the high point of village community life. The Quarrymen were drawn to the fête in a carnival procession of decorated floats, for form's sake set back as far as possible from the Band of the Cheshire Yeomanry. There was a troupe of morris dancers on the church green, and a crowning of the Rose Queen. At first glance, the unloved and passing novelty of skiffle doesn't seem very community-spirited. The Woolton villagers didn't care for it; skiffle was rough-and-ready music to be played, not listened to. But it had interesting roots.

The name, and the ethos, originates in the 'rent parties' of 1920s Prohibition-era Chicago, where partygoers drank illicit alcohol, listened to jazz and blues played on cheaply improvised instruments such as washboards and washtub (or tea-chest) basses, and paid a small contribution towards the rent to join in the music-making.[56] Skiffle is 'participatory', in Turino's terms. Turino finds this aspect common to musics as far apart as the Shona of Zimbabwe, the Peruvian Aymara and Midwestern American dance. Like so much American music (including the song 'Nelly Gray'), when skiffle crossed the Atlantic, it was 'whitened', exchanging its African American blue notes for Lonnie Donegan's European-sounding harmony and vocal style (although, confusingly, Donegan's 'Take this Hammer' and 'Rock Island Line' still sang of slavery).[57] Also, participation in British skiffle became an oddly one-way street. In one direction all were welcome to join, since it was so cheap and easy to play. At its brief high point in 1957, it is estimated that there may have been as many as 50,000 skiffle bands in Britain.[58] Although skiffle drew in Britain's youth, it didn't give much back, because skiffle sounded, frankly, boring to those on the outside. This is why the Beatles took off on their musical journey, in search of something more sophisticated.

This journey has a literal, physical, track, continuing from Woolton in a geographical circuit around Merseyside's pubs, theatres, ballrooms and dance halls, before and after their apprenticeship years in Hamburg. Beatles fanatics can recount this circuit like a catechism:

- 17 December 1960 (just back from Hamburg): the Casbah Coffee Club.
- 24 December: across the river to the Grosvenor Ballroom in Wallasey.
- 31 December: back to the Casbah.
- 5 January, 1961: north of the city to Litherland Town Hall.

- 6 January, swerving west to Bootle, St John's Hall.
- 7 January, back into town to the Aintree Institute.
- 9 February, the Cavern Club...[59]

Music is physically always on the march. However, the Beatles' soundtrack was also, in a deeper sense, a journey through musical styles. Turino divides the world's music into four artistic practices, or fields, which he calls the *participatory*; the *presentational*; *high fidelity*; and *studio audio art*. They climb ever higher orders of abstraction, a mini-evolution of music or, if you will, a stairway to heaven.

THE PARTICIPATORY FIELD: The Beatles-Quarrymen begin with the participatory practice of skiffle. Turino thinks that their journeymen period in Hamburg was also participatory, because they performed essentially as a dance band, and the dancers actively contributed to the events' sound and motion. Participatory musics across the world have many features in common.[60] They cater for a wide range of abilities; their success is gauged by the intensity of people's involvement rather than by artistic quality; they have open forms, without clear beginnings or endings, so people can join in and fall out whenever they like; they are made up of cyclic repetitions of easy-to-remember short units; because performances are only loosely scripted, participants need to pay acute attention to each other in the moment, creating a heightened sense of synchrony and immediacy; and densely overlapping textures, wide tunings, unrelenting loudness and fast pace are a gentle cover for the less able participants. All these features are present as much in the Bira ancestral ceremony of northern Zimbabwe as in the old-time string bands of the Appalachian mountains before they evolved into bluegrass. While this kind of music can be fun to play, the repetition and absence of contrast makes it boring for outsiders. The endless repeats of the words 'Cumberland gap' in Donegan's eponymous skiffle hit soon outwear their welcome. And only die-hard Beatles fans dig deep into their early anthologies.

THE PRESENTATIONAL FIELD: When the Beatles become more accomplished, they play for an audience that listens. Several things happen to their music, and an excellent example is 'Please Please Me', their first UK No. 1 hit, and the first presented on national TV.[61] The form of the song is closed, in that it has a clearly defined beginning and ending (an 'intro' and an 'outro'). Note the contrast between verse and chorus, and the contrast within the verse itself, with the repeated opening phrase answered by a longer and more harmonically complex middle phrase lifting the verse to a perfectly judged climax. Of course, repetitive songs like 'Twist and Shout', performed in 1963 on *The Ed Sullivan Show* on the high tide of Beatlemania, show that the line between pop and skiffle was fuzzy. The screams of the hysterical audience certainly *participate* in the song; each 'ooooh' and shake of Paul and George's heads shamelessly milks the screams in a call-and-response pattern.[62] The twists elicit shouts. Yet I doubt that the British social classes really came together in November 1963 when Lennon invited the Queen Mother to participate in the song at the Royal Variety Performance: 'For our last number I'd like to ask your help. Would the people in the cheaper seats clap your hands? And the rest of you, if you'll just rattle your jewellery.'[63]

THE HIGH-FIDELITY FIELD: Most music in the West is consumed as recordings rather than live. The Beatles were pioneers in that, and they were lucky to work with fabulous sound engineers and producers. A perfectionism creeps in, a degree of control not possible when they performed their music in front of an audience, as they rarely did after 1966, the year of *Revolver*. Perhaps their most finely wrought album, *Revolver* also understands the mystery of the high-fidelity practice: a recording is rarely, if ever, a passive capture of a live performance; rather, it is manipulated to enhance the *illusion* of liveness. The effect of liveness is very much an illusion, because the track is an impossible, imaginary object stitched together in a studio from different takes like a cinematic film. Compression, equalisation, reverb, echo, close miking and separation of individual parts: the aim is to make every detail in the music transparent to the listener. Yet this total clarity is as idealistic as those crystalline landscapes of the fifteenth-century Flemish school – say, Van Eyck's *Adoration of the Mystic Lamb* – where a ray of gold leaf above the lamb's ear in the middle ground is as razor-sharp as a blade of grass in the foreground. In a live performance, the drum sounds bleed into the texture like haze in a perspective; recordings are made for the ear of God.

These are some of the effects in 'Tomorrow Never Knows', *Revolver's* final track.[64] The tamboura (an Indian gourd instrument) is given a fade-in. Ringo's drums are damped and compressed. Harrison's guitar solo is overdubbed, recorded backwards, treated with a fuzz box and Leslie cabinet (which modifies the sound by rotating the loudspeakers).

George Martin also put Lennon's lead vocal through the Leslie because 'he wanted to sound like the Dalai Lama singing on a hilltop'. McCartney's tape loops, mixing laughter and distorted guitars, pan wildly between left and centre of the sound image.

THE STUDIO-AUDIO ART FIELD: In 'A Day in the Life', the last track of *Sgt. Pepper*, the balance is tipped from adding special effects to a song one could imagine being performed in a presentational setting, to an entire track as a unified sonic object, assembled from diverse materials. A track becomes, in a sense, an abstract painting. The famous orchestral 'freak out' in the middle even resembles the avant-garde music McCartney admired at the time by composers such as Stockhausen, whose face features on the album cover.[65] At their stratosphere, the Beatles converge with abstract art music.

In their short and concentrated career ascending these four stages, the Beatles recapitulate the entire history of music. Except that 'history' is the wrong word, as it conveys progression, whereas Turino rightly observes that each of these 'fields' has its own merits. One can get as much joy from participating in simple musical games as from listening to complex art. It is also questionable whether 'Hey Jude' heard live at a gig, with audiences swaying, holding hands and trailing off into an infinite mantra, is the same object as when you listen to it through headphones in your armchair. *Hamlet* in the theatre is a different beast from Olivier's film. And Maggie May sails on, last heard of in *Pirates of the Caribbean 5: Salazar's Revenge*, sung by Paul McCartney in a cameo playing Captain Jack Sparrow's uncle.[66]

One shouldn't get too dewy-eyed about music's capacity to bring people together. The other lesson from the Kop is that football anthems are a continuation of war – the Boer War – by other means. Music can be weaponised in many ways. When General Noriega was holed up in the Vatican Embassy in Panama City in 1989, the US army blasted him for fifty-one days with irony-tipped bullets of rock: U2's 'All I Want is You'; The Clash's 'I Fought the Law'; Van Halen's 'Panama', and many others. The opera-loving general surrendered on 3 January 1990.[67] Music is still used as a technique for interrogating prisoners at Guantánamo Bay; according to one report, 'it fried them'.[68] And in the Iraq War the American military used Metallica to disorient prisoners held in shipping containers. In the words of US psychological operations Sergeant Mark

Hadsell: 'These people haven't heard heavy metal. They can't take it. If you play it for 24 hours, your brain and body start to slide.'[69]

Military music can take more subtle forms. After America entered the war in 1941, 'When You Wish Upon a Star' – sung by Jiminy Cricket in Disney's 1940 *Pinocchio* – was recruited as propaganda for the war effort (just like Vera Lynn's 'We'll Meet Again').[70] Yet it became Hitler's favourite tune, which he loved to whistle for guests at his dinner parties. Albert Speer reports that the Führer also whistled it as they stood at the Palais de Chaillot overlooking a conquered Paris, thereby gamely tossing its sentimentality back in America's face.[71] People often say that 'jazz and blue jeans' won the Cold War.[72] Yet it is hard to believe, given its fringe interest today, that high classical and even avant-garde music was sponsored by the State Department as an arm of American foreign policy, a means of winning the culture wars in Europe against Russia. In a memo to his Secretary of State, dated 24 October 1953, Dwight D. Eisenhower urged John Foster Dulles to include 'the singing of a beautiful hymn' within the remit of psychological warfare.[73] Eisenhower charged the American National Theatre and Academy (ANTA) with the mission of cultural diplomacy. The aim was to wean high art-music from its associations with communism and demonstrate its compatibility with American democracy. In 1959 Leonard Bernstein, perhaps the ANTA's most successful special agent, toured Russia with the New York Philharmonic, and lectured luminaries such as Boris Pasternak as to why their heritage should look up to the Great American Songbook.[74]

If Karl Marx was right, and history repeats itself as farce, then music's Cold War was a dry run for the rich comic fare of the Eurovision Song Contest. Now, Lordi (winners 2006) and Verka Serduchka (runner-up 2007) notwithstanding, Eurovision provides a serious service (see **Figure 3.3**). Two hundred million viewers laughing at each other and voting together enacts what the cultural theorist Benedict Anderson famously called an 'imagined community'.[75] For a few hours each year, Europe experiences itself as a coherent totality. Turkey, seen off from the gates of Europe since the Battle of Vienna in 1683, and indefinitely excluded from membership of the EU, won Eurovision in 2003, the year of the Iraq War. Since 2003, it has finished six times in the top ten, years when Britain is still being punished for that war, and now for Brexit, by being voted near the bottom.[76] Britain also submitted lousy songs, of course.

Figure 3.3 Verka Serduchka and friends

The Case for Classical

Classical music was conspicuously absent from the map of children's favourite genres in the Youth Music report. Following Turino's work, we can now see why. Classical music would seem to be the least 'participatory' music in our culture, because of both its technical challenges and the perception that the music (primarily) of dead, white, European males is distant from young people's values. Not only has classical music become a soundtrack, consumed like most of the West's music as recordings rather than live, it appears to be not a very engaging one. But what would happen if you gave every child in a school a musical instrument (and not just the children, the teachers and dinner ladies too), and then love-bombed the school with support from the local symphony orchestra? And what if that school came from the most deprived ward in the city, and classical music was used as an instrument of social and civic regeneration?

Some people claim that the Friary, formerly Saint Mary of the Angels Catholic church at West Everton, is one of the finest examples of Italian Renaissance architecture outside Rome. The church was converted into a recording and rehearsal space for the Royal Liverpool Philharmonic

Orchestra (RLPO). West Everton Children's Orchestra, from its outset involving the eighty-four pupils, teachers and dinner ladies of Faith Primary School, have rehearsed there since 2009 as part of the RLPO's In Harmony programme, originally inspired by Venezuela's El Sistema. It is thrilling to see an entire school, even the head teacher, immersed in music; even more rewarding to see them give a concert downtown in the Philharmonic Hall. According to the RLPO's website, In Harmony 'uses orchestral music-making to improve the health, education and aspirations of children and young people in Everton'.[77] The ward of Everton, where the school sits, has an IMD (index of multiple deprivation) of 67.5, the highest in Liverpool, measuring deprivation of income, employment, education, health and housing.[78] What can music really do to help?

The results of the Venezuelan model are rather mixed. Started by the politician José Abreu in 1975 in an underground parking garage, El Sistema is credited with having lifted 700,000 children out of poverty, drugs and crime. An electrifying concert by its flagship Simón Bolívar Orchestra in 2007 in the Albert Hall was possibly 'the greatest Prom of all time', according to the *Daily Telegraph*'s arts editor, Paul Gent.[79] And El Sistema's most famous graduate, Gustavo Dudamel, went on to be music director of the Los Angeles Philharmonic. Sir Simon Rattle, Liverpool-born conductor of the London Symphony Orchestra (and previously the Berlin Philharmonic), calls El Sistema 'the most important thing happening in music anywhere in the world'. Indeed:

> If anybody asked me where is there something really important going on for the future of classical music I would simply have to say here, in Venezuela … I say I have seen the future of music in Venezuela and that is a resurrection.[80]

The apparent success of El Sistema also speaks to the idealistic image of the orchestra as a model for a harmonious society and a perfect world.[81] It is an image, originating in the European Enlightenment, of a hundred or more individuals working together in synchrony to make beautiful sounds. The orchestra is utopian, which is why Leonard Bernstein performed Beethoven's 'Ode to Joy' on Christmas Day 1989 in Berlin to mark the falling of the Wall. Does it not follow that the experience of playing in an orchestra gives a child a sense of discipline and social responsibility?

It is possible, however, that the Venezuelan miracle has feet of clay, at least according to a systematic exposé by the musicologist Geoffrey Baker.[82] First Baker goes after the facts: the alleged figure of a million or so recruits to El Sistema has no basis in evidence; the vast majority are middle-class children in stable lives free of drugs; hardly any children from deprived backgrounds make it from the school (the 'núcleo') to the orchestra; there is a high drop-out rate, and a culture of physical and sexual abuse. As a social development project, El Sistema is bogus, yet it has received $500 million in loans from international development banks. Next he goes for its principles. The hierarchical, pyramid structure of an orchestra offers a conservative, authoritarian model of society out of kilter with the progressive politics of Hugo Chávez, the country's long-time leader when El Sistema was set up. Education – especially music education – should be imaginative and child-centred. Yet orchestral playing fosters mechanical routine and passive submission to an adult conductor. If the orchestra is indeed a social model, then it harks back to the industrial age of standardisation and centralisation. It can hardly prepare children for our uncertain, rapidly changing world, an information age that thrives on intuition, imagination and flexible problem-solving.

Whatever the veracity of Baker's claims (the debate sparked by the book is lively),[83] the fact is that they don't apply to Liverpool In Harmony for the simple reason that it is nothing like El Sistema. In Harmony has grown since its inception to encompass a wide range of community settings, including a nursery and a family centre. It is keenly targeted at a specific area of the city, and it operates under the wing of the RLPO. The final valuation conducted by the National Foundation for Educational Research (NFER) is exquisitely nuanced and sensitive. It finds 'no quantitative evidence that children who participated in In Harmony achieved better at school or attended school more regularly than their peers in comparison schools'.[84] On the other hand, the report attests that well-being was enhanced in all sorts of subtler and less quantifiable ways. Parents engaged better with the school. Watching their child play an instrument was a source of pride and raised the family's aspirations. Parents and relatives set foot in the Philharmonic Hall, where the In Harmony orchestra performed once a year, for the first time. They got on a train to London for the first time, to hear the children at a family Prom in the Royal Albert Hall. Widening travel throughout Liverpool was symbolised by crossing the A580, the motorway that divides Everton from the prosperous city centre containing the Philharmonic and St George's Hall. Belying the image of a port city ever on the move, disadvantaged communities can get left behind. In this respect, music afforded mobility in two ways: the practical business of getting from A to B literally widened horizons, and by putting a little bit of magic in the families' lives, music enabled them to imagine new realities.[85]

The usefulness of classical music, then, is a lot less direct than its critics suspect. Listening to Mozart doesn't really make you smarter – there truly isn't any 'Mozart Effect'.[86] But the discipline required to play it in an orchestra might open up the whole family's horizons, and *that* might make you smarter in the long run. Similarly, playing in an orchestra isn't at all like slaving in a nineteenth-century factory under an authoritarian boss, the conductor. The skills entailed in performing and conducting are far subtler than that, and it is easy to see how they transfer into life skills. So what does the conductor actually do? Sir Roy Vandervane, the fictional conductor in Kingsley Amis's wickedly funny satire, *Girl, 20*, despite being incompetent, gets excellent results simply by buying the musicians a beer, so that they like him.[87] Yet satire aside, the results of conductor-less orchestras have been controversial, and often linked with the opposite ideals of either early twentieth-century Soviet communism or modern American management theory.[88] The conductor's hands give timing; his or her face and entire body give expression. One scholar has even analysed conductors' eyebrow movements.[89] Eyebrows up, with head aside: 'I suggest.' Eyebrows central, again with head aside: 'I implore.' Eyebrows up, eyes towards a musician: 'Accent that note.' Eyes narrowed: 'Play more precisely', and so on... More broadly, the conductor mirrors the split attention of the audience, divided in his or her case between the whole army of musicians and the individual players. Crucially, only the conductor has a global ear, since the players are preoccupied with their own parts: the conductor has an overview, or 'overhear'.

It is even more complex than that in the strings (if not the other sections), because the musicians' own attention is also divided. First they watch each other's visual cues (typically, the bow of the leader or concertmaster), and only then do they watch the conductor: that is, the synchrony within the army takes precedence over that between the army and their general. Also, strangely, the orchestra lags behind the conductor's beat, between twenty and fifty milliseconds.[90] This is a well-known phenomenon called 'melody lead', and it is not specific to conducting; you hear it in romantic piano playing, where the right hand plays slightly ahead of the left, creating an effect called 'rubato'. And it is not always the melody that takes the lead. The reason jazz sounds so laid-back is often because the melody lags behind the accompaniment. And in classical string quartets, the violins and cello often follow the viola (which is why great composers such as Mozart and Beethoven loved to play viola in their quartets, to sit in the hot seat).[91] Interestingly, the conductor-orchestra time lag closes at those breathtaking moments when everything slows down and quietens to a hush. In other words, the orchestra catches up with the conductor at those precise points when the audience's attention is most sharply in focus, when the entire hall holds its breath. I can only describe such moments as points of religious revelation.

The Temple and the Cave

At the end of the road, music is a religion. Parts 2 and 3 of this book will show that religion was also the start of our journey. Soundtracks begin and end there. Yet the road forks, each track starting (and ending) with a kind of church. One church is a temple; the other is a cave. I never take the bait when critics of music education provocatively declare (and I summarise) that 'the songs of Stormzy [or Adele or Taylor Swift, take your pick] are as finely crafted as Mozart', as a dig at the supposed imbalance of the school curriculum. There has long been a space in our schools for popular and classical – why would there not be? Both musics afford an experience of an altered state of consciousness (abbreviated by psychologists as ASC), if not of 'spirituality' in the sense of any established religion. A work that persuaded a lot of ethnomusicologists that, across all of world cultures, there were two distinct types of ASC was the French anthropologist Gilbert Rouget's seminal *Music and Trance* (*La musique et la transe: esquisse d'une théorie générale de la musique et de la possession*).[92] In brief, Rouget argued that music could induce two kinds of altered state, 'trance' and 'ecstasy', with the following features:[93]

Trance	*Ecstasy*
Immobility, silence, solitude, sensory deprivation, recollection	Movement, noise, in company, sensory overstimulation, amnesia

At first glance, it is obvious how these two categories map onto the experiences of sitting quietly in a concert hall and leaping around in a mosh pit. Rouget's ideas have received a lot of criticism, however, with scholars pointing out that musical experience has less to do with the quality of music being played than where it is played. For instance, one is just as likely to hear repetitive drumbeats in a Stravinsky concert as in a techno rave. Conversely, there is reflective music within the popular music world, indie subgenres being characterised by their 'undanceability'.[94] It is more pragmatic to talk not about the musical styles themselves, but about 'trance-like' and 'ecstatic' etiquettes associated with different venues, what the French sociologist Pierre Bourdieu calls a 'habitus'. The most visible marker of that is bodily motion. So what is trance-like in the psychology of attending a concert, and why exactly is a concert hall like a church?

The Leipzig Gewandhaus, originally a wing of the textile guild hall, was built in 1781 and invented the nineteenth-century concert hall (see **Figure 3.4**).[95] It has a horseshoe design, which means that a large part of the audience sat on opposite sides of the hall, with an excellent view of each other, but with an occluded view of the orchestral stage. The horseshoe was actually modelled on the double choir of Bach's church in Leipzig, the Thomaskirche. Just as the two choruses in Bach's *St Matthew Passion*, performed in the Thomaskirche in 1727, face each other, the audience's referent in the Gewandhaus is not the orchestra but the community. The musical community evolved out of the Lutheran congregation. The worshipping listeners looked at themselves.

Liverpool's first Philharmonic Hall, completed in 1849, was also a horseshoe. When the hall burned down in 1933, it reopened in 1939 in the rectangular shape favoured by modern concert halls, with the audience's sightlines absolutely centred on the stage. The attention of the audience swivelled from itself to the music. In some ways, you might say that the audience became more passive. Modern concert etiquette frowns on chatting or moving, so today's audience sits stock-still and silent, and often in dimmed light. The modern concert hall

Figure 3.4 The original Leipzig *Gewandhaus* concert hall

looks less like a church, but *feels* more like one. It has helped to cultivate a quasi-religious contemplation of music, and a worship of our canonic composers like saints or demigods. As Western organised religion began to fade after the Enlightenment, music stepped into the God-shaped hole. For atheists like me, the ritual of attending a concert delivers a spiritual experience. Yet despite being quiet and still, the modern audience is far from passive. It exercises a regime of prayer in the way it listens.

As I sit and fight the temptation to move – the urge to move to music is as irresistible as blinking – I imaginatively reconstruct these gestures in my head. EEG (electroencephalography, a technique of reading the brain's electrical activity) has shown that listening to music fires the same mirror neurons in our brain that are associated with motor activity.[96] Because we *can't* move, the focus of our attention is the person who stands in front of the orchestra doing a little dance, the conductor. Melodramatic and fanciful though the conductor's gestures can sometimes seem, they are a vital proxy for our repressed actions.

I also entrain to the rhythms of the orchestra. 'Entrainment' is the process by which people align their rhythmic and cyclical behaviours with each other (there will be a lot more to say about entrainment in future chapters).[97] Given that 'symphony' means 'agreement' or 'concord' of sound, would it be idealistic to imagine that music causes the entire body of musicians and audience to synchronise their heart-rate and breathing patterns? Yes, because experiments have found no evidence for that.[98] But what these experiments do show is that heart-rate variability clusters around the main boundaries of the music – beginnings, middles and endings, and that these are literally *breathtaking* moments. In other words, the audience's synchrony fluctuates around nodal points, especially when the music slows down and goes very quiet, when you can hear a pin drop. At such moments we see not a synchrony of movement but a coordination of stillness. The entire hall holds its breath.

Furthermore, my mind wanders and I remember things, exactly as Rouget describes. There is no need to apologise if you daydream or if your attention fluctuates in the middle of a long programme. It would be superhuman to hold your concentration for forty-five minutes. Psychologists have found that listeners oscillate between 'future-oriented' and 'analytic' attention in everyday conversation as much as in concerts.[99] These principles are all too familiar. When you follow a speaker and you think you've missed a word, one ear (as it were) goes back to check if you've heard the word correctly, while the other ear keeps listening in real time. Your attention is momentarily split: listening for detail ('analytic'), and listening for the story ('future-oriented'). In a concert, you can hop back and forth between attending to what, say, the clarinet is playing, pulling back to take in the whole orchestra, and then moving back in to focus on the dialogue between the cello and the viola. There is no right or wrong to how you listen.[100] However, while there are no rules, there are some interesting principles. It turns out that it is easiest to change gears – to switch levels – when the music is well ordered or 'hierarchical' (with clear organisation between the whole and its parts).[101] In a well-ordered work, the composer, in a sense, has already done the hearing for you. Conversely, it is harder to change focus when the music is over-complex or even muddled (i.e. poorly composed). Of course, experienced music lovers can be particularly skilled at listening, a facility that comes with practice. And there are also nodal points when the entire audience's attention comes together, such as when it is time to clap.

I suspect that many of the 2,000 people at the Phil come to be alone, to enjoy their personal feelings within a lonely crowd, pinned down by the music and free of distraction. If people want ecstasy (or recreational Molly, MDMA), then there is plenty of that to be had at the Zanzibar, the East Village Arts Club, Studio 2, Lomax and dozens of other venues that dot Liverpool City. They forgo the stillness of the temple for the frenzy of the cave. Caves are where it all began. The Cavern is where it all began. Dark, dank, cramped, sweaty, and with terrific acoustics, the original Cavern Club in Matthew Street heaved with an ecstatic mob, the flesh-and-blood singers standing within reach. But in what sense is a cave also like a church?

DJs are skilled at raising the heart rate of ravers from the normal 60–100 BPM (beats per minute) to 140 or even 180, inducing an altered state of consciousness. Techno music in particular has been correlated with many other heightened physiological effects: an increase in systolic blood pressure and in levels of neurotransmitters, peptides and hormonal reactions. Lasers and strobe lights activate alpha and theta brain waves. Prolonged dancing, leading to fatigue and hyperventilation, lowering of blood sugar and hypoglycaemia, produces hallucinations. Overheating at raves releases endogenous opiates. Sleep deprivation and fasting before a rave enhances the effects of the driving rhythms.[102] All these effects have been found in 'ecstatic' religious traditions, from the Pentecostal churches of the American Deep South to the dancing dervishes of Sufi Islam.

Neither the temple nor the cave came first. Before trance and ecstasy became established as religions, they were really the same thing, at the still point of the turning world, as T. S. Eliot would say, where the fire and the rose were one.[103]

CHAPTER 4

IMAGINARY LANDSCAPES, INVISIBLE CITIES

The ancient Greek philosopher Pythagoras lectured to his disciples behind a screen so that they could hear his voice without being able to see his face. Pythagoras' disciples were called the *akousmatikoi*, meaning 'those who hear', and the term 'acousmatic' came to define the condition of musical listening in the West.[1] Western music, especially Western classical music, is 'acousmatic' in a double sense. When we hear a violin play a musical pitch in a concert hall, that note doesn't refer to any source in the real world – as when a bark refers to a dog, a creak to a door, or a footstep to a foot – even when we can see the violin perfectly well. Instead, we enjoy the sound of the note in itself. This acousmatic quality is enhanced when we attend to the music as a recording, when we can't see the performers at all.

Acousmatic listening is unnatural because, in the real world, hearing is part of an ensemble of senses whose job it is to pick up information about the environment. This is one reason why, as we saw in Chapter 3, music was normally an accompaniment to something else, especially to work-related activities. Yet around 1800, because of the rise of middle-class leisure and changes in the philosophical weather after the French Revolution, all this changed, and it became customary to treat music as abstract. On the other side of the 1800 watershed, we see a French philosopher such as Jean-Baptiste Dubos, who claimed in his *Réflexions critiques sur la poésie et sur la peinture* of 1719 that music was only a valid art if it represented reality, like painting and literature:

> The basic principles that govern music are similar to those that govern poetry and painting. Like poetry and painting, music is an imitation. Music cannot be good unless it conforms to the general rules that apply to the other arts on such matters as choice of subject and exactness of representation.[2]

After 1800, however, audiences learned to accept music in itself as an autonomous structure, not because it 'painted' or 'expressed' anything. A musical work could stand proudly by itself like a physical object, even though it was obviously less physical than a sculpture or a painting, and less so than a poem, whose words at least referred to real things. Musical works, such as Beethoven's symphonies, were now propped up through the internal scaffolding of formal coherence, where every note was heard to refer to another note *within the work*. To be sure, programme music continued to flourish, such as the tone poems of Liszt and Richard Strauss, or one-off works like Debussy's *La mer*. However, the boot was now on the other foot, and music that told stories or painted pictures became the exception that proved the rule, and was even viewed with grave suspicion. Eduard Hanslick, the greatest music critic of the nineteenth century, friend of Brahms and foe of Wagner, and the polar opposite of the eighteenth-century Dubos, firmly believed that programme music was an abomination that ought to be stamped out.[3] The triumph of musical works was now sealed by enshrining them in scores, which were then treasured as monuments of Western culture. Western classical music constitutes what the philosopher Lydia Goehr calls an 'imaginary museum of musical works', imaginary because they exist only in people's heads.[4]

Treating music as an abstract, self-contained object might be seen as typifying everything that is wrong with the Western tradition. On the other hand, immersive virtual environments have recently emerged in their purest form in video gaming. Otherwise put, gaming is anticipated by acousmatic music. Another way of saying this is that classical music, insofar as it is an art at all, is a type of fiction, which is why music is different from mere sound. There is no object that music refers to, just as Hamlet wasn't a real person. Once we begin appreciating music as a fictional art form, we no longer need to make apologies for it: for instance, that music is valuable because it heals you, because it equips you for jobs, or that because it has any of those practical roles we explored in Chapter 3. Certainly, music does all that, and more. But music need not be always applied music.

The first thing to note is that acousmatic music isn't abstract at all. Rather than classical music disengaging from the world, it really digests and refines it, by analogy to how we distil grape juice into wine, or the scent of a flower into perfume. These origins in a source are retained, but concentrated, refined, lifted up and magically transmuted. We will see in this chapter that the secret of how music does that lies in the phenomenon of *mimesis*, an imitative faculty that Darwin detected in so-called primitive peoples, and that biologists ascribe to the animal kingdom. The paradox is that Western classical music has refined biological mimesis to the nth degree.

So what does music imitate? Not specific objects (like trees or faces) as the philosopher Dubos required, but qualities of motion and emotion, including all those soundtracks that we followed in Chapter 3. But these are now no longer tracks through a city, but pathways through the invisible cities and imaginary landscapes of musical works. We will continue to see in Parts 2 and 3 of this book how important travelling and walking are to the musical human, not least because australopithecines, our primal hominin ancestors, were essentially walking apes. I will argue that listening to a sonata or a symphony is akin to 'walking' through a virtual landscape whose pathways are musical processes. The breadth of musical landscapes is particular to the Western classical tradition, and is certainly not shared by the three-minute culture of pop songs. I'm wary of pitting classical against pop music, Mozart against Stormzy. However, I believe that the consciousness-raising experience of 'walking' through a classical 'landscape' – whose breadth can stretch from twenty minutes to several hours – represents one of the pinnacles of Western culture.

En route I shall put together some heady ideas: that walking, like human gesture, expresses emotion, and that the steps of a musical journey are like the steps of a logical argument. We will finally confront the problem of what emotion really is, a thread that runs throughout this book. I will ask why we hear music as movement; why immersion in music is like a fish swimming through the sea; and why the sea of music is as oceanic as religion. And this will bring us to the larger mystery of how the musical work reflects Western religion's strange obsession with explaining pain. Like its religions, mythologies and dramas, the West's musical works are fixated both on pain and on a logical order that rationalises this pain as a necessary point on a path towards redemption.

In short, my argument will lead us down the garden path along the following steps: motion – emotion – imitation – religion. We will begin our journey by considering what is so distinctive, or metaphorical, about musical 'space'.

The Mysteries of the Musical Space-motion Continuum

The first two notes of 'Somewhere Over the Rainbow' 'rise' an octave while Judy Garland duly looks up in the Kansas sky, perhaps towards Oz. The melody then gently 'descends' back home, arcing down rather like the rainbow itself. I've put scare quotes over the words 'rise' and 'descends' because musical notes don't really rise and descend, or move at all. It's one thing to hear a marching band approach or depart, or track left to right, when the physical source of sound is on the move. But when the notes emanate from a musician who is standing still, there is actually nothing to see: just vibrating air. So is talking of music in terms of motion through space just a metaphor? When Shakespeare's Romeo compares Juliet to the sun ('But soft, what light through yonder window breaks? / It is the east, and Juliet is the sun'), he doesn't mean that Juliet is a ball of fiery gas. He is talking metaphorically, and perhaps Dorothy is singing metaphorically.

Musical 'space' and 'motion' are, if not figures of speech, then at least distinct from space and motion in the real world. One difference is that when a note moves up a step – say, C up to D – it doesn't need to travel through all the intermediate positions to get there, as when a bird flies between two branches. A musical scale flips from one note to another like the numbers on a digital clock face, as opposed to the constantly moving hands of an analogue clock. A second mystery of musical space is that it is a spiral, like a DNA molecule. If you climb up the scale, you eventually, after eight notes, end up where you started: the octave is the same note as the first note (the tonic), but with the acoustic frequency of vibrations doubled. You can hear this octave if you sing 'Some-where' in your mind. 'Where' is both as far away as you can travel from home ('Some'), and the same note raised to a higher power. A single word, and one octave leap, magically stakes out the height of the rainbow through a leap of imagination.

There are further rotations of this spiral at the centre of the scale, whose middle notes (the third and fifth steps) also echo the stability of home, albeit more distantly. As we saw in Chapter 2, the simplest frequency ratios of the musical intervals (after the 1:1 of the unison) are, in reverse order, the octave (2:1), the fifth (3:2) and the third (5:4).[5] As Dorothy's melody descends, it hits the fifth on the word 'high', and the third on 'dreams', reaching the home of the tonic on the final syllable of 'lullaby'. In other words, as a musical scale goes up and down the octave, it swings back and forth between pockets of instability (dissonance) and stability (consonance). We will learn the reason for this oscillation later, and its surprising connection with walking.

There is in fact a simple, knock-down argument for why up–down motion in music is real and not metaphorical. It corresponds to the rising and falling motion of the vocal cords in our larynx.[6] When we sing a high note, the larynx is tensed; when we sing a low one, it relaxes. Our singing experience even shapes how we hear non-vocal music. So although playing a very high note on a piano doesn't require any more effort than playing a low one, our vocal cords sympathetically contract when we hear it as if it did. Moreover, there is evidence that our association of musical pitch with height is innate and hard-wired into our brains.[7] Experiments have shown that one-year-old babies matched rising and falling tones with arrows pointing up and down,[8] and that pitch height is even registered by very young children who have been congenitally blind from birth.[9]

The world of music is full of examples of how cultural knowledge overwrites these innate associations. Ancient Greek music theory speaks not of high and low pitch, but of 'sharp' and 'heavy'. In Bali and Java, they have 'small' (= high) and 'large' (= low). The Kisedje of Brazil associate pitch with age, so think in terms of 'young' (= high) and 'old' (= low).[10] And pianists of course play on keyboards which 'rise' from left to right. But that doesn't at all mean that pianists don't carry innate pitch height in their minds, just as absence of this sense is not proven by the fact that the Kaluli of Papua New Guinea, who associate melodic contour with waterfalls, have no concept of rising melodies because waterfalls don't rise.[11]

There is also a neurological basis for why sounds in general evoke movement. Our sense of hearing is closely linked to our vestibular system, which is responsible for keeping our balance when we are walking. Listening to music activates the premotor cortex, basal ganglia and cerebellum, motor areas associated with movement. Indeed, people need only to imagine music – not necessarily to actually hear it – for these brain regions to be activated.[12] The most elegant theory of why we hear and imagine music as motion, even tying together the spiral of musical space, was proposed by the philosopher Charles Nussbaum.[13] It all goes back to the fish.

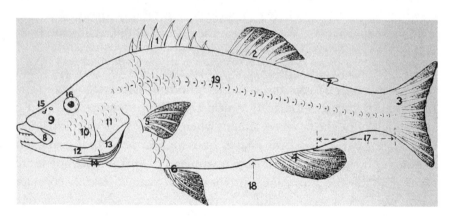

Figure 4.1 A fish's lateral line

Fish don't hear very well. But they are excellent at detecting motion through water; namely, the periodic – i.e. repetitive and cyclical – swimming movements of other fish. They do this through a system of hair cells arranged head-to-tail across their body called the lateral line (see **Figure 4.1**).[14] It is more accurate to say that fish feel sounds rather than hear them, and this tactile dimension is recaptured when very low bass notes make our nether regions rumble. In no sense did the human ear evolve out of the lateral line (it grew, rather, from the fish's gill). We hear through the organ of Corti, the core of the cochlea, which contains a set of hairs sensitive not to periodic pressure waves, as in fish, but to frequency (see **Figure 4.2**).[15] The organ of Corti is a miniature, highly superior version of the lateral line. If you uncoiled the cochlea, the smaller hairs – those responsive to the highest frequencies – would lie nearest the brainstem, and the largest hairs would be furthest away.[16] In this respect, evolution has flipped the lateral line from the horizontal head-to-tail axis of the fish to the vertical head-to-toe axis of humans. This is akin to turning a piano keyboard on its side, so that the pitches now rise instead of moving left to right. And indeed nineteenth-century acousticians such as Hermann von Helmholtz pointed out the resemblance between the organ of Corti and the harp-like arrangement of strings sitting horizontally within a grand piano.[17]

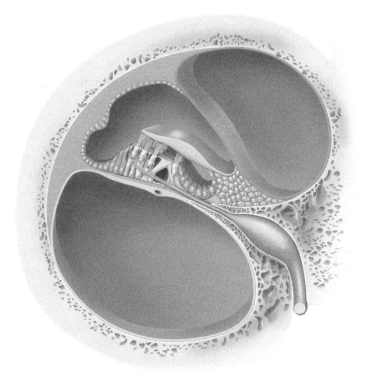

Figure 4.2 The organ of corti

Nussbaum's story now moves in to explain the connection between hearing music and walking. Adapted to a vertical life on dry land,

and subject to gravity, walking involves periodic (regular, repetitive) swings away from and returns to a centre of stability, informed by the vestibular system's sense of balance. This periodic return to stability reminds Nussbaum of the spiral of musical space, the way a scale oscillates between degrees of consonance and dissonance; ultimately, the periodic return of the octave.[18] Just as walking in a line combines direction with cyclic repetitions, a scale of notes coordinates 'movement' 'up' and 'down' through musical space with cyclical returns to stability. There are several extremely suggestive messages we can take away from Nussbaum's just-so story. Human hearing is an evolutionary blend of ancient and modern systems: a primeval system orientated to periodicity, and a younger system sensitive to frequency. Or in other words, our liking for octaves is an evolutionary memory of when we were fish. The second lesson is that listening to music really is related to our experience of walking upright in a gravitational field. A further thought is that when we say music 'touches' us, as when a fish feels the tactile vibrations of water, we are not talking metaphorically at all.

In Schubert's song cycle *Winterreise* (*A Winter's Journey*), a jilted lover walks through a snowy landscape in search of spiritual redemption. The twenty-four songs alternate different styles of walking – trudging, ambling, shuffling, even running helter-skelter in panic – with moments of standing still, as when the lover stops to consider a linden tree ('Der Lindenbaum'). The styles of walking even take on aspects of nature, so that the lover can jerk like frozen tears ('Gefrorne Tränen'), flit like a will o' the wisp ('Irrlicht'), rush like a raging river ('Auf dem Flusse'), or hover like a pair of crows ('Die Krähe'). The piano is very good at capturing the rhythms of the human gait, blended with poetic imagery. Music doesn't need words to express motion. The slow movement of Schubert's mighty Ninth Symphony is like those vast mountainous landscapes that Schubert loved trekking through in southern Austria. Walking through a landscape is intrinsic to Western music; it is not a metaphor. But that doesn't mean that there aren't further mysteries to how we imagine it. To go further down that path, we need to consider a famous thought experiment by the philosopher Ludwig Wittgenstein.[19]

The image in **Figure 4.3** shows a pair of protuberances jutting from a circle. You can choose to see them as either the ears of a rabbit or the beak of a duck. You can even flick from one to the other at will. Wittgenstein uses this illusion to explain his distinction between 'seeing' and 'seeing *as*'. Seeing that a leaf is green is just a perceptual act. But imagining that a drawing represents a duck rather than a rabbit is a procedure that can be prompted. You can decide, be told, or even be taught to see something in a particular way. And although Wittgenstein didn't infer this, his idea also applies to music. You can choose or be guided to hear music one way or another.

Figure 4.3 Rabbit or duck?

When listening to music, we can adopt the external viewpoint of a spectator. For instance, imagine listening to Vaughan Williams's *The Lark Ascending*. The violin, impersonating the lark, seems to fly through the sky: it is an object moving through a landscape. But sometimes it is the landscape that moves while we stand still. This happens when we survey a well-known piece in our minds. Think of any work or song you know well – it could be *The Lark Ascending*, Beethoven's Fifth or even 'Somewhere Over the Rainbow'. If you are familiar enough with it, you will be able to bring the beginning, middle or end of the music to the mind's attention at will. It's no different to mentally thinking of the various rooms of your house.

Imagine now that you are inside the music, rather than a spectator. Hearing or imagining the gallop from Rossini's *William Tell* Overture, you feel yourself carried away on a horse. Rather than observing the music move past you, you are moving with the music. This happens in most dance music, and in dance-like music such as Bach's *Brandenburg Concertos*, as well as in music with a lot of kinetic drive, such as Beethoven's *Eroica* Symphony. You give in to the music's motion, you identify with it. Alternately, music that doesn't have much sense of directed motion, such as Debussy's *La mer* or the majority of Renaissance polyphony, has the opposite effect. Now it is the music that moves while you stand still and feel the sound wash over you. This is like the two ways of imagining time. Sometimes you feel yourself travelling down the path of life; at other times, you worry that life is passing you by.

In all these four examples – (1) external, moving object; (2) external, moving landscape; (3) internal, you move; (4) internal, you stand still – your choice is prompted by an aspect of the music.[20] Vaughan Williams's lark moves because the orchestral accompaniment is comparatively slow, so that we hear the bird as a figure against a ground. With dancing or galloping music, on the other hand, the whole orchestra moves together. The reason that Palestrina's masses and much other early music tends to wash over us like the waves of the sea is that too much is going on in the texture for us to grasp or predict a line of direction. But we don't need prompts in order to decide to hear music in various ways. Dorothy's song from *The Wizard of Oz* is not exactly a blank slate. But it is simple enough to run our thought experiment. Consider the opening two notes again, the octave leap of 'Somewhere'. First, imagine those two syllables, respectively, in low and high locations, perhaps the base and apex of the rainbow. What you are doing is hearing the snippet of music as two places in musical 'space'. Now, imagine them as a single note in motion, rising up the rainbow. You have switched your focus onto the music's 'motion'. Duck-Rabbit, Space-Motion. Welcome to music's space-motion continuum.

Motion Conveys Emotion

Dorothy's rising octave conveys another quality: a sense of yearning. When one note moves to another in music, it is not like the Newtonian motion of an inanimate object, say a cricket ball whizzing through physical space. A note seems to have a life of its own so that it 'wills' its journey to the next note.[21] Or – to flip from rabbit to duck – we may feel that there is a life force flowing between the notes. We enjoy, in turn, a sense of anticipation as the melody 'rises' to the top, and then an emotional reward when it reaches it. Climactic or very high notes in melodies typically induce a frisson of pleasure that psychologists call 'the chills' (or even 'skin orgasm').[22] The top A at the end of 'Nessun dorma' never fails to deliver, and Pavarotti (the 'King of the High Cs') shamelessly milks the note much longer than Puccini's score asks for.

What do musical motion and emotion have in common, apart from six letters? Neuroscience tells us that the brain's motor and reward systems are united in the striatum, deep within the subcortical basal ganglia of the forebrain. The upper, dorsal part of the striatum is responsible for action and prediction. The lower, ventral striatum is connected to the oldest and most emotional part of the brain called the limbic system. A team of neuroscientists working at McGill University in Montreal, led by Robert Zatorre, discovered a direct link between these brain regions and musical 'chills', based on the release of dopamine.[23] Dopamine is a pleasure-inducing neurotransmitter associated with food, sex, drugs and also music (unlike the other three, you can't have too much of music; it is just as addictive, without being bad for you in excess). Using positron emission tomography (PET scans), Zatorre's lab measured how dopamine was released in the brains of eight subjects listening to their favourite pieces. The order of events is fascinating. When music starts to build to the climax during the anticipation phase, dopamine pours into the dorsal striatum. When the musical climax arrives, it triggers an emotional reaction in the ventral striatum. This is why listeners experience as much pleasure in imaginatively 'moving' towards the musical goal as when they reach it.

The job of a composer, then, is to manipulate the anticipations of the listener. That was the view of the great music theorist Leonard Meyer, the first person to crack the riddle of musical emotion.[24] Meyer showed that all music was based on patterns, some of which are natural (or psychologically hard-wired), such as the expectation that a scale will continue in the same direction that it began, and some of which are learned, such as the convention that a verse in a pop song will lead to a chorus. Composers tread a tightrope between novelty and redundancy. Too much change and the listener is lost. Too little, and the listener is bored. Emotion is induced when a pattern is interrupted or subverted in some way. It is like when someone creeps up behind you and says 'Boo!'

Emotion in music, as in life, originates in the fear of the startle reflex. Musical emotion is the distillation of surprise, and we discussed the shocks in Haydn's *Surprise* Symphony in Chapter 1. But Meyer found that emotion also arises when a pattern is fulfilled, when it reaches its goal, just as Zatorre confirmed. Writing in the 1950s, Meyer proposed ideas that took a further half-century to test with modern neuroscience. The evidence rests that musical emotion swings back and forth between the subversion and resolution of expectation, between anticipation and climax. Some of the most vivid examples are in opera, because it raises this principle to high drama.

The joke in opera is that Wagner's *Tristan und Isolde* is the most drawn-out sexual climax in world history, around five hours. More accurately, the lovers' consummation, expressed by the harmonic resolution of the yearning 'Tristan chord' introduced in the opening bars, is interrupted exactly halfway through the opera. In Act II, Scene 2, at the point when they are about to kiss, the pair are discovered by Isolde's husband, King Mark, and the 'Tristan chord' is interrupted. Much, much later, when Tristan lies dead of his wounds on a beach in Brittany, the chord is resolved when Isolde pours out her soul in an ecstatic 'love-death' (*Liebestod*). The subversion-resolution rhythm is also fundamental to comic timing. At the end of Mozart's *The Marriage of Figaro*, the Count is furious to have discovered his wife apparently *in flagrante* with his servant. He lifts her veil; it turns out to be his wife's maid, Susanna, and the Countess emerges from her hiding place. In the space of seconds, rage turns to surprise, then to wonder, culminating in a hymn of forgiveness. Although it begins in comedy, Mozart's dizzying succession of reversals recalls the *peripeteia* of ancient Greek drama, or even the transformation scene at the end of Shakespeare's *The Winter's Tale*.

What is going on here, according to Meyer's most distinguished follower, the music psychologist David Huron, is 'contrastive valence'.[25] Emotion is most intense when our evaluation of something switches from negative to positive; indeed, the intensity is proportionate to the contrast. Judging from the hundreds of millions of views it has received on YouTube, contrastive valence on a global scale was elicited by the singer Susan Boyle's audition video for the British talent show, *Britain's Got Talent*.[26] The video is a test case of social stereotyping, and has become a subject of learned academic studies.[27] Presented as an ungainly middle-aged woman, Boyle stands on stage, and is mocked by both the judges and audience. As soon as she starts to sing 'I Dreamed a Dream' from *Les Misérables*, derision turns to surprise and steadily mounts to ecstatic enthusiasm. The audience rise to their feet; their enthusiasm climaxes with the melody's own high point, the goal of its rising scale. It is a perfect emotional storm, an extraordinary coming together of surprise, contrastive valence, melodic anticipation and climax, catching fire virally across the planet. The immediate response of Piers Morgan, one of the judges, could hardly have been scripted better: 'That was the biggest surprise I have had in three years of this show.' I am not ashamed to admit that I blub whenever I watch this video; whether cynically or, more likely, through happenstance, it presses all the emotional buttons. It is instructive to compare it with Anne Hathaway's equally remarkable Oscar-winning performance of 'I Dreamed a Dream' in the film of *Les Misérables*. Hathaway makes us cry because we sympathise with Victor Hugo's tragic heroine. The Boyle video makes us cry because it subverts a pattern, a social stereotype.

Anticipation is possible only because humans have a grasp of regular time intervals. The neuroscientist Aniruddh Patel has linked our ability to predict what comes next to the evolution of walking.[28] In other words, walking may have taught our brain its sense of time, and time is perhaps the brain's 'internal simulation' of the periodic motion of footsteps (averaging about one step every 100 milliseconds). This is a lovely theory that neatly wraps together music, emotion, anticipation and walking. But how significant is it that monkeys can't be trained to tap in time with a metronome? Or, indeed, that EEG scans of brainwave patterns in rhesus monkeys suggest that they don't even perceive regular beats?[29] Do we shy away from the inference that animals who don't walk upright on two legs, and who lack a sense of time (including animals such as human babies), by definition have no emotion? Tell that to a barking dog or a howling infant. The theory is on the back foot, and needs more work.

What Darwin has to teach us about musical emotion

Rare is the thinker who sparks not one intellectual revolution but two. Charles Darwin's *On the Origin of Species* is his best-known work. Not far behind in importance is *The Expression of the Emotions in Man and*

Animals, the book that did most to shape our modern understanding of emotion.[30] *The Expression* detonates two explosive claims. The first is that there is a continuity between the emotions of people and animals. That will be a focus for Part Three of my book. But as a taster, I would suggest that there is no reason to doubt that the rage of the T-Rex in Walt Disney's *Fantasia* comes from the same reptilian brain as the rage of Stravinsky's music that accompanies it. I will park that idea for now. The second explosion is Darwin's idea that emotions serve an adaptive role in helping humans and animals survive in a hostile environment. Whether or not we share the same emotions as animals (and I think we mostly do), emotions function in a similar way. Emotions are not irrational decoration or garnish, as opposed to the rationality of concepts and language. Darwin showed that they were rational in their own fashion, and absolutely central both to evolution and to modern everyday life. As we shall see, this is very good news for music, the emotional art par excellence. The idea blasts a path for a theory of musical evolution.

Darwin's Eureka moment happened during a visit to London Zoo, where he encountered a puff adder:

> I put my face close to the thick glass-plate [in front of the puff adder] with the firm determination of not starting back if the snake struck at me; but, as soon as the blow was struck, my resolution went for nothing, and I jumped a yard or two backwards with astonishing rapidity.[31]

Had Darwin met the snake in the wild, then his instinctive recoil might have saved his life. As it was, this instinct is so entrenched in our nature that it is impossible to resist, even when our rational mind tells us we are safe. In Darwin's words, 'the nervous system [...] sends its order to the motor system so quickly, that no time is allowed for [us] to consider whether or not the danger is real'.[32] Emotions, then, far from being irrational, are in some ways smarter and faster than reason. They afford a 'quick and dirty' appraisal of a situation, with a direct bearing on our actions and possible well-being.

The 'quick and dirty' affective appraisal isn't the end of the story. It triggers physiological responses (such as activity in our autonomic nervous system and changes in the facial musculature) and motor responses (how the organism deals with the situation). And finally these yield to a more discriminating 'cognitive appraisal' ('It's a snake!') or reappraisal ('It's behind glass', or possibly, if in the field, 'It's only a stick'). According to Jenefer Robinson, a contemporary philosopher much influenced by Darwin's theory, 'emotion is not a thing or a response or a state or a disposition; it is a *process*, a sequence of events'.[33]

Science doesn't progress in a steady line. It is more like the medieval goose dance of Echternach in Luxembourg, where processing pilgrims, hopping from right to left foot like a goose, alternated between three steps forwards and two steps back.[34] It took a very long time for Darwin's ideas on emotion to be taken seriously. For much of the twentieth century, psychology was dominated by the behaviourism of B. F. Skinner, which held that humans were glorified lab rats subject to 'operant conditioning' and with no inner life, certainly no emotion. After the 1980s, however, the humanities and social sciences undertook an 'affective turn', led by emotion theorists such as Magda Arnold, Richard Lazarus, Keith Oatley and Nico Frijda.[35] Following Darwin, these 'appraisal theorists' held that emotion helped pick out and focus attention upon something crucial in the environment that impinges on our well-being.

Emotional appraisal isn't anticipation; anticipation predicts what will happen in the future, whereas appraisal perceives and evaluates what is taking place right now. Emotion is a mode of sensory perception, like eyesight and hearing. Nevertheless, appraisal is directly related to my running idea that emotion involves walking down a path, but now in a quite different way. An emotional appraisal induces a tendency to act in a certain manner; in short, what the psychologist Nico Frijda terms an 'action tendency'.[36] Fear makes us flee. Anger makes us attack. Love makes us touch what we love. Emotion is also appraised in terms of how it helps or hinders our personal goals. Happiness means our goal is achieved. Blocking our goal makes us angry. Losing our goal, as when we lose a loved one, causes sadness. So if we imagine life as a pathway through the world towards a goal of personal well-being (i.e. evolutionary survival), then emotions are the ways we walk this pathway.

It is obvious how this model of emotion maps onto the idea that music is a pathway through an imaginary landscape. Happy pieces unfold musical 'action tendencies' towards successful goals. Sad pieces seem to lack the will to live, and their pathways meander without any clear goal. It doesn't matter whether you adopt the viewpoint of the actor or the spectator, the rabbit or the duck; whether it is the object or the landscape that 'moves'.

Many of these pathways have actually already been explored in real life, in the journeys of music through the city outlined in Chapter 3. Here is the trick, or, if you prefer, the miracle: the same principles apply in everyday life as they do in the inner life of music. The musical human becomes the human in the music. This constitutes the double life of music.

The Double Life of Music

Let's make a return visit to that teenage bedroom in Chapter 3, where music was a soundtrack for a love affair. What kind of music do lovers choose to script the early stage of a relationship? It must be relaxing, so song rather than dance. It needs to be quiet and soft enough to talk over, or to not talk at all, letting the song's amorous qualities speak *for* the lovers ('music is the language of love', and so on). It would be good if the song were slow, to set the cautious tempo for the encounter. And if the music oscillated in intensity, scripting the hesitant approaches and withdrawals of early intimacy.

Any number of love songs would be suitable. A classic that springs to mind is Whitney Houston's 'I Will Always Love You' from the film *The Bodyguard*. My point is that all the features of amorous behaviour such music might accompany are also present *inside* the song. Remember how the track begins, with Houston singing quietly, breathily and alone (without accompaniment), in a low register, and with those strangely hesitant breaths between her words. As Houston gets into her stride, she stretches out her words with those soaring vocal runs characteristic of gospel music, whose effect here is to compound an emotion of trembling uncertainty. This is a perfect set-up for the song's killer blow, when she finds certainty on an extremely long, held tonic note swelling at the top of her register (the first note of the scale, but up an octave), with the words that complete the sense of the song. The melodic climax is underscored by the first entry of guitar and synth strings.

And then she repeats the cycle all over again, dropping back down and rising to a climax twice more, each wave higher and more confident than the one before. The second verse is more intense because the rhythm section, absent till now, finally comes in, and she sings louder and with more conviction. In verse three she is joined by the saxophone. And for the third climax Houston pulls the old trick of jacking up the key, and her voice breaks into a falsetto up a fifth for the final stratospheric 'you'. I remember Houston's song in the early 1990s stunning British pubs into silence, as drinkers succumbed to collective swooning and the musical 'chills' at the final climax. Never has the term 'skin orgasm' felt more accurate to describe how music can induce waves of pleasure running all over your body.

'I Will Always Love You' builds from hesitancy to erotic climax. *Tristan und Isolde* also does that; in fact, all love music has this shape, and that is why it sounds like love music. The shape of love – or, in Darwinian terms, its 'action tendency' – is cumulatively widening waves towards a climax. You don't need to see the video of Houston pining for Kevin Costner to get this, nor do you need to know anything about Whitney Houston, or even understand the words. The shape is in the music. This is the sound of sex. It is no accident that such music can also script sex. The crucial point, though, is that music mirrors and internalises everyday behaviour. It turns out that music is not abstract after all. Or rather, it *is* abstract, according to the technical sense of something abstracted from concrete reality and rendered in concentrated form. To stay with the simile I introduced earlier, it is like distilling the essence of a flower into a perfume.

Music in the West has a 'double life' because it both accompanies our activities and mirrors them within its sounds, gestures and formal patterns. What we hear in 'I Will Always Love You' also applies for all the other emotions.

When General Noriega was besieged in the Vatican Embassy, as I recounted in Chapter 3, the US Army didn't bombard him with Céline Dion. They used hard rock, because its aggressive power chords express the emotion of anger. The screeching violins in the shower scene of *Psycho*, courtesy of Bernard Herrmann, are sonic analogues of Anthony Perkins's stabbing gestures. But they go equally well with Janet Leigh's screams of terror: Hitchcock knows that anger and fear are two sides of the same coin. Albinoni's *Adagio*, cited by the *Daily Telegraph* as No. 5 in its poll of the top seventy-eight funeral songs (strangely, No. 1 is Monty Python's 'Always Look on the Bright Side of Life'), is sad because it is saturated with weeping gestures called 'appoggiaturas'.[37] *The Wall Street Journal* ran a feature on why Adele's 'Someone Like You' makes people cry, and they also put it down to its appoggiaturas – descending, sigh-like ornaments that clash with the harmony.[38] But sad tunes also tend to droop in descending contours, mimicking the way grief pulls us down and saps our energy. Conversely, when we're proud, we stand up straight and puff out our chests. Elgar's *Pomp and Circumstance Marches* audibly do that. We catch the revolutionary fervour of the 'Marseillaise' from its opening fanfares; these drive the music forward just as military music propels armies. The biggest stroke of genius in all film music was to use double-bass rumbles to suggest an approaching shark. Long before *Jaws*, Berlioz used the same idea in the slow movement of his *Symphonie fantastique* to evoke the distant thunder of an approaching storm. Spielberg couldn't resist recycling this genius idea twice more, for the T-rex in *Jurassic Park*, and the tank in *Saving Private Ryan*.

Musical happiness is more elusive because, in some ways, all music makes us happy; we even enjoy sad music at some level. It turns out that happy music is formally simpler and more conventional, because Darwinian happiness – its 'action tendency' – is goal-fulfilment.[39] 'Happy Birthday to You' is a perfect little gem of conventional simplicity and goal-fulfilment. Happy music loves symmetry and repetition: a concise opening phrase ('Happy birthday to you') is answered by a modified repeat. Happy music needs to wander off-course so as to be able to return in triumph. The song's second half is more continuous (i.e. without the symmetrical repeat), more complex, attains the melodic high point ('Happy BIRTHDAY dear X...'), and smuggles in a final repeat at its end. 'Three Blind Mice', 'Twinkle, Twinkle Little Star' and Beethoven's 'Ode to Joy' all work on the same principle: opening repetition, digression, return. They also epitomise happiness's liking for step-wise descending patterns, simulating the law of gravity. What goes up must come down, in a nice balanced arc.[40]

Because of its simplicity and predictability, the 1950s dance genre of skiffle (see Chapter 3) epitomises another strand of happy music: its 'participatory' nature. We are never happier than when we are socially connected; when we can participate in the music-making or when we dance. Dancing makes you happy because it fully engages your body in pleasurable activity, thereby reinforcing a feedback loop: happiness makes you want to dance, and dancing makes you happier (through what psychologists call 'peripheral feedback').[41] However, these very qualities also render happy music suspect in the eyes of Marxist philosophers such as Theodor Adorno, prince of the melancholy science of critical theory.[42] Music that is easy on the ear – because predictable – can often be shallow and artistically not very interesting. It is easy to mass-produce in the factories of popular culture, such as the pop and rock industries or purveyors of advertising jingles. The dubious link between standardised music and money is cashed out when easy listening is used to lubricate the shopping experience, as we saw in the arcades of Bold Street and Liverpool One. But this doesn't mean that happy music always succumbs to this shallow pitfall. The Beatles' journey, from skiffle to *Abbey Road*, is one of gradually deepening happiness – from the ridiculous to the sublime. Another version of deep happiness is

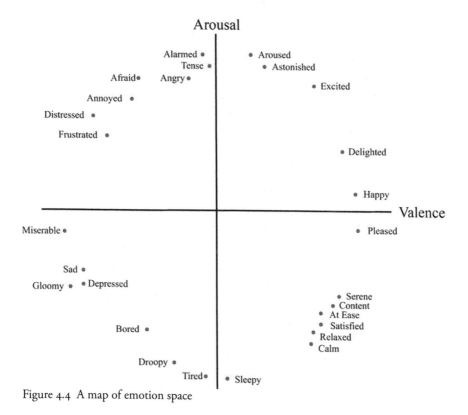

Figure 4.4 A map of emotion space

classical sonata form, the most prestigious type of music in the West.[43] The form is the quintessence of symmetry, goal-orientated development and triumphant return. Ideas are presented in an exposition, elaborated in a development section, and repeated and resolved in a recapitulation. The default emotional setting of classical music is happy, which is why we like it so much.

It is surprisingly practical to map emotional space. **Figure 4.4** is based on the psychologist James Russell's circumplex graph of emotion along the two axes of valence (pleasant or unpleasant) and arousal (high or low energy).[44] The five basic emotions – happiness, sadness, anger, tenderness and fear – can be plotted in terms of these parameters. Happiness is pleasant and high-energy. Anger also has high arousal, but is unpleasant. Sadness is low-energy and unpleasant. Tenderness is low-arousal and pleasant. Fear is like anger, but includes elements of unpredictability. Experiments conducted by the music psychologist Patrick Juslin discovered that listeners associate these emotions with how a melody is performed. So Juslin asked a guitarist to play 'When the Saints Go Marching In' in different ways, and then asked the listeners to identify which emotions they felt were being expressed.[45] When the tune was played loud, staccato (detached articulation), fast and in the major key, listeners heard it as happy. This flipped to angry when the guitarist changed major to minor. When played soft, legato (smooth), slow and in the major key, it sounded tender. When soft, legato, slow, but now in the minor, listeners heard sadness. And when played with unpredictable contrasts, it sounded frightening. These acoustic parameters work across the entire spectrum of classical and popular music, for any pieces you care to imagine. Here is a set of random examples: George Harrison's 'Here Comes the Sun' (happy); Adele's 'Hometown Glory' (sad); Carly Simon's 'Nobody Does It Better' (tender); Rage Against the Machine's 'Killing in the Name' (anger); the British dubstep artist Burial's 'Ghost Hardware' (fear). With his uncanny mix of electronic sounds, glitches and unpredictable contrasts, hovering just above audibility, Burial presents the modern sound of urban anxiety.

Fear is nature's most primal emotion, a creature's way of coping with a hostile environment. Scientists have taught a single-cell slime mould called *Physarum polycephalum*, an organism so primitive that it lacks a nervous system, not to flinch from certain bitter substances.[46] To ask whether this organism experiences fear in the same way we do is to look at emotion the wrong way round. It is the case, rather, that what we call 'fear' is just a name for an extremely fundamental coping mechanism. What is so fascinating is that this primeval reflex is still around aeons of evolutionary time later, in the most sophisticated forms known to human culture.

Schubert's Fear

Fear stalks the landscape of Schubert's *Unfinished* Symphony. The first thing you hear is a mysterious, dark, slow theme whispered almost inaudibly by the double basses.[47] Why do we find this theme so threatening? We are biologically programmed to associate low and slow sounds with large objects (think the roar of a bear). When this sound is very quiet, we automatically adjust for distance, so it sounds far away. John Williams uses exactly the same principle as Schubert in *Jaws* (although, paradoxically, sharks are silent). The symphony pauses for effect, and then the violins react to this threat by trembling. This is a freezing response, the first action tendency of fear.[48] The beats of the lower strings (cellos and basses) mimic the palpitations of a scared heart. Schubert's distant threat takes nine minutes to arrive. The ominous low theme comes back with a vengeance at the start of the development section, now loud and nasty, and all hell breaks out: a storm of orchestral fireworks. In Darwinian terms, this is the action tendency of attack. Despite the interval of nine minutes, the listener infers a journey across the musical space-movement continuum, an imaginary path from A to B. We hear that the threat has 'moved' towards us, across Schubert's virtual landscape.

This is the primitive undercurrent of the *Unfinished* Symphony. It is overlaid by a culturally more modern story, the conventional plan of sonata form. Sonata stories share the shape of the stereotypical fairy tale, as catalogued by the great Russian folklorist, Vladimir Propp.[49] In folk tales the world over, from *Puss in Boots* through *The Wizard of Oz* to *Star Wars*, a hero or heroine leaves home, has adventures, possibly culminating in a battle, and returns home to triumph or tragedy. In music, we call 'home' the 'tonic' key – the key based around the first note of the scale. This key is generally used in much of the first part of the music, the exposition. Leaving home is called 'modulation', and it is usually to the 'dominant' key, built on the fifth degree of the scale. The second half of the exposition normally sits in the dominant key. Adventures and battles happen in the development section, in even more distant keys. And the hero/heroine returns home in the recapitulation. Most music, from Haydn through Brahms, Mahler, Sibelius to Shostakovich, rings the changes on this basic tale. It is part of the music lover's mental furniture.

As I said earlier, as part of the 'double life of music', the same principles of everyday life apply within music's inner life. That was Miracle no. 1. Here comes the next move of the trick, or Miracle no. 2. The five quadrants of emotion space, mapped by Russell and Juslin, are staging posts on the hero or heroine's journey in sonata space. As the musical protagonist walks the 'landscape', he or she undergoes a succession of emotional experiences. It is rather like the various emotional gaits traipsed by the jilted lover in Schubert's *Winterreise*, although there the emotions were walked by successive songs. But it is the same principle. Our journey through life is an ever-changing emotional gait. After opening with fear, Schubert's symphony modulates to love in the tender second theme – the famous, standout melody of the work. The exposition climaxes in triumph. But this happy conclusion is premature and superficial. It reminds me of the notorious poster of *Jaws*, showing a woman happily swimming on the ocean's surface, serenely oblivious of the danger below. This danger surfaces in the development section and consumes the music. The movement dies in tragic grief, the fifth and final emotion.

In music, as in horror films, nobody actually dies, unlike in the reality of nature 'red in tooth and claw'. Music's imitation game is cleverer than that of cinema, however, because it is abstract. The life of music mirrors everyday life without there being anything to see. How does music do that?

Mimesis

Music can imitate anything. It may not be very good at painting the visual impression of something, say a teaspoon in a glass of water. But it has a fantastic capacity to express motion and emotion: people's struggles, aspirations, triumphs and tragedies. Musical expression is as endlessly resourceful as onomatopoeia, hand gestures or the rising and falling intonations of the human voice, as when we are stuck in a foreign land and are forced to communicate with our hands or vocal sounds. Musical imitation could even be said to exemplify a more general human compulsion to mimic. Darwin called this compulsion a 'faculty', based on experiences gained on his voyage on the *Beagle*. The journal of the *Beagle* records the interactions of its crew with natives of Tierra del Fuego.

> They are excellent mimics: as often as we coughed or yawned or made any odd motion, they immediately imitated us. Some of the officers began to squint and make monkey-like faces; but one of the young Fuegians (whose face was painted black with a white band over his eyes) succeeded in making far more hideous grimaces. They could repeat with perfect correctness each word in any sentence we addressed them … All savages appear to possess, to an uncommon degree, this power of mimicry.[50]

The encounter becomes even more interesting when the sailors entered into the spirit of mimicry, and began imitating the Indians imitating them. Captain FitzRoy of the *Beagle* noted his impressions in his own journal:

> They expressed satisfaction or good will by rubbing or patting their own, and then our bodies; and were highly pleased by the antics of a man belonging to the boat's crew, who danced well and was a good mimic.[51]

Reviewing these reports, the anthropologist Michael Taussig asks, 'Who is mimicking whom?'[52] Exactly the same chicken-and-egg problem happens when adults imitate baby talk through infant-directed speech or 'motherese'. As we saw in Chapter 2, people (and they don't necessarily have to be parents) discover this faculty when they instinctively talk to a young child. What is so fascinating about language is that, the further back we go – when we strip away syntax and semantics – the more imitative it gets. What language loses in articulation, it gains in mimesis.

In the early twentieth century the primitive roots of mimesis fascinated a stream of thinkers. The German philosopher Walter

Benjamin thought that 'the gift of seeing resemblances is nothing other than a rudiment of the powerful compulsion in former times to become and behave like something else'.[53] The French writer Roger Caillois audaciously linked mimesis to insect biology, as when an organism such as a stick insect mimics its ecological niche to hide from predators. Caillois believed this demonstrated life's instinct to merge with its environment: 'the human desire to recover its original insensate condition, a desire comparable to the pantheistic idea of becoming one with nature … [and] returning to prenatal unconsciousness'.[54] Similar claims were made in the anthropology of religion, and it is no accident that the hero of Caillois' narrative is the 'praying mantis' (in French, 'la mante religieuse'). The leap from biology to religion, at first glance astronomically wide, is actually no leap at all. The sociologist Émile Durkheim taught us how the earliest religions mediated with the Divine by imitating animals – that communing with animals bridged humans with nature and supernature. Darwin himself describes the 'corrobery', an Australian Aboriginal dance ceremony, including an emu dance 'in which each man extended his arm in bent manner'.[55] Running with Darwin's idea, Durkheim's *The Elementary Forms of Religious Life* observed that religious rites, such as those of the Arunta (or Arrernte) Aboriginal people, are essentially imitative. The dancers jump like kangaroos or fly like winged ants; they mimic the squeak of a bat, the call of a wild turkey, the hiss of a snake, the croak of a frog.[56] The power of mimesis, so it is broadly believed, is that it affords control. We imagine that we can move aspects of the world by imitating it, a principle that is fundamental to the ancient tradition of sympathetic magic. This pre-scientific world view survives in the voodoo practice of pricking a wooden image of our enemy.

Mimesis is what music does, with one foot in biology and another in religion. A composer imitates nature and the world. He or she does so not superficially – like Vivaldi in *The Four Seasons*, or the bird calls in Beethoven's *Pastoral* Symphony. Music taps into the inner life of human experience, its motions and emotions.

Mimesis of mimesis, as in the imitative circle between the Fuegians and the sailors, or baby and caregiver, brings us to Miracle no. 3. When we listen to music, we imitate *it*. We identify with the music. Not just beating in time, even inwardly; not just tensing up or relaxing with it. At a far deeper level, we inhabit the music, skin, body and soul.

We walk its path. Not alongside the music: we *are* the music while it 'walks'. We become the personas in the music and take up their motions and emotions. We mind-meld with Stravinsky's clown Petrushka and live his jerky rhythms. We walk the stately funeral march from Handel's *Saul*. We can even experience what it is like to be an inanimate building. Listening to the finale of Schumann's *Rhenish* Symphony, a work inspired by Cologne Cathedral, the music fills us with the church's size and weight so that we feel ourselves stooping and lurching. Musical mimesis is also mental karaoke in a British pub. We don't necessarily need to sing along with Whitney Houston. Just listening to her we find ourselves inwardly and physically in sync with her voice and her feelings.

Music's double life, then, is due to the mimesis of mimesis. This is why Western music is participatory despite its apparent divorce from creative music-making. Our music is participatory in a dual and interlinked sense. First, we fill our lives with music as a soundtrack, as we saw in Chapter 3. Second, we sink ourselves into the music in the act of focused listening. These two sides are interconnected because we participate in music's imitation of our world in circles within circles.

Musical mimesis is by no means restricted to the West; we have already visited the Kisedje Mouse Ceremony. My next chapter will go deeper into the origins of music in the religious imitation of animals. But I want at this point to shade the distinctive borders of Western music by means of two examples of world music that use mimesis in a quite different way. They suggest that traditional musics outside the West haven't raised the idea of walking through a landscape to such a high level of abstraction.

The ancient Kazakh shamans of Central Asia invoked the spirit world by imitating totemic animals and birds.[57] 'Aqqu', a traditional piece played on the two-stringed horsehair fiddle called the *qobyz*, is the epic tale of the White Swan, the Kazakhs' most important ancestral spirit. It is still performed today by *qobyz* virtuosos such as Raushan Orazbaeva, and her rendition of 'Aqqu' is filled with sound effects imitating the calls and flight patterns of swans, as well as other scenes from the epic. The audience is given a textual programme so that they can follow how the successive sound effects illustrate particular episodes in the myth. They hear swans in flight; swans circling; landing on the lake; taking off and flying away; a galloping horse as a boy gives chase; his grandmother wailing; the boy fighting his enemies; more swan cries fading into the distance – all these effects evoked through nuanced instrumental techniques in a kind of musical onomatopoeia. Raushan claims to have learned these techniques through careful birdwatching, and that, when she played 'Aqqu' beside a pond full of birds, they even mistook the sound of her *qobyz* for that of a swan, and responded with similar calls.

Now, all these sound effects hold together and make sense because the audience is following the story in their programme sheets. In no respect are the individual sounds understood to follow each other in themselves, as one note 'moves' to another in the pathways of Western music. The epic story certainly moves, but this progression is guided by the words of the epic, not driven from within the music itself. More importantly, it is even doubtful that you would hear the *qobyz* as a swan unless you were primed to do so.

My second example comes from China. The *qin*, a seven-string Chinese zither, produces such a quiet and delicate sound that it was traditionally played alone for oneself rather than in public. Performing the *qin* was an extension of spiritual meditation on the path towards personal enlightenment.[58] As with the shamanistic *qobyz*, the *qin* player sought access to the spirit realm via the imitation of nature, guided in this case by Daoist philosophy. Through its vibrating strings, the *qin* was a sympathetic resonator, sounding out the harmony in the depths of nature. Also like the *qobyz* tradition, the music of the *qin*, the earliest record of which goes back to the Tang Dynasty (AD 618–907), is deceptively programmatic. On the one hand, it gives the impression of being soaked in nature imagery. The 150 surviving *qin* anthologies are accompanied by poems, stories and programmes referring to rivers, mountains, flying birds, boats floating on the water, birdsong and even the dripping of a woman's tears. Even the hand and finger postures bear imitative meanings. Here are a few of these postures, as named in the *Taigu yiyin* anthology of 1413: 'the leopard catching its prey'; 'a crane calling in the shade'; 'the lonely duck looking for the flock'; 'a fish beating its tail'.[59] The celebrated *qin* piece, 'Wild Geese Descending on a Sandbank' (Ping sha luo yan), according to a handbook compiled in 1868, purports to express a string of honking and flapping effects: wild geese land on the shore; they call to each other; dialogue of honking between birds in the air and birds on shore; the lonely goose in the air finally lands to join its friends, etc. However, exactly as with the

Kazakh 'Aqqu', the meaning of these sounds is only evident from the accompanying written programme. Indeed, rival versions of Ping sha luo yan supply contradictory interpretations of the music.[60]

As with 'Aqqu', traditional *qin* music is a succession of isolated moments. This is compounded by the music's extremely free rhythmic notation. There is no linear continuity from one moment to the next, because the music is a series of free-floating molecules. Broadly speaking, its stillness gives the listener a foretaste of spiritual tranquillity. It is a blessed relief from the agony of time, the goal-driven temporality that is the especial torment of Western consciousness.

Sticking with birds, to understand the agony of Western time, one need only compare 'Aqqu' and 'Jiao'an Qinpu' with the swans that populate classical music, from Tchaikovsky's *Swan Lake* (whose theme was stolen from *Lohengrin*, Wagner's 'swan knight') through Saint-Saëns' *Carnival of the Animals* to Sibelius's *Swan of Tuonela*. All these Western birds are incarnated within a distinct theme (you can hum it), which is as bounded as the peculiarly Western notion of the individual human subject – an image of humanity with which much of the world disagrees. As bounded individuals, we identity with these swans as they float purposefully, if languidly, down the river of time. There was a famous performance of *Lohengrin* when a foolish stagehand released the mechanical swan, meant to carry the hero to shore, too early. Having missed his boat, but without missing a beat, the tenor Leo Slezak turned to the audience and asked: '*Wann geht der nächste Schwann?*' ('What time's the next swan?').[61]

The Spiritual Path

The founding myth of Western music features not swans but those mysterious bird-women (alternatively, fish-women) hybrids known as Sirens (see **Figure 4.5**). Greek mythology has it that Sirens lured sailors to their deaths on the rocks through the irresistible beauty of their singing. In Homer's *Odyssey*, Odysseus, sailing home from the Trojan War, is determined to hear the Sirens' song in safety, so he has his men lash him to the ship's mast and stops their own ears with wax. Overcome by the music, Odysseus begs his men to untie him so that he can plunge into the sea. But they don't hear his pleas, and they row on. This is a powerful allegory of the dangers and safeguards of identifying too closely (through mimesis) with the potentially overwhelming power of music. It was seized upon by Theodor Adorno and Max Horkheimer, authors of one of the most influential political tracts of the twentieth century, as a parable of the emergence of Western civilisation through the subjugation of nature:

Figure 4.5 *Odysseus and the Sirens*

> The bonds by which [Odysseus] has irrevocably fettered himself to praxis [i.e. the ship; the manual labour of rowing] at the same time keep the Sirens at a distance from praxis: their lure is neutralized as a mere object of contemplation, as art. The fettered man listens to a concert, as immobilized as audiences later, and his enthusiastic call for liberation goes unheard as applause. In this way the enjoyment of art and manual work diverge as the primeval world is left behind.[62]

Many of the themes of my book converge in this passage. The ideas that the musical human diverges from animal song (the Sirens are half-bird or half-fish); that civilisation distances us from musical nature and immobilises the listener; that the price of musical sophistication is abstraction; but also that, in compensation for such distancing, abstraction is a safeguard against losing ourselves through mimesis. Let's unpack these ideas.

Adorno, who wrote a lot about mimesis, was rightly sceptical of Caillois' and Benjamin's rose-tinted view of this faculty. To utterly lose yourself by identifying with an object is to die, which is why Freud's name for mimesis was the 'death drive'. We experience this most viscerally when we surrender to something greater than ourselves: the infinite, God, water and music. William James, the father of modern psychology, and brother of the novelist Henry, grasped the link between religion and the oceanic:

> Religious rapture, moral enthusiasm, ontological wonder, cosmic emotion, are all unifying states of mind, in which the sand and grit of the selfhood incline to disappear [...] [It is] a sea *in which we swim*.[63]

More than literature, more than painting, music is also a watery medium in which we swim. The oceanic metaphor is prominent in many of the reports compiled by Alf Gabrielsson, a psychologist who studied ordinary people's 'strong experiences with music'. A middle-aged woman is at a concert of Respighi's *The Pines of Rome* and writes that 'the sound effect that arose gave me the feeling of being sucked into a heaving ocean of notes/music'.[64] Listening to Bach's *St Matthew Passion*, another woman hears 'how it gushed and bubbled within me'.[65] A man attends a performance of Shostakovich's String Quartet No. 8 and feels 'as if I was being carried along on waves'.[66] Why does sound in general, and music in particular, feel so immersive, like a medium in which we are submerged? As we saw earlier, Nussbaum argues that musical perception has 'a quality of immediate touch',[67] which he traces back to the lateral line of fish. Implicit in Nussbaum's argument – one I find as compelling as it is plausible – is that the 'oceanic' feeling we get from being immersed in music is an evolutionary memory of where life began.

Music's oceanic quality allies it with religion. Indeed, a key strand of Parts 2 and 3 of this book is that music and religion sprang to life at the same time. A musical tone instantly communicates a sense of the numinous. It feels wholly 'other', like a ray emanating from the spirit realm. This is why music was such a natural accompaniment to ritual from the dawn of time, a kind of sonic pageantry. Wrapping ritual in music rendered it mystical. If the numinous is music's base-line, then intensifying its speed, loudness or complexity can lead to altered states of consciousness inducing religious ecstasy, as we saw at the very end of the last chapter. The sensory overload from a barrage of musical impressions can create a trance-like 'twilight state', as John Pfeiffer has termed it. According to Pfeiffer, a philosopher of religion, in the 'twilight state ... you are ready to believe beyond belief, so totally and enthusiastically that the message comes through with a halo, with the force of religious revelation'.[68]

Like Odysseus, we can baulk at plunging into an oceanic 'twilight state'. In quite different circumstances, I once had occasion to experience the dangerous pull of the Absolute. I had climbed the tower of Rheims Cathedral, which is terrifyingly high even for the jaded modern tourist. Looking over the side, I was engulfed not just by vertigo, but by an almost irresistible compulsion to jump. It is possible that church architects factored in such terror to give Christians a taste of awe in the face of the Divine. When I saw Hitchcock's *Vertigo*, I recognised how cannily the screen composer Bernard Herrmann had found the music for this feeling. We see James Stewart reeling on top of the church tower, immersed in, tugged by, Herrmann's dizzying, spiralling harmonies.[69] He pulls back. Western music pulls back.

So how does Western music pull back? There are two answers to this question. The first answer is that it is protected by the abstraction afforded by musical structure. Musical forms are the fetters that tie Odysseus to the ship's mast, just as religious ritual was both a vehicle of religion and a safeguard against getting too close to the Divine. Musical form and religious ritual essentially performed the same double function. To grasp, then, why the abstraction of Western music was so necessary, we need to get our heads around its puzzling, self-medicating role as both poison and cure. As the German poet Hölderlin wrote, 'Where danger is, deliverance also grows.' Poison and cure don't just grow next to each other: they may even be the same plant.

The second answer involves the peculiar nature of Western religion. The Graeco-Judaeo-Christian tradition is vastly complex, and will engage us more directly in later chapters. But Nussbaum hits the very large nail on its head when he points out that Western religion, philosophy and art have an unusual fascination with conflict, pain and the general 'horror of the contingent', meaning the seemingly absurd chaos and arbitrariness of the cosmos. From Plotinus to Hegel, philosophers have subscribed to the *principle of plenitude*, believing that a world of fullness and variety – containing all its defects and contradictions – is superior to a sanitised world, *so long as these tensions are demonstrated to be logically necessary.*[70] Greek tragedy, Christ's Passion, the classical symphony: what these have in common is that they embrace dissonance and then explain it. An abstract work of music is like a divine plan: everything makes sense to the last detail. This formalist coherence, where every note is heard to lead ineluctably and satisfyingly to the next along a necessary path towards a kind of 'home', simply didn't evolve outside the West. Western abstraction may look deceptively like the renunciation of sensuality, which is such a key feature of Eastern religions, especially Buddhism. Yet Buddhist rejection of an empty and impermanent world is the exact opposite of the Western principle of plenitude.[71]

Whether one likes it or not – and to non-Western ears, the fixation with unity and goal can sound laboured and over-bearing – this fact is a dart to the heart of the musical human in the West.

Gateway to Part Two

Motion – emotion – imitation – religion. The journey has taken us to a striking pass and flipped the argument. Chapters 1 and 2 told a story of music's decline. The cheery news in Chapter 3 was that our modern lives were actually full of music, albeit of the applied sort. Here in Chapter 4 we have seen how music in everyday life is absorbed within musical works; that listening isn't passive at all. There is a life within the music. More than that, we learned that music's abstraction is a necessary safeguard against getting too close to nature and the Divine, and that what happened to the musical human is part of the bigger story of Western civilisation. The mood music gets brighter when we see that musical nature is not so much 'killed' as refined.

Part Two is overtly a history of the musical human from bone flutes to Beethoven. At every stage of this story, we will see the music of the West side by side with the music of 'the rest', often to the former's disadvantage. I will always emphasise that, despite Western music's beauty spots, there were equally viable alternatives elsewhere. Our itinerary will be off-piste, taking in sights off the usual European tourist tracks: Sumeria, Egypt, Athens, Rome, the Mayan and Aztec empires, Muslim Spain, as well as parts of India, Africa, China and Japan.

But at a deeper level it will also be a series of variations on the West's founding myth of Odysseus and the Sirens, a cost-benefit analysis of Western musical 'progress'. Adorno and Horkheimer's commentary on this myth tells a familiar tale. Throughout history, humans became just as much slaves to reason as they were initially to nature, myth, ritual and religion. The ancient myths foresaw the double bind of reason: the more heroes try to escape their fate, the more they are ensnared by the tragedy's diabolical logic. Oedipus digs his grave deeper and deeper as he seeks to reason his way out of Thebes' predicament and solve the Sphinx's riddle. In the West, the violence of reason unfolded in a series of waves: the centralised control of the Christian Church, colonialism, empire, slavery, globalisation and modern bureaucracy. It would be just as one-sided to blame the musical human for the West's collective fate as it would be to ignore its astounding achievements. The task, rather, is to appreciate the vast cost of these achievements in the lives of non-Western others, and – drilling down deeper – in the musical human's animal nature.

PART TWO

HISTORY

CHAPTER 5

ICE, SAND, SAVANNAH AND FOREST

In the beginning … was sound. We are still picking up echoes from the Big Bang 13.8 billion years ago. When Arno Penzias and Rob Wilson, two astronomers working at Bell Labs, Holmdel, New Jersey, noticed faint microwave signals emanating from the Milky Way in 1963, they first attributed the noise to interference caused by pigeon droppings falling on their antennae.[1] It was a telling mistake: we will see that birds tend to hover over the origins of music in all sorts of strange ways. But is astronomers' talk of 'bangs' and 'noises' only a metaphor? The new science of asteroseismology claims that stars ring or vibrate just like musical instruments because of turbulence trapped in their outer layers. Of course, stars resonate at frequencies that are much too low for the human ear to hear. Yet by speeding up these frequencies into audible sound, asteroseismologists, such as Bill Chaplin at Birmingham

University, have developed a tool for figuring out what is happening inside galaxies.[2] The composer Trevor Wishart closed the circle by sonifying electromagnetic spectra into acoustic spectra.[3] Wishart's piece *Supernova* puts a wonderful new spin on the myth of the 'music of the spheres', which has haunted the West for thousands of years. For instance, in his *Harmonics*, written in the second century AD, the Egyptian mathematician Ptolemy compares three types of stellar movements (the rise and fall of the planets) with three kinds of melody.[4] Until Chaplin and Wishart came along, it would have taken a divine ear to perceive such music.

Centuries before they ever heard of a Big Bang, musical humans told origin myths about how the world came about through music. The Maidu Native Americans of Northern California believed that the world was created when the Earthmaker sang over a lump of clay.[5] The Keres of Laguna Pueblo of New Mexico, USA, attributed creation to their goddess Tse che nako: 'In the center of the universe she sang.'[6] Closer to home, St John wrote that 'In the beginning was the word,' and that word was presumably sung, like most religious scripture. Japan has a particularly delightful myth. The Shinto sun goddess, Amaterasu, sulks with her brother and hides in a cave. Her sister lures her out through a song and dance that turns into a striptease, much to the delight of 8 million gods who are watching.[7] The story links the origin of music not to the creation of the world, but to the return of summer and fertility.

Myths aside, what are the facts? As we saw at the start of this book, the historical record trickles away bit by bit as we go back in time beyond the European Middle Ages, past the music of ancient Greece and Mesopotamia, until we are faced with the supposed silence blanketing the prehistoric savannah. Our initial pessimism was unwarranted, because the early world was anything but silent. In this chapter, I will assemble evidence through four main tools: (1) the archaeology of musical instruments; (2) images of music and dance in prehistoric rock art and ceramics; (3) the social and material conditions of early *sapiens*, entailing a theory of mind; and (4), last but not least, the living fossils of contemporary hunter-gatherer and sedentary musical cultures.

We can trust to first principles. If you are a member of a nomadic, foraging tribe, trekking hundreds of miles across the tundras of southern Europe 40,000 years ago, what musical instruments do you take with you? Grand pianos? Not invented. Drums? Still too heavy; better to carry a small child. You take portable lithic objects like flint axes, if anything at all. Better still, you bear nature's instrument, your own voice.

The Portability Principle

You can deduce a surprising amount from the archaeological record of musical instruments. As surviving instruments get heavier and heavier to carry, they tell a story of how early *sapiens* settled down into increasingly stable societies, culminating in the city state.

2.6 million years ago: Pleistocene, Lower Paleolithic

Oldowan tools, named after the stone choppers found in the Olduvai Gorge in Tanzania, would have produced percussive sounds when struck against rock by *Paranthropus* (a slightly more developed australopithecine, our earliest hominin ancestor).[8] Is this the first music? The question is moot at this stage. As we will see in Part Three, the first ensemble music was probably a by-product of coordinated hominin labour. So we shall also leapfrog over the Acheulean pear-shaped hand-axes of *Homo ergaster* 1.5 million years ago, which may or may not have been used to create deliberate sounds. While it is extremely likely that, half a million years ago, the first *sapiens* in Africa would have produced music by banging rocks together, sonic use-wear patterns are impossible to identify.[9] So let's leap on ahead to mature *sapiens* 40,000 years ago, and the world's first purpose-built musical instrument, which was a flute.

40,000 BC: Upper Paleolithic, Ice Age

In 2008, a team of archaeologists explore the Hohle Fels cave in the Swabian Alps in Germany, and discover a voluptuously proportioned figurine of a woman. The so-called 'Venus of Hohle Fels' is the oldest undisputed representation of a human.[10] As well as other figurines of mammoths, rhinos and tarpans (a prehistoric species of wild horse), they also find a flute. Hohle Fels is very close to another cave at Geissenklösterle, where other flutes were discovered in 1992 (see

Figure 5.1).[11] A member of that earlier expedition called Wulf Hein reconstructed one of these flutes. It has five finger holes, with a V-shaped notch for the mouthpiece. You can hear Hein playing pentatonic melodies (based on five-note scales) on this flute on YouTube, including 'The Star-Spangled Banner'.[12]

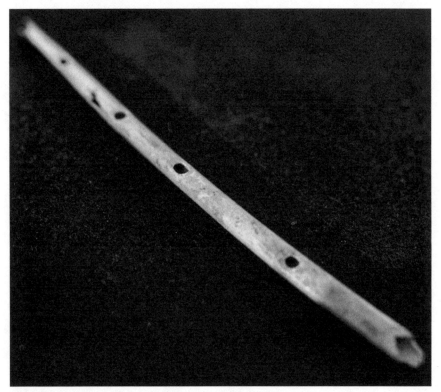

Figure 5.1 Vulture-bone flute found at Hohle Fels

25,000 BC: Last Glacial Maximum

Another Venus, probably also another fertility symbol: the 'Venus of Laussel' bas-relief. She was discovered carved into a block of limestone in 1911 in the Dordogne, south-west France. She is holding a horn striated with thirteen lines.[13] The horn's crescent, shaped like the horn of a cow, also looks like a crescent moon, while the lines might represent the thirteen lunar cycles. Our primal association of music with animals and astronomy is in place. We can assume that mammoth or bovine horns would have been blown at that time, although animal remains biodegrade, and we have hardly any surviving evidence until the invention of metallurgy in the Bronze and Iron Ages. But, in essence, what we have so far in epochal succession are three great families of musical instruments: percussion, woodwind and brass (made from horn). Enter the strings.

2000 BC: Neolithic

Between 1950 and 1955, archaeologists dug up a series of tablets in Nippur, Iraq, bearing cuneiform script.[14] This is the world's oldest decoded music notation. It tells you how to tune a lyre, gives examples of a seven-note scale (close to our Western do-re-mi), and even some melodies of Hurrian cult songs. The tablets, now housed in the British Museum, bring three inventions together: strings, notation, melodies. These three key developments all arrive at the same historical moment. What made this possible was the invention of farming 10,000 years ago, because strings were made from twisted animal guts. Lyres and harps are large, delicate and impractical to carry long distances. Like farmers, instruments now put down roots in settled communities. These roots dug deeper as instruments became even heavier after the arrival of metal.

1700 BC: Bronze Age

The earliest metal instruments include bronze bells created during the Chinese Shang Dynasty (1750–1046 BC). The Shang bells housed within the Smithsonian Institute in Washington D.C. get larger and heavier through the centuries.[15] A small bell, dated around 1600 BC, would have hung mouth down from a cast loop held by a clapper. Another, more diminutive specimen might have been worn on a collar of a domesticated animal, perhaps a dog or a pig. A *nao* bell dated 1200 BC is a different proposition: not suspended but socketed into a base pointing upwards, and pounded by a hammer. It would have formed part of a series of bells of varying sizes producing different notes. From the Shang bells of 1500 BC to the 'Marquis Yi of Zeng' chime-bells of 400 BC discussed in Chapter 1, instruments brought together music with ritual glorification of an emperor. This heavy, static music was the sound of a city state.

You can tell an enormous amount from looking at and listening to instruments. The above sketch outlines the evolution from tribe to village to city state. It mirrors the growth of technology from Paleolithic flint knapping (banging rocks) to Neolithic cattle herding (plucking gut strings) to Bronze Age metal forging (striking bells and gongs). In social terms, it signals a drift from egalitarian to hierarchical and centralised communities. And it is a record of a new way of thinking. According to Tim Ingold, probably the foremost authority on hunter-gatherer societies past and present, their worlds are stamped by the three hallmarks of 'immediacy, autonomy, and sharing'.[16] Always on the move in search of food or even just water, they live lives 'oriented forever in the present'. We will see that hunter-gatherer music has an egalitarian playfulness in its very structure. Sedentary minds, by contrast, are far more planned and future-oriented, often in harmony with the cycle of the seasons. What crops up in agricultural communities is an obsession with ritual; in music this translates into sheer repetition. With city states, playfulness and ritual yield to the glorification of centralised power. Through the ages, music has been a loyal handmaiden of spectacle.

Put in these terms, the prehistory of the musical human looks simple and straightforward. The reality is far more interesting. And we need to tread lightly because the archaeological record is fickle and hostage to fortune, or at least to subjective interpretation. Something might turn up tomorrow to upend the narrative. Indeed, instruments already have, but have been interpreted as outliers. For instance, an object that looks like a Neanderthal flute has been dated as 67,000 years old, trumping the *sapiens* flute by 30,000 years.[17] The apparent vestige of an elephant-hide drum has been dated at 37,000 years old.[18] There are 24,000-year-old mammoth bones painted in ceremonial red ochre and bearing repetitive marks indicating their having been struck like a xylophone,[19] and a 15,000-year-old image of a hunting bow being played like a violin.[20] Indeed, our modern violin is basically two hunting bows rubbed against each other, strung with the guts of the beast we have killed. Some archaeologists think early *sapiens* drilled holes in the phalanges of reindeer to create a whistle. Others argue that the holes were just a way to get at the delicious bone marrow.[21] Common sense also comes into play. Even if animal horns and hides biodegrade, why shouldn't early *sapiens* have played them? Ghana is famed for its pre-colonial trumpet music played on elephant tusks; tusk trumpets might have been around for as long as mammoths and elephants.[22] That elephant-skin drum might be authentic after all, even though we think that the technology to stretch skin or leather over a wooden frame is fairly recent. There is no evidence that the conch shells dug up in ancient Mesoamerican tombs were blown like trumpets, but we can infer that they probably were from later Maya and Inca hieroglyphs.[23] And so it goes.

Musical instruments evolve. They rise and thrive, or fall into extinction like dinosaurs. The Bronze Age *lur* – a long blowing horn without finger holes – went extinct with the Vikings, although its name survives in the contemporary Swedish word for telephone, as well as a brand of butter, Lurpak (packaged with images of *lur*s).[24] There are families, or species, of instruments. Idiophones (e.g. xylophones) vibrate themselves. Membranophones (e.g. drums) vibrate through skins or membranes. Chordophones (e.g. pianos and violins) produce sounds through vibrating strings. Aerophones (e.g. flutes and oboes) vibrate columns of air. Five thousand years ago the ancient Chinese classified instruments according to what they were made of: stone, wood, silk, bamboo, bronze, leather, gourd or clay.[25] In each species, one can track lines of evolutionary descent. The Tanzanian rock gongs of the Serengeti are some of the sonic wonders of the world (see **Figure 5.2**).[26] They are

Figure 5.2 A Serengeti rock gong

pitted with depressions, each of which produces a different metallic note, and are the progenitors of the modern xylophone. The Mesolithic music bow – the ancestor of the violin – generated two diverging evolutionary lines towards the harp and the lyre (see **Figure 5.3**).[27] Harp strings enter directly into the hollow body of the instrument, while on a lyre the string vibrations are transmitted via a bridge. Harps get bigger, bulkier and less portable, and one day find themselves inside grand pianos. Lyres become smaller, and eventually turn into guitars. We can track the start of their evolutionary branch in images found in ancient Israel. The very first illustration of the harp is a rock etching in Megiddo (Armageddon) in the north-western Valley of Jezreel. A rock etching in the Negev, dated 2,000 years BC, outlines the asymmetrical, box-shaped lyre that migrated from Akkadian Mesopotamia. A ninth-century BC seal shows a mature twelve-string Canaanite lyre decorated with a flower. This is the kind of lyre played by King David (1010–970 BC). The Hebrew word *kinnor* is often mistranslated as 'harp'. David really played a lyre.

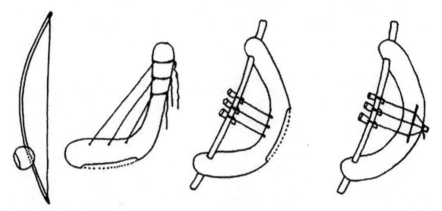

Figure 5.3 The evolution of the harp and lyre from hunting bows

It is interesting that, once civilisation becomes more settled, portability becomes an option again. The Boy David with his lyre was a strolling minstrel, with the same whiff of disapproval as the fly-by-night pop guitarist. Harps and, later, pianos, were respectable because they didn't really move. The ancient quarrel between harps and lyres lays down the battle lines for the modern power struggle between pianos and guitars. In late eighteenth-century Europe, the guitar rather than the piano was the amateur instrument of choice. There was the distinct possibility that the bourgeois Victorian home would have featured not an upright piano but a guitar. Having conquered the musical world in the nineteenth century, a century later the wheel turned again and the guitar became pre-eminent.

An important rule of musical evolution is that primitive instruments are often not displaced, but linger on. So, for instance, the practice of banging rocks together is still with us in the metallic form of cymbals. Cymbals haven't evolved much over thousands of years and are the coelacanths of the orchestra (coelacanths, once thought to have become extinct 66 million years ago in the Late Cretaceous, were discovered swimming off the coast of South Africa in 1938). This means that when *sapiens* disappears, reduced to a smear between geological strata, alien visitors might stub their tentacles against the odd cymbal lying around in the desert. The aliens would be wrong to extrapolate from this that we had no violins or oboes. Reciprocally, we would be wrong to make similar assumptions about Ice Age orchestras because no wooden instruments have survived. The Schöningen spears and artefacts show that *Homo heidelbergensis* could fashion wood with great precision 420,000 years ago.[28]

Another rule is that the portability principle misses the most important instrument of all: the landscape itself. Sounding stones, including stalactites in caves and rock gongs in deserts, have been found with paint and striations showing where they have been hit. Hominins and *sapiens* exploited the natural resonance of caves. Archaeoacousticians mapping the sound qualities of caves found that points of maximum resonance are marked with rock art.[29] Flute shards tend to lie close to these points, and away from areas in the cave where more practical business was conducted. The numinous resonance of caves indicates the nexus of music, landscape and the Divine.

The landscape is obviously too heavy to carry. It doesn't matter, because people carried themselves from one cave or sounding stone to another. Most importantly, *sapiens* carried a cave inside their bodies: their mouths. The nomadic Tuva tribes of Outer Mongolia practise multiphonic singing where one person can shape their mouth cavity to generate overtones that sound like several voices singing at once.[30] Tibetan chant works on the same principle, as does the Jew's harp – an ancient Asiatic instrument with a tongue that you twang (made from reed or bamboo, later metal) in your mouth. Climbing the harmonic series, from deep fundamental to higher partials, Tuvan, Tibetan and Jewish harpists believe that they are ascending to the

Divine. The rising overtones are a stairway to heaven. We can assume that prehistoric shamans knew this principle very well.

The flute found in the cave at Geissenklösterle was made from the radius bone of a griffon vulture. Why is that so significant? Quite simply, while the drawings and artefacts discovered in the Blombos Cave in South Africa suggest that humans were cognitively mature 60,000 or 70,000 years ago, they lacked the opportunity to make flutes because Africa had very few birds with appropriate hollow bones. The archaeological record shows that during the Middle Palaeolithic, when humans crossed from Africa to Europe, swans, vultures, geese and eagles were present in the following Eurasian and African countries:

Swan: Azerbaijan, France, Germany, Holland, Russia
Vulture: Azerbaijan, France, Georgia, Germany, Greece, Portugal, Romania, Spain
Goose: Azerbaijan, Bulgaria, France, Georgia, Germany, Italy, Holland, Poland, Russia, Spain, UK
Eagle: Azerbaijan, Bulgaria, France, Germany, Greece, Italy, Portugal, Romania, Russia, Spain, Libya (a single example)[31]

As the archaeologist Iain Morley emphasises, with the single exception of eagles in Libya, there seems to have been a dearth of suitable birds in prehistoric Africa. It is not that African *sapiens* were incapable of carving instruments; it was that they lacked opportunity. Confirmation that instrumental music started in the West, indeed in Germany, would have mightily pleased nineteenth-century musicologists. Less convenient for advocates of Europe's musical supremacy is that a counterpoint every bit as rich as a Bach fugue probably originated in ancient Africa (albeit it would have been vocal, not instrumental).

Hunter-Gatherers

Think yourself back to that cave at the Geissenklösterle site in Germany 40,000 years ago. It helps to watch Werner Herzog's glorious film *Cave of Forgotten Dreams*, which, though set mostly in the Chauvet Cave in France, features a scene with Wulf Hein playing his flute outside

Geissenklösterle. Hein gazes across a forested valley. It would have been filled with ice, because the mountain was encased in a glacier 2,500 metres thick. Reindeer and mammoths wander across the tundra munching a kind of grass we can trace from ancient pollen grains. Hein wears a garment tightly stitched from reindeer fur, and reindeer-leather boots. He looks like an Inuit.

Let's call this Inuit-like hunter Orpingalik (for reasons I'll disclose later). What was life like for Orpingalik in the middle of the last Ice Age? There were nine months of winter in the year, and only a few hours of precious daylight in the working day.[32] Part of a small tribe of forty souls, moving on every few weeks following the reindeer and mammoth in their annual cycle to the breeding grounds, Orpingalik lived in an igloo-like structure made of skins. The cave was reserved for gatherings after dark, like a modern town hall. A lot of time is spent sitting around the fire in the cave telling stories, and the stories turn into song, almost always danced. Solidarity for these people is as important as food and shelter, which is why craftsmen like Orpingalik are released from hunting to devote hundreds of hours to crafting a flute, a thing with no obvious survival value. Every part of life has a song, much of it involving hunting. There are songs to bless the spears, to rouse the men, to celebrate a kill. One song imitates the bleat of a calf, to lure the adult mammoth over a cliff. There is a song to teach children where to collect an ancient strain of cloudberries. These songs are largely made up of nonsense syllables meant to imitate the language of a totemic goddess, who is half-woman, half-bird. When Orpingalik plays a flute made from bird bones, he speaks directly with this goddess. However, most of the tribe play small rattles and clappers, sometimes tied to their arms and legs like a sonic decoration of their bodies. So the sounds they make directly follow the rhythms of their dance.

Who creates these songs? In principle, anyone can, although the tribe especially prize the songs heard by their shaman, Takutjartak (another name explained below), during his dreams. Takutjartak is a spirit traveller, and journeys through layers of the cosmos to commune with his ancestors. It is partly his skill as a singer that keeps this loose community together, stopping members defecting to other tribes. Everyone in his tribe owns a signature melody, to which they can invent new texts as they occur to them on their travels. One person thought of some words during a long vigil spear-fishing. Songs record travels through the terrain. There is a song associated with this particular cave; another with the nearby Hohle Fels; another with the glacier, which is alive and sings back. The tribe believe that singing these songs awakens and refreshes the ancestral spirits sleeping in the landscape. And the tribe itself has a signature song, which helps identify it when approaching other tribes during their midwinter trek to the ceremonial meeting grounds. Sound travels great distances. During one of these festivals, Orpingalik's people foraged tools and songs from a tribe as far away as Isturitz in the Pyrenees.

What were these songs like? Wulf Hein amusingly plays the American national anthem on his reconstructed flute. But what Orpingalik plays doesn't sound like tunes to our ears. Most of his songs last only a few seconds, and are like bursts of feeling. They are not melodies, but atoms of music repeated in subtle variations, or just repeated. For the singers, assembling these fragments is a skill, a test and a game. And the accompaniment – handclaps, body slaps, rattles – goes its own way and is strangely not in time with the song. Often everyone sings together, the women and children an octave above the men. Other times, they pursue independent lines, as in a conversation. Everyone joins in at their own level, entering and leaving the conversation as they choose. Although the individual songs are short in themselves, it is the chain of songs – in their hundreds – that matters, and the chain can run all night. During the midwinter festival, the succession of songs lasts for many weeks. By our standards, these people have an incredible memory.

How can we know all this, in the absence of archaeological record? My story is obviously a thought experiment, albeit not wholly without evidence. Everything in my account is borrowed from the practices of contemporary hunter-gatherer societies, including the name of Orpingalik, an Inuit shaman who was interviewed by the Danish explorer Knud Rasmussen in 1921.[33] Modern hunter-gatherers are scattered across the planet, in landscapes ranging from rainforests, deserts and grassy plains to polar ice caps.[34] In nearly all cases these societies are egalitarian and nomadic, and their music is predominantly vocal with percussion accompaniment, with no use of metal. Obviously, while we will never know what Palaeolithic music actually sounded like, contemporary hunter-gatherers furnish us with an astonishingly rich quarry of facts about what it *might* have sounded like. These facts constitute a field of possibilities and educated guesses.

It is clearly false to believe that hunter-gatherers are frozen in amber and that they have no history, because their main historical event is of course their collision with the West. On the other hand, treating these societies as passive victims of colonisation does a huge disservice to the dignity of survival. For instance, Inuit traditions continue to thrive two centuries after first contact with Europeans. And it is extraordinary to consider that the Australian Aboriginal people, geographically isolated for 60,000 years, met Captain Cook in 1778: this is one second to midnight in their enormously long historical clock.

Mapping contemporary hunter-gatherer music over the prehistorical timeline involves speculation of a rather higher order, however. From the Ice Age to the invention of agriculture between 12,000 and 9,000 years ago there was a gradual climatic warming, interrupted by a cold snap (12,900–9700 BC) called the Younger Dryas. There was also the diffusion of early humans, radiating from central Africa to Asia and Australia, Europe, and then across the Bering Strait to Alaska, eventually migrating south through the Americas. Let's consider what the diffusion of the musical human might have sounded like, by reviewing in turn the musics of four geographically diverse hunter-gatherer communities: African Pygmies, Australian Aboriginal people, Alaskan Inuit and Native Americans.

Long into the night before the BaYaka Pygmies of Cameroon set out on an elephant hunt, the women perform a song they call 'Yele'.[35] It makes the animals feel *kwaana* – soft, relaxed and sleepy – and easier to kill. The BaYaka are dispersed in the rainforest in small groups of fifty to a hundred people, coming together from time to time (especially in the dry season) in larger communities to perform spirit plays. BaYaka life has a rhythm of aggregation and dispersal. They have no sense of hierarchy or personal property, sharing all food and items, and the playfulness of their social interactions animates their music, which they believe comes from their ancestors in dreams. This playfulness informs the most famous aspect of Pygmy music, BaYaka included: its polyphony. A Pygmy song comprises several melodies sung simultaneously in counterpoint and in different metres. Pygmy polyphony is an inconvenient truth for music historians who believe that music evolves from the simple to the complex; that is, from simple one-voiced texture to complex counterpoint such as Bach fugues. Because of course there is nothing simple about Pygmy music, just as there is nothing 'primitive' about Pygmy society. Anthropologists such as Ingold turn the usual narrative on its head to hold up hunter-gatherer egalitarianism as a model for later 'civilizations'.[36] For Western musicology, the idea that counterpoint originates in Africa – notionally before the 'out-of-Africa' dispersal – and that music was originally polyphonic (and thus not melodic) is nothing short of a scandal. I shall return to this scandal again and again in this book.

The question, then, is why? Why might polyphony, rather than melody, be closer to the musical source? As with many evolutionary questions, the answer lies in the convergence of a range of separate strands.

A community of people is most physical when bodies weave together in a danced song. In dance, Pygmies 'mix themselves together' (*bosanganye njo*) both physically, by intertwining their arms and legs, and musically, by interlocking their melodies.[37] The musical polyphony emanates from the counterpoint of bodies. Another strand is the Pygmies' distributed sense of self, distinct from the individual, bounded self of the modern West. Pygmies think collectively, without hierarchy. There are many other factors. The interwoven melodies are like the crisscrossing animal trails in the undergrowth. It is simply more efficient to hunt a different trail from your neighbour, just as it is to sing a different melody, since this distributes risk. Likewise, the skill to negotiate polyphony can be exported to the skill of interpreting animal tracks: music teaches hunting. A further set of factors pertains to the Pygmies' relationship with their environment, the rainforest itself. The forest's hubbub of animal cries and bird calls also constitutes a kind of polyphony. If hunting is poor, the Pygmies use a *molimo* trumpet (fashioned originally from elephant tusks) to talk to the forest in a ceremony that may last several weeks.[38] The signalling behaviour across bird populations in dawn choruses is particularly suggestive.[39] Because the choruses are so dense, birds need to break through by singing louder and at higher pitch (a phenomenon well known in noisy cities); and by double-coding their signals, so as to reach out to both rivals and potential mates. The Pygmies' relationship with birds is quite subtle. Unlike some hunter-gatherers (such as the Kaluli of Papua New Guinea),[40] they don't imitate the actual melodies of the birds. Instead, they double-code their polyphony. A wonderful aspect of Pygmy song is that alternate notes are yodelled; yodelling in many parts of the world is used for long-distance signalling, either for herding animals (as in the Swiss mountains) or, in the Pygmies' rainforest, for hunting. Pygmy counterpoint is double-coded because the voices alternately talk to each other within the song and reach out through yodelling across long distances. Pygmy counterpoint and dawn choruses are examples of convergent evolution adapting to an ecological niche.

When the ecological niche changes, so does the music. Two hundred miles north of the BaYaka, the Bedzan Pygmies of the Tikar Plain live on the edge of the desert, away from the rainforest, and their music doesn't have any yodelling.[41] Perhaps in compensation for that, Bedzan polyphony has the most extreme variability of any Pygmy music. Every time they sing a song, it is different; they have no concept of a song being a stable or repeatable structure. This makes sense: if a song is like a game, a sport or even a hunt, then music is an activity – like jogging or jumping – not a thing. And this has dramatic consequences for how a people transmits its music to the next generation. It is not the song that is remembered and handed down, but the skill to create it. Better to teach a child to fish than to give him a fish.

Far away from the natural resonance of the forest canopy, the musical human of the Australian deserts adapted to a very different ecology. No longer pressed down by a hostile, noisy and opaque jungle, hunter-gatherers could spread out over vast distances. Sight lines opened up; indeed, to use a word popularised by Bruce Chatwin's famous book on Aboriginal people, *songlines*. Sixty thousand years ago, the first Aboriginal people crisscrossed the Australian continent with songs, both marking their territory and, allegedly, even absorbing its very contours into the lines of their melodies. This is Chatwin:

> The melodic contour of the song describes the land over which
> the song passes ... certain phrases, certain combinations of musical
> notes, are thought to describe the actions of the ancestors' feet. An
> expert song man ... would count how many times he has crossed a
> river or scaled a ridge – and be able to calculate where, and how far
> along, the songline he was ... A musical phrase is a map reference.
> Music is a memory bank for finding one's way about the world.[42]

This is beautiful prose. Yet one wonders who Chatwin had been speaking to, because his romanticised account is mostly wrong. Admittedly, what the Aboriginal people introduced into world music was an all-encompassing linearity, intimately linked to journeying through a landscape. But not quite as Chatwin imagined it.

Aboriginal songs can't contain maps because they are too short, over in a matter of seconds.[43] Nor can they capture the specific contour of the land, because their songs tend to have the same contour: they descend. It is not a single Aboriginal song in itself that is a map, but an enormously extended chain of songs, each song tagging an object or place in the environment. By dancing, singing and painting mythical stories associated with these sites, Aboriginal people awaken totemic spirits sleeping in their landscape: totems such as Honey Ant, Emu, Fire, Water. The world was made by these spirits in the ancient time that Aboriginal people called the 'Dreaming' (*Jukurrpa* in Warlpiri; *Altyerre* in Arrernte). The chain is sung, song after song, en route to and from communal gatherings in the dry season, so that the songlines trickle through the desert like the water that drives Aboriginal migration. Unlike their colonial invaders, Aboriginal people don't think of the desert as an arid and empty space to be avoided, but as a world replete with spirit, music and meaning. They lack the nature/culture distinction beloved of anthropologists.

Like the Pygmies, Aboriginal people sing in counterpoint, albeit in a slightly looser idiom called *heterophony*. The layers of a heterophonic song comprise not different melodies, but subtle variants of the same melody. The Yolngu people of north-eastern Arnhem Land say that the individual voices are threads woven together into the tail of a possum.[44] There is a counterpoint of another sort in the interaction of melody and text. Aboriginal songs have many more words than Pygmy songs; the Africans tend to start off with a single word and then devolve into wordless vocalisation. It is unclear why words, and with them conceptual meaning, became so important in Australia. The contrast would have delighted Enlightenment philosophers like Rousseau, who would have pointed to the step from vocalised to texted song as a step towards civilisation (albeit in the wrong direction, away from 'nature'). Be that as it may, words and music interact in much more irregular fashion than in modern Western song. Melody, words and indeed rhythm go their separate ways, their cyclic repetitions cutting across each other (for example, the words may be repeated in an AABB pattern within a

single melodic phrase).[45] Note the word repetitions in this Yolngu song
about a possum:

> beginning,
> possum-fur string,
> ever-travelling, tip
> appearing,
> wafting, possum-
> fur string, wafting,
> woven
> spiritual essence,
> beginning,
> possum-fur string,
> night-travelling[46]

As well as the possum-tail metaphor, Aboriginal people use the landscape
metaphor of 'spreading out' to describe how textual and melodic cycles
intermesh with each other within a song.[47] Their music spreads out
through the landscape, just as Pygmy polyphony is a network of forest
trails.

Distinctions in world culture must always be cautious. One striking
aspect of African art is the dearth of representations of dance in rock
painting, compared to other continents.[48] This is an enigma, given the
centrality of dance in African culture. If there is an anti-representational
bent in African music, then it is borne out in the Pygmy avoidance of
mimicking the sounds or motions of the animals with which they are
otherwise so entangled. Aboriginal dance, by contrast, loves to imitate
animal gestures, such as the preening of the brolga (a kind of crane) or
the jumping of the kangaroo.[49] Moreover, this penchant to mimic is
strongest in the northern regions of Australia, where rock art is most
figurative, and fades in central and southern Australia, whose more
geometric rock art favours tracks and circles.[50] I wonder if the visuality
of Aboriginal music flows from Australia's vast open spaces. Even before
you see a person coming towards you, you might hear their *ikwe*, their
signature melody. A procession of women approaching the ceremonial
ground (always from a south-westerly direction) might be a distant
blur; but the kind of song they sing – perhaps a *djanba*, or maybe a
wangga or a *lirrga* – would be audible and instantly recognised.[51]

Most of Australia has been searingly hot for at least a million years, and was hardly touched by the Pleistocene ice. The early humans dispersing north through Asia and Europe adapted to conditions that were in many ways far harsher. In principle, why would vocal polyphony – the sound of the Pygmies and Aboriginal people – not thrive in a cold climate? When people are singing several melodies at once, the words get garbled (as they famously do in Mozart's operatic ensembles). This doesn't matter for Pygmies and Aboriginal people, because their belief systems value the acoustic sound of music far higher than its words. But it might be inferred that words become a matter of life and death in extreme weather conditions, where people shelter in cramped spaces such as igloos, and the imperative is to avoid conflict. Not just words, but playfulness and humour, to defuse tension. It is comforting to think that, far from being the grim and dour place of our imaginings, the Ice Age might have been filled with laughter. Ice Age song would have been monophonic – everyone singing the same music in unison – so as to convey words with crystal clarity. These words would have been social and educational in intent, and probably very funny. We don't have a shred of historical evidence for this hypothesis. Yet that is exactly what happens in the music of contemporary hunter-gatherer societies across the circumpolar region, ranging across the Chukchi of Russian Siberia, the Ainu of Hokkaido in Japan, the Sami of Lapland and the Inuit of Greenland, Alaska and Canada. We do know that this was the course of circumpolar migration to the Americas: from Asia through Europe across the Bering Strait to North America. We also know that cultures across this region share linguistic, archaeological and even genetic histories. Luca Cavalli-Sforza's discovery that genetic and linguistic trees correspond with each other is especially fascinating.[52] That is, he found that the evolution of a people's language shadowed the evolution of its genes. The idea has inspired ethnomusicologists to find similar distribution patterns within the 'genes' of shared musical practices. This is to consider ways of playing and singing as analogous to genes handed down across generations of musicians.[53]

The Inuit arrived in Alaska relatively late, in AD 900, displacing the Tuniit (or 'Dorset'), the last surviving remnants of the Palaeo-Eskimos who had travelled from Siberia 3,000 years earlier.[54] Much, though not all, of their ancient Eskimo lore was throttled by Christian missionaries after the 1920s, whereas Siberian Chukchi culture was deep-frozen by communism. As we will see below, comparing Inuit with Chukchi music reveals the evolutionary direction of travel, from Siberia to Alaska.

When the Inuit shaman Orpingalik met Knud Rasmussen in 1921, he explained to the explorer 'how a song is born in the human mind':

> Songs are thoughts, sung out with the breath when people are moved by great forces and ordinary speech no longer suffices. Man is moved just like the ice floe sailing here and there out in the current. His thoughts are driven by a flowing force when he feels joy, when he feels fear, when he feels sorrow [...] But it will happen that the words we need will come of themselves. When the words we want to use shoot up of themselves – we get a new song.[55]

Many of Orpingalik's songs survive, and they contain a tremendous amount of humour. One song aims a barb at Orpingalik's old song fellow, Takutjartak: 'A good large arrow I threw at your fat ass. It was very annoying for you. You run away fast.' This was meant in jest. Much of Inuit music comprises teasing, jesting and gaming songs, designed to deflect direct conflict in this exceptionally hostile environment. The best-known gaming song is a species of throat singing called *katajjait*.[56] Two women stand so close to each other their mouths are almost touching. They fire off a series of vocal sounds into each other's mouths in a rapid-fire alternation of inhalation and exhalation, continuing to the point where one of the women is too exhausted to pant any further, and loses the game. The duel is the tip of a social iceberg. There are songs with narrative family trees going back generations. Songs that tell you the weather, or where to pick juicy cloudberries and blueberries. Songs that teach children the names of birds, and their nesting patterns. Or teach them physical coordination, such as skipping games and juggling games. Songs whose dance steps mimic sledging, harpooning, cutting up animals or plucking feathers to teach youngsters all manner of activities. And of course a majority of songs involve hunting, such as one that entices seals by imitating the crying of pups.[57]

By far the most important are the Inuits' drum-dance songs (*inngerutit*), performed on a large tambourine (*qilaat*) made from driftwood or lashed-together bones, and played by a stick fashioned from a caribou rib.[58] Drum-dance songs were originally contests. Two men would face each other, singing, dancing and drumming, mocking their opponent and amusing their audience. But the sound of the drum itself was deadly serious, and speaks to the centrality of drumbeats in shamanistic culture worldwide. The terrifying sound of the drum has two aims: frightening away evil spirits, and inducing a trance-like state in the Inuit listeners. The centrality of the drums compensates for the relative simplicity of the songs themselves – simplicity relative to the richer textures of Pygmy and Aboriginal counterpoint. It is as if the importance of words and sociality has edged out music. There is another way of looking at this, going back to the analogy of melody with forest trails and songlines. Trails don't last very long in the featureless Arctic tundra, because as quickly as they are traced they are covered with fresh snow. So the Inuits' trails are constructed in their minds; they are even more imaginary than Aboriginal songlines. It is as if the mesh of trails has evolved into a more abstract web of culture. This level of abstraction might have been forced on *sapiens* by the Ice Age, and it may mark an important advance towards the social complexity entailed by Neolithic sedentary culture, and the cognitive revolution associated with the invention of agriculture.

We must not forget that the Inuit are a modern culture. Drums are, perhaps surprisingly, a modern instrument: the technology to bake ceramics, or to stretch a skin over a wooden frame, is more recent than making string instruments, probably being developed around 7000 BC. The earliest known image of a frame drum – played by a shaman who is flying like a bird – survives in a Siberian cave painting, dated 2,000 years BC.[59] The Ice Age Orpingalik might have dampened reindeer hide with urine and shrink-wrapped it over rolled-up tree bark by drying it on his fire. But we have no physical evidence of that. More likely he banged out his dance songs by hitting a sounding stone or a stalactite.

Nevertheless, we can extrapolate some aspects of Inuit music back to Siberia, where it probably originated. The Siberian Chukchi have their own version of female throat-singing duels (*katajjait*) called *pic eynen*. They also practise drum-dance songs. However, throat-song games and drum-dance songs are never performed in the same ceremony by the Inuit, whereas they are by the Chukchi.[60] For the Chukchi, these two games form a unity; by the time this musical tradition has travelled west (or east) to North America, it has split apart into two distinct kinds of music, played at different times by women and men. There was an 'out of Siberia' musical dispersal, paralleling the tribal dispersal, evolving from unity to diversity. We can, with reasonable logic, extrapolate this dispersal back to the cave at Geissenklösterle 40,000 years ago, and conjecture that lots of hunter-gatherer music, which has since then evolved apart, would have originally been sung and played together.

America, the last continent to be reached by the 'out of Africa' migration, is host to 200 First Nation tribes who display virtually every feature of the music of the Pygmies, Inuit and indigenous Australians, in assorted combinations.[61] Native American culture is egalitarian, has no notion of private property, has loose tribal affiliations (with individuals leaving and joining a tribe at will), and was historically nomadic, following the buffalo herd's movements across the rolling grasslands in search of water.[62] Music, ascribed a supernatural origin, was heard in dreams by the medicine man. Songs are accompanied by an assortment of percussion instruments, rattles and bull-roarers, made from dried gourds, tree barks, spiders' nests, deer hooves and turtle shells. What dates Native Americans as young hunter-gatherers, closest in style to the Inuit, is their love of the frame drum. Like the Inuit, their music is also monophonic, and often sung in unison. And much of it also centres on hunting: bison are lured over a cliff by a song imitating a bleating calf, just as the Inuit sing like a seal-pup to attract its mother.

What marks Native American song as younger still is its self-conscious interest in ritual and history. The Choctaw of Mississippi have kept alive a particularly vivid oral history stretching back 8,000 years to the Palaeo-Indians and the age of mammoths.[63] Choctaw say that their songs were granted them by their creator, Shilumbish Chito, during their mythic migration. Even today they claim that, on the morning after a good sing, they can hear their ancestors' voices. While the Inuit like to dance in a line, Native Americans prefer circular dances. For the Choctaw, the circular dance symbolises the sacred world, which is shaped like a circle cross-cut with the four directions, representing wholeness, balance and continuity. This is mirrored in the circularity of their songs, which are built in four phrases. The cross-cut circle of the Choctaw parallels the Tibetan mandala, the universal symbol of cosmic harmony. And this is further reflected in the Choctaw's circular concept of historical time, which they see as layered. History moves not in a line from past through present to future, but up and down through layers of time, just as the dreaming shaman journeys through levels of the cosmos, from ancestors' time to now time and back again. Songs are sounding icons of circular history in their circular repetition and in their interaction of repetition with variation. In a good Choctaw song, the singers overlay musical motives on top of basic patterns staked out by a strong song leader, often the shaman himself. It is a perfect metaphor for the persistence of the past through layers of innovation. With their circular rituals, the Choctaw knock on the door of a new world of sedentary societies governed by the rotation of the seasons.

We cannot know for certain that these four hunter-gatherer cultures echo the flow of *sapiens* out of Africa and east to west. In the end, my account is what evolutionary scientists call a just-so story: a high-end parable. On the other hand, for these modern cultures from far-flung corners of the Earth to share common musical practices testifies to a prehistoric core: the story must have a kernel of truth. This idea also has consequences for us. Reversing the telescope, it is just as extraordinary that fragments of this ancient world have lived on in the corners of our own consciousness. Hare and Coyote, the shape-shifting trickster gods of the Native Americans, still chase each other in modern cartoons in their new shapes of Bugs Bunny and Wile E. Coyote to the music of *Looney Tunes*. We bring cosmic trees into our homes at Christmas and sing songs around them. And the Tungus (Siberian) grandmaster of shamans, aka St Nicholas, rides through the sky drawn by eight caribou familiars to the music of Neolithic bells.[64]

Sedentary Music*

About 12,000 years ago global warming melted the Pleistocene into the Holocene, humans settled down into 'sedentary' communities, discovered farming, and history began. This, at least, is the short version of an immensely complex story.[65] The truth is full of twists, turns and surprises. For instance, archaeologists now believe that settlement happened before the discovery of agriculture rather than the reverse. Thus the earliest sedentary villages were in the Natufian

---

* 'Sedentism' – adjective 'sedentary' – is the term favoured by anthropologists for the practice of settling in one place for an extended period.

region of the Levant in 12,000 BC, while agriculture (the domestication of plants and animals) arrived somewhat later, around 9000 BC, in the Fertile Crescent of the Middle East.[66] Equally surprising is that what sparked off this chain of events seems to have been a new kind of religion. Building a religious temple such as a stone circle might take many hundreds of years, and to do that people needed to settle, and settled communities had to be fed. We can presume that music played a central role in the founding of these religions, and that it partook of the cognitive revolution, which depended on these dramatic social and material changes. How did sedentary societies think?

Hunter-gatherers live in the moment, but farmers have one eye on the seasonal calendar, very much orientated towards the future. They keep their other eye on the past, because, dwelling in a fixed place, they accumulate knowledge, which becomes tradition. In other words, if you settle a large number of people together, this is what happens: they watch each other carefully, and over time group observation establishes a cultural niche, which eventually feeds back to change people's behaviour. Through tradition, both memory and behaviour become much more collective. And arching over tradition is religious ritual. What brings all these elements together – religious ritual, the seasonal calendar and everyday village life – is the idea of the circle, something we came across earlier in Choctaw society. Even today, music in contemporary sedentary communities typically circles around a village's central plaza. But the very first recorded settlements, such as Jericho, were also circular.[67] According to the Bible, the walls of Jericho fell after the Israelites marched around them seven times blowing ram's horns.

We saw earlier that the new technologies of sedentism (ceramics and metallurgy) brought string and metal instruments, as well as the first framed drums. Settled communities in the Neolithic era discovered how to make ceramic cooking pots; stretching a skin over a pot created a drum. They also learned to work metal, leading to bells and gongs, and gut from farmed animals was turned into string instruments. More generally, instruments could now afford to grow in size, weight and delicacy. Heavy gongs or sets of bells didn't need to be carried. A fragile harp wouldn't undergo the knocks and scrapes of a long journey.

The social complexity of villages also increased the variety of instruments. We can infer from pictures on plaster walls or ceramics that instruments were played together in richer combinations. To penetrate deeper into Neolithic music, we can make two sorts of educated guesses. As before, we can map from what we already know of contemporary sedentary musical cultures across the world. Secondly, it is a fair bet that Neolithic music was built on the same principles as other aspects of farming life, such as the stabilising force of circular rituals. The modern idea of a piece of music as a permanent, settled entity was probably hatched at the same time as sedentism about 10,000 years ago. As we saw earlier, hunter-gatherer music tends to be made up not of fixed melodies, but of musical atoms, assembled like a game on the move, so that the music is different each time it is performed. Neolithic people would have repeated music and handed it down to their children. If you repeat bits of melody in the same order, you essentially create a tune. This is, of course, highly speculative, but if you follow the logic of a stable society, then it is likely that Neolithic music invented tunes.

Exhibit A for this theory is a temple on a hilltop in Anatolia, ancient Turkey, discovered in 1994 by Klaus Schmidt. Göbekli Tepe, dated 10,000 years BC, is the oldest and most exciting archaeological dig on the planet, and arguably the turning point of history (see **Figure 5.4**).[68] Göbekli Tepe is not actually a hill but an artificial mound forming a series of megalithic enclosures or sanctuaries. Within these enclosures are circles of T-shaped monolithic pillars, each one suggesting the contour of a human standing upright with arms outstretched. Towering over the circles are central monoliths six metres tall. The stones are decorated with images of bulls, foxes, snakes, spiders and scorpions, and might have served a religion based on the overcoming of fear associated with dangerous animals. For musicians, the megaliths of Göbekli Tepe are interesting because they are also sounding stones.[69] Delicately striking your hand against the centre of these hollow pillars produces a drumbeat with an infrasound resonance of 14 Hz. Sounds as low as that bypass the ear to affect the body directly, as when your body 'hears' the rumble of an underground train. Archaeologists believe that the ground beneath the stones is hollow, like the circles at Xaghra in Malta and Epidauros in Greece, which were ancient underground bath systems. In effect, the underground box beneath Göbekli Tepe functions as a transducer (an energy convertor) for the megaliths' resonance. It is a soundbox for a gigantic harp formed of stone 'strings'.

Figure 5.4 An artist's impression of the building of Göbekli Tepe

At Göbekli Tepe, Mohammed didn't come to the mountain; the mountain came to Mohammed. Its sounding stones are not fixtures of the natural landscape, such as a mountain or a cave. People purposefully constructed and ordered them. The megalithic enclosures would have been spaces for religious rituals dominated by music, servicing nearby villages. The most famous example of an Anatolian village at the dawn of agriculture is Catal Höyük, a thirty-four-acre site near the modern Turkish city of Konya.[70] A catacomb of tightly clustered one-roomed mud-brick homes, accessible through holes in their roofs, Catal Höyük would, in its heyday between 7200 and 5700 BC, have housed as many as 10,000 people. It was in every sense a settled community. Although no musical relics survive, much is revealed in the imagery painted on Catal Höyük's plaster walls (see **Figure 5.5**). In one painting thirty people are dancing around a huge bull.[71] While Neolithic rock art contains many images of animals and people, they are rarely displayed interacting together. Representing humans and bulls in the same visual space tells us that cattle were central to Catal Höyük inhabitants' lives and rituals. The fresco includes one of the earliest representations of a framed drum. One character plucks an instrument that looks like a primitive bowed harp. Others rub two bows together, as if they are playing the single-string bows (*malunga*s and *berimbau*s) of southern Africa. The fresco, then, portrays an early orchestra made up of drums with plucked and bowed strings. The shapes of the people, and their multicoloured skin tones, suggest that the orchestra comprised both men and women, and people from different ethnic groups. The room looks as if it might have contained an altar for religious ceremonies involving singing, playing and dancing.

Figure 5.5 A Catal Höyük wall painting showing hunting bows

In fact, Catal Höyük is filled with such altars, each one indicating that music would have been performed within the home. The domestication of music, a by-product of farming, marks a hugely significant moment in its journey: a journey from the landscape (cave or mountain) to the temple (Göbekli Tepe's megaliths) to inside people's permanent dwellings. If repetition is the basis of ritual, then Catal Höyük's houses show how ritual emerges literally from the ground up. The dwellings are all the same shape and size; and, over thousands of years, they were made and re-made in the same space on top of ancestors buried beneath their floors. We can imagine that Catal Höyük's music was made and remade in the same way, and that it was as standardised as the hundreds of virtually identical ox-head sculptures and terracotta figurines of fertility goddesses unearthed in their altar rooms.

Standardisation suggests an absence of social hierarchy. Judging from its equal-sized living spaces, Catal Höyük was as egalitarian as hunter-gatherer societies. But as agriculture gradually became more secure, the accumulation of wealth from good harvests led to social inequality. Some people break their backs to grow the food; a more leisured class manages, guards or prays over it. Four thousand years downstream from Catal Höyük, the villagers participating in musical rituals at Stonehenge in 3000 BC were as status-conscious as audiences in modern concert halls, with the top people standing at or near the centre of the stone circle, and the riff-raff tapering off towards the edges. That is the theory proposed by archaeoacoustician Rupert Till.[72] Stonehenge's remarkable acoustic properties have long been celebrated. 'It hums,' says Thomas Hardy's Tess of the D'Urbervilles. 'Harken!' As Tess's boyfriend Angel listens, 'the wind, playing upon the edifice, produced a booming tune, the note of some gigantic one-stringed harp'. Stonehenge would have created sounds in three ways: as a 'temple of the winds', as Hardy heard; as an arena for music-making on drums and other percussion instruments; and as an assembly of sounding stones to be struck. The smaller bluestone monoliths, distinct from the larger sarsen stones, were dragged all the way from an area in Wales called 'the ringing rocks'. The effort to transport, curve and polish the bluestones, plus the wit to face their concave surfaces towards the centre of the circle, bespeaks a culture capable of very long-range planning: 1,500 years, to be precise, much longer than the time to build the European cathedrals.

Stonehenge was a Neolithic venue for ecstatic partying, and it is not an accident that modern rave culture likes to bask in its glory. Neolithic ravers at the Henge would have played clay or wooden drums, pieces of wood, or just clacked small stones together. Within the circle, the sound will have been reflected back from each stone and amplified, producing an effect not dissimilar from the Whispering Gallery of St Paul's Cathedral, or the Echo Wall of the Imperial Vault of Heaven in the Tian Tan Temple of Beijing, but with the added effect that this was happening in the open air. We can't know exactly how it would have sounded because half the stones are missing. Using digital computer modelling, Till reconstructed the original effect. He estimates that the high-frequency notes of small drums, played dead centre, would have produced the best sound. And, importantly, that the reverberations would have been most powerful for participants standing in the middle of the stone circle; less good for people outside the sarsen ring, but still within the surrounding bank and ditch; and least effective for an audience beyond that. For people lucky or important enough to be occupying the centre, this was literally the best seat in the house.

Again and again we have seen that music's prehistory doesn't move in straight lines. Neither rock art nor sounding stones disappear with the arrival of farming, especially when we spread our purview to consider the world beyond the Fertile Crescent. In Kupgal, South India, the locals refer to the Neolithic granite boulders overhanging the cliffs as 'musical stones'.[73] When struck, these boulders produce deep, gong-like sounds. They can only be played by young men, cattle herders, strong enough to climb the vertical rock faces just below the peak of the hill. The boulders are covered with petroglyphs (rock carvings or engravings) of anthropomorphic figures and cattle, sometimes in sexual congress. Near the cliffs are mounds of ancient cow dung, attesting to a Neolithic cattle pastoralism. The inaccessibility of the jagged musical stones makes perfect sense in the hierarchy of cow culture, where those in closest contact with the herd have the highest status. As for what the music sounded like, there are plenty of modern examples of sedentary cultures involved with cattle. We met the Tutsi tribe of Rwanda in Chapter 1. Another example is the Nuer people of South Sudan.[74] Nearly all their songs are about their cattle, and they help to pass the long hours tending them at pasture in the Nile Valley. In Nuer initiation ceremonies, the initiate must compose a song in praise of a bull. Nuer cattle songs are accompanied by side-blown bamboo flutes or pan pipes, and never by drumming. Why? One plausible reason, proposed by the biomusicologist Nils Wallin, is that 'tonal patterns in the high pitch range present acoustic features which have the strongest recognition effect on cattle'.[75] Apparently, flute music calms cattle, whereas drumming upsets them. As we shall see in the next chapter, the Nuers' ancient Egyptian forefathers knew this perfectly well, which might be why their music was dominated by the gentle lilt of flutes and harps – still the signature sound of pastoral music in

Western classical music (think Debussy's *Prélude à l'après-midi d'un faune*). Pitched high up above the village, the rock gongs of Kupgal were presumably too far away to frighten the cows.

Maddened by the noise, a terrified cow runs through the streets of Bhaktapur, Nepal, chased by a procession of musicians clashing wooden sticks and cymbals, and hitting small barrel drums called *dha*s.[76] This is the ancient festival of Gaijatra, still performed annually on the first day of the second fortnight of the month Gula during the monsoon season (out of respect for animals, the cow is nowadays substituted by bamboo sticks topped by cow horns). Gaijatra commemorates the people of Bhaktapur who have died in the previous year. The cow conducts their souls across Vaitarni, the sacred river dividing the world of the living from that of the dead. As the musicians process through the town from one shrine to another until they reach the central plaza, they trace the course of a circle. The circular procession not only maps the geography of the town, it symbolises the circle of the seasons, the cycle of life, the shape of the cosmos and the hierarchy of the Hindu caste system.

Most importantly, all this is conveyed in sound by the cyclical form of the music they play. The music of the Gaijatra 'stick dance' (as it is called) is not freely improvised, like the hunter-gatherer music I have discussed. It is as fixed and ritualised as the social conventions that support a farming settlement. The pattern goes like this. Every seventh step, the dancers turn to face each other to click sticks, not unlike the English Morris dance – another example of an agricultural ritual. This happens in the first part of the dance. When the procession approaches an important shrine, the lead dancer cues the others to accelerate so as to click sticks every third beat, so that the music becomes more exciting as the metre quickens. Most music across the world gets faster and more intense as it proceeds; virtually every Western pop song does that. There is nothing mysterious about progressive intensification in music. It is the inevitable consequence of seeing musical time as a cycle oriented towards a climax; indeed, like a calendar. As Gaijatra rises and falls in waves of intensity, it mirrors the circle of the seasons. This kind of highly ritualised music is lacking in the literally open-ended, participatory songs of hunter-gatherers. If every member of the tribe is to enter and leave the song as they please, then the song can't be crafted with a beginning, a middle or an end.

One of the many fascinating aspects of animals and music, as we shall see in Chapter 9, is that animals intensely dislike human music. This is thought-provoking, in light of the ultimate origin of music from animal vocalisation. It also reflects upon an emerging theme of this book: the entanglement of human music with animals at all stages of history and evolution. One might even venture that a defining characteristic of the musical human is our obsession with animals. Music partly originates in the percussive banging that *sapiens* used in order to drive out dangerous animals from their caves – and, by extension, animal-shaped spirits. Music literally creates a space in which to settle: positively, because of its magical aura; and negatively, as an aversive force to keep out evil and to demarcate a boundary between civilisation and nature, the village and the forest. Thus music even antedates settlement. That was the lesson of the temple at Göbekli Tepe: evidence that religion – and music – motivated sedentism. In sum, these are some of the many things music can do. It creates a space. It maps the borders of the settlement, the line between the human world and the realm of animals. It mediates between the human and the Divine. And it explains the role of animals and agriculture in the origins of music. The most spectacular example of that is a village on the other side of the world from Nepal, in the Amazonian rainforest.

The Kisedje Indians of Mato Grosso, Brazil, a people mentioned in earlier chapters, have an origin myth to explain where agriculture came from. They believe that in ancient times they subsisted on rotten wood, until one day a mouse taught them how to grow maize and sweet potatoes. At the climax of the Mouse Ceremony, a rite of passage for an adolescent male and the climax of a year filled with ceremonies, a Kisedje boy symbolically transforms into a mouse. Each season of the year has its own rite. The Gaiyi Ceremony marks the end of the rainy season. Mouse Ceremonies happen when the corn is ripe. The Garden Song is sung when clearings are burned. The Bee Ceremony celebrates the cutting of the gardens, when men swarm like bees from house to house in the village. Each social group has its own kind of songs, and places where they are permitted to sing them (the village plaza, the houses, the forest). The Kisedje's songs create as well as reflect society. For example, brothers-in-law or enemies who might never normally speak to each other might well sing together. Interestingly, the Kisedje make a clear analogy between the formality of their songs (i.e. the length and structure of the phrasing) and the formality of the setting. The most 'classical' music, as we would say in the West, happens in the prime site: the village's central plaza.

The anthropologist Anthony Seeger, who spent many years with the Kisedje, believes that a Kisedje village is a concert hall, with concerts lasting a full year, and the villagers as orchestra.[77] The village is structured like a theatre, with a circle of thatched houses around a cleared central plaza. As the male singers circle the plaza (and only men are allowed to do this), they are answered by women weeping in their homes, while old men and children shout, call out or giggle. Every sound made during this performance is considered 'music'; although there is a clear concentric hierarchy – with the importance of the music radiating from the plaza – the Kisedje don't consider that there is a boundary between performers and audience. This leads us to reconsider the meaning of polyphony, the idiom of the Pygmies and the Aboriginal people. In one sense, Kisedje songs lack counterpoint: their music is sung either in unison or single-voiced. They don't have much interest in instruments, not even percussion. Kisedje music is essentially vocal. However, there is a broader kind of 'counterpoint' in the totality of the sounds and noises surrounding the performance.

While the Kisedje speak of distant 'ancestors', it would be a fantasy to think of their tradition extending back into the ancient past, or to imagine their culture as timeless. The Kisedje have a concrete context and history: they are just one part of a patchwork of tribes settled in the Upper Xingu National Park in Brazil, having been displaced in the nineteenth century by colonial conflicts further north.[78] They have particularly strong inter-tribal relationships with the Arawak, Carib and Kamayura Indians, each of whom have their own distinctive and equally complex musical cosmography. For instance, Kamayura music is dominated by flutes rather than voices, and they associate the power of flutes both with tribal strength and with the very act of settling in their part of the forest. All tribes believe that they learn new songs from outsiders. If hunter-gatherers forage songs, sedentary cultures take them prisoner. Hence it is not the specifics of their musical culture that may have been shared by sedentary humans 10,000 years ago, but the mechanism by which they use music to create spaces, boundaries and concepts of outsiders.

A further myth to discard is that sedentary societies necessarily come after nomadic ones. It is common sense that settlements can collapse if conditions fail, and the people can go back on the road, as indeed seems to have been the case in North America (or, back in the Middle East, with the wandering Israelites in the Negev desert). One object lesson is the Pueblo Indians of Arizona, who discovered farming and built circular villages in AD 500, and left behind many images of music and dance. An image on a clay pot shows a group of people dancing with arms interlinked in a circle, and a solitary flautist standing nearby.[79] The point of circle dancing is that it restrains individual bodily freedom (i.e. arm movement) in the name of the social collective. The nomadic Hopi Indians, who descended from the Pueblo, also dance in a circle. But they dance today as individuals, no longer with arms on each others' shoulders.

The Maya

Historians still debate whether early humans trickled through the bottleneck of Mexico to South America, or via primitive boats across the Pacific. Either way, Palaeo-American culture climaxed with a series of city states founded by civilisations such as the Maya, Inca and Aztecs. A temple-wall painting from the ancient Mayan city of Bonampak in Mexico shows what happens when music becomes urban (see **Figure 5.6**). Two trumpeters blare out of the picture. Others in this twelve-man orchestra, perhaps part of a theatrical procession, play drums, rattles and ocarinas (small flutes shaped like a whistle).[80] The mural is dated AD 775, well into the Mayan Classic Period, but the music it portrays could plausibly have sounded three millennia earlier in the Preclassic Period (2000 BC–AD 250). The trumpets were wooden; the Maya didn't acquire metallurgy until AD 800. It is also remarkable that string instruments of any kind were alien to the American continent until they were introduced by the Spanish.

Figure 5.6 Detail from Mayan temple wall painting at Bonampak

Late in the post-contact, or colonial, period of Mayan history, after their defeat to the Spanish in 1523 under Pedro de Alvarado, we have an eye-witness account, dated 1624, of wooden trumpets being used by the Maya to enact the sacrifice of a prisoner taken in battle:

> Tied to a stake, he is attacked by four dancers disguised as a jaguar, a puma, an eagle and another animal. They try to kill him to a terrible din caused by yells and the calls of some long twisted trumpets that look like sackbuts and whose frighteningly dismal sounds are enough to scare the wits out of anyone.[81]

Incredible detail on a vase pulled out of a lowland Maya area tells its own story. K731, as it is labelled, features the Mayan maize god emerging from the split carapace of a turtle (the turtle looks otherwise alive and well). Coming up behind in a canoe is another god beating a turtle carapace with a deer antler.[82] Mayan astronomy calls Orion the Turtle, and they believed that the Earth sits on the back of a celestial turtle swimming in the primordial sea (Terry Pratchett's *Discworld* novels borrow this idea). The image on the vase blends music with agriculture, astronomy and animal worship. This is the heart of the Mayan musical cosmography. Even today the modern Maya of Guatemala beat a turtle-shell drum with two ears of corn in their Las Posadas ceremony, to assure a good harvest. They have also kept the expression, *lahb*, which in the Mayan language Ch'orti' means 'to stroke a drum with the dexterity of a tortilla maker'.

Like the Inca and Aztecs, the Maya amplify the ritual agrarian and hierarchic aspects of sedentary societies around an autocratic king. El Mirador, a Mayan city that flourished in 600 BC, occupied a site of ten square miles, and contains La Danta, the world's largest pyramid, seventy-two metres high. On top of La Danta sacrificial victims had their hearts ripped out to the fearsome sound of conch shells blown like trumpets. Down below in the central plazas, huge processions sang to the sun or the maize god. The most vivid record of such processions, depicting an Inca harvest festival that took place in April 1535 in the Inca city of Cuzco, Peru, was observed and recounted by the Spanish colonist Juan de Betanzos:

> These things happened in April 1535 when in the Valley of Cuzco
> they harvested the maize and other crops. Each year after the harvest
> it was the custom of the rulers of Cuzco to make a great sacrifice
> to the sun [...] They formed two lines, each of more than three
> hundred lords. It was like a procession with one choir facing another,
> and they stood very quietly waiting for the sun to rise. When the
> sun was partly risen they began to intone a song with great order and
> harmony. While they sang each one tapped one of his feet, like our
> singers of polyphony, and as the sun rose they sang higher.[83]

As they sing, the great Inca king sits on his chair in a tent watching, occasionally walking out to join the choirs. This continues from sunrise to sunset. 'And since until midday the sun was rising, their voices grew, and from midday on they diminished, carefully following the progress of the sun.'

It wasn't all spectacle and religion: the Maya also enjoyed music at home and at court. Ocarinas and other instruments have been dug up in the remains of household kitchens, and would have been played for family entertainment. A collection of figurines was discovered sitting around a monkey-faced singing shaman. One figurine is a deformed dwarf depicted blowing a trumpet while he boxed (Maya boxing imitated the swipe of a jaguar's paw); another dwarf plays her rattle while she dances.[84] Playful buffoonery aside, the Maya took singing extremely seriously as a virtue of lordly accomplishment. Glyphs (non-religious hieroglyphs) on murals represent singers with a red dot on their cheeks and a flower coming out of their mouths.[85] The red dot means 'lord'; the flower shows that the singer impersonates the god of music, who always wears a floral headband in murals, because the Maya associate music with fragrance (both are carried by the wind). This bundle of symbols says, essentially, that Maya singers were male and highly respected. By extension, the most accomplished singers were princes and kings.

How did the Maya songs of the sun really sound? Appalled by these heathen practices, the Spanish destroyed virtually everything they could get their hands on, perhaps also including music parchments. We can't be sure whether the Maya's complex system of glyphs included music notation. Yet if we take a broader view of how notation works, maybe something did survive. The line of a musical score is really just a shadow of the music's undulation through time. Waving your arm along with the music is cruder, but also a kind of notation in its way. In Mayan art, speech scrolls unfold out of people's mouths in undulations that denote the intensity of sound.[86] The thunderous reverberations from the mouth of the rain god, Chaak, are evoked by the jagged lines of his speech scrolls. The oscillations of skilful rhetoric are suggested by speech scrolls with whiplash contours. The din of battle is denoted by parallel chevron lines on Maya drums. They might have sounded like the noise that so horrified Hernán Cortés during the battle for Tenochtitlan, the capital of the Aztec Empire, in 1523:

> Once they had gained their victory, the people of that city, in order to terrify the alguacil mayor and Pedro de Alvarado, took all the Spaniards they had captured dead or alive to Tlatelulco, which is the market, and on some high towers which are there sacrificed them naked, opening their chests and tearing out their hearts as an offering to the idols. [...] All during that day and the following

night the enemy celebrated with drums and trumpets so loudly it seemed as if the world was coming to an end.[87]

The world coming to an end was theirs, not ours. One sound that may have survived sleeps in the very stones themselves. Every year during the spring equinox, the pyramid of Kukulkan in the ancient Mayan city of Chichen Itza in Mexico casts a shadow in the shape of the plumed serpent Quetzal, representing the god's annual descent from heaven. If you clap your hands in Kukulkan, the pyramid answers back with a chirped echo, the drawn-out falling tone of the plumed Quetzal bird.[88] Once again, birds hover over the origins of music.

CHAPTER 6

THE TUNING OF THE WEST

Each age has its own sound. As the ear of God hovered above the Middle East around 12,000 BC, perhaps as He pondered which tribe to elect as His Chosen People, it would have heard a lot of drumming. The soundscape in 4000 BC was sweetened with harps and flutes. At 1700 BC, it was jabbed by the piercing tones of the aulos, a kind of double oboe. The Romans loved trumpets. The epochs of the ancient world chart a symphony in four movements:

I: Ice Age. Thrilling percussion.
II: Bronze Age. Pastoral idyll, slow movement with harps and flutes.
III: Iron Age. A collapse into a new Dark Age. Music is faster, louder and more shrill.
IV: Roman Empire. Triumphant military processions with trumpets.

The sounds tell the ancient story of stability, collapse and return to order. For thousands of years, harps and flutes are the predominant instruments of the Egyptian Old Kingdom. We can tell that from iconography. Then something happens, sending shockwaves through the Egyptian soundscape. A detail from a papyrus written sometime during Dynasty 19 (1307–1070 BC) is a picture of joyful cacophony (see **Figure 6.1**).[1] A musician blows an aulos, marching behind a

Figure 6.1 Animal musicians in a Dynasty 19 papyrus

crocodile, a lion and an ass strumming lute, lyre and harp. Apart from the native harp, all these much noisier instruments are new to Egypt. What happens is the Hyksos invasion of 1720 BC. The Hyksos is the possible name for the mysterious Sea Peoples, Viking-like ocean-faring hordes emanating from Western Asia, who swept across the Eastern Mediterranean during the second millennium BC.[2] The Sea Peoples are often blamed for tipping the world into its first Dark Age. Historians pinpoint the year civilisation collapsed to 1177 BC.[3] But Hyksos music had been destabilising Egypt for over 500 years, since 1720 BC. The aulos made music more shrill. The lyre (smaller and lighter than the harp) made music more portable. The number of strings on the harp went up from four to sixteen, allowing music to become much louder. The Hyksos introduced the multi-fretted lute, a signature instrument of Central Asia unknown in Egypt. The genius of lutes is that they can play an unlimited variety of semitones and microtones. By contrast, the pitch of a harp string is fixed. All this means that Egyptian music acquired a much more flexible and elaborate tuning system. Through contact with Asia, the rigid music of Egypt began to melt. And so starts the great story of Western music's love affair with the sinuous and exotic sounds of what the West disparagingly calls 'the Orient'. We hear this 'Orientalism' (Edward Said's term – see chapter 2) in Mozart's flirtation with Turkish marching bands (see the *Rondo alla Turca* from his Piano Sonata no. 11 in A major, K. 331), and the Moorish sighs of the Spanish guitar. This love affair began in ancient Egypt.

Egypt's relationship with 'the Orient' was part of a system of exchanges spanning most of Asia. Much later, this system would coalesce into a network of trade routes, stretching from China to the Mediterranean, called the Silk Roads. We will explore the musical Silk Road in Chapter 7. The point to stress now is that the traditional Eurocentric view of ancient music, fostered by our obsession with classical Greece and Rome, is way out of kilter. Its true centre of gravity was Asia Minor. To modern ears, ancient Greek music sounds Arabic. This is because the medieval Muslim world was a custodian not only of Greek wisdom (the philosophy of Plato and Aristotle) but also of Greek scales, transposed into the Arabic modes called *maqams*. The star of the musical Silk Road was the lute. In its travels across Asia, Africa and Europe, the lute assumes many guises: the Middle Eastern oud, the Chinese pipa, the Indian veena and the European guitar. The star of the ancient world is the lyre, David's instrument as well as Homer's. Homer improvised his *Iliad* and *Odyssey* accompanying himself on a four-string lyre called a *phorminx*.[4] The brute fact that the number of lyre strings had narrowed from the more usual seven (or more) to a mere four bears witness to the collapse of civilisation of which Homer sings (the Trojan War is dated 1184 BC; Homer lived between 800 and 700 BC). Homer's recitation had to make do with just four notes, D, E, F and A. Had he composed the *Iliad* a thousand years earlier, he would have enjoyed the full gamut of our modern seven-note scale. Music history during the first Dark Age really had run backwards.

Taking the Eurasian landmass as a block, can we infer a common ancient musical language, a sister of the Indo-European ur-language originating in Sanskrit? We saw in Chapter 2 that 'creation' and *kriti* (the South Indian song genre) share the same Sanskrit root, 'kr'. *Atem*, the modern German word for breath, derives from the Sanskrit *Atman*, meaning soul or universal spirit. Are there similar connections in world music? Remarkably, there are: between traditional Japanese scales and the ancient Greek scale called the *enarmónion*. Given the enormous geographical, historical and cultural distances between these scales, scholars have hypothesised an extremely ancient 'major-third-trichord belt' ('trichord' because three notes: a semitone and a major third) extending from east Asia to the Mediterranean, including the music of India, Mongolia, Tibet, Cambodia, Indonesia, Korea and Japan, but *not China*.[5] To understand the significance of this primordial language, and the absence of China, we need a little lesson in ancient music theory. What exactly is the *enarmónion*?

A Lesson in Ancient Music Theory

Recall the principle of the octave from Chapter 4. If you keep on climbing the modern Western scale, you eventually get back 'home', but an octave (eight notes) higher than you started: Do-Re-Mi-Fa-Sol-La-Ti-*Do* (or C-D-E-F-G-A-B-*C*). Rising up by step is actually a contemporary way of thinking. The older, more natural course is not to add notes but to divide intervals, beginning with the octave as the purest musical sonority, with the simplest acoustic ratio of 2:1 (it resonates twice as fast as the fundamental). As we saw in Chapter 4, the next simplest intervals are the fifth (ratio of 3:2) and fourth (ratio of 4:3). You hear the harmonious triangle of octave, fifth and fourth at the monolith scene of Stanley Kubrick's *2001: A Space Odyssey* (courtesy of Richard Strauss's *Also Sprach Zarathustra*), and in the military signal known as 'The Last Post', played annually by a troop of buglers next to another monolith, the London Cenotaph, to commemorate the dead of the two world wars.

The fourth (which it can be shown theoretically to be an inversion of the fifth) is the most important interval in ancient melody, persisting well into the European Middle Ages. The Renaissance taught us to like thirds at about the same time that Europe discovered sugar. This is why Mozart, who is full of thirds, sounds sweet. But this is a corruption of our older, savoury taste for fourths. The Greeks seized upon the interval of the fourth as the basis of their music, and called it the *tetrachord* (literally, 'four notes'). This doesn't mean that ancient Greek music was confined to four notes. Rather, the Greeks understood scales as tetrachords chained together.[6]

The original *enarmónion* was an interval of a tetrachord with a half-step sitting on the boundary note, thereby cleaving the fourth into a semitone plus a third. In other words, the scale had three notes (a *trichord*), consisting of a little step and a larger one. This – from our perspective – ungainly succession of a step and a leap forms the primitive core of Western music, and survives in the Japanese *Kumoi* and *In* scales, and the *pelog* scale of Balinese gamelan.[7] It is notable that Japan and Bali are both islands, and are also islands of history. As with the living fossils persisting in the Galápagos Islands, such as iguanas and giant tortoises, ancient species of music have survived in Bali and Japan. We surmise that the Greeks learned this scale from the Egyptians because the first-century Jewish historian Flavius Josephus defined the Egyptian harp as *órganon trígonon enarmónion*.[8]

What is most significant about the *enarmónion* is its unevenness. The 'step' (the semitone) fits four times into the 'leap' (the major third): one interval is four times the size of the other. Surely there was a more equitable way of filling in the fourth of the tetrachord? This was indeed what happened across most of Eurasia. There was a drive to equalise the size of scale steps. The Romans, picking up from later Greek tendencies, popularised the modern European seven-note scale. The Chinese stuck with the older five-note pentatonic scale (think the children's tune 'Chopsticks', played on the black keys of the piano), but levelled off the contrast by eliminating half-steps or semitones. This brings us back to the interesting role of China, a topic I shall pursue in Chapter 7. China, as I mentioned earlier, stands aside from the pan-Asian 'major-third-trichord belt' embracing Greece, India, Mongolia, Tibet, Cambodia, Indonesia, Korea and Japan. In all these regions, the *enarmónion* is still a major player, now side by side with younger scales, but not in China, or indeed the West. The reason why musical irregularity – irregular interval sizes – should have been stamped out in both Rome and China is simple. Both were empires, and from East to West, empires govern through bureaucracy and standardisation.

It is a truism that ancient history climaxes, at the birth of Jesus of Nazareth, in a face-off between the Roman and Chinese empires.[9] This view has a musical grain of truth. Rome and China trod opposite paths to the same goal of a modern, regularly spaced scale. In Rome, musical modernity took the form of the European seven-note scale. China reached the solution of an 'anhemitonic' (i.e. without semitones) pentatonic scale. At this point in our story of the musical human, abstraction is far from a preserve of the West; it is more a symptom of empire in general. In short, we are not trading in the shop-worn, orientalist fiction that the West was somehow more 'rational' than the East. However, as we begin to sharpen our focus on a Western music going its own way, the particular flavour of its abstraction becomes ever clearer.

Its distinctiveness is forged from elements I have yet to stir in, including the music of Mesopotamia (the Sumerians, Akkadians, Babylonians and Assyrians), Egypt, and, most importantly, the Israelites. A continuous and living stream links the hymns and laments of Babylon, the Jewish psalms and the Christian chants that constitute the bedrock of European music. European music results from the confluence of this stream with the genius of classical Greece, whose dramas were operas all but in name. What consolidated and promoted this marriage was the organisational heft of Rome. The Roman Empire, as we shall see, contributed very little that was original to music. But what it did do was spread Graeco-Judaic (evolving into Christian) music around the Western world.

The Christians asked: who invented music, who tuned the West, Athens or Jerusalem? One legend has it that the Greek philosopher Pythagoras discovered the musical proportions from the sounds produced by a blacksmith's hammers. Advocates of Jerusalem pointed to Genesis 4:21, which cites Jubal as 'the father of them that play upon the lyre and organ'.[10] In the Middle Ages, the two myths were merged, airbrushing the pagan philosopher while giving full credit to Jubal. According to the thirteenth-century Franciscan monk, Aegidius Zamorensis, 'Tubal [sic], the son of Lamech by his wife Ada ... was the first to discover the proportions and consonances of music, so that the work of the shepherd ... might be turned into pleasure.'[11] Had the Church's memory been longer, it would have traced music's ancestry back to Mesopotamia, the cradle of Western civilisation.

With Athens and Jerusalem as parents, and Rome as midwife, the birth of European music was attended by a Good Fairy and a Bad Fairy.

The Bad Fairy arrives late and curses the child: 'She will never know a home, nor the feeling of true freedom. Ageing but never dying, cloaked in complexity, she will wander without end across the face of the Earth, and few will have ears to hear her.' The Good Fairy turns to the parents and says: 'I bless your child with the gifts of formal perfection, spiritual fervour and eternal life. She will be loved throughout the world. Best of all, everyone will know her name.'

Singing to the Moon

The first recorded name of a composer in the history of the world is that of a Sumerian princess called Enheduanna (2285–2250 BC).[12] The daughter of King Sargon the Great (2334–2279 BC), Enheduanna served the cult of Inanna (Ishtar) as high priestess in the temple of the moon god Nanna in the city of Ur. Ur occupies the site of Tell el-Muqayya in present-day Southern Iraq, and was the birthplace of Abraham, whose name means 'Father of Multitudes' in Akkadian. Another reason to remember Ur is its ziggurat, the vast stepped pyramid completed by King Shulgi in the twenty-first century BC, a version of which would have existed during Sargon's reign. Its surviving foundations are impressive enough, but the ziggurat would have originally climbed thirty metres towards the heavens. It was the original Tower of Babel. It might also have been the inspiration for Jacob's Ladder. For the British archaeologist Sir Leonard Woolley, who had discovered Enheduanna's name and image inscribed on a calcite disc in 1927 during his excavations of Ur's temple complex (see **Figure 6.2**), the ziggurat brought to mind a vision 'which showed to Jacob ladders set up in heaven and the angels ascending and descending on them'.[13] The ladders were the ziggurat's triple staircases; the ascending and descending 'angels' might have been 'priests in robes of state bearing the statue and emblem of Nannar'. Because there were no mountains on the planes of Mesopotamia (unlike Moses' Mount Sinai), the Sumerians built homes for their gods on top of artificial mountains, ziggurats. Enheduanna would have sung her hymns to the moon god at the top of her Tower of Babel, strumming one of the fabulously ornate Lyres of Ur, the world's oldest surviving string instruments.[14]

Figure 6.2 Enheduanna, the world's first composer

The ancients didn't distinguish poetry from song, so Enheduanna is also the world's first recorded poet. Through the Babylonian religious tradition she helped to found, she became the fountainhead of both the Jewish psalms and the Homeric hymns. Her forty-two liturgical works were copied and re-copied for 2,000 years, and continued to resonate in world culture long after her death. Faint echoes can be heard in the hymnody of the early Christian Church.[15] What did Enheduanna sing on top of the ziggurat? We need to wait nearly a thousand years till 1400 BC for the first surviving notated melody; all we have are Enheduanna's words. But the raw intensity of these words gives us a flavour of what her music might have sounded like. Here is a section of her 153-line hymn, *The Exaltation of Inanna*:

In the van of battle, all is struck down before you.
With your strength, my lady, teeth can crush flint.
You charge forward like a charging storm.
You roar with the roaring storm.

You continually thunder with Ickur.
You spread exhaustion with the stormwinds, while your
own feet remain tireless.
With the lamenting *balaj* drum a lament is struck up.[16]

Enheduanna in her ferocity comes across like a character from *Game of Thrones*: Daenerys Targaryen, 'stormborn' rider of dragons. Except that Enheduanna really existed, which we know thanks to the Sumerians' invention of writing, originally a modest tool for administering flood defences on the banks of the Tigris and Euphrates.[17] Hence to the Mesopotamians' long list of contributions to world civilisation – cuneiform script, mathematics (including the sexagesimal system), astronomy (including the prediction of lunar eclipses), medicine, irrigation and the twelve-month calendar – we can add composer. But we recognise these achievements only because of writing, the most important invention of all. Cuneiform script records information about music and musicians, as well as the notation of music itself.

Nevertheless, the cognitive revolution occasioned by writing (mass storage and retrieval of information; the administration of a state; the manipulation of abstract symbols; the reproduction and dissemination of culture) was really the symptom of an underlying power structure.[18] Power, symbolised by gigantic architecture such as city walls and ziggurats, was concentrated in the king, and the authority of a king was legitimated by the heavens: in practice, priests. So power pivoted on the partnership between the two buildings of palace and temple, the apex of a hierarchy dramatically steeper than in earlier hunter-gatherer and sedentary social models. Thanks to writing, we know an enormous amount about the hierarchies of Mesopotamian music.

Palace and temple employed different kinds of orchestra.[19] The palace orchestra (the *Nar*) comprised mostly string instruments. The temple orchestra (the *Gar*) was dominated by percussion, perpetuating these instruments' primordial role of frightening away evil spirits. Orchestras were hierarchical in themselves, and were led by a 'chief musician'. We actually have the names of hundreds of chief musicians, not just aristocrats such as Enheduanna. See for instance the *Gar* musician called Ur-Utu, whose prosperous social status we can deduce from records of his salary and ration allocation. Or Risiya and Warad-Ilisu, the two most notable (male) *Nar* musicians of Mari in the eighteenth century BC.

Princesses aside, the status of female musicians was normally pitiable. While Risiya and Warad were allowed to own land, and were even entrusted with diplomatic missions, women who sang or played were part of the king's harem. Terracotta statuettes of women playing timbrels (a kind of tambourine) depict them naked, with an emphasis on pubic hair – a far cry from the blank Greek ideals of the human body.[20] The sexualised representation of female musicians harks back to older fertility cults. Yet world music would never shake off its stigma of prostitution. In the Semitic languages of the ancient Middle East, including Akkadian, Egyptian, Hebrew and Arabic, the root word *Šmᶜ* means both chantress and concubine, and is related to the Akkadian verb *shemu*, 'to hear'.[21]

Outside the palace and temple music accompanied every walk of life, the high and the low, designated by some hundred genres of song noted by the cuneiform scribes. There was music in the workplace, in fields and animal enclosures, in the nursery and the tavern. Musicians enlivened weddings and funerals, religious processions and festivals, often side by side with jugglers and magicians. '*Alala*' was both an exclamation of joy (the origin of 'yell'?) and the refrain of a work song with alleged fertilising powers. The text of one song sings: 'The king of Urartu's fallow field I brought back the alala-song. I let his people intone again the call of the sweet alala-song.'[22] Musicians also went to war, and were prized as booty. A captured musician helped transmit music across the palace networks of the Middle East. The Sumerians had a rich stock of words for classes of musicians, for types of instruments, for tuning and performing techniques and for the various activities of making music: 'musicianship' (*narutu*); 'to sing joyously' (*nagu*); 'to play a musical instrument' (*zamaru*); 'merry-making' (*nigutu*); 'to hit' or 'to beat' (*tuku*).[23] Importantly, they didn't have a single word for music in general. This is entirely characteristic of world cultures outside the modern West. Only we seem to have abstracted the wealth of musical practices into a single word.

Figure 6.3 shows a fragment of an Old Babylonian instruction text written in Akkadian cuneiform script.[24] It was discovered at Nippur, and dated *c.* 2000 BC. The text teaches a novice musician how to tune a twelve-string lyre. One or two lines are missing from the lower right corner of the tablet, but the cuneiform can be discerned and translated.

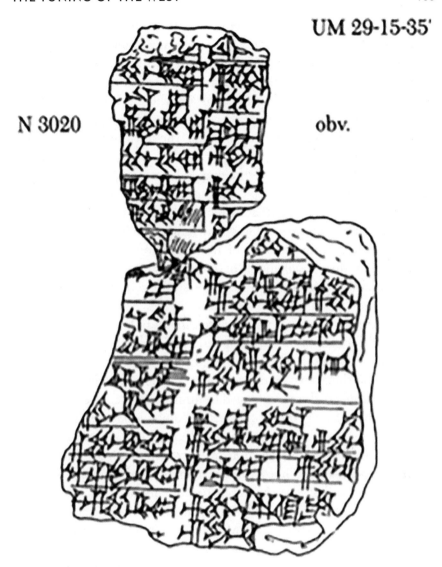

Figure 6.3 Cuneiform script of old Babylonian instruction text

Li-pí-it-es-tár	Hymn title
geze-en-nu-um	test/tune
si-hi-ip ni-id qá-ab-l i-im	paired mode
ze-en-nu-um	tune

First, the text gives the title of the hymn. The second line instructs the player to 'test' the string, which was done by sounding it against another string. 'Paired mode', mentioned in line three, means the type of scale the tuning will generate. This of course depends on which notes the strings are tuned to. Once a lyre string is tuned, the note can't be changed (in contrast to lutes, whose tuning is much freer because their strings are stopped by a finger placed anywhere across their length). A twelve-string lyre can only play twelve notes, although these can be preselected from seven different 'modes'. The last line of the text tells the player to tune the string, which he would have done by Babylonian procedures translated as 'tightening', 'loosening', 'making right/perfecting', 'raising/tuning up', 'setting' and 'coming down'. Tuning was 'epicentric', meaning that, after fixing the pitch of the central string, the musician worked his way outwards in concentric pairs of strings, alternating intervals of fifths and fourths. The Sumerians thought that these oscillations of intervals sounded like the zigzag contour of a thunderclap from Adad the storm god, in which a terrific clap is followed by a series of diminishing ones. A commentary on an astrological text called the *Enuma Anu Enlil* says: 'If Adad throws forth his voice like a *pitnum* ...' (a tuning system for a lyre).[25]

Babylonian scales have seven notes; five of the twelve strings double these notes at the octave for extra resonance. There are seven scales. The seven heptatonic scales are arranged in tuning charts as a seven-pointed star with mystical significance. Where is the *enarmónion*, the core of the ancient major-third-trichord belt? It is there, embedded in the most commonly used of these seven-note scales, which the Babylonians called *isartu*, and which the Greeks named Dorian: **E-F-G-A-B-C-D**. One of these seven scales, *embubu*, looks like our modern diatonic scale.[26] While *embubu* was theoretically an equal point of the star, it was, in practice, hardly ever used. The Middle Assyrian song catalogue cites thirty-two types of song, only two of which use our modern scale.[27] The scale's long path to world domination starts here, but 4,000 years ago it was reserved for special occasions. While it sounds normal, even natural, to our ears, for the Babylonians *embubu* would have carried a sense of gravitas.

It is impossible to exaggerate the importance of tuning for the Babylonian mind. In a universe governed by number, and the magical correspondences between music, mathematics, astronomy and the calendar, a mistuned lyre meant a mistuned cosmos, with potentially dire consequences. Enki, the Babylonian god of music, was represented by the number forty which, in the sexagesimal system, has a ratio of 40:60, the same in acoustics as the interval of the fifth, and the same proportion, according to the Babylonian calendar, as the length of the shortest day to the longest night at the winter solstice.[28] Get that ratio wrong on your lyre, and the harvest was at stake. We take musical instruments for granted, but for the Babylonians they were as special and potent as a loaded weapon. Indeed, an instrument was a god, which is why lyres were often shaped as a cow – an avatar of Inanna – as well as strung with cow-gut ('My good divine wild cow,' Enheduanna hails her in her hymn). In 2120 BC King Gudea of Lagash designated that year of his reign in honour of a *balag* (a harp/drum hybrid). The name of his favourite *balag* was 'Great Dragon of the Land'.[29] All this puts a spin on the alarming (to modern sensibilities) Babylonian concept of *Isaru*, by which the tautness of a harp string is compared to the erection of the male member, as in: 'Let my penis be like the taut cord of the harp, not to withdraw from her.'[30] A weapon, a goddess, a sex object. If John Lennon were alive in 2000 BC, he would have written: 'Happiness is a warm lyre.' The ancient world was far less prudish than ourselves in mixing sex and religion. The highly erotic *Song of Songs*, a jewel of the Old Testament, is indebted to Mesopotamian love songs.[31] Echoes of Enheduanna reverberate in one of Bach's greatest masterpieces: 'The Bridegroom comes, who like a roe and young stag leaps upon the hills.' Bach set this line in a cantata (BWV 140, *Wachet auf*) whose text is based on the *Song of Songs* and, via the long and winding road of tradition, Sumerian hymns.

But what of the actual music? The oldest notated piece of music in the world is the so-called 'Hurrian Hymn No. 6', written on clay tablets, excavated from the Royal Palace of Ugarit in the 1950s, and dated about 1400 BC. Tantalisingly, the tablet names four Hurrian composers: Tapšihuni, Puhiyana, Urhiya and Ammiya. Even more frustratingly, the song remains as out of reach as Tantalus's apples. While it is fully notated in Akkadian cuneiform – thus qualifying it to be the world's oldest song – nobody agrees how to interpret the symbols. Oceans of ink have been spilled deciphering it, generating thousands of pages of quasi-mathematical charts and tables, and performing versions as far apart as, say, Abba's 'Dancing Queen' is from Beethoven's Fifth, so out of proportion to this little scrap of text. One interpretation sounds like an anodyne Christian psalm; another like an impassioned Muslim chant.[32]

The lesson here is that the vast majority of normal Mesopotamian people would have found this score just as impenetrable as modern scholars. Indeed this speaks to the reality that most people today find *any* kind of musical notation somewhat forbidding. And that is exactly the point. In a society of enormous inequalities, literacy was restricted to the tiny elite who used writing as a tool of power as daunting as a ziggurat or palace. Writing – especially in its most arcane form of *musical* writing – glowed with an aura of magic. It was displayed on walls and monuments because, not in spite of, its obscurity, in order to intimidate. Mystery also shrouded Mesopotamian religion and religious hymns. Enheduanna sang to Nanna in an inner sanctum at the top of the ziggurat; the moon god was represented as a figurine sitting on a plinth within a niche (*parakkum*). This was far from the open-access columned porticos of Greek temples. Akkadian prayers were individual, not congregational, with none of the social dimension of Jewish synagogues, Greek choruses or the Christian Church. On the one hand, the elitism of Mesopotamian musical culture suggests that it wasn't as modern as it seems. On the other, perhaps it was all too modern. A remote figure, sitting in her office within the temple complex she administered, her hair coiffed by Ilum Palilis, her personal hairdresser, and dictating her songs to her scribe, Sagudu (both of whose images flank her own in the seal Woolley discovered), Enheduanna was, in every sense, the world's first *classical* composer.[33]

Blinded by the Sun

The south wall of Ramses III's temple at Karnak is engraved with sumptuous scenes of singers and musicians processing as part of the Opet festival, held in the second month of the lunar calendar. Statues of the gods Amun, Mut (his wife) and Khons (their son) sail along the Nile from their shrine at Karnak to the temple at Luxor. The exterior west wall shows the barques of the gods being greeted by rows of female worshippers standing on the river bank. They hold papyrus umbrels and sistra, a kind of rattle. The queen wears a vulture crown. The second row of worshippers is led by a woman playing a circular frame drum.[34] It is obvious that the ancient Egyptians prized music, and recognised that its use in public rituals such as processions was an effective way of knitting the country together. Much less clear is music's role in ancient Egypt's

3,000-year history, or the impact of this gigantic culture on the history of music. We all think we know ancient Egypt, from King Tut to Cleopatra. But the page marked 'music' in Egypt's history is mostly blank.

Sometimes turning points in world history can be precisely dated. The Bronze Age ended and the Iron Age began in 1177 BC, the eighth year of Ramses III's reign. Egypt was assaulted yet again by the Sea Peoples, after which it lost much of its Mediterranean influence and became a second-rate power.[35] All across the Eastern Mediterranean and Aegean, empires fell (the Hittite, Akkadian, Assyrian and Ugarit) and palaces disappeared, as well as the administrative structures that underpinned them, including writing. The long Golden Age disintegrated into a Dark Age of continuous warfare and illiteracy. Ramses left us a vivid account of the Sea Peoples' attack in an inscription on the walls of his mortuary temple at Medinet Habu, near the Valley of the Kings:

> The foreign countries made a conspiracy in their islands. All at once
> the lands were removed and scattered in the fray. No land could
> stand before their arms, from Khatte, Qode, Carchemish, Arzawa,
> and Alashiya on, being cut off at [one time]. A camp [was set up]
> in one place in Amurru. They desolated its people, and its land
> was like that which has never come into being. They were coming
> forward toward Egypt, while the flame was prepared before them
> [...] They laid their hands upon the lands as far as the circuit of the
> earth, their hearts confident and trusting.[36]

We now know that the enemies Ramses describes were the Hyksos, and we also know what their musicians looked like. A wall painting in one of the Beni Hasan tombs, twelve miles from Minya, portrays a group of foreign-looking people arriving in Egypt resembling modern-day Bedouins.[37] The women's brightly coloured, patterned garments contrast with the lighter hues of Egyptian dresses. A bearded man carries a lyre. As I said earlier, the Hyksos had actually introduced the lyre and many other colourful new instruments – the lute, the double oboe (aulos), larger harps, a clay drum called the *darabukka* – when they briefly ruled Egypt during the Second Intermediate Kingdom. (They also brought the horse and chariot). When the Hyksos were kicked out, these instruments stayed and were stirred into the cosmopolitan melting pot of the New Kingdom.

The genius of Egypt's civilisation was to adapt and endure for three millennia. The comparison with Mesopotamia, outwardly so similar to Egypt, is instructive. Both were riverine desert kingdoms with powerful monarchs, mighty gods, advanced technologies, limited literacy and gigantic public works. But whereas Mesopotamia was a collection of separate city states constantly at war with each other, Egypt enjoyed unity, stability and historical continuity along the 300-mile length of the Nile, thanks partly to its geographical isolation, which bred extreme conservatism. Egypt's ultra-conservative attitude to music was noted by Plato. The Greek philosopher writes that Egyptian tunes were 'enacted by law and permanently consecrated; [...] prescribed in detail and posted up in the temples'. Tradition was enshrined in pictures: 'It was forbidden by painters and all other producers of postures and representations to introduce any innovation or invention [including] any other branch of music, over and above the traditional forms.'[38]

From our general knowledge of hieroglyphs, we are aware how much this civilisation valued public images, which it festooned on every inch of its temples, tombs, statues and papyrus. We can even track Egypt's rise and fall according to the frequency of its musical pictures. As the Old Kingdom declined after its Sixth Dynasty, around 2181 BC, images of music become a lot more sparse. Their number peaks during the New Kingdom, when Egyptian civilisation reaches its apex, especially under Eighteenth Dynasty pharaohs such as Akhenaten and Tutankhamun. Banquet scenes are a staple part of tomb paintings, showing the tomb owner and his wife feasting at table, regaled by musicians playing harp, lute, lyre and double oboe – all Hyksos instruments. These scenes dry up at the end of the Ramesside period; there is not a single surviving banquet scene for 600 years after the death of Ramses XI (1107–1078 BC), the last Pharaoh of the Twentieth Dynasty and of the New Kingdom.[39] Their absence is eloquent, if silent, testimony to a long period of musical austerity in the Iron Age.

Not all change can be laid at the Hyksos's door. Change can also come from within. The seventeen-year reign of the Sun King, Akhenaten, is the lifespan of a mayfly in Egypt's grand scheme of things. Yet Akhenaten, famous for his experiment with monotheism, put a depth charge under Egypt's placid surface. Some of the aftershocks are responsible for the dramatic changes in music under Ramses III. What are these changes? The challenge for us is that none of the music seems to have survived, because the ancient Egyptians, unlike the Sumerians, appear not to have developed a system of music notation. Why not?

In hieroglyphs of the Old Kingdom, the word 'sing' appears regularly with a picture of an arm. The ancient Egyptians indicated the music not in a written score, but through a series of hand and arm gestures given by a chief musician presiding over an ensemble. This was the Egyptian art of chironomy. The chironomist was much more than a conductor: a modern conductor essentially only mimes the music in order to spur the orchestra, whereas the chironomist fed the players their actual pitches, intervals and rhythms. The *Mr Bean* episode in which Rowan Atkinson conducts a Salvation Army band exemplifies the fantasy that our gestures can directly create the music.[40] By putting more swing into his arms, Mr Bean changes the music from a Christmas carol to jazz. This is precisely how chironomy worked in Old Kingdom Egypt. A painting in a Fifth Dynasty tomb of Niankhkhnum near Memphis shows a group of eleven people, five of whom are musicians (playing two harps, two flutes and a clarinet) while *six* are chironomists. Crazy micro-management, with more chiefs than Indians? Unlikely. One or two conductors would have been present, but at least four of the gesticulating figures probably symbolised not individual chironomists but a selection of notes arranged in sequence, as in a comic strip, in order to sketch out the tune. This is the same principle as a cue sheet or chord chart for a jazz improvisation.

We can also have a good stab at what these notes were, because the eagle-eyed painters were incredibly precise. At the tomb of Ptahhotep at Saqqara, a single chironomist gives two signs to a harpist, one with outstretched palm, the other pinching thumb and index finger. These correlate with the two notes played by the harp in the same picture, and we can gauge what they are because of the length of the strings. A string twice as long vibrates at half the frequency. The ratio of the shortest string to the longest in many of the harps in Egyptian paintings was 4:3, which is a perfect fourth or tetrachord, the boundary of the primordial *enarmónion* scale. As I mentioned earlier, the early Jewish historian Flavius Josephus defined the Egyptian harp as *órganon trígonon enarmónion*.

There was a wider, cosmic significance to these gesticulating bureaucrats, however. What they were ultimately doing was imitating, even identifying with the goddess Merit, the personification of music itself. Merit created order (the Egyptian word *Ma'at*) in the universe through song and gestures. Typically depicted with outstretched arms about to clap, she was a chironomist goddess. This is not such an unfamiliar idea. It is what we all do when we bound around in the privacy of our homes 'conducting' Beethoven Nine or 'Bohemian Rhapsody', or playing air guitar. We become little dancing gods or goddesses, shaping the cosmos through our gestures. Chironomy also spoke to the intensely visual sensibility of early Egyptians, and the link between vision and sociability. The Mesopotamians might have endorsed Mrs Thatcher's notorious claim that 'there is no such thing as society'. Theirs was a world of power and forced compliance. Egypt, by contrast, was a constellation of little village communities held together by political persuasion and a state religion, which is why they invested such huge sums in visual spectacle.[41] The visual also permeated day-to-day life, where all private and official business was conducted through face-to-face communication rather than through texts, because only 2 per cent of the population could read or write.[42] In exactly the same way, musicians in an Egyptian band, just as in a modern jazz band, didn't need notation because they watched each other closely and could anticipate each other's moves. This is probably why chironomy disappeared during the New Kingdom, when Egypt's visual culture reached its climax, and spectacular monuments – hitherto confined to the outskirts – moved into the centre of cities.[43] Musicians had become so visual they no longer needed to be prompted what to do by external parties.

And then the Sun King ascended the throne and plunged music into darkness. Amenhotep IV (1380–1336 BC), known as Akhenaten, one of the most controversial characters in Egyptian history, banned the worship of all gods except the sun disc Aten, an aspect of the god Ra, and himself, as son of the sun.[44] Did he give the Jews the idea of monotheism, as Freud proposed?[45] And what is the connection between monotheism and Akhenaten's stricture that musicians playing in his presence, or before the god, should be blindfolded, or even blinded? The tomb of Meryre at Akhenaten's capital, Amarna, has a painting of seven temple musicians, all old, bald and with pot bellies (signifying well-nourished high status), squatting next to another old man who is playing the harp.[46] The artist has taken pains to represent their eyes as narrow slits, to indicate that they were blind. Reliefs at Karnak show palace musicians wearing blindfolds. Presumably, Akhenaten thought that blinded musicians were better attuned to the wavelength of the god; this also plays to the common belief that nature compensates the blind with sharper hearing. Or maybe the blindfolds just prevented the men from ogling palace beauties such as Nefertiti, since female musicians were allowed to play with their eyes open. In any case, although the maverick Pharaoh was posthumously airbrushed from history – his temples torn down, his statues smashed, the old gods restored – the image of the blind spiritual harpist would cast a long shadow.

Ramses III was assassinated in 1155 BC by a minor wife and was buried in the Valley of the Kings. When the Scottish travel writer James Bruce discovered his tomb in 1768, he found pictures of two blind harpists.[47] This wasn't unusual: the epidemic of blind harpists in Ramesside tombs is partly due to the popularity of an Egyptian literary genre called 'harpist songs', poems that lamented the futility of life.[48] The crucial difference was that harpists in harpist songs used not to be blind, but now they were. We don't know what Ramses III's harpist sang. But we do have the text of the harpist song in the tomb of Paser, vizier to his grandfather, the great Ramses II. 'How weary is the nobleman,' the song begins. 'Verily, bodies have perished since the days of the god.'[49] A suitably gloomy opening, but harpist songs give the lie to the myth that this afterlife-obsessed civilisation was a death cult. Actually, the thrust of these songs is to seize the day: 'Spend a happy day, nobleman. Ignore all evil and remember happiness.' The Egyptians believed that the afterlife was an extension of *this* life, and an opportunity to reconnect with dead friends and ancestors.[50] Harp songs, then, were sensuous and life-affirming, a call to make merry. Whoever wrote the 'Song of the Preacher' in Ecclesiastes (read annually at the Feast of Tabernacles) borrowed from them, as well as from their cousin, Siduri's song in *Gilgamesh*, which consoled Gilgamesh for the death of his friend, Enkidu.[51]

So we come full circle. In the wake of the Sea Peoples' invasions, banquet scenes disappear, and the lone harpist – always sitting somewhat aloof from the other musicians at dinner (see **Figure 6.4**) – steps forward, loses his sight and becomes the star of the show. The collapse of entertainment music (or at least of its representation) in favour of devout harp songs signalled not just austerity, but a breakdown in the connectivity of human relations (including justice and retribution), of the world order that the Egyptians called *Ma'at*. The songs of the blind harpists epitomised the resurgence of state-sanctioned piety in Ramesside Egypt.[52] Piety was a natural reaction to this new world of uncertainties. The spotlight now fell on the individual's subjection to an all-powerful, capricious god, rather like the relationship between Job and Jehovah portrayed in the Old Testament. Freud claimed that Moses was an Atenist priest who fled Egypt after Akhenaten's death. Although the historical record of Jewish captivity in Egypt turns out to be hazier than Freud thought, it is delicious to imagine Moses playing his harp in the temples of Karnak or Amarna, blindfolded, and worshipping the one and true God. Presently, the blind harpist will become David with his lyre, but with a neat twist. David will be fully sighted, and God will disappear.

Figure 6.4 Egyptian banquet scene with blind harpist

The Great Trump

After Moses shepherded his people across the Red Sea, the Israelites thanked Jehovah in a song of praise. The menfolk, led by Moses, began: 'I will sing unto the Lord, for He is highly exalted: the horse and his rider hath He thrown into the sea...' Then Miriam and the women answered with similar phrases: 'Sing ye to the Lord for He is highly exalted' (Exodus 15:1). Moses' first biographer, the Jewish philosopher Philo (born 30 BC), tells us that 'the Hebrews formed two choruses out of the men and the women and praised God'.[53] This call-and-response pattern, where one chorus answers another, is characteristic of Jewish religious music. Another word for it is 'antiphony'. When David returned from defeating the Philistines, the women greeted him antiphonally with a responsorial song. A cheerleader sang 'Saul has slain his thousands', and then everyone else answered 'and David his ten thousands'.[54]

Jesus would have heard, or even participated in, responsorial antiphony in the Jerusalem Temple. The older rabbis of the Talmud who were alive before the Temple was destroyed in AD 70 recorded how this was done.[55] A solo cantor might sing the entire melody, the congregation responding after each half-verse with a refrain. This was how they sang the *Hallel*, a prayer based on six psalms (nos. 113–118) performed on holy days such as Pesach (Passover). Otherwise, the soloist and congregation could alternate half-verses, which is the form of the *Shma Israel*, the centrepiece of morning and evening prayers.

The Israelites didn't invent responsorial song. A long line of influence stretches through the Assyrians and Egyptians back to North and West Africa. Artaxerxes II of Persia liked to be entertained at dinner by his concubines singing antiphonally. An ancient Sumerian lament was sung by alternating groups of female singers.[56] As late as the 1930s, Nubian rowing parties on the Nile preserved an ancient Egyptian practice whereby a leader improvised a short snatch of melody and the other men answered him.[57] It goes back ultimately to the linguistic 'parallelism' of ancient African oral literature,[58] and bounces back again to the leader-chorus alternation typical of sub-Saharan song today. Then and now, the idiom reflects a loose tribal organisation around a strong leader, be that leader a king, a cantor, a rower on the Nile or a prophet. Handel kept the same responsorial pattern when he set the so-called 'Song of the Sea' ('Shirat Ha Yam'), Moses and Miriam's song of praise, in Part Three of his oratorio, *Israel in Egypt*.

Laying aside the tangled issues of chronology – of when, or even if, Moses and the other prophets actually existed – the stand-out question, surely, is what is a nomadic tribe doing roaming the Middle East in the late Iron Age? The participatory ethos of ancient Jewish music is a throwback to the group singing of hunter-gatherers in the Palaeolithic era. In other words, the chorus is much more central to the Israelites than to the Mesopotamians or the Egyptians, which is to say that theirs was a much more sociable, less hierarchical, culture. Jewish music delivers the shock of the old. In two other respects, however, Jewish culture was very modern indeed.

The first innovation that set the Jewish nomads apart was their literacy, because hunter-gatherers (according to anthropologists) aren't supposed to read or write. Hebrew inscriptions began to appear in the ninth century BC. By the end of the eighth century, the time of the prophet Isaiah, Aramean scribes had spread literacy through much of the Assyrian empire on the back of the Phoenician alphabet (much easier to read than cuneiform or hieroglyphs). Israelite society as a whole became literate. The telltale signs are the many clumsy or mis-spelled inscriptions on ceramic pots, obviously written by ordinary people rather than by professional scribes. In Mesopotamia and Egypt, by contrast, literacy was in the hands of a tiny elite.[59]

The second novelty was that their single god was both invisible and rootless. The norm for all of history (Akhenaten excepted) was that gods resided in particular places, temples or parts of the landscape, such as mountains, caves, streams or glaciers. Indeed, the spirit was an emanation of the landscape, just like an echo, so to awaken the spirit meant awakening a sound. David, before he established the First Temple, sang to his god under open skies, a god he couldn't see or worship in a statue. God lived instead in the written law of the Torah, and 'The Torah is not in Heaven', as Deuteronomy 30:12 reminds us.[60] The Torah was carried within the Ark of the Covenant; God, like his chosen people, was ever on the move. There is something profoundly mobile about a text. Just as Jewish history is stamped with exile and diaspora, its texts were disseminated and handed down through the ages. The core musical texts were the psalms.

All of life is in the psalms, but they mostly praise God. Some scholars think that Psalm 104, written by David, was influenced by Akhenaten's 'Great Hymn to Aten':

> Singers, musicians, shout with joy,
> In the court of the sanctuary
> And in all the temples of Akhenaten,
> The place of truth in which you rejoice.[61]

There is a tradition that ancient Jewish singers cried out at the top of their lungs to catch God's attention. On Mount Carmel, Elijah taunted the priests of Baal: 'Cry aloud: for he is a god; either he is talking, or he is pursuing, or he is on a journey, or peradventure he sleepeth, and must be awakened.'[62]

What did they sing? The *Mishnah* (the Oral Torah, the first major work of rabbinic literature) is forceful on the point that all scripture must be recited to a melody: 'If one reads the Scripture without a melody, or repeats the *Mishnah* without a tune, of him the Scripture says, *Wherefore I gave them also statutes that were not good.*'[63] So what were these melodies? Remarkably, the music of Jewish scripture survives in the tradition of cantillation, a vocal outpouring halfway between melody and recitation. It is notated in a system of Masoretic accents (*ta'amim*) similar to the dots and dashes applied to consonants in written Hebrew to indicate vowels.[64] Each accent means not a single pitch but a group of two or three notes, each group (or motif) having its own name. (Much of the evidence of how to interpret them turned up in the Dead Sea Scrolls). This is the cantillation of the sentence, 'Then Moses called for all the elders of Israel' (*Wayikra moshe Le chol zigne Israel Qadma Tvir Pashta Tarcha*), as preserved by the Babylonian Jews of the Diaspora. Each word has its own motif: *wayiqra* is sung to the Masoretic accent called *qadma*, which means 'preceding'; *moshe* is sung on *tvir* ('broken'); *lcholziqne* on *pasha* ('stretcher'); *Israel* on *tarcha* ('burden'). A competent reader would automatically know which musical accent went with each word. The accents, little packets of notes, flowed like dance steps joined together by a skilful dancing master – *pas simples, pas doubles, reprises, branles.*[65]

Psalms dance, and this takes us to the most extraordinary connection of all. The *ta'amim*, the Masoretic accents, were written traces of those visual chironomic hand gestures we saw in ancient Egypt. Consider these two passages from the Old Testament. 'These are they whom David caused to minister over the hands of song of the house of YHWH' (1 Chron. 6:31). And: 'The Levites stood with cymbals to praise YHWH according to the hands of David' (Ezra 3:10).[66] One of David's hands indicated the notes of the scale; his other hand showed the ornaments to be applied. One of his hands becomes the accent at the top of the Hebrew text; his other hand ends up at the bottom. Masoretic terms such as 'palm' (*tifha*), 'ladder' (*darga*) and 'rising and falling' (*oleh we-yored*) give the game away. One can infer that the melodies of the First Temple, built by King Solomon in the tenth century BC, were originally conducted through chironomic gestures, as in Egypt; and as literacy spread to the whole population and the psalms were written down, the gestures were gradually transformed into textual markings. But, in effect, the Israelites 'danced' their way through their psalmic cantillation, just as the Egyptian chironomists imitated their dancing goddess, Merit.

The psalms also mention a variety of instrumental accompaniments. There are references to string instruments, *neginot* (Psalms 4, 6, 54, 55, 67 and 76); an eight-stringed harp, *hasseminit* (Psalms 6 and 12); a lyre, *haggittit* (Psalms 8, 81 and 84); and a wind instrument, *mahalat* (Psalms 53 and 88). Fifty-five psalms have the word *lamnasse*, meaning choirmaster. However, the 'harp' mentioned in Psalm 137 ('By the rivers of Babylon … We hanged up our harps') is no such thing. The word *kinnor* doesn't mean 'harp'; it is a lyre (although in modern Hebrew a *kinnor* is a violin).[67]

Why, then, did the Christian Church Fathers ban musical instruments as sinful? Plainsong, a direct descendant of psalmic cantillation, is still performed *a cappella* today, without instruments. The answer is a curious tale of how instruments were both tainted and hallowed by blood and sacrifice. The First and Second Temples had orchestras with a rich array of instruments. During Jesus's time, one psalm was sung each day in the Temple, performed by twelve Levite musicians, including trumpeters, at the climax of the service when the lamb was slaughtered. Indeed, instruments were tolerated in the Temple on the Sabbath precisely because they accompanied the sacrifice and helped to underscore its significance.[68] What is the link between instruments and blood? The clue is the central role of the ram's horn, the shofar. The Old Testament refers to the shofar seventy times, more than any other instrument.[69] 'With trumpets and the sound of the shofar, shout for joy before the King Adonai' (Psalm 98:6). The sound of the ram's horn reminds the Jews of when Abraham killed a ram instead of his son Isaac, and signifies the substitution of human sacrifice with that of animals. Human sacrifice continued to be practised by the Phoenicians, to their god, Baal. They were a people with whom the Jews had otherwise much in common. The shofar is the symbol of the Jews' covenant with God.

Blasts of the shofar punctuate every kind of Jewish ritual. It is the sound of how God first revealed Himself to Moses on Sinai. The shofar announces the new moon, convenes assemblies, heralds important announcements, crowns a king, wages war (and felled the walls of Jericho), declares the presence of God and awakens a slumbering soul. It is blown on Rosh Hashanah, the Jewish New Year, and Yom Kippur, the Day of Atonement. Most importantly, the shofar – or 'trump', as it is normally mistranslated (short for 'trumpet') – sounds three times in world history. The First Trump was on Mount Sinai. The Last Trump will be on Judgement Day. But the Great Trump will sound at the end of days when the Messiah is enthroned.[70]

Whether or not the Jews stole the idea of monotheism from the Egyptians, their religion discarded its central plank. Judaism had no place for the afterlife, a Kingdom of the Dead, or what the Christians called 'Heaven'. Instead, the Jews grounded salvation here on Earth but at the end of history, through what is called eschatology.[71] This linear view of history, of progress, is perhaps their main gift to Western civilisation, including classical music. And to Western music in particular, Judaism gave four blessings through its influence on Christian liturgy:

1) A canon of sacred books
2) A practice of reading and discussing them in public
3) The institution of people praying together in a congregation
4) A collection of 150 hymns, the psalms.[72]

Western classical music has a canon of sacred musical books we call scores, enshrining a collection of many hundreds of musical masterpieces. We read and discuss these scores at universities, sometimes in public. The institution of worshipping this music is called a public concert. The Judaeo-Christian Church, then, helped to create the template for how Western classical music evolved. I outlined this system in Part I of this book; Chapters 7–8 will tell the story of how this unfolded.

The other half of the template was forged by the Greeks. Greek music was as sociable as that of the Jews, but starkly opposed to it in many ways. Both musics featured a chorus of people singing and dancing around a single wind instrument. The shofar was the voice of God, and led the Jewish chorus in unity. The aulos shrieked like a Daemon, and provoked the Greek chorus into tragic conflict.

Tragedy!

Our word 'music' comes from the Greek *mousikē*, which literally means 'of the Muses', the nine personifications of the arts and sciences.[73] So music was originally just one of the crowd: Euterpe, Muse of song, held hands with Terpsichore (dancing), Melpomene (tragedy) and their sisters. Our Western habit of abstracting melody out of language, bodily movement and drama – narrowing its meaning into something called 'music' – would have offended the Greeks' richly interconnected vision of the world. This is why the musical form that became most characteristic of Greek culture was not individual song but the plural chorus. In the dithyramb, fifty singer-dancers, in the grip of a wild emotion, leap and chant in a circle around a single musician playing an aulos, a kind of oboe with two pipes blown simultaneously.[74] They are conjuring the death-agony and rebirth of Dionysus, a fertility god related to the Egyptian Osiris and the Eurasian Atys/Adonis. The sound of the aulos must have been extremely powerful to penetrate the sound made by fifty singers. It is clear that the Greeks found the aulos terrifying. Aristotle called it 'orgiastic', meaning it caused religious frenzy, and Longinus claimed it sent listeners out of their minds.[75] For Aristophanes, the aulos was a 'deep roaring [*barybromon*] pipe'.[76]

Dithyrambs, like the Jewish choruses, are a throwback to hunter-gatherer group singing and dancing. The Greeks' backward step is especially odd as they were much more settled than the Israelites in sophisticated city states. Stranger still is the fact that choruses (paeans as well as dithyrambs) were a relatively late arrival, what in Chapter 2 I called an 'invented tradition'. They were imported during the 'Classical' period from Phrygia (Anatolian Turkey) and Crete. Pindar described the dithyramb as a drunken party of the gods, and this gets to the heart of the creative chaos at the heart of Greek polytheism.[77] Artistically, having lots of gods makes sense. At their height, dithyramb groups competed at festivals in theatres like rival teams in today's football stadiums. The war of football chants, discussed in Chapter 3, is an exact analogy.

A dithyramb plus three speakers is a tragedy, arguably the premier art form of Western civilisation. Greek tragedies were sung, and were closer to operas than to what we call 'plays'. By the same token, the Greeks' greatest composer was Euripides, the third and youngest of the trio of tragic dramatists beginning with Aeschylus and Sophocles. Euripides is the Greek Wagner. At the climax of his tragedy *Herakles*, Hercules, rendered mad by Hera, slaughters his entire family.[78] The most affecting point of the drama is the chorus in which wife, father and children beseech Hercules for mercy: 'The *khoros* [chorus] of his children stood there – a beautiful form, and his father, and Megara.' We don't have the music, but the chorus would have been accompanied, like a dithyramb, by an aulos. The aulos had traditionally been used in Greek cultic rituals involving animal sacrifice. Once again, we see a striking parallel with the Israelites. Just as the shofar is a symbolic substitution for Abraham's sacrifice of Isaac, the aulos in *Herakles* expresses the horror of child murder for the delectation of a refined audience. 'I'll pipe you down with fear,' threatens Lyssa, Hercules' nemesis. The *khoros* understand only too well the danger of the aulos: 'Move away, children,' they sing, 'flee! This tune that is being piped destroys.'[79] According to Aristotle, it was the job of tragedies such as *Herakles* to make the audience feel the aesthetic emotions of pity and horror.[80] Sacrifice is turned into religion by the Jews, into high art by the Greeks. The horror at the centre of Greek music is greatly distanced from its origin in ritual violence, but it still gives us pause for thought. Why do we enjoy it? How have we come to this?

Greek music's origins – its true origins, rather than the imagined ones of invented tradition – were very different. It enters the world stage with the epic poems of Homer. The *Iliad* and *Odyssey* were sung solo by the bard, accompanied by a primitive four-string lyre called a phorminx.[81] The great Homer scholar Albert Lord convincingly demonstrated that these epics were not written down or composed but improvised by spinning out a chain of clichés, or formulas; and that this tradition was very much alive in the oral Serbo-Croat epic poetry of former Yugoslavia in the 1950s when Lord wrote his great book, *The Singer of Tales*.[82] The *Iliad* is a string of formulas, endlessly varied: 'rosy-fingered dawn', 'wine-dark sea', 'swift-footed Achilles'. England's national epic, the Anglo-Saxon poem *Beowulf*, was also improvised and sung this way. We can infer that there were musical formulas too. Each verse was sung to the same parabola of emotion, the vocal contour rising and falling in pitch in two grand waves.[83] Sometimes the bard would sing against the grain, choosing not to fall or rise at certain points in order to emphasise an important word or for rhetorical effect. Because ancient Greek was a pitch-accent language, a basic melody was already wired into everyday speech. Every word included one syllable that was emphasised, not, as English is, through stress, but by speaking (or singing) it higher, by as much as a fifth.[84] So we can tell that the speech-melody in the opening verses of the *Odyssey* was distinctly more dissonant and open-ended than that which opens the *Iliad*.[85]

The *Iliad* is particularly full of music. Helen despairs that both she and Paris 'are doomed to be a theme of song among those that shall be born hereafter'.[86] She would have been tickled that this, essentially, is what the *Iliad* is: a song about Helen of Troy. In Book 9, Achilles sings and plays his silver-bridged phorminx for his lover, Patroclus. The Polyxena sarcophagus, discovered not far from the ruins of the real city of Troy, refers to the myth that Achilles danced in his armour at the tomb of Patroclus.[87]

Whether or not the Trojan War actually happened (and in some fashion it probably did), the Asiatic spirit of Anatolian Troy prevailed over native Greek music. The Greeks credited most of their musical instruments to Assyria, Asia Minor and Phoenicia. The philosopher Aristoxenos claimed that the *enarmónion* was brought to Greece by a legendary Phrygian piper called Olympus.[88] This was false on both counts. But it shows that the Greeks believed that both the aulos and the *enarmónion* – the pan-Asiatic mother tongue of music – were invaders from Anatolia (present-day Turkey); and, indeed, that they were interlinked.

Homer's epics merely described violence. Music in classical Greece actually enacted it. Aulos versus lyre. East versus West. This was Greek warfare in a musical nutshell (or tortoiseshell, which lyres were made from). The Greek intellectual miracle mediates conflict, *Agon*, at every level, from the dialectics of philosophy to the snares of tragedy. Nietzsche, in *The Birth of Tragedy*, framed it as a cosmic battle between two gods, Apollo and Dionysus: Apollonian reason and light versus Dionysiac emotion and daemonic darkness.[89] Apollo's instrument was the lyre, although Hermes invented it, and it was perfected by Orpheus. Dionysus played the aulos, fashioned by this agrarian god from a reed plucked from the field. Apollo and his lyre weren't welcome in tragic drama. Lyre-strumming Orpheus came to a sticky end, torn limb from limb by the Bacchantes, Dionysus' crazed female groupies, leaving just his head bobbing in a river, singing forlornly. In Euripides' play, *Antiope*, Zethos, a military man of action who favours the aulos, launches an attack on his lyre-playing brother, Amphion. *Antiope* is an allegory on the fratricidal conflict between the two instruments.[90] Why did lyre and aulos hate each other?

Partly it was class warfare. The lyre, or kithara in its mature form, was the instrument of those snooty dinner parties called *symposia*, in which intellectuals philosophised. Pictures on Attic vases reveal how 'love of wisdom' ('philo-sophy') shaded comfortably into love of attractive boys playing kitharas. Boys are shown using their lyres to fend off bearded symposiasts, a far cry from the sanitised 'mad pursuit' pictured in Keats's *Ode to a Grecian Urn*. Aristophanes' *Clouds* pokes fun at the lyre's pederastic reputation. An old philosopher, called 'Better Argument', reminisces about the 'good old days' when naked boys walked in orderly fashion for lessons with their lyre teacher, the *kitharistes*, all the while 'keeping their thighs spread open'. And the Athenian statesman Aeschines was aroused by the sight of young Alexander (before he was 'great') singing to his lyre at a Macedonian symposium.[91]

The lyre was also the instrument of music theory, that most esoteric, possibly effete, of sciences. In short, the tuning of the West happened through the lyre. The lyre was ideal for visualising tuning systems because it displayed strings side by side, and the strings held their tuning. The aulos was useless because it was tuned through the muscles of the mouth, and its pitch notoriously wobbled. Aristoxenus, the greatest music theorist, complained that the 'pipes are in flux and never stay the same'.[92] On the basis of the lyre, Aristoxenos devised a 'Perfect System' of classifying the many scale-types, or 'modes', much superior to the Mesopotamian system to which it was indebted.[93] For example, each mode (Dorian, Iastian, Ionion, Locrian, Lydian, Phrygian and many others) was associated with a particular ethos or emotion, impacting both the listener and society. The 'Perfect System' enclosed music in a shell of beautiful abstraction. The question that niggled was whether the theory corresponded to what any living and breathing musician actually did, including those fascinating *auletes* (aulos players) sweeping in from Anatolia.

Interlopers and troublemakers, the *auletes* were the musicians of the *demos*, the democratic mob. What Plato and Aristotle chiefly disliked about them was that aulos players were professionals, even though professional competition undeniably raised standards.[94] This is why *auletes* spearheaded the 'New Music' revolution in fifth-century Athens, at the apex of Greek civilisation. 'New Music' (what the Greeks called 'Theatre Music') was more complex, more virtuosic, more emotional and more self-consciously 'primitive' and Dionysiac the newer it became. For instance, the wildly dithyrambic 'Hymn to Poseidon', by a composer called Arion, sings of dolphins dancing in a circle.[95] The aulos was much more flexible than the lyre; it could play the cracks between the notes, the microtones. And of course the two pipes could play in counterpoint with each other. Their restless, sinuous melodies writhe like Medusa's snakes. A good *aulete* could imitate virtually anything: the sound of thunder, of wind, animal cries, screeching axles and pulleys, buzzing wasps. The Spartan armies played the aulos on the march, and this may explain why Athenians, Sparta's mortal enemies, were conditioned to find their sound viscerally terrifying.[96] Most importantly, an aulos could 'modulate', that is, change key. Earlier melodies, including the choruses of Aeschylus, were confined to the same mode, and thus to the same emotion. Euripides, the most advanced of the New Music composers, wrote melodies whose feelings and modes shifted to reflect the words, just as the words were freed from conventional forms (the verses were 'astrophic', not divided into stanzas, and 'polymetric', using a variety of metres). This malleability (*metabola*) gave Plato another reason to denounce the aulos as an agent of disorder, because he associated it with the destabilisation of Athenian society, and justifiably so. Athens was riven by constant struggles between the *demos* and the aristocrats.[97] If great music must be sacrificed for the greater good, then so be it.

New Music created the extra bonus of music notation. Once music became too complex to be entrusted to an oral tradition, it had to be written down. This is why we are blessed with about 150 fragments of Greek music. It's not much, and the fragmentation is immensely frustrating. But this represents a quantum leap in our knowledge of ancient music. Of the 2,200 note successions in this corpus, 47 per cent are adjacent, so we can infer that Greek melodies moved mostly by step. They also arch, starting with an ascent and falling at the end of the song.[98] The jewel in the crown is a fragment from the opening chorus (the antistrophe of the first stasimon, or song) of Euripides' play/opera, *Orestes*. The chorus sings its distress to Orestes in an agitated dochmiac metre, a complex rhythmic pattern of eight short notes split into groups of three and five (similar to modern Bulgarian folk rhythms):

I grieve, I grieve – your mother's blood that drives you wild. Great prosperity among mortals is not lasting: upsetting it like the sail of a swift sloop some higher power swamps it in the rough doom-waves of fearful toils, as of the sea.[99]

Here is a taste of how the Greeks notated the music.[100]

Π	Ρ	C	Ρ	Φ	Π
κ α τ ο λ ο		φ υ ρ ο μ α ι		Z μ α τ ε ρ ο ς	
[ka - to - lo - phy - ro - mai				ma - te - ros]	

The notation is alphabetic, on three levels. The bottom line gives the chorus's words. The top line tells you the notes they sing. Π is a B flat; P is a microtone, a tiny pitch below; and C is an A natural. So we recognise that P (the microtone) comes back on the next syllable ('mai'). There is also a third line of notation: the big Z between the two words indicates the pitch G, to be played by the aulos. It is squeezed between the words for convenience; in reality, the G would be played continuously as a drone accompaniment.

What does this sound like? A musical sob, or a plaint, almost exactly as in a song by Adele or Barber's *Adagio for Strings*. Our modern name for this motif is 'appoggiatura', and it conventionally expresses sadness. Some aspects date the music as *c.* 420 BC: the dochmiac metre; the microtones (the *enarmónion* scale originally would not have split its semitone into two quarter-tones; the bunch of closely packed notes in the New Music was called a *pyknon*). But this combination of appoggiatura with driving rhythm also gives us Mozart's Symphony No. 40, a work of rage, pity and horror. This is dumbfounding. We have waited aeons for ancient music to reveal itself. Bone flutes are just bits of bone. Mesopotamian scores are undecipherable. Finally we lift the curtain over Greek music, take a peek, and what we find is … our own reflection looking back at us, across a distance of two and a half millennia. Ancient Greek grief doesn't sound very different from grief in Western classical music. There is no question that Mozart (or Adele) could have copied from Euripides. The point, rather, is that Euripides, Mozart, Adele and we ourselves partake of a continuous Western tradition. We are still Greeks.

To a great extent, the musical human comes of age in the New Music of Euripides in fifth-century Athens. Music breaks free from language: the appoggiaturas in *Orestes* are repeated incessantly, independent of the words' tonal accents. Musical form is born, and form frames the chaos. Perhaps the Greeks' greatest contribution to civilisation is to explain death as a necessary moment within artistic form. In musical terms, they find a way to structure extreme dissonance and disorder, even to make it sound inevitable. They complement the achievement of the Jews in redeeming death through time. Jewish history, Greek form. Both cultures disdain the Egyptian temptation of an afterlife (the Greek Hades is no heaven). Step by step, the Christians would meld history and form into classical music, at a time when Europe was effectively still Roman. So what did the Romans ever do for us?

Gonzo Fiddles While George Burns

Episode 210 of the *Muppet Show* constructed an entire routine around the name of its guest star, legendary American entertainer George Burns.[101] Burns puffs his cigar and chats urbanely to camera in his dressing room while the Great Gonzo plays his violin, and the gag runs on and on. Nobody needs to mention Nero because we all know that the mad emperor set fire to his capital and admired the view while playing the violin. It's not relevant that Nero's instrument was in fact the kithara, and that, on 19 July in AD 64 he was thirty-five miles away from Rome in his residence at Antium. As Karl Marx thundered, history repeats itself, 'the first time as tragedy, the second as farce'.[102]

Music in ancient Rome was in many ways a farcical repetition of Greek culture. There is no more vivid example of that than Nero himself. Earlier in AD 64, the citizens of Naples, together with a large contingent of Alexandrian sailors on shore leave, witnessed a treat when the most powerful man on Earth, the Trump of his day, stepped on to the stage of the city's theatre dressed as a Greek *kitharode*, a lyre player. A long purple robe, a chiton, rolled luxuriously down over his feet, covered by a mantle adorned in gold, and there was a golden wreath in his hair.[103] Nero sang indefatigably into the sunset, egged on by the 'regulated applause' (*plausus compositus*) and 'regular cadences' (*certi modi*) of bussed-in cheerleaders.[104] If the Roman historian Suetonius is to be believed, the captive audience wasn't allowed to leave 'even for the most necessary purposes'. Expectant mothers went into labour. Men were lowered down over the theatre walls by friends, or pretended to be dead and were carried off on stretchers.[105] The critics, writing safely after Nero's death, were not kind. The satirist Lucian wrote that 'his voice was naturally hollow', and that 'his songs had a sort of buzzing sound to them'.[106] Roman coins that portray Nero as a *kitharode* show him with his chin raised high over his chest, so that he seems to be looking at the sky. This was typical of how singers were represented at that time. Lifting the chin raised the larynx, producing a voice that was high, hard, loud, guttural and nasal – a quality of voice still found in the Middle East, but which sounds harsh and strained to Westerners.[107] Despite his limitations, Nero took his art extremely seriously, studying for many years with the most famous *kitharode* of the day, a Greek called Terpnus.[108] To improve his voice, he submitted to a gruelling physical regime, which included purging and lying on his back with heavy weights piled on his chest. More dedicated singers had a *fibula* (a kind of safety pin) inserted through their member, reflecting the belief that sexual activity damaged the voice.[109] Indulging his fantasy till the very end, Nero dreamed about murdering the Senate, burning Rome down and sailing off to Alexandria to see out the second act of his life as a professional musician.[110]

Nero plays to all our lurid imaginings of Roman music, many of which are documented in the iconography. Wall paintings at Pompeii show the orgiastic music associated with the cult of Dionysus. The noise of the tympana (a large frame drum) and cymbala (a pair of cymbals) drowns out the screams of those being violated.[111] The Roman Senate had banned such festivals in 186 BC, but they must have continued in Pompeii until the eruption in AD 79. At the other extreme of Roman life, gladiators in the arena hacked chunks out of each other to the accompaniment of wide-bored horns and 'water organs', whose sound was powerful enough to stand up to the surrounding mayhem.[112] The water organ, or *hydraulis*, was the world's first keyboard instrument, the air pushed through the pipes by a flow of water. Not for the first time in world history, technology was put in the service of violence and gratification. Rome took this principle further than before, so that instruments became bigger and louder. Their lyres had more strings; their *tibiae* (a Roman version of the aulos) had more holes and slides.

During the great famine of AD 383, the city kicked out all the foreign tutors but kept the choirs, music teachers and 3,000 dancing girls. The Romans, who clearly loved their music, got their priorities right.[113] The essence of musical culture in Rome was that it was *popular*, of the people, and this may account for why not a scrap of it seems to have been notated or written down. All ancient cultures were oral to a degree, but in Rome memory was especially valued. Cicero called the song that helped children remember their twelve times tables a *carmen*; the tune for learning the alphabet was a *canticum*, according to Saint Jerome. Saint Augustine got fed up with the *odioso cantio* ('beastly jingle') of *Unum et unum duo, duo et duo quattuor*.[114] Adult Romans exercised their memories on the hit tunes doing the rounds in the theatre. If Athens had their tragedies, then Rome most prized its comedies, such as the plays of Terence and Plautus. As with Greek tragedies, these dramas were operas in all but name, with singing, dancing and instrumental interludes. But they were sung and played for laughs. During the brief, seven-month reign of Nero's successor, Emperor Galba (assassinated in AD 69), we have a record of how the audience behaved at an Atellan farce (a kind of pantomime originating in southern Italy). The public took up a line from a popular song (*notissimum canticum*), which went 'Onesimus has come from his villa', and repeated it over and over again, with all the appropriate gestures.[115] And when the actor Fifius collapsed into a drunken stupor, the audience chanted in unison, '*Mater te adpello, exsurge et sepeli me*' ('mother, I call on you, rise up and bury me'). This level of audience investment and participation is not that far removed from *The X Factor* or *Britain's Got Talent* (or *Carry On Cleo*). It is revealing, then, that Roman origin myths are less dignified than the Greek dithyramb. The historian Livy ascribed the origin of music drama to the audience's obscene reactions to citizens' attempts to placate the gods during the plague of 363 BC. As the performers danced and played, delinquent youths mocked and mimed them with rude gestures and verbal insults (one can imagine their modern descendants chucking beer cans). The pantomime became the first comic play when authors added plot and dialogue.[116]

The need to keep the citizens happy with bread and circuses even led to the formation of the world's first international music union. This was by mutual arrangement. After the defeat of Macedonia in 167 BC, Greek musicians poured into Rome, and were recruited to play in the triumphal games organised by General Anicius Gallus to celebrate their own conquest.[117] The musicians then unionised into a guild of 'Dionysiac artists' (*Dionysiaci artifices*), vastly improving the organisation of public festivals. Such was their efficiency that, under Claudius, the Romans could take their games and festivals to every major city in their empire, while the Greek musicians established a 'union with all the members of the world' (*sunodos ton apo tes oikoumenes peri ton Dionuson … techniton*). Emperors from Augustus to Diocletian (died AD 316) obliged by granting them immunity from taxation.

Musicians were equally prized as the vanguard of the Roman army. Military brass instruments, regimented into the four ranks of *tuba*, *cornu*, *bucina* and *lituus* (essentially all varieties of trumpet, bugle and horn), were literally the army's cutting edge. Army musicians were considered to be full soldiers, rather than minstrels or slaves, and were paid the going salary (*c*. AD 160) of 120 denarii per year. Caesar's *Gallic Wars* tells of how he tricked the Gauls by planting trumpeters in empty encampments.[118] Suetonius writes movingly of how Caesar's decision to cross the Rubicon turned on a trumpet signal: 'When Caesar hesitated before his destiny, a man of rare and beautiful cut, a miraculous apparition, seized a trumpet (*tuba*) from another musician, and crossed the river sounding the *classicum* (the imperial fanfare) with all his might.'[119] So a trumpet calls at a crossroads of world history. This is why the great rhetorician Quintilian thought that the trumpet *was* Rome; the sound of the *tuba* symbolised nothing less than Rome's military might and glory. The trumpet was to Rome what the shofar was to Israel and the aulos to Greece.

We should not be so surprised, then, that this outward-looking, culturally omnivorous empire, overrun by foreign artists, failed to nurture much home-grown musical talent. Like Rome, Britain in the eighteenth and nineteenth centuries, the world's other great imperial colossus, was mocked by the Germans as a 'land without music' ('*Land ohne Musik*'). It made sense for Roman and British aristocrats to get the best musicians money could buy, and the best were foreign. Just as Emperor Hadrian's favourite court composer was the Cretan Mesomedes, George I and Queen Victoria brought in Handel and Mendelssohn. Adding insult to injury, while Roman music was neglected at home, imperial muscle promoted foreign music around the world. It also made music rather simple. Mass culture, then as now, is an empire of pop. Cicero, the champion of clear oratory, mocks the 'flexiones' of the Greek New Music.[120] Fussy microtones and the *enarmónion* disappear and are replaced by the regular steps of the diatonic scale, the basis of Western music ever since. So this is how populism, imperial bureaucracy and the tuning of the West intersect, around a common scale. A landmark in this development, and another monument of the historical record, is a little song discovered inscribed on a second-century grave stele in

present-day Turkey, then part of Hellenistic Rome. The world's oldest
surviving *complete* piece of music is the so-called 'Seikolos song'.[121] (The
Orestes chorus was only a tiny fragment; 'Seikolos' is a whole.) Here are
the words:

> While you live, shine
> have no grief at all
> life exists only for a short while
> and Time demands his due.

'Seikolos' is miraculous because, to all intents and purposes, it sounds
perfectly modern to our ears. It is disposed in regular four-bar phrases,
is diatonic, and is in A major, with a dance-like iambic lilt much
simpler than *Orestes'* agonised dochmiac metre. It actually recalls the
engaging tunefulness of Mesomedes a century earlier, so we can guess
that its style was fairly prevalent. We won't find this tuneful style again
in Western music for more than a thousand years. It must have been
going on, in fields and taverns. But there was an embargo on notating
it, enforced by the Bad Fairy, making another appearance in this story.
She had returned in the guise of the Christian Church.

CHAPTER 7
SUPERPOWERS

The Holy Roman Empire had become a laughing stock long before Napoleon dissolved it in 1806. By its end, it was neither holy, nor Roman, nor an empire, as Voltaire famously quipped.[1] But the title was fit for purpose when Pope Leo III crowned the Frankish king Charlemagne 'Emperor of the Romans' on Christmas Day, AD 800. Modern historians tend to stress the persistence of the Roman polity after its official demise in AD 476, when the barbarian Odovacar deposed Romulus Augustulus.[2] Ceding political power to the Franks, Rome itself slipped seamlessly into being a capital of the Western Church, and of the music which glorified that Church. Rome was now an empire of song, or at least of chant, based on Hebrew psalmodic recitation, now sung in Latin.

The New Rome ran its empire not with soldiers but with singers, sent out to every corner of Christendom to ensure, quite literally, that all Christians sang from the same hymn sheet. One even reached the northern tip of England near Hadrian's Wall, the frontier of the old Roman Empire. Shortly after the Anglo-Saxon abbot, Benedict

Bishop, established a monastery at Wearmouth (near the modern city of Newcastle-upon-Tyne) in AD 674, he imported an arch-cantor (*archicantator*) of Saint Peter's basilica in Rome called John. According to the Venerable Bede, England's greatest early historian, this was done so that John might 'teach the monks ... the mode of chanting throughout the year'.[3] John taught the English how to sing the psalms in the Roman way.

How the soundscape had changed since Emperor Hadrian had sailed up the Tyne a few centuries earlier in AD 122 to inspect the building of his wall.[4] Had you stood in AD 122 at Vindolanda, the Roman fort not far from Wearmouth, you might have heard Hadrian himself singing ditties in Greek by his favourite court composer, Mesomedes the Cretan, vying with Pictish battle cries and Roman trumpet signals (but not bagpipes, a Middle Eastern instrument taken up by the Scots only after AD 1000).[5] Later, you would hear plainsong sung in Latin. The language of music changed from Greek to Latin. Why, one might ask, were seventh-century musicians across Europe and the Mediterranean basin bothering with a dead language? The universal imposition of Latin was a fitting symbol for the formality of the emerging classical music. Chant, sung in Latin, would underpin 'official' Western music for more than a thousand years. First, it would be sung by itself, as plainsong. Later, it would be taken up as the scaffolding for polyphonic masses and motets by the canon of great Western composers, such as Machaut, Dufay, Josquin and Palestrina. Chant only loosens its grip at the end of the sixteenth century, the onset of the modern age when the West really takes off. This chapter investigates how we get to that point, when Western music breaks away from the other musical superpowers of India, China and the Islamic world.

Despite the fixation of music historians with the West, the point needs shouting that before the Renaissance, Europe was very much a poor relation to the other superpowers. The Gupta Empire in India, the Umayyad and Abbasid Caliphates in the Middle East and the Song Dynasty in China all experienced a 'renaissance' (a cultural and technological efflorescence) far earlier than Europe. This is the case also for their musical achievements. Why, then, did Western music conquer the world after the sixteenth century? There is a temptation to look for musical equivalents to guns, germs and steel, picked by the American writer and polymath Jared Diamond as the West's three secret weapons.[6] Western music's three 'killer apps' are notes, notation and polyphony. These increasingly come to define Western music in the period up to 1600, and they are characteristically absent in the other great musical civilisations, each of which emphasised other dimensions neglected in the West. The Islamic world had ornament. India had emotion, affiliated to ultra-refined taste. China put colour, or timbre, at the centre of its music (in the West, these are peripheral). Ornament, taste and colour represent paths not taken by Western music.

On the other hand, the other civilisations didn't develop staff notation – the by now universal system of writing music – nor the West's idea of layering music vertically, akin to visual perspective. Perhaps this vertical dimension of harmony and counterpoint is the single most divisive feature of Western classical music. Not only does it cut itself off from the more horizontal mainstream of Asia and the Middle East; it even turns its back on its own popular and folk traditions of song and dance. This is how and why, more than the other traditions, Western music's killer apps kill nature, as I proposed at the start of this book.

It would be tricky to lay the blame entirely at the feet of religion, because, as I have argued in earlier chapters, music and religion were originally two sides of the same coin. The question, rather, was how religion was institutionalised and managed. Judaeo-Christianity was just one of a number of compassionate faiths that arose in the so-called Axial Age after 800 BC, alongside Buddhism and Hinduism in India, Taoism and Confucianism in China, followed a little later by Islam, in response to population growth and market competition.[7] What set Christianity and its music apart was its problem with sex. The other religions had a pragmatic attitude to erotic pleasure, smuggled into the temple in the guise of an ecstatic union with the Divine. By contrast, the Christians' preoccupation with original sin made them suspicious of music that was excessively sensuous. Music was sinful if it was too elaborate or too colourful, if it had instruments, or if it could be danced.

Western music was seduced by sin in the thirteenth century, interestingly around the same time that India discovered the ecstatic, Sufi-inspired genre of Qawwali, and Yuan Dynasty China invented opera. The agent of global change was Islam and the Mongols on the backs of horses, a distant echo of how the Hyksos had ridden horses to effect similar musical revolutions nearly 3,000 years earlier (see

Chapter 6). In the West, the music of the al-Andalus, the name for the Muslim-ruled Iberian Peninsula, inspires the French troubadours to sing of courtly love, and ignites the long fuse of the musical Renaissance, which flares up two centuries later. What was it about the year 1300 that brought the four musical superpowers together in a kiss of ecstasy?[8] (Four rather than five: sub-Saharan Africa's vast contributions to music, especially rhythm, are missing from the historical record, largely because of the absence of literacy.) Adopting a global perspective, we will look at these four musical civilisations not separately but as colliding billiard balls. The emphasis will be on movement, clash and fusion, never more so than in the traffic of the Silk Road. What was the musical Silk Road?

And With a Chant to Bind Them

Birds cropped up a lot in Chapter 5 in the origin myths of many world cultures. The West's musical origin myth also concerns birds. Pope Gregory the Great (AD 540–604), supposed inventor of Gregorian chant (the byword for medieval plainsong), was often pictured receiving dictation from the Holy Spirit in the form of a dove cooing in his ear. If this was true, then it would have occurred slightly before the Angel Gabriel began reciting the Quran to Mohammed in AD 610. (As we shall see, whether or not Quranic recitation is 'song' was much debated by Islamic scholars.) For the Christians, chant is a perfect embodiment of the Holy Spirit. Surging upwards in mounting waves of melody, chant is also a kind of prayer: work of the soul. Such soul-work was also sung in the Hindu and Islamic traditions (recall Tyagaraja's 'Sogasuga' in Chapter 2), but interestingly much less so in China. Once again, China stands apart from the Eurasian mainstream. Just as Chinese isn't an Indo-European language, and Chinese pentatonic scales aren't part of the ancient 'major-third-trichord belt' (see Chapter 6), Chinese melody doesn't fit the global tendency of religious music to intensify towards an ecstatic climax.[9] Perhaps, as we shall see, this has something to do with the Chinese attitude towards time.

Pope Gregory didn't really invent chant. His hagiographers gave him credit for that because he was a great Church reformer.[10] Christian psalmodic chant began within the private homes of Jesus-believing Jews in the fourth century, before and after Emperor Constantine legalised Christianity in A D 317.[11] It then migrated to the deserts outside Alexandria in the mouths of anchorite fanatics who starved themselves and chanted round the clock. Fuelled by their fervour, psalmodic chant swept like a craze across the Mediterranean, returning to the towns, where the presence of a congregation and a bishop made it both louder (less of a solitary, low-energy mutter) and more tuneful. When chant entered the basilica, it acquired its characteristic resonance, that echo of voice against stone, which is the soul of chant.

It is extraordinary, yet on reflection logical, that the anchorites aimed to fill up every hour of the night and day with chant. At Byzantium, the Christian Church's eastern arm, there was even a Monastic Office of the Sleepless Monks, tasked with singing constantly.[12] Given that chant was the breath inside you, and the spirit of the cosmos, how could music not be constant? There is a surprisingly spiritual foundation, then, for our modern need for ubiquitous music, music everywhere and at all times. It also drove the Church's mission to fill up every hour, or Office, of the night and day with an appropriate chant, and thence every day of the liturgical calendar. The word for this process was 'Properisation', named after the 'Proper', the collection of chants for the entire year.[13]

As the Christian Church grew in strength, it used chant to bind Christendom together. There was an obvious reciprocal relationship between Europe's political fragmentation, in the wake of the collapse of the Roman Empire, and the new empire of song. Cutting across warring languages and polities, Latin psalmody unified Europe on a more spiritual level. Which was not to say that the Roman Church didn't also acquire a corporate identity consciously modelled on the old power structures. A document called the *Ordo Romanus I*, dating from A D 700, tells us how the Papal Mass was conducted.[14] Arrayed like a Roman emperor, the Pope processes in pomp in a cavalcade from the Lateran Palace to the church of S. Maria Maggiore. The nobles sit in a part of the church called the 'senate' (*sanatorium*). The celebrants of the mass are disposed in a quasi-military chain of command: Pope, archdeacon, subdeacons, archcantor, lower cantors, the lead singer called a prior. The chants themselves are not melodies, but a collection of melodic ideas improvised in real time by the singers, cued by signals coming down the chain of command from the Pope. This is not a million miles away from the chironomy of ancient Egypt or the 'hands of David' in the First Temple: how musicians were directed through hand gestures.

The whip of imperial discipline was cracked on all sorts of targets, to standardise, control and ultimately purify a properly Christian music. The Church banned, or severely restricted, all of the following:

- Instruments. The early Church Fathers looked at instruments as something evil, and were perplexed that the Hebrew psalms were so full of references to them.[15] Like angelic choirs, Christian monks sang *a cappella* (without instrumental accompaniment), a stark departure even from the Bible, because angels don't play instruments – not even harps.
- Women. There were no female voices in Christian choirs. The Church's vendetta against sex was curiously in tension with the central Christian idea of the Incarnation, of a God made flesh.
- Dance. The Church frowned on secular or popular music; not just dance, but all the sounds of the tavern or the theatre, including catchy tunes and showy ornamentation.
- Language. Perhaps most odd was the exclusion of the people's common tongue in favour of Latin. The music of the other great faiths reached out to the populace in their own spoken language, the beautiful Arabic of the Quran being the most striking example. Latin erected a stony barrier.
- Freedom. Charlemagne clamps down on the freedom of monks to chant pretty much any note they liked. He orders all chant to be composed and sung in one of eight modes, the so-called Octoechos, throughout the Carolingian empire.[16] This was music's original *lingua franca*: Frankish muscle imposing Roman law.

These strictures pave the way for Western music's most powerful tool, invented by an eleventh-century Italian monk called Guido d'Arezzo (991–1033). Guido invented staff notation, our musical score. The lines and spaces of a staff map the notes of a musical scale. This was much more intuitive and easy to read than the ancient alphabetic or diacritic notations ('diacritic' marks are the signs and accents added to letters, as in Hebrew). Previously, learning chants was achieved through a lifetime of arduous repetition and rote learning. Monks, who laboured for years to memorise chants, could now read them off the page at sight. It was an enormously labour-saving device, intended, according to Guido, to give the 'foolish monks' more time for study and prayer. When Guido put his scores into the hands of Pope John XIX himself, and the Pope took delight in instantly reading a versicle of an antiphon, music notation received the imprimatur of the entire Church.[17]

A cost-benefit analysis reveals that staff notation introduced a whole variety of enzymes, if not toxins, into the musical bloodstream. The visual element detached music from the muscle memory of larynxes and fingers. The natural site for music was in the body; suddenly, music was enshrined on the page, like a fairy-tale princess whisked out of her cradle and imprisoned in a picture. The visual element detached music from place and community; widely disseminated through scores, the home of music was now everywhere and nowhere. The ladder of precise notes in a stave rips music from speech, whose pitches slide naturally into each other. Most important, notation allowed the Church to bind the Empire even more tightly, assuring ideological purity without the need to physically send out singers. 'Purity' is a dubious word. Guido wrote that notation would allow monks to keep their ascetic devotions *cum puritate* ('with purity'), so that, essentially, they wouldn't think about sex.[18] But 'purity' also epitomises the Christian spirit of total renunciation. It communicates the tang of cold air at an all-night vigil, and the burning sand at the feet of the desert anchorites.

Point Counter Point

First notes, then notation. The third killer app is polyphony, or counterpoint. Again, it seems to have been born in church: specifically, the church of Notre-Dame de Paris in the twelfth century, in a two-voiced texture called *organum*, whence it spread to all Western music.[19] One needs to tread carefully here, because the supposed evolution from 'monophony' (single-voice music, like chant) to 'polyphony' (multiple independent lines) built the master narrative of Western musical supremacy, the grand historical march from simplicity to complexity. The narrative is false.

I argued in Chapter 5 that the polyphony of the African Pygmies was a better fit for the collective and participatory nature of hunter-gatherer music. Limbs entwine with limbs, like interweaving melodies in the great dance. In fact, the enforced monophony of Christian chant was an aberration, because most world music, both then and now, is polyphonic. Or more strictly speaking, heterophonic: voices going their own way, with different versions of the tune. Here is the Welsh churchman Gerald de Barri describing what went on in large parts of the British Isles in 1198:

> When they made music together, they sing their tunes not in unison, as is done elsewhere [he means in monasteries], but in part with many simultaneous modes and phrases. Therefore, in a group of singers (which one very often meets with in Wales) you will hear as many melodies as there are people, and a distinct variety of parts.[20]

A quite different view was proposed by the fourth-century missionary, Niceta of Remesiana (present-day Serbia). Niceta thought that chant ought to be sung with 'Christian simplicity [so that] all must seek to blend their voices within the sound of a harmonious chorus'.[21] 'Christian simplicity' was ever the mask for dictatorial control, and woe betide a novice monk whose voice stepped out of that 'harmonious chorus'. The Church fathers were Neoplatonists, following Plato's suspicion, in his *Laws*, that counterpoint was a symptom of civic 'conflict and confusion'.[22] The citizens of Plato's ideal city, his *Republic*, sang in unison. And that is why Saint Augustine would have associated polyphony with the chaos of barbarian hordes sweeping over the Roman world.[23] Imposing unison singing (or singing at the octave) was, to coin a phrase, 'taking back control'.

Plato tolerated polyphony so long as it was out of harm's way in the 'music of the spheres', the eight-note counterpoint traced by the eight revolving celestial bodies (Sun, Moon and the known planets).[24] But such celestial counterpoint was far too good for imperfect mortals. This makes Dante's narrative in his *Divine Comedy* deliciously ambiguous. Dante's musical story moves in three steps from hellish cacophony in the *Inferno*, where the demon Malacoda makes 'a trumpet out of his asshole'; through the penitents in the *Purgatorio*, who sing Gregorian chants in unison; climaxing in the *Paradiso* with the community of the blessed singing rich polyphony.[25] Dante paints an unforgettable picture of an astronomical clock whose intricately meshing cogs comprise singing spirits. Is Dante saying, like Plato, that polyphony is too good for us?

The point is that the kind of polyphony Dante would have heard in fourteenth-century Florence was nothing like that practised in Pygmy rainforests or Welsh taverns. It was highly regulated according to mathematical ratios, each voice striking a perfect consonance (a unison, octave, fourth, fifth, third or sixth) against another. By Dante's lights, the much freer heterophony of the Welsh (or Tuscan) peasants was literally diabolical: that is, cacophonous. It was curious that only the West achieved this hierarchical, controlled kind of polyphony, because in so many other respects Europe was technologically far behind the other superpowers. The astronomical clock, for example, the inspiration for Dante's contrapuntal clock of souls, was invented in the West in 1271, half a millennium after I-Hsing built one in China in AD 725.[26] The crucial difference was that it never occurred to the other superpowers to practise this ideal kind of polyphony in reality: it remained in the stars. By contrast, the Christian West *incarnated* polyphony within real living people, just as God was incarnated in the human person of Jesus Christ. The analogy was rehearsed by many of the Church Fathers. A Christian resonates with Christ as an octave does to a unison, by the ratio of 2:1, because Christ, having a dual nature, divine and human, was contrapuntal in Himself.[27]

News from Elsewhere

It is 8 February 1434, at Chambéry, the Savoyard court of Philip the Good of Burgundy, the most powerful secular ruler of the age. His court composer, Guillaume Dufay, is the pre-eminent musical genius at the twilight of the Middle Ages, the creator of sumptuous polyphonic motets and masses. They are gathered there to celebrate the marriage of Louis, Duke of Savoy, to Anne of Lusignan, daughter of King Janus I of Cyprus.[28] Dufay is about to be humiliated. We know this thanks to a verse in the court poet Martin Le Franc's epic, *Le Champion des dames*:

> You have heard the blind men
> Play at the court of Burgundy
> Haven't you? Surely you have.

Has there ever been anything like it?
I have seen Binchois shamed
And fall silent before their fiddling.
And Du Fay vexed and scowling
Because he has no melody as beautiful ...

What shamed Dufay, and his colleague, the composer Binchois, was the virtuosic playing of Juan Fernandez and Juan de Córdoba, a pair of itinerant blind minstrels from Spain. Their instrument, the vielle, was a species of violin with a longer neck and body, evolved from the Arab rebab. One always suspected that there was a popular musical counterculture, opposed to everything the Christian Church stood for. Here we are afforded a peek behind the curtain to discover it in its full glory. Confronted by a music more visceral and free than anything he could have imagined, Dufay made a fool of himself by writing an instrumental dance in the Iberian manner, nicknamed the 'Portugaler'. This little piece has generated a great deal of scholarly fuss, because it is like nothing else Dufay composed.[29] It is very sectional, with lots of fast notes, as if allowing the musicians to enter and leave wherever they choose, in the 'participatory' style of popular dance music (such as skiffle) I discussed in Chapter 2. He never tried his hand at this kind of music again. But it does show which way the wind was blowing. From the East.

The East pressed on the Holy Musical Empire from three sides. There was Byzantium (Constantinople), the Oriental Church. There was the fallout from the Crusades to liberate Jerusalem. And there was the Islamic influence via Spain, where the blind minstrels had strolled from. Byzantine Church music was older, purer, sung in Greek rather than Latin, and was steadfastly opposed to newfangled Western harmony or polyphony. Sylvester Syropoulos, Grand Ecclesiarch of the Hagia Sophia in Constantinople, then the biggest church in the world, heard some Dufay motets sung at the Council of Ferrara-Florence in 1439 and found them 'incomprehensible'.[30] Commensurate with its size, Hagia Sophia employed 160 singers, who would have made a tremendous sound. It is said that what prompted Charlemagne to order the roll-out of the Octoechos (the eight modes) throughout his dominions was that he heard some Byzantine chant.[31] The modes, of course, were Greek.

All the treasures of Greek music theory were housed at Byzantium, and when a little of this (much more was to come via the Arabs) was handed down to the West via Charlemagne, a great line of transmission was laid down from ancient to modern music. Thereafter, this conservative tradition drifted increasingly eastward, first to the Greek and then to the Russian Orthodox Church, where it can still be heard today.

The Crusades against the Arabs were very selective in what they brought back. Their appetite for the Greek knowledge safeguarded by Islamic civilisation (including Euclid, Plato and Aristotle) didn't extend to Greek-influenced Arab music theory, or indeed to Arab music itself. The Crusades impacted on music indirectly by enthusing generations of troubadours – roving aristocratic singer-songwriters – to sing of courtly love. A much more direct influence came from Moorish Spain, the al-Andalus, because the first troubadours sang in Arabic.[32] Arabic love song was the direct model for French love song. It lit a fire under European music.

The Path of Ornament

Western polyphony sacrificed the older art of ornament. Compared to the music of the rest of the world, Western melody is rather plain, and necessarily so. Decoration needed to be pruned if notes were to mesh together in a harmonious contrapuntal grid. Islamic art walked an entirely different path. Europe always took a condescending view of Islamic ornament – praising its wealth while regretting the fact that Islamic art never 'grew up', like the West, and painted people. It is not quite true that Islamic painters avoided figural representation, although portraits tended to be tucked away in miniatures rather than displayed in public spaces. See this beautiful image of a lutenist singing to a noble lady in an Andalusian garden, '*Chant de luth dans un jardin pour une noble dame*', contained within the thirteenth-century manuscript *Histoire de Bayâd et Riyâd* (see **Figure 7.1**). Nevertheless, it is certainly the case that ornament is central in the art of the Islamic superpower stretching from Mecca and Baghdad through North Africa and medieval Spain. Where did ornament come from, why couldn't the West get its head around it, and how did it display itself in music?

Figure 7.1 A *Muwashshah* sung in an Andalusian garden

We'll begin where we left off: in the al-Andalus. Only eighty years after the death of the Prophet (AD 570–632), Muslim forces crossed into the Iberian Peninsula in 711, and established Córdoba as the cultural capital of the Umayyad Caliphate. More populist than the courtly music of the rival Abbasid Caliphate based at Baghdad, Andalusian music was epitomised by a song genre called *Muwashshah* which managed to combine artfulness with catchy tunes.[33] Often, these were composed and sung by highly trained slave girls – unheard of in the sexist West. The great Arab historian Ibn Khaldun (1332–1406) tells us that *Muwashshat* (the Arabic plural) 'were appreciated by all the people, both elite and masses, due to the ease of understanding them and the familiarity of their style'.[34] The word *Muwashshah* derived from *wishah*, meaning a woman's girdle embroidered with alternating colours; the poem similarly alternated long and short verses. French troubadours were impressed by the richly ornate melodies, and the fantastically intricate metrical schemes. The Berber poet Al-Tifashi (1184–1253) mentions an Andalusian singer who improvised for two hours on a single line of poetry; another who made seventy-four embellishments (*hazzat*) to a single phrase.[35]

Astonishingly, for things we take so much for granted, it was Andalusian poetry that popularised complex end-rhymes and the sonnet form, best known in the West in the sonnets of Petrarch and Shakespeare.[36] Ibn Zaidun (1003–1071), the most celebrated writer of *Muwashshat*, also gave us the ideal of unrequited love as an ennobling passion, a yearning for an unattainably distant beloved (Dante's Beatrice is a Western imitation).[37] We can add these artistic achievements to the long list of Islamic inventions, including algebra, Arabic numerals (borrowed from India), the three-course meal, domestic hygiene such as bed sheets and undergarments, and the words 'magazine' and 'tariff'.[38]

'Jadaka Al Ghayth' ('The rain that falls upon you'), the most popular *Muwashshah* sung today, probably offers only a distant echo of how these songs sounded in the eleventh century. However, it captures an essential paradox of Islamic music by fusing ornate decoration with driving rhythm. The West has plenty of elaborate melody; Gregorian chant is its earliest example. However, it virtually never combines it with dance. Chant is literally timeless. When regular metre was drip-fed into Western Church music after the thirteenth century, either the decoration was stripped out, or it continued timelessly in the great polyphonic masses.[39] But listen to the Tunisian singer Sonia M'Barek perform 'Jadaka Al Ghayth', and you will be struck by how she effortlessly picks out every single note with a trill, slide, shake or turn.[40] This is much closer than Western song to the natural pitch fluidity of the speaking voice, how in talking we slide from one pitch to another. Meanwhile, the drums, zither, lute and violins keep the rhythms chugging along.

The blend of melodic and metrical ornament is intoxicating yet as light as air. In the grandest works of Islamic music, such as multi-movement song suites called *nawba*, music that sometimes lasts several hours, these two extremes alternate, chivvying each other along as the music accelerates towards an ecstatic climax. The *nawba* is introduced by a short, free-rhythm instrumental improvisation called a *taqsim*. The voice enters and the rhythms become more regular and the melody more complex. Over successive movements the music turns faster and simpler, reaching a pitch of ecstasy called *tarab*. This climax was both sexual and divine. The philosopher Ibn Hazm (994–1064), another towering intellectual figure from Córdoba, carved out a space for ideal beauty in the passion between lovers. Thereafter, erotic desire would be accepted as a metaphor for divine love.[41]

It is a cliché that music is like architecture. But in some cases architecture can be music. A familiar masterpiece of Islamic ornament is the Nasrid palace and fortress complex in Granada, known as the Alhambra Palace. The Alhambra is a symphony of the two extremes of Islamic ornament, the curvaceous arabesque and the linear geometrical, analogous to melody and metre in Andalusian song. Like the *Muwashshat* once sung in its courtyards (see **Figure 7.1**), the Alhambra takes the visitor from garden to sky. Gardens designed as a sequence of connected courts lead the eye, through a series of arches and columns, to arabesques of vine tendrils imaged in cut-tile mosaics within the living quarters. Tessellated polychrome tiles in the royal bath-house drum a subtle geometric rhythm against a white background.[42] Their senses already overstimulated with shape and colour, visitors' minds are overwhelmed by the star decorations and *muqarnas* roofing (ornamental vaulting) of the dome of the Comares Hall, a metaphor for the Seven Islamic Heavens.

Mohamed and the Quran are ambivalent about music, and its position within Islam has always been deeply controversial.[43] Officially, music was *haram*, unlawful, and the Prophet disapproved of reciters using melodies from love poetry. In 1999 the Lebanese singer Marcel Khalife was prosecuted by an Islamic court for setting lines of the Quran in his popular songs.[44] Yet the Call to Prayer (*adhan*), thrice repeated with increasing ornamentation in the *Rast* mode, and the whole performed five times every day, is arguably music in all but name.[45] By the same token, *zikr* – the rhythmic chanting of the name of Allah – is as physiologically stimulating as the whirl of the Sufi dervish.[46] All the same, Islam is careful to designate the Quran itself 'recitation' (*tajwid*), even though the sound of its Arabic is said to be as beautiful as music. Muslims are privileged to access the sonic beauty of their religious text; English-speaking Christians had to wait until the Tyndale Bible of 1526 for that pleasure, and then only second-hand, through translation. The Quran's link with music could be indirect and subtle. Umm Kulthum, the greatest Middle Eastern singer of the twentieth century, whose rapport with her nation was so powerful that Egyptian generals timed their battles around her radio broadcasts, was often said to have honed her voice by reciting the Quran.[47]

The broader point is that the sonic beauty of oral recitation is like the beauty of calligraphy, flowing naturally out of Arabic's cursive writing. Sound and writing are ornamental, just as music is a sonic calligraphy. The West finds it hard to grasp ornament because it is locked into thinking of it as, by definition, 'superficial' and less significant than 'structure'. But the tables can be turned to question the West's superiority complex about realism. Representing anything, not just a human figure, creates an aesthetic space apart from reality, a boundary between life and illusion. This is why Western music inhabits a realm apart from its audience. Gregorian chant had little regard for the listener, since it was sung by monks for themselves. By contrast, Islamic arabesques or geometric lattices spill out of the decorative surface into the surrounding world. The Arabic word *wajd* signifies the interactive circle of mood connecting the musicians with its listeners, an ambience.[48]

The telltale difference is how Islam received the wisdom of the ancients during its period of *falsafa* from the ninth to the twelfth century during the Abbasid civilisation, specifically in the geometry of Euclid.[49] When we enjoy the complex tessellations of six- and twelve-pointed stars in the ceiling of the Alhambra, all those dodecagons, equilateral triangles and rhombic modules, geometry has become a concrete thing.[50] In the West, it remained an invisible underlying principle, at least until Picasso and Mondrian in the twentieth century. If Christianity incarnated God in Christ, then Islam incarnated geometry in the world. Both are legitimate, yet opposite, paths to the Divine.

How did Islamic musicians follow this path? In their peculiar take on the mathematical proportions enshrined within the Greek modes, the musical branch of *falsafa*. When Charlemagne learned the Greek modes from Byzantine singers in the ninth century, the Western Church made a mistake that has continued to haunt European music. It treated modes as abstract scales, so that ever after music and scales came to inhabit separate realms. The Arabs understood that modes were not scales; they were maps, or blueprints, for improvisations. The Western scale is just a ladder of pitches. An Arab mode, called a *maqam*, tells the musicians so much more: which notes should be emphasised; how high or low the melody should extend; its characteristic motives; even the mood of the piece.[51] *Rast*, the most common *maqam*, always starts on the tonic note, and is dignified and plain. *Mahur* starts on the fifth, and is more animated. Some modes move in an arch structure, rising and falling. Others descend. And so on. *Maqam* closes the gap between innovation and tradition, and ties performers to a great brotherhood of music, in tune with Islam's egalitarian spirit.

Islamic ornament blossoms the closer it gets to Persia, the home of Rumi with his gardens of poetic metaphors, and of Sufi mysticism, and the further it retreats from Greek centres of gravity. An argument could also be made that Islamic music blazes most brightly when it interacts, or even clashes, with other cultures. This happened, for instance, in the thirteenth century under the Delhi Sultanate, when Muslims colonised large parts of India, as we shall see in the next section. A backward glance at thirteenth-century Spain underlines the fact that musical cultures are most vital when they are syncretic; that is, when they bring together diverse peoples. The court of King Alfonso X of Castile and León (1252–1284), composer of 420 *cantigas*, was a meeting place for Christians, Muslims, Berbers and Jews, and a refuge for troubadours fleeing the Albigensian Crusade.[52] Pictures of music being played at his court feature instruments from all these traditions. And the *Muwashshat* were taken up by the Spanish Jews and sung in Hebrew.[53] Sadly, some superpowers are more syncretic than others. Saladin (1137–1193), the first sultan of Egypt and Syria, and founder of the Ayyubid Dynasty, tolerated the faiths of the peoples he conquered, but when the Christians sacked Jerusalem in 1099 during the First Crusade, they slaughtered every man, woman and child, and burned alive those Jews sheltering in the synagogue.[54]

The Path of Taste

Western music lost its sense of taste. *Rasa*, the Sanskrit word for taste or flavour, is central to Indian aesthetics. King Nanyadeva (1057–1147), who ruled Mithila for fifty years, founded the Karanataka Dynasty, and in his spare time wrote the *Bharatabhasya*, one of the great treatises of ancient Indian music theory, noted that the flavours of music cannot be described in words.[55] What do we gain by thinking of music like a good curry? When Westerners talk of musical 'taste' (as in, 'that gentleman has fine taste in piano sonatas'), it is a comment on the social refinement of the person, not the quality of the music in itself. *Rasa* theory says otherwise, that flavour resides in the music, rather than in the listener. Putting taste centre-stage highlights the immediacy and interconnectedness of musical experience. *Rasa* is really a metaphor for emotion, so that emotion is felt to emanate from sound, rather than residing in how listeners feel, as the West thinks. Equally, the emotion of *rasa* is a metaphor for the cosmically immersive nature of Indian philosophy, where listening to sound, *nad*, is the same as meditating on the 'One'. The aromatic haze of a sitar drone, perhaps played by Ravi Shankar, is a sonic icon of Hindu or Buddhist mindfulness. Shankar has even claimed that it reveals the 'essence of the universe'.[56] The problem is that sitars and drones only arrived in India in the sixteenth century with the Mughal conquests, long after King Nanyadeva and his predecessors. When did Indian music acquire its taste, and from whom?

Few musical artefacts survive from the Harappan civilisation of the Indus River valley in modern Pakistan, *c.* 2500 BC. The outstanding example is a four-inch bronze statuette of a dancing girl.[57] We don't know what music she was dancing to. But she already displays the curvaceous pose so emblematic of Indian art, compared with her rectilinear Egyptian and Mesopotamian contemporaries. India is a water-world, and perhaps the fluidity of its art pre-dates the Aryan invasions from the sandy central Asia of 1700 BC, in the Indo-European migration that developed the Vedic civilisation. The four books of the Veda contain the entirety of India's pre-Buddhist religious wisdom, and Vedic recitation, based on cantillation of the Sanskrit hymns of the *Rigveda*, represents the very oldest recorded music on Earth.[58] Depending on whether you agree that recitation is 'music' at all and not just heightened speech, then the *Rigveda* has more than an edge on the 'Hurrian Hymns' of 1400 BC, discussed in Chapter 6. The roots of music are more exposed in India than in the Fertile Crescent or in Africa. That said, this cantillation is as primitive as can be, just two or three notes wobbling around the main reciting tone. We know that thanks to another living fossil in an island of history: Vedic chant is still performed in this way in modern Sri Lanka.[59]

Vedic chant suggests that music evolved by expanding outwards from one or two notes to fill the entire octave. We recall that the Greeks and Sumerians thought the opposite, that music originated by subdividing the octave into ever smaller intervals. Which is correct?

It depends whether your starting point is a musical instrument (the Greek and Sumerian lyre string) or the human voice, which is of course inarguably both older and more natural. So, the Indians have it. Indeed, they believed that the whole universe is contained within the sacred syllable *Om* (pronounced *aum*) intoned during every Vedic ceremony. According to the *Mandukya Upanisad* (the sixth, and shortest, of the 108 ancient Sanskrit scriptures called *Upanisads*), the first three phonemes of the syllable express, respectively, the states of waking (*a*), dreaming (*u*), and deep sleep (*m*), with the silent fourth quarter denoting the ungraspable infinite.[60] The acoustic overtones of the *Om* mantra enact the eternal emergence and return of sound to the world soul, the *Atman* (the Sanskrit root of our 'atmosphere'), whose breath is the soul of music. You don't need a sitar string, then, to taste the *Atman*: it is all there in the Vedic mantras, three millennia ago.

Although voice and the breath were always fundamental to Indian classical music, it valued instruments much more than the West, which made do without them for its first thousand years. The singer tuned him or herself to the resonating strings of a *veena* or *tanpura* (later, a sitar), just as the listeners gave themselves to the sound, and the music dissolved into the world soul. This is conveyed by India's most ancient and prestigious musical genre, the *Dhrupad*. *Dhrupads*, still performed today, bundle together all the main threads of this tradition, as listed below.

Raga

In polytheistic India, the hundreds of ragas are the plural gods of music, Krishna, Ram, Shiva and countless others. A raga is half-scale, half-melody, but it is quite unlike the Greek mode or Islamic *maqam* with which it is often compared.[61] Ragas have divine personalities, and, indeed, are often associated with a specific deity. An Arab *Muwashshah* or Persian *Ghazal* can shift (or 'modulate') from one *maqam* to another in the same piece.* This is prohibited to a *Dhrupad*, which must devote itself single-mindedly to one god at a time.

---

* *Ghazal* songs are musical settings of the ancient Arabic poetic form of the same name. They consist of between five and fifteen rhyming couplets, and are of an amatory, tender nature.

Meditation

Dhrupads begin with an unmetred improvisation called an *Alap*, which may last as long as an hour. The *Alap* starts by circling the *sa*, the raga's tonic note in the middle register, and then gradually expands to fill two or three octaves. It reveals the raga one note at a time. Unlike in the West, Indian music meditates, Zen-like, on the individual note in all its majesty. It is said that a note, *swar*, contains the entire universe, and that it even has a divine soul.[62] Ornaments are not tacked on externally (as they are even in Islam); they are the microscopic detail within the note. To listen to a *Dhrupad* means meditating on its notes and the emerging raga.

Rasa

To meditate is also to savour the taste of the raga, its *rasa*.[63] The literal meaning of *rasa* is 'sap, juice, essence', because *rasa*, like so many parts of Indian thought, is a process. It is a process of purifying the personal and transitory into the spiritual and permanent, distilling grape juice into wine. There are thirty-three transitory emotional states, or *bhavas*, such as world-weariness, anxiety, envy, joy, pride and perplexity. Music distils them into the nine permanent emotions: erotic (*shringara*), comic (*hasya*), pathetic (*karuna*), furious (*raudra*), heroic (*vira*), terrible (*bhayanaka*), disgusting (*bibhatsa*), marvellous (*adbhuta*) and peaceful (*shanta*). The goal of *rasa* is *moksa*, a spiritual delight purged of all worldly and personal conditions.

Evolution

As the *Alap* reveals the raga, and yields to the firm pulsations of the faster *Gat*, the music enacts the gradual emergence of form out of matter: the evolution of the world. *Dhrupad* improvisation is also the closest equivalent in music to the generativity of speech: how people compose sentences out of the linguistic deep structures in their minds.[64] *Dhrupad* could also be heard to recapitulate the history of Indian music: the proliferation of *desi* regional styles out of the central core of *marga* devotional music after AD 500, in the wake of the Gupta civilisation. The essence of Indian music is to look behind the surface profusion (of gods, of cultures, of decoration) to an underlying spiritual unity.

A catalyst of this abstract way of thinking was of course Buddhism, which originated as a reforming movement within Hinduism itself. The young Siddhartha, the future Buddha, had enjoyed music, and mention is made in the *Nidānakathā*† of him being provided with 40,000 dancing girls.[65] On the renunciatory path to Nirvana, however, the mature Buddha turns away from music as a dangerous sensual distraction; indeed, as a variety of the 'thirty-two kinds of feminine tricks which provoke lust' described in the *Lalitavistara*.**[66] While the original Buddhist dogma of the Theravādins viewed music as the epitome of sin, after AD 200 the softer Mahāyāna strain, happy to use music as a celebration of Buddha's life, diffused through much of Asia including India, Tibet and Japan. Japanese music, which we will get to in Chapter 8, is arguably the most 'Buddhist' of all. In stark contrast with the ascetic Buddhist orthodoxy, most Indian music accommodated transcendence and meditation to the sheer gorgeousness of sound, which in Chapter 4 I described (following Nussbaum) as the 'principle of plenitude'. In this respect, out of all world musics, it is Indian music that is closest to the Christian West.

One might imagine that this unique tradition should have come to a juddering halt after the first wave of Muslim invasions, when Mahmud of Ghazni entered India from Afghanistan in 1018. But the opposite was true: Islam brought out the best of North Indian music, while the Carnatic south split off and guarded the old ways. The first fruit of Islamic influence was rhythm. Drumming, always important in India, became even louder. The Rjarajesvara Temple at Tanjore in 1051 boasted seventy-two drummers out of its 157 musicians. By the sixteenth century the proportion of percussion instruments had risen further: the royal band of Mughal Emperor Akbar comprised one pair of cymbals, twenty-three wind instruments and forty-two drums.[67] But the most striking innovation was the concept of *tala*. *Tala*, the pattern of metrical cycles that underpin raga, is today one of the most basic and familiar aspects

---

† The *Nidānakathā*, forming the introductory chapter of the *Jātaka*, narrates the biography of the Buddha, and was written down at least fifty years after his death in the fourth century BC.

** The *Lalitavistara*, focusing on the Buddha's maturity, was probably compiled much later, around the third century ad.

of Indian music. Yet this was a Sufi import of the thirteenth century, inspired by Islamic *zikr* repetition (the ecstatic incantation of the name of Allah) and the whirl of a dervish's dance.[68] Ancient Indian theory had always discussed *tala*, but only as an abstract, underlying principle of formal proportion. Islam's contribution was to flesh out *tala* as real music; to *incarnate* it, just as it incarnated geometry in the decoration of its palaces.

The second major Islamic contribution was the Sufi/Hindu hybrid of Qawwali.[69] Nusrat Fateh Ali Khan (1948–97), the greatest Qawwali singer of the twentieth century, could trace his lineage back, through the chain of *guru–sisya* (teacher–disciple) relationships common in Asia, to the founding of Qawwali during the Delhi Sultanate in the thirteenth century by the Sufi saint Amir Khusrow. Khusrow's fusion of Persian, Arabic and Turkish styles with Hindustani devotional music was a model of Asian syncretism, and a mirror image of the Arab-Spanish synthesis happening on the other side of the Islamic Empire. Qawwali is more viscerally exciting than the austere *Dhrupad*. *Dhrupad* is a solo meditation, whereas Qawwali is sung by a group of men egging each other on and showing off in a competitive spirit, whipping up the music to ever higher peaks of divine ecstasy. Cumulative intensification had always been part of *Dhrupad*, albeit held in check by its balanced contemplation of the raga. Qawwali ruthlessly upset this balance for the sake of drama. Was this Islamic? It is more likely that its drama reached out to the home-grown tradition of Indian theatrical music, until now poles apart from the music of devotion. In other words, the tide was flowing towards fusing the sacred with the secular.

And this takes us to the third impact of Islam on Indian music, at the courts of the great Mughal emperors.[70] The word 'Mughal' comes from 'Mongol', and Babur, the founder of the Mughal Dynasty, was born in modern Uzbekistan and was the great grandson of Timur (known to the West as Tamerlaine). Babur's luxurious court, with its sumptuous *naubat* orchestras, began the Golden Age of Indian classical music. *Naubat* meant 'orchestra of world domination', and under Akbar, Babur's grandson, the Mughals' enemies stood no chance against the *naubat* artillery of Persian drums and cymbals (*damama, naqara, duhul* and *sanj*), double-reed woodwind (*surna*), trumpets (*nafir*) and horns (*sing*), all dutifully listed by the historian Abu'l Fazl, the chronicler of Akbar's reign.[71] These can be discerned in a painting, *Attempt to assassinate Akbar at Delhi*, produced in 1590 or earlier by Bhagwari Kalan (see **Figure 7.2**). [If you look in the top-left corner, you can see the musicians.]

Figure 7.2 *Attempt to assassinate Akbar at Delhi* by Bhagwari Kalan

The musical jewel in Akbar's crown was Tansen (1500–86), Indian music's most legendary figure. Such was the power of Tansen's performance of *Dhrupad* that it was said that he could bring on rain, make night fall and ignite lamps. This was also the Golden Age of the *Dhrupad*. Absorbing Islamic decoration, it grew closer to the luxuriously ornate genre called *Khayal*. It is extraordinary, however, to speculate how the marriage between Islamic and Hindu music was managed, given the differences between the two religions, fault lines that would eventually split India from Pakistan. Hinduism was polytheistic, caste-based, non-proselytising, venerated idols and worshipped the cow. Islam was monotheistic, egalitarian, proselytising, iconoclastic and avoided pork. And, crucially, Hinduism was much more tolerant of music itself. How would the twain ever meet?

Persian culture had its own concept of *rasa*; according to the seventeenth-century Mughal poet Sundar: 'The path of *rasa* [is] understood by everybody.'[72] A connoisseur at Babur or Akbar's court was called a *rasika*, one who savoured the taste of the arts. Not just any *rasa*, however, but one *rasa* in particular out of the set of nine: the emotion of ecstatic love, *shringara rasa*, which exactly corresponded to the word *'ishq* in Persian. In short, the Muslim-Hindu marriage altar was built on the common ground of *'ishq-shringara rasa*. The 1,004 *Dhrupad* texts preserved from the time of Emperor Shah Jahan (1592–1666) were dedicated to love, *'ishq-shringara rasa*. The venerable *Dhrupad* was recast as a genre of love, often as a panegyric to the Mughal emperor as irresistible lover.[73] Shah Jahan, the subject of innumerable *Dhrupads*, mourned his beloved wife Mumtaz Mahal so deeply that he constructed the most beautiful building in the world to remember her by, an architectural marriage of ornament and taste. We know it as the Taj Mahal.

The Path of Nature

The great sinologist Joseph Needham, author of *Science and Civilization in China*, reckoned that ancient China produced on average fifteen inventions every century.[74] Most had profound consequences: gunpowder, paper, magnetic compasses, stirrups, cast iron, all varieties of bridge technology. Perhaps more interesting are the 'sleeper' inventions, the ones that bided their time. Many centuries before Leonardo sketched his helicopter, the Taoist philosopher Ko Hung (AD 283–343) reported the following in his *Pao Phu Tzu*:

> Someone asked the Master about the principles of mounting to
> dangerous heights and travelling into the vast inane. The Master
> said: 'Some have made flying cars with wood from the inner part of
> the jujube tree, using ox leather [straps] fastened to returning blades
> so as to set the machine in motion.'[75]

What Ko Hung is referring to is the technique of attaching a rotary blade to a man-carrying kite. There is no reason to disbelieve that it worked, although Ko Hung's account shades into the oriental legends of flying carpets, genies and shamans (and the cruel Emperor Kao Yang's love of executing prisoners by making them participate in aeronautical experiments suggests that often it *didn't* work). The helicopter turns up again in eighteenth-century Europe as a toy called the 'Chinese top', as did the kite, and both were duly refined in the West into propellers and early aircraft wings. But not in China. I shall delve into what became known as the 'Needham Question' – why, despite its enormous head start, Chinese science allowed itself to be overtaken by the West – in the next chapter. For now, let's consider an example of a sleeper invention in music, something discovered in ancient China, but unaccountably never taken further there.

The Marquis Yi of Zeng ruled a small state in the middle of the Yangzi region, and died in 433 BC. When the People's Liberation Army liberated his tomb in 1978, the world learned that the Marquis had been serenaded in his afterlife by a rich ensemble of mouth organs, zithers, drums, woodwind and percussion instruments.[76] The star of this ensemble was the set of sixty-five bells suspended on bronze racks (see **Figure 7.3**). Why? Because the bells furnished the players with a reservoir of chromatic notes from which they could extract a twelve-semitone scale. Chromatic scales were only available to Western musicians with the invention of the keyboard in the late Middle Ages (i.e. the black and white keys of the modern piano). The Marquis Yi bells prove that China had discovered the scale seventeen centuries earlier.

Figure 7.3 The Marquis Yi of Zeng Bells

The puzzle was that the individual bells were inscribed with the names of the five-note (anhemitonic, without semitones) pentatonic scale; indeed, they constitute the earliest concrete evidence for this scale in China. So, if Chinese music favoured pentatonic scales, why did the Marquis Yi bells supply all the semitones across three octaves? The solution to the puzzle attests to the pragmatism of Chinese thought. Once forged and shaved, a bronze bell couldn't be retuned, unlike the string of a lyre or zither. So in order to fit in with the other instruments in the ensemble, the bells were constructed in pentatonic scales beginning on different notes. For example, one scale of bells might start on C (C, D, E, G, A), another on F sharp (F sharp, G sharp, A sharp, C sharp, D sharp), respectively using both the white and black notes of the Western keyboard. Because these transposed scales don't overlap, they fill in all the half-steps in the imaginary keyboard. This is why three flutes tuned to different bells could play all twelve semitones of the chromatic scale between them. The scale was literally unthinkable for the West for thousands of years, lost in arithmetical speculations based on the divisions of string lengths. Much more practical, Chinese musicians took as their starting point not intervals (fourths, fifths, etc.) but notes themselves. Theirs was a bell culture; Western music had – and continues to have – a string culture.

The acoustic partials generated by a bell are so complex that they can't be expressed in simple arithmetical ratios, unlike the tone of most other instruments.[77] This makes them practically useless for music, which is why the West exiles bells to church towers. Chinese acoustic science was then the most advanced in the world. The Yi bells' asymmetrical design (oblate rather than circular, covered in thirty-six nipples called *mei*, and producing different pitches when struck on the side or the centre) both broadened the range of overtones, and gave them a fast attenuation so that the sound died away quickly. The bells could be hit again and again, unlike Western bells, with their lingering resonance. The Confucian temple orchestras depicted on bowls and vases during the period of the Warring States (481–221 BC) show musicians going at it hammer and tongs upon suspended chime-stones and bells.[78] This ancient bell culture is echoed in the modern gamelan of Java and the Dayak long-house gong ensembles of Borneo (two more examples of ancient musical practices preserved on islands of history). Even after bells handed over to zithers and flutes as favoured instruments during the Han Dynasty (206 BC–AD 220), the name for the tonic note, the note that gave the tuning to the other instruments, was the 'Yellow Bell'. And bell culture explains the Chinese interest in the physical nature of musical material, and why they classify instruments according to what they are made from: the eight categories of metal, stone, clay, leather, silk, wood, gourd or bamboo. By contrast, ancient India, Greece, and to a mixed extent the West, categorise instruments in terms of how they produce their sound, through hitting, vibrating, blowing, etc.

The Chinese, then, were far more concerned with the nature of sound, its timbre: a complex package of sound waves and overtones. Pitch (the frequency by which an elastic body vibrates in the surrounding air) is much easier to organise than timbre; this is why we have scales of notes, but no scales of orchestral tone colours. Because there are as many timbres as there are instruments to play them, they are like the 50,000 characters of Chinese script, each of which indicates both a word and a concept. Far older than alphabetical scripts such as Sanskrit, Greek, Latin and Arabic, the Chinese system reflects a way of thinking that is radically distinct. In his archaeology of the human brain, Colin Renfrew concludes that 'Chinese thought and Western thought [are] the products of two largely independent trajectories of development'.[79] Chinese exceptionalism is manifest also in music. The West – and also, in most regards, India and the Middle East – walked the path of pitch. Taoism (from *Dao*, 'path') led Chinese music down the path of nature and timbre.

Taoist harmony with nature is expressed through its elusive concept of *qi*. Similar to the Greek *Pneuma* and the Sanskrit *Atman*, *qi* is the life force that blows through the universe. But it is a peculiarly grounded, even human life force, because *qi* is powered by the interaction of two contrary forces called Yin and Yang, which squabble, mix and breed almost like people. Most importantly for musicians, the clash of Yin and Yang makes noise. According to Sun Xidan, 'The *qi* of Earth ascends above, while the *qi* of Heaven descends below. Yin and Yang rub against each other, and Heaven and Earth jostle up against each other. Their drumming creates peals of thunder.'[80] And when *qi* blows through bamboo, it makes music, in harmony with the wind and breath. This is why Chinese music's origin myth is based on bamboo pipes as a channel of *qi*, while the West prefers a vibrating string. Inevitably, its origin myth once again features birds: in this case, pairs of amorous phoenixes. Legend states that the Yellow Emperor ordered Ling Lun to pick bamboo growing in the Jie Valley by Mount Kunlun.[81] He bored twelve holes, inspired by the calls of six male and six female phoenixes. Long before the twelve-semitone scale was a reality in the tomb of the Marquis Yi, it was the stuff of legend.

The sound of *qi* becomes less abstract and metaphorical and more concrete and practical after the Warring States period, when China settled down into a unified imperial power under the Qin and Han. The Qin emperors hated music, and made a bonfire out of instruments. But the Han recognised music's power as a tool to measure the health of the nation, and as a medicine for its ills. According to their *Canon of Filial Piety*: 'In changing customs and altering manners, nothing surpasses music', and this included rubbing out 'alien customs and depraved music'. In their enormous task of unifying disparate peoples across a vast region around a central authority, the Han used music as a civilising force, as captured by this oft-quoted passage by the philosopher Xunzi:

> When music is central and balanced, the people will be harmonious and not indulgent; when music is solemn and dignified, the people will be uniform and not disorderly. If the people are harmonious and uniform, then the military will be strong and the city-walls secure, and enemy states will not dare attack.[82]

Hence the meanings of music were standardised, just like weights, measures and the Chinese script. China's so-called 'correlative cosmology', the system by which all aspects of the cosmos (including music) were networked in a web of associations, can seem fantastically superstitious to us. Why was it auspicious, for example, to play pipes in spring, zithers in the summer, chime-bells in the autumn and drums in winter? Because a bamboo pipe obviously helps trees to bud in spring. Silk worms fattening on mulberry leaves during the summer enjoy the sound of zither strings made from silk. Autumn is when the Yang forces of nature retreat, and bells are sounded when an army retires. Finally, that most primeval of instruments, the drum, assists the winter sun during the crisis of the solstice.[83]

Meanwhile, to assure compliance, folksongs and ceremonial music from the far reaches of the empire were funnelled for approval through a central Music Bureau (Yue Fu).[84] It is testament to the staggering longevity of Chinese civilisation that the Yue Fu, established by the Han, closed its doors for the last time in 1911 only with the collapse of the final dynasty, the Qing.

This practical, civilising use of music reflects the triumph of Confucianism, the Han's state religion. But it went against the contemplative and somewhat passive nature of Taoism. In some ways, these two religions represent the Yin and Yang of Chinese culture, and the tension between them throbs even at the heart of its most prestigious instrument, the seven-string zither called the *qin* (or *Guqin*, its modern version). A *qin* is a long, flat, hollow wooden box, about three feet long, with the silk strings stretched out lengthwise. Its soft, delicate sounds made it an ideal instrument for the gentleman scholar, who is typically portrayed in Chinese prints playing it in lonely bamboo groves on high mountains, where its sounds meld with the wind and the silence. The *qin* is an instrument both of nature and of spiritual reverie. There are many pictures of Confucius meditatively playing the *qin* in his garden, or teaching it to his disciples (see **Figure 7.4**). Yet the calm image misleads: in the sage's *Analects*, the instrument features in a far more worldly – i.e. Confucian – capacity as a tool, even a weapon, of politics. In one passage, the Master fobs off a petitioning visitor with the excuse that he is too ill to see him, but then takes up his *qin* and plays it through the door, making sure that the departing guest can hear that Confucius is in perfect health.[85] In another, he rejects the petition of a man from the north, whose wild playing on the *qin* displeases him.[86] Much later, during the cultural efflorescence of the Tang Dynasty, Wang Wei (AD 699–759) – poet, painter, composer and perhaps China's greatest all-round artist – gently skewers Confucianism in a poem that alludes to a legend in the *Zhuangzi*, an ancient collection of Chinese fables.[87] An anecdote relates how one day an old fisherman, drawn by the sound of Confucius playing his *qin*, moors his boat and sits down to listen to the Master deliver a lecture under an apricot tree. After a long conversation, the fisherman, unimpressed, walks off because he prefers the Tao.

Figure 7.4 *Confucius playing a qin under an apricot tree* by Bai Yunli

In playing the *qin*, timbre is all; it is much more important than pitch. There are traditionally 1,070 finger techniques, communicated by 200 Chinese characters.[88] Modern players use about forty, each one producing a different colour of sound. For instance:

- Plucking a string in the inward–outward direction (*mo, t'iao*).
- Sliding along a string in the left–right direction (*chin, fu*).
- Hitting a string in the downward direction (*yen*).
- Picking a string upward and releasing it (*chua-ch'i, nien*).

- Pressing down and pushing the outermost string outward and releasing it (*t'ui-ch'u*).[89]

Qin notation is not a 'score' but a tablature, because each character tells you not how the notes sound, but how it is produced by the appropriate positions, postures and movements of the fingers. Most importantly, rhythm is not specified. In some ways, the music comes across like free-floating atoms of colour, worlds away from the great arcs of intensification of the Indian *Dhrupad*. Time seems to stand still; the music is a series of moments. This compounds the exceptionalism of Chinese music: just as its pentatonic scales stand aside from the ancient 'major-third-trichord belt' (see Chapter 6), its concept of time fits the model neither of the 'arrow' (the Judaeo-Christian West) nor the 'cycle' (Greece and India), to invoke the distinction between two models of time made famous by Stephen Jay Gould.[90] Yet just because Chinese time lacks linear (or cyclical) direction, and the classical Chinese language is tenseless, this does not mean that ancient China had no notion of time. It is the case, rather, that Chinese time was qualitative rather than quantitative, as epitomised in the concept of an event being 'auspicious'.[91] The anthropologist Clifford Geertz's advice on asking the time in Bali applies also to ancient China. Don't ask what the time is; ask what kind of time it is.[92]

Water and Clouds over Xiao Xiang, composed by Guo Zhuwang during the Song Dynasty (1127–1279), is one of the most famous *qin* pieces still performed today.[93] Yes, the music is a succession of fragmentary moments. But each moment is as auspicious as the sixty-four hexagrams in the *Book of Changes* (or *I Ching*). And it bristles with motion, and with opposite motions (akin to Yin and Yang), which fight, blend and proliferate like the colours in a turning kaleidoscope. Depending on which metaphor you prefer, the fingers 'dance' over the fingerboard like acrobats, leap like T'ai-chi warriors or draw calligraphic marks on the air. These moments may not be goal-directed, but they certainly move on the spot. The ancient Chinese experience of time is perhaps best preserved in Japanese traditional music of *gagaku* and the *shakuhachi*. It is yet another example of ancient China's 'sleeper' inventions, transforming Western music in the twentieth century in the works of Debussy, John Cage, Messiaen, Stockhausen and Boulez.

Water and Clouds over Xiao Xiang expresses the composer's sadness and patriotism as, riding the two rivers, Xiao and Xiang, he gazes across at the Jiuyi Mountain to find it obscured by clouds and rising mist. This reminds him that Mongolian intruders have invaded his country.[94]

The Road of Silk and Horses

Four musical superpowers, each with a superpower. The West had polyphony (with notes and notation). Islam had ornament. India pursued taste. And China's power was colour or timbre. Far from standing in stately isolation, these giants of ancient music bumped, jostled and blended. And cultural blood flowed between them through the arteries of the Silk Road, the system of trade routes stretching from the steppes of Central Asia to the Mediterranean and North Africa, from China to Rome. The Silk Road continues to fascinate because it shunts the spotlight of history from Europe to Eurasia. As Peter Frankopan has observed, if ever there was a misnomer, it was the word 'Medi-terranean', the 'centre of the Earth'.[95] By the same token, all roads nowadays lead to China.[96]

The Silk Road was also a musical superhighway for melodies, scales and modes, instruments and performance techniques. Caravans laden with silk, cotton, gunpowder and spice might also have carried lutes. 'Yoke lutes' (with two arms extending from their body to a crossbar) first show up in Mesopotamian stone carvings towards the end of the third millennium BC, but they probably arose much earlier in what is now Afghanistan. Lutes were taken by the Hyksos to Egypt around 1650 BC, and arrived in Greece much later, where they were called *pandoura*, from which are derived the words mandolin, tanbur, tambour and tambourine.[97] The lute travelled to India and became a *veena*, evolving a thousand years later into the long-necked sitar; also to China (*pipa*), Korea (*pip'a*), Japan (*biwa*) and Persia (*barbat*). From Persia, the *barbat* enters the Arab territories by AD 600, and becomes the *oud*, their word for 'rod' (giving us our word, 'lute').

In the hands of Islamic music theorists, the *oud* was the perfect instrument to visualise new kinds of scales unknown to the Greeks. They could slide their finger in between a major and minor third, creating a quarter-tone midway between 'happy' and 'sad' intervals called *wusta Zalzal*, the beauty spot of Arab melancholy. Lutes reach Western Europe via the courts of Andalusian Spain. Several centuries later, Frederick II

(1194–1250), the most sophisticated Holy Roman emperor since Charlemagne, was so enamoured of Moorish culture that he preferred to reside in Sicily, where he encountered lutes, and introduced them to Germany. Their journey took them to Italy and Holland, where they were painted by Titian, Caravaggio and Vermeer, and soon to England, taken up as the natural instrument of the gentleman courtier. Holbein's painting *The Ambassadors*, housed in the British National Gallery, displays a handsome lute, its eleven T-shaped pegs typical of Italian lutes of that time, alongside a globe, a book and a musical score, all fitting accoutrements for diplomat intellectuals.[98] One of the eleven strings is broken, and this has been read as a symbol of death (echoing the skull at the base of the picture), and a portent of the break-up of Christendom consequent upon King Henry VIII's imminent divorce and excommunication. In Chinese terms, the harmony of the empire was broken.

For good or ill, broken strings actually became the mainframe of Western instrumental music. The polyphony strummed on a lute is an illusion, because the fingers can create at best only the semblance of continuously independent melodic lines. Scholars of French baroque music call it *stile brisé* or *stile luthé* (literally, 'broken style' or 'lute style'), and seventeenth-century lutenists such as Chambonnières and Couperin introduced it to harpsichord music.[99] Bach's keyboard suites are transcriptions of the *stile brisé*'s broken counterpoint. Bach follows in the lute's long, long history, trekking on the musical Silk Road. Yet even today, across gulfs of time and space, any guitar player happening upon an almond- or melon-shelled lute hanging for sale in an old Silk Road bazaar, perhaps the renowned bazaar at Kashgar at Xinjiang, could pick it up and play it, instantly reconnecting with music's millennial timeline.[100] Lute DNA is in our blood. Or from the lute's point of view, an ancient shelled animal has evolved, but has remained recognisably the same species.

Much more than a path to convey objects and ideas, the Silk Road signified the spirit of motion itself. Central Asia was a nomadic horse culture, a seething vortex of tribes (Huns, Tartars, Mongols, Turkmen, Kazakhs, Uzbeks, Uyghurs and countless others) whose lives were intimately involved with those of horses. The mobility of horses gave nomadic people the military edge over the agrarian lands in the south, and allowed them to unify Eurasia into vast confederations of tribes and villages. Their obsession with horses was recounted in oral epics such as the *Manas* of the Kyrgyz people of Kyrgyzstan.[101] Comprising 500,000 stanzas, twice the length of the *Mahabharata*, and twice that of the *Iliad* and *Odyssey* combined, this sung poem must count as the longest piece of music in the world, ever. Epics are long because they are poetic journeys; the *Manas* is the longest because the Eurasian steppes afforded its journey a vast geographical expanse. The *Manas* is all horse. Tales of noble or magic steeds fill its verses. The poetic metre (trochaic tetrameters) mimics that of a galloping horse. When it is performed well, listeners huddled in their yurt have claimed to hear the patter of ghostly hooves raised from the spirit world.[102] And the effect on the audience can be to match the giddy exhilaration of actually riding a horse, a taste of what the shamans of Mongolia and Siberia experience undertaking their spirit journeys on the backs of magical winged mounts.

Eurasian epics are normally sung unaccompanied. The instrument most characteristic of Central Asia is not the lute but the two-stringed horse-headed fiddle, the Mongolian *quyurci* (or *morin khuur*), a wooden trapezoid sound-box, the end of whose long neck is carved with the face of a horse, sometimes with leather ears (see **Figure 7.5**).[103] The longer, male string is woven from the tail of a stallion; the shorter, female string

Figure 7.5 Mongolian horse-headed fiddles and zither

is taken from a mare. A traditional Mongol ballad sings of how two horses belonging to Genghis Khan (Cinggis-qan) ran away because their master didn't recognise their fine qualities. The Great Khan gave chase: 'Mounting his brown horse Alcul, taking his golden fiddle [*aryasun quyurci-ji*], Genghis stuck his white *zal* bow in its case, making the fiddler Aryasun his guide.'[104] Legend has it that the first *quyurci* was constructed from the bones, skin and hair of a magical flying horse. In Marco Polo's (1254–1324) vivid account of the Mongolian (or 'Tartar') army squaring up to its enemy, *quyurci* are played on horseback by thousands of soldiers:

> Soon both armies were drawn up in battle array and only waiting for the sound of the kettle-drums. For the Tartars [*sic*] do not dare to start a battle till their lord's drums begin to beat; and while they are waiting it is their custom to sing and to play very sweetly on their two-stringed instruments and to make very merry in expectation of battle.[105]

Polo counted '760,000 horsemen' on both sides. If even a fraction of his estimate is true, then this stands as the biggest musical performance in recorded history, easily dwarfing Victorian *Messiah*s and Mahler's *Symphony of a Thousand*.

It is more accurate, then, to see the Silk Road as a road of silk and horses. The Chinese sent out silk and imported horses. This transaction was physically embodied when the first two-string violins drifted over the border from Mongolia into China during the Song Dynasty (960–1279) and developed into the earliest Chinese fiddles, the *erhu* and the *huqin* (the character *Hu* in both words signified that the *erhu* and *huqin* were instruments of 'barbarians').[106] Like the *qin* zither, the *erhu* and *huqin* had silk strings. But their bows were made from the hairs of a horse's tail. These silkworm/equine hybrids are sonic metaphors of the road of silk and horses. We echo that metaphor today when we scrape our Western violins with horsehair bows, although our strings are made not from silk but from gut or steel.

The deep historical origins of bowing are murky. We found images of single-string bows on the walls of Catal Höyük 9,000 years ago in Chapter 5, and these might go back to the African hunting bow. But we can be absolutely certain that the practice of bowing a string with the intent of producing music was first established in Central Asia. From there, the idea of bowing was a fellow traveller of the plucked lute along the same silken roads. While *quyurci*s travelled south to engender *erhu*s, their northern and western journeys produced the Arab *rebab*, the Andalusian *vielle*, the medieval European *rebec* and the modern violin.

The most spectacular product of this transaction between silk and horses was Chinese opera, invented in the Yuan Dynasty (1271–1368), when China was governed by the Mongols led by Khubilai Khan (1215–1294), grandson of Ghengis.[107] It is fitting that opera, this child of the Silk Road, had many parents. One inspiration was the Mongols' somewhat broad taste in culture, and their love of genres that mixed singing, dancing and sung poetry with storytelling. Another was the reality of living under foreign occupation. Disenfranchised from art music, Chinese intellectuals had to put down their *qin*s and embrace the kind of vernacular folk traditions they had previously disdained, but which would entertain their new rulers. Opera resulted from this alliance between the serious and the popular. Yet another parent came from the south, the Indian folktale genres of *Jakata* and *Panchatantra*.[108] The novelty of these genres is that they alternated passages of prose and poetry, with the verse passages occurring at key points where they are sung with instrumental accompaniment. This is what operas do both in China and, much later, in the West: alternate spoken 'recitative' with sung arias. The idea was conceived in India in 300 BC.

Yuan opera couldn't be more different from Western opera. The actors impersonating the gods and heroes in Monteverdi's first opera, *L'Orfeo* of 1607, are essentially singing statues. Pinned on their plinths, they face the audience, strike a thespian attitude, open their mouths to make their sound, but otherwise don't move a muscle. Western opera has been fixed and static ever since. In absolute contrast, the multimedia entertainment that was Yuan opera was total theatre: a kaleidoscopic mixture of story, music, voice, movement, make-up, costume, stage design. Its modern descendant, Beijing opera, sees the stage as a platform upon which to display the performers' four skills (*gong*): song (*chang*); speech (*nian*); dance-acting (*zuo*), which includes pantomime; and martial arts (*da*), encompassing acrobatics.[109] Yuan opera was as richly varied as the Silk Road itself, the very spice of life. The all-singing, all-dancing, all-moving Yuan actor was like a *qin* performance gesture or a Chinese ideogram sprung into 3D animation. All the separate aspects of total theatre – language, music, action – are absorbed into a unified arc of energy. The motion may begin with the contour of a Chinese speech tone, turn into the contour of a melody, spiked by a gesture in the drums, and then be flicked by an outstretched arm or the movement of a gaze so that it curves downstage, becoming the performer's physical movement through space as he or she traces an S-shaped curve, crossing upstage and circling back in the opposite direction, all laced with acrobatic leaps and martial manoeuvres.[110] It is exhilarating to follow such lines of flight culminating with the crackle of electricity at the tip of a pointing index finger. Here is a suitably 'horsey' example, taken from a monologue in a comic military opera from around 1300:

> I had my halberd and he had a two-edged sword – in a trice he hacked off a great piece of my left arm. I leapt from my horse, opened my kit, sewed the piece back on, and met him again. This time he had a knife-pike and I my bow, but before our mounts crossed he sliced off a great piece of my right arm. Down from my horse, opened my kit, sewed it back on, and again we met. He had now a great flanged broadaxe and I my double-edged sword. This time he whacked both man and horse in two. Down I got, opened my kit, sewed everything together, and met him again. Ten times we met until I was patched all over ... finally he cried in admiration, 'You can't fight worth a copper, but sure can sew.'[111]

Farcical and bawdy, this kind of stuff recalls the Elizabethan jigs Shakespeare enjoyed, a homegrown English version of total theatre, which also blended comic acting with song and dance, stage fighting and pantomime. But whereas Shakespeare absorbed this multidimensional total theatre into his comedies, it never made it into Western opera, with one or two distinguished exceptions such as Mozart's *The Magic Flute*. Opera in the West was still, stillborn, and yet still born all the same, in the cultural nativity we call the Renaissance.

Why the European Renaissance strangled the life out of the musical human is a subject for the next chapter. None of the four superpowers was safe from the tide of history, however, not even China under the Mongols. In Xanadu did Kubla Khan a stately pleasure-dome decree. Pride of place in the Great Khan's orchestra was an organ outfitted with a mechanical peacock, which swayed in time with the music.[112] This clockwork marvel, the essence of Chinese technical superiority, is also a kind of death. What starts in myth with singing phoenixes ends with an avian robot: clever, polychrome and multicultural to be sure, but silent.

CHAPTER 8
ENDGAMES

It was a map that gave us our first planetary view of our world (See **Figure 8.1**). Abraham Ortelius' *Theatrum Orbis Terrarum* (1570) confirmed, you could say, a shift on the Earth's axis from a polycentric planet – bumping along through evenly matched superpowers colliding like billiard balls – to a monocentric, capitalist world.[1] But the shift had started somewhat earlier, perhaps when the Earth became a single unit in the gift of a divine authority. This happened with the Treaty of Tordesillas of 1494, through which Pope Alexander VI bisected the Atlantic and Pacific oceans with imaginary lines carving up the New World between the Spanish and Portuguese empires, and then with the Treaty of Saragossa (1529). The Spanish got their hands on North and Central America, and the Philippines. The Portuguese grabbed the bigger share: South America, and large chunks of Africa and India. And so begins the great narrative of Westernisation, in which European models of technology, capital, even of reason itself, spread across the globe on sailing ships, through an alliance of naval exploration, missionary Christianity and colonialism.

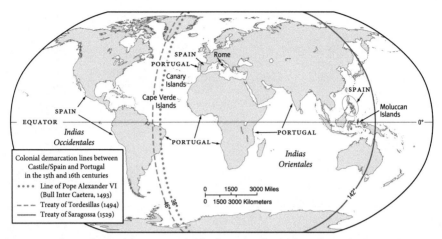

Figure 8.1 How the world was carved: Abraham Ortelius' *Theatrum Orbis Terrarum*

The monocentric world was a contrapuntal world. Counterpoint, composed in the masterworks of European sacred polyphony, took over the globe on the same ships as missionaries and conquerors. In this respect, it was business as usual, where music helped cement the compact between popes and kings. But in another respect, the stakes were far higher. The Holy Roman Empire had united Europe first through Gregorian chant, afterwards through polyphony. Now this process spilled out of the Mediterranean Basin and flowed across the seven seas. The victory of counterpoint was absolute and global. The most dramatic example of that is the musical conversion of the indigenous peoples of Mexico in the wake of the Spanish invasion.

In 1519, Cortés lands in Mexico. This picture shows the massacre of Aztec musicians by the Spanish at Tenochtitlan in May 1520 (see **Figure 8.2**).[2] Their Christian sensibilities upset by the Aztec practice of human sacrifice, the Spanish chose to execute the musicians first (followed by the dancers), in the spirit of shooting the cheerleader or army bugler. As we saw in Chapter 5, the criminal destruction of every shred of Aztec musical culture at the hands of the Spanish left virtually nothing for the historical record. And yet the speed of the Indians' conversion was breathtaking:[3]

Figure 8.2 *The Massacre at the Festival of Toxcatl*

1527   Fray Juan Caro starts teaching polyphony at a school in Tetzcoco.

1530   An Indian choir performs regularly at Mexico Cathedral.

1532   Twelve years after the massacre, the missionary priest Pedro de Gante writes to Emperor Charles V telling him of 'singers that could sing in Your Majesty's chapel, so well, that if it is not seen it will not be believed'.[4]

1559   The Indian cathedral choir performs Spanish motets to commemorate Charles V's death.

1575   Hernando Franco, the first in a succession of visiting Spanish composers, arrives in Mexico, taking up a position as cathedral chapel master.

1617   The birth of Juan de Lienas, the first great indigenous Mexican composer of which we are certain. Indian composers had surely been active far earlier, but this is hard to prove, because they adopted Christian Spanish names.[5]

Long before Lienas wrote his sumptuous Requiem, *Salva Regina* and *Magnificat*, the Franciscan missionary Gerónimo de Mendieta (1525–1604) noted in his *Historia Eclesiástica Indiana* (begun 1571) that 'only a few years after the Indians began to learn the chant, they also began to compose'. Mendieta goes on to confess that their pieces 'have been adjudged superior works of art when shown to Spanish masters of composition. Indeed the Spanish masters often thought they could not have been written by Indians.'

Across the opposite hemisphere, precisely the same conversion was being effected at Manila in the Philippines, Spain's transpacific entrepôt in the trade route between America and Asia. Ships from Mexico conveyed not just musical manuscripts and musical instruments (organs, guitars, harps and bandurrias), but the skilled craftsmen who built them. Intramuros, Manila's walled city centre, contained the thickest concentration of convents and churches anywhere in the world, and these interiors resounded with sacred music performed in Latin by Filipino singers. The world's first global city, and a node of the earliest worldwide web of trade and cultural exchanges, Manila was also the most musically diverse. One of the first instrumental groups to arrive was a recorder consort made up of African slaves donated by a Portuguese captain, playing Italian polyphony.[6]

Manila's importance also lay in being a jumping-off point for musical missionaries into Asia; that is to say, Jesuit missionaries who were also musicians. The Spanish Jesuit Juan de Santa Marta (1578–1618) composed a contrapuntal mass in jail in Miako (modern-day Kyoto) while awaiting execution (he was crucified). There followed a hiatus, when the Japanese Shogunate famously shut its doors against Western influence until the Meiji restoration of 1868. The Jesuit Tomás Pereira (1645–1708) fared better in China, where he amused the Kangxi Emperor with the unheard-of party trick of notating music and performing it back. His colleague, the missionary-composer Teodorico Pedrini (1671–1746), presented the Emperor with sonatas he had written in Beijing in the style of Corelli.[7]

Counterpoint takes over the globe as the vanguard for the triumph of Western classical music as a whole. This chapter asks why. What was it about Western classical music that made it so viral, akin to Shakespeare, the English language, capitalism, technology, even cricket? Cricket is a particularly good comparison, because the many former colonies of Britain who adopted the sport (such as India, Pakistan, South Africa and the West Indies) made it their own, just as Mexican *indios* made Spanish counterpoint their own.[8] The chapter also asks who are the losers. The casualties of globalisation include the many folk traditions that indigenous peoples had to give up in order to fit in with their rulers. Cortés massacred not just Indians musicians, but the music they played. The cultural theorist Edward Said borrowed the metaphor of 'counterpoint' to capture this darker side of globalisation.[9] At first glance, the interweaving voices of a contrapuntal texture are a nice analogy for multiculturalism.[10] The metaphor quickly darkens when we realise that not all voices are equal. Cultural counterpoint is not some happy-go-lucky open society of relaxed pluralism, but a power struggle between 'voices' that are dominant, and those that are dominated (or 'subaltern'). In the global counterpoint between the West and the rest – the 'counterpoint' between counterpoint and the world – music that didn't fit was left out of the group picture, quietly expunged, or worse.

Global 'counterpoint' continues to threaten the many traditions of 'classical' music outside the West.[11] Venerable musical traditions are scattered throughout the world: Thailand, Laos, Cambodia, Vietnam, Indonesia, Japan, China, Korea, North and South India, North and South America, the Middle East and all across Africa. Many of these are as elitist as Western classical music, and similarly involve the transmission of a hallowed canon of great works. So in what way does the classical tradition of the West differ from this multitude of alternative musics? The single most significant difference is *how* the music is transmitted.[12] Through most of the world, music is handed down orally through the great chain of master–apprentice relationships. In Western music, by contrast, works were enshrined in scores, and the scores were floated, as it were, on the open sea like messages in a bottle. This bred a critical, even aggressive, attitude towards the past, so that Western music history became a process of constant experiment and reinvention. Outside the West, apprentices deferred respectfully to their master, and the musical past he or she represented.

One could say, then, that Western colonial aggression turned in on itself, in a constant attack on its own musical past. This mania for eternal revolution was the engine that drove the West's musical 'progress'.

During the course of the twentieth and early twenty-first centuries, Western globalisation has been overtaken by two musical counter-flows, even tidal waves. The first wave came from Africa, flowing across what the postcolonial theorist Paul Gilroy called the 'Black Atlantic', the musical traffic of generations of African slaves.[13] Seeding a multitude of genres in both North and South America and the Caribbean, from blues, jazz, rock, funk and rap to rumba, reggae and reggaeton, this wealth of music travelled back to Africa to inspire new traditions such as highlife and Afrofunk, the cross-currents and confluences becoming too complex to chart. The second, later, wave emanated from Asia. The 1905 cover of the first edition of Claude Debussy's orchestral score *La mer* borrows from

Katsushika Hokusai's (1760–1849) woodblock print, *Under the Wave off Kanagawa*.[14] The image is iconic of the *japonisme* craze that flooded France in the nineteenth century, but it can also stand for how the Asian ethos captivated all of the West, with its liberating models of consciousness and time. As we shall see at the end of this chapter, this extended to our love affair with animé film scores and J- and K-Pop bands.

These two waves are, in historical terms, the return of the repressed. Global music history is capped by the ultimate irony that, for complex cultural and economic reasons, Western classical music is in a far healthier state in China, Korea and Japan than in Europe or North America. One might venture a prediction that Southeast Asia will be a sanctuary for Western music for many hundreds of years, long after its demise in the West itself, just as ancient Greek culture was safeguarded by Islam until the European Renaissance. Similarly, the most interesting rock and folk music in the world is happening today in Asia, Africa and South America.

Renaissances

Modern music began on 6 October 1600. In other words, the history books tend to agree that music of the 'common practice period' – music you are likely to hear performed regularly in the West – started with the premiere of the first European opera. *Euridice*, by Jacopo Peri, turned out to be a misbegotten, and now forgotten, misfire.[15] But it was quickly outdone by the West's first operatic masterpiece, Monteverdi's *L'Orfeo* of 1607. Opera was invented and improved in a series of experiments; indeed, it arose as an intellectual exercise prompted by the father of the father of Western science.

Galileo, whose telescope proved Copernicus' theory that the Earth went round the Sun, was the son of another scientist. Galileo senior, Vincenzo Galilei (1520–91), was a composer, writer, music theorist and acoustician.[16] Vincenzo's systematic experiments on the physical properties of vibrating strings (he proved that interval ratios were proportionate to the square root of the tension applied to a string) taught his son two lessons.[17] Don't trust ancient authorities, and test everything. In fact, it is not going too far to claim that Galileo junior learned experimental protocol from music theory. The experiment in question sought to recreate ancient Greek music drama. As a member of the Camerata de' Bardi, an intellectual and artistic think tank based in Florence, the cradle of the European

Renaissance, Vincenzo came across three hymns written by Mesomedes the Cretan, Emperor Hadrian's favourite composer, whom we met in Chapter 6. Inspired by Mesomedes, Vincenzo wrote a truly epoch-defining essay titled *Dialogue on ancient and modern music* (*Dialogo della musica antica e della moderna*) in 1581.[18] In this essay Vincenzo Galilei attacked the prevailing styles of music, and advocated a new style called 'monody'. Monody, a kind of directly outpouring speech-song of the soul, emulated the emotional text-setting which the Florentine Camerata believed was invented by the ancient Greeks, but which was since then lost to Western civilisation. The essay threw down a gauntlet to Italy's composers, and the result was opera. Peri tried his hand first, then Monteverdi succeeded.

Galilei's intervention was remarkable at several levels. Deliberately leapfrogging over 2,000 years of Western history to ancient Greece was a revolutionary act – a deeply provocative rejection of tradition and authority. He probably wouldn't have been able to decipher Mesomedes' hymns, which at that time represented the entirety of surviving Greek music. He was motivated, rather, by the ideal of Greek music drama. And yet Galilei could never have guessed just how right his intuition would prove to be, that the music drama of fifth-century BC Athens comprised the West's last period of musical revolution, as we saw in Chapter 6 in Euripides' 'New Music'. That is, now that contemporary scholars have gathered evidence that fifth-century Greek tragedy was the West's first modern music, it emerges that, in the grand scheme of things, Euripides and Monteverdi are two musical mountain peaks, towering almost exactly 2,000 years apart.

And there is more. Vincenzo's invention of monody double-stamps the musical renaissance as simultaneously restorative and revolutionary. It is common sense that, lifting something out of context – in this case, removing a lost Greek art out of history – is a wilfully impertinent act of abstraction. It goes hand-in-glove with the birth of Western experimental science. This odd blend of 'going forward by going back', literally going back to the future, distinguishes the Italian Renaissance from all the other renaissances blossoming outside the West. Mughal India, Ottoman Turkey and Ming Dynasty China also enjoyed a cultural efflorescence in the sixteenth century, comparable to what was unfolding in Europe. These other renaissances certainly produced glorious monuments of culture. But they were essentially conservative, not radical; they lacked what the British art historian Kenneth Clark, quoting the great Italian art historian Giorgio Vasari, called the 'spirit of criticism', that awkward scepticism towards authority that shaped the Galileo family.[19]

The image of the Italian Renaissance cast by Clark's magisterial television series, *Civilisation*, was very much of its time, and has not weathered well. Clark's traditional account foregrounded Italian humanism's principles of clarity, light, grace and good manners. To be fair, he conceded that Florentine culture was founded on the cut-and-thrust of trade and banking. But the 'spirit of criticism' was downgraded in favour of the spirit of harmony and proportion, qualities we discern, say, in the Pazzi Chapel in Florence, or in the art of Raphael. In music, this is borne out in the traditional view of Palestrina's smoothly flowing counterpoint as all sweetness and light.[20] One might line up any number of Renaissance personalities to argue against that view, testifying instead to the muscular violence beneath the skin of the Renaissance body. There is no more vivid exhibit than this painting of Ercole d'Este, Duke of Ferrara (1431–1505).

Figure 8.3 *Ercole d'Este* by Dosso Dossi

Duke Ercole started his career as a warrior. After a humiliating defeat to the Venetians at the 1482–4 War of Ferrara, Ercole changed tack and became the biggest art patron in Italy, and owner of the finest musical establishment.[21] Ercole's patronage of artists and composers was ostensibly a compensation for military failure. In reality, it was a prosecution of war *as* culture, deploying culture as a political weapon. Ercole co-opted painting, sculpture, drama and music to represent himself as a strong man, and he liked to parade at court in military armour.[22] This famous portrait of Ercole dressed as a soldier by Dosso Dossi presents him as an Italian *conquistador*, a brother-in-arms of Cortés (see **Figure 8.3**). Ercole commissioned Josquin des Prez, the greatest composer of the day, to make him a musical portrait too, and the resulting *Missa Hercules dux Ferrariae* took the letters of Ercole's name and fashioned them into a melody. The melody, or *cantus firmus*, spells Ercole's name in musical pitches, and it recurs incessantly in every voice of the mass. Duke Hercules, the musical armed man, is thrown into battle against the voices of Josquin's counterpoint. Counterpoint is a battle.

Let's draw together all the violent threads of this story. Ercole recruited Josquin into his cultural battle against the other courts of Italy. Cultural competition between the Italian states – a long-distance echo of that between the ancient Greek city states – was also a small-scale version of the rivalry between Europe's nations. After all, Ercole had stolen Josquin from France. The French, Italian, Iberian, English and German-speaking lands tried to outdo each other in acquiring the most prestigious painters, poets and musicians. The West was much less unified than the other musical superpowers; it was a seething cauldron of languages, cultures and religions. Counterpoint's war of voice against voice was a perfect symbol of that.

This is why Vincenzo Galilei's rejection of counterpoint in favour of 'modern' monody was really just the latest battle in a much longer and larger culture war. In the same way that Galilei distanced 'modern' music from 'ancient' Renaissance counterpoint, theorists of Renaissance counterpoint caricatured medieval music as primitive. They conspired in a myth that music was reborn from thin air, *ex nihilo*, in the fifteenth century after languishing in the lowest depths of Gothic barbarism. The details concern dissonance technique: what constitutes a consonant sonority versus a dissonant one. The Renaissance theorist Gioseffo Zarlino argued that major thirds are consonant, as we still hear them today.[23] Medieval theorists heard thirds as dissonant, and favoured the simpler harmonic proportions of fourths and fifths. Tastes change. But the break between harmony based on fourths, and harmony based on thirds was itself a musical revolution.

There are musical revolutions right the way through the history of Western classical music. Their manifestos are the slogans of style periods: 'Renaissance', 'baroque', 'classical', 'romantic', 'impressionist' and so on. Each one was considered in its time a kind of rebirth, a 'renaissance', the dawn of a modern age. Nevertheless, our problem is not so much that identifying the birth of musical modernity is a fool's errand. The point, rather, is that Vasari's 'spirit of criticism' – the instinctual rejection of the ancestor – seems to be baked into Western music from the outset. If we are forced to pick out a single defining feature of the musical human in the West, it is this critical attitude towards the past. The long, long chains of master–disciple deference in the music of India, China, Africa and Islam are broken in the West into a long, long *via negativa*, the negative path.

And yet something substantive does change at the beginning of the seventeenth century in Europe. This is the moment when the West starts to outstrip the rest of the world technologically, if by no means culturally or artistically. As I said earlier, it was not unusual for a nation or empire to experience an artistic efflorescence. As in Italy, this happened in the sixteenth century in the Mughal Empire under Akbar the Great, in the Ottoman Empire under Suleyman the Magnificent, and in the Ming Dynasty in China. Also as in Italy, these high points felt like a restoration of past glories, especially under the Ming after the Mongol invasion. The question of why modern science took off only in the West is especially pertinent in China, given that they had invented double-acting piston flamethrowers in the tenth century.[24] This has become known as the 'Needham Question', after the author of *Science and Civilization in China* (see Chapter 7). There is no satisfactory answer to the Needham Question, apart from the general point that China after 1500 was stultified by bureaucracy, cultural homogeneity and lack of internal competition. Elsewhere, post-Gupta India was strangled by the caste system and poor respect for manual labour – which partly explains why the Mughals were not receptive to Western technology.[25] The case of the Ottomans is more complex, because they were most directly and adversely affected by the discovery of America.[26] Enriched by silver plundered from the New World, European merchants bought up Ottoman raw materials and set off a chain reaction, whereby reduced domestic productivity in the Ottoman lands led to a black market and to a rigid bureaucracy.

There can never be any question of Western music being any better (or worse) than non-Western music. That said, Western music splits away from the musical mainstream at the same time that Western science really takes off, and it acquires three of science's characteristics: a liking for big names, an experimental method and a sense of historical progress. Foundational for all these traits was an obsession with preserving music in notation.

Because of Western music's unique fixation with writing notes down in scores, it is the only musical superpower with a fully recorded history. Walk into a good bookshop and you can hold 400 (or even 1,000) years of this history in the palm of your hand.[27] This is an astonishing yet in some ways deeply troubling achievement. Astonishing, because no other world culture has a comparable music history. To be sure, as we saw earlier, a modern-day Qawwali singer can proudly trace his lineage back to the thirteenth-century Amir Khusrow. Yet what he is proud of is the continuity of this tradition, not historical change. Moreover, like other oral traditions, Qawwali lacks the notated evidence to record such change, above broad novelties such as the modern incorporation of the harmonium organ.[28] On the other hand, what makes Western music history so troubling is that it is really a history of scores, not of people, albeit the scores are notionally attached to 'big names' such as Handel, Mozart and Brahms.[29] Handel, Mozart, Brahms and hundreds of others are known to us as composers of these scores; what they were like as flesh-and-blood people may intrigue us (Beethoven scrupulously ground exactly sixty coffee beans for his morning cup of coffee; Wagner loved to swan around his flat dressed in silk gowns), but it is not pertinent to music history. Otherwise put, there are plenty of bad composers who led far more eventful lives than Bruckner, who practically did nothing, went nowhere, and had no love life. We don't care about that because Bruckner was a wonderful composer, and we don't care about lots of bad composers who were interesting people.

Musical manuscripts have been around far longer than 400 years, of course. What changed after 1600, as a kind of afterbirth of modern science, is that European music escaped the clutches of the Christian

Church. The contrapuntal idiom excoriated by Monteverdi's friends as the '*prima prattica*' ('the first [or old] practice') was the style of Church music. The '*seconda prattica*' was secular and new. After Monteverdi and Galileo, European composers reversed the direction of their musical telescopes from God to Man. To adjust Alexander Pope's epithet from his *Essay on Man*, they decided that 'The proper study of the musical human was the musical human.' The abstraction of scores afforded composers a clinical, hermetic environment in which to play with musical ideas and invent harmonies and forms. The score became a laboratory, a test tube. This is why, after 1600, composers were like scientists.

The West's musical renaissance raises the curtain on what is called the 'common practice period'. The epic drama that follows, with its long chain of dramatis personae (Monteverdi–Schütz–Bach–Mozart–Beethoven–Schubert–Schumann–Brahms–Wagner–Mahler–Schoenberg…),   has been chronicled to exhaustion elsewhere, and outlined very much in brief in Part One. As I stated at the outset, my interest is not in the kind of music history found in the standard textbooks ('who wrote what and when'), but in the musical human's deeper, more global history. There is a darker drama happening on the other side of the curtain, a side beyond the limelight of opera houses and concert halls. The question is: who pays?

The Crimes of Colonialism

Beaches are interfaces not just of land and water but of civilisations. As the natives stood on the shore watching the unfamiliar ships approach, their attention would have been hooked by the sounds of trumpet calls, drum beats, whistles, even psalm singing.[30] Musicians were shoreline ambassadors in the first encounter between natives and invaders. In a new land, music really comes into its own as a universal language, the opening gambit of spiritual conversion. Encountering the Tupinambá Indians of Brazil in 1578, the French missionary Jean de Léry sang them Psalm 104. 'In truth you sang marvelously well,' they responded through a translator, 'but we do not understand your language, so explain your song.'[31] And so what begins on a beach ends in a church.

But the dance between missionaries and indigenous cultures could be complex and many-sided. The Jesuits in south-eastern Brazil took up a popular Amerindian dance called the *cateretê* in order to sweeten their message, and today it is widespread in the country as a devotional dance to Saint Gonçalo.[32]

The dark side of colonialism, however, has been thoroughly exposed. Here is the opinion of the early nineteenth-century Colombian liberal Pedro Fermín de Vargas:

> To expand our agriculture it would be necessary to Hispanicize our Indians. Their idleness, stupidity, and indifference towards normal endeavours causes one to think that they come from a degenerate race which deteriorates in proportion to the distance from its origin … it would be very desirable that the Indians be extinguished by miscegenation [interbreeding].[33]

Soon the Indians would indeed be exterminated, by gun and microbe.

The difference with music is that normally nobody dies when you play a wrong note, although the appalled Spaniards encountered exactly such a practice among the Aztecs. According to the sixteenth-century historian Bernardino de Sahagún, if one of their singers or drummers (*teponaztli* players) made a mistake, 'immediately the chieftain ordered him seized, and the next day had him summarily executed'.[34] No, the civilised musical sanction was rather more nuanced. Thus the 1585 constitution of Mexico City cathedral decreed that erring musicians would be fined or dismissed. The 'violence' inheres in the submission of the Aztecs to Spanish counterpoint, at the expense of their indigenous music. As Fermín de Vargas might have put it, the Indians' music was extinguished through miscegenation with that of the West. Here are three further points on the spectrum of refined violence:

1. Music could whitewash and misrepresent. In 1733, Vivaldi wrote an opera, *Moctezuma*, about the end of the last Aztec emperor. The plot is ridiculous beyond belief. Moctezuma and his wife Mitrena agree to the marriage of their daughter, Teutile, to Cortés's brother, Ramire, and Cortés magnanimously forgives Moctezuma and allows him to

rule Mexico as Spain's vassal. The score (once lost, and rediscovered only in 2002) is one of Vivaldi's most sumptuous.

2. In Werner Herzog's film *Fitzcarraldo*, Klaus Kinski dreams of building an opera house at Iquitos, on the Peruvian Amazon. He fails, but the entire population of Iquitos troops down to the beach to hear Caruso perform Verdi's opera *Ernani* on a ship. 'This God doesn't come with cannons,' Fitzcarraldo announces, 'but with the voice of Caruso.'[35] A real opera house was opened at Manaus, northwest Brazil, in 1892.

3. El Sistema brought disciplined orchestral playing to Venezuela, as we saw in Chapter 3. But why was the youth of Venezuela drilled in symphonies rather than in salsa or merengue, its own traditional music?

The ultimate crime of musical colonialism is to take away an occupied people's indigenous music. We don't know what the Aztecs sang, but it might have been similar to the Andean polyphony still being performed today by the Q'ero at Cuzco in Peru, the historic capital of the Inca Empire. Their music recalls the free, 'primitive' counterpoint of which Dante so disapproved. In a typical performance, five or more Indian women sing simultaneously, telling their stories and complaining about their everyday lives. Only sometimes do they meet on a particular phrase or note; the lines are perfectly happy to go their own way.[36]

Counterpoint, then, was probably rife in pre-contact South and Central America, albeit of a much freer sort than Spanish polyphony. Ironically, both the Aztecs and the Spanish shared the metaphor of thinking of music as 'florid'. Remember the Maya and Aztec custom, described in Chapter 5, of depicting music on glyphs as volutes of 'song-flowers' emanating from a person's mouth.[37] Thus it was strangely fitting that the Aztecs were invaded by a Catholic nation. In the European wars of religion, Protestant England rejected polyphony, both at home and abroad, as a musical symptom of Catholic idolatry. This is why, when the English colonised North America, they imposed upon the Indians not contrapuntal masses but pared-down puritanical hymn tunes.[38]

Many more churches were built in Africa and Asia. Western tonality – the kind of chords you hear in Bach or Mozart – was unrolled like a giant carpet over the entire African continent, smuggled in through hymn tunes. Even the national anthems of African states were carefully purged of traditional rhythms. For instance, the dance-like 'Osee Yee' appendix of the Ghanaian anthem, composed by Philip Gbeho (1905–1976), was struck out by the censors.[39] At first, Western Church music ate like an acid into African identity. According to a Kenyan Sabaot woman: 'These new songs [hymns] are breaking us up … Our children are lost, these church styles are rotting our culture.'[40] Since the 'Africanisation' drive of the 1960s, however, the occupier has become more accommodating. African church services now absorb many of the hallmarks of traditional music: polyrhythmic handclapping and drumming, call and response, multilayered harmonies, vocal effects and cries, as well as body movement – such as a singer's characteristic downward rippling motion from the head to the legs. This begs a question: when does a colonising force become naturalised?

A fascinating example is the case of the Indonesian church of HKBP (Huria Kristen Batak Protestan), with 4 million members, one of the largest Protestant religions in Asia. The story of its founder, the German-born Lutheran missionary Ludwig Ingwer Nommensen (1834–1918), vividly portrays musical colonialism in action. Setting up his mission in Sumatra, where his predecessor was speared to death, Nommensen's violin playing was literally disarming. Facing a hostile Toba crowd, Nommensen 'took down his violin and played until his arms ached, showed them his watch, and told them stories about Europe until they forgot their displeasure and left'.[41] One time, he waded into a crowd in the throes of a powerful *bius* ceremony, whipped up into hysteria by *gondang* gong rhythms (similar to gamelan), and denounced their ancestor spirit (*sombaon*) as Satan. You would think such a foolhardy act meant certain death. Yet Nommensen cleverly appealed to the Toba's own customs, explaining that *bius* clashed with their customary laws of hospitality (*adat*). His first powerful convert, Raja Pontas Lumbantobing, was baptised in 1865, and the rest fell like dominoes. Many were drawn into church by the authoritative roar of the organ. Although Indonesia, like China, was a gong culture, gongs ceded to church bells. And then in the twentieth century, *gondang* – once banned from services and weddings – was gradually readmitted, but now purged of its ancestral spirits. HKBP had grown strong enough to go native.

How does musical colonialism look from our point of view? Western music has been infected by 'orientalism' – a distorted image of the Orient – since the first Crusades against Islam. After Constantinople fell to an Ottoman Army commanded by Mehmed II on 29 May 1453, it became clear that Europe could easily become a colony itself. Fear of the Ottomans runs like a red thread through subsequent Western music, up to Beethoven and beyond. When Constantinople fell, Europe went crazy for a song nicknamed 'L'homme armé' ('The Armed Man'), one version of which, by the Renaissance composer Antoine Busnois, has the words:

> It will be fought for you
> Against the Turk, Master Simon,
> Certainly it will be,
> And the axe will beat him.[42]

The 'L'homme armé' melody is made up of vocal imitations of military trumpet signals. Europe was flooded by more than forty masses based on this tune. That is, the tune was threaded through the counterpoint as the main structural voice, the *cantus firmus*. The 'L'homme armé' melody was, essentially, a sonic icon of the Turkish threat, and every great Renaissance composer proved his mettle by writing a 'L'homme armé' mass, in effect marshalling the forces of counterpoint against Europe's historical enemy. The greatest example is the *Missa* 'L'homme armé' by Josquin, and it was the model for the mass he wrote for the armed man of Ferrara, Duke Ercole. We have come full circle.

By another imponderable historical coincidence, Manila was founded the same year as the Battle of Lepanto, 1571, when the Ottoman navy was defeated by the Holy League (all the maritime Catholic states in the Mediterranean apart from France). This was the turning point in Christendom's campaign against Islam, after the Turkish high-water mark of 1453. We like to think of Westernisation as linear and inevitable. Yet if European counterpoint had fallen to Islamic ornament, musical Westernisation would never have happened. After their defeat, the Ottomans were lampooned all along the streets and canals of Venice in ballads:

> My song, go to Selim,
> and beg him not to drink so much wine,
> but to recognize Christ as his God.[43]

Such verses indicated a sea change in Europe's musical attitude towards the East: from terror to mockery.

A third battle fended off the Turks from their deepest incursion yet, to the very gates of Vienna. The 1683 Ottoman Siege of Vienna had two apparently opposite musical repercussions. One response was outwardly respectful. Every major European ruler, including Frederick the Great of Prussia, succumbed to the fashion for Ottoman Janissary music, and incorporated a Turkish military band (a *mehter*) within their army.[44] Benedetto Ramberto, in his *Libri tre delle cose de Turchi* of 1539, describes a *mehter* of 200 mounted and walking trumpeters and drummers, a band that would have made a terrifying din.[45] Including a *mehter* in your army was tantamount to inoculating it with a strain of the Ottoman virus, stealing the enemy's strength. The other response was mockery through the *alla turca* style, best known in Mozart's *Rondo alla Turca* and his opera, *Die Entführung aus dem Serail* (*The Abduction from the Seraglio*): see the ridiculous treatment of Osmin. Laughter aside, the *alla turca* sound was a shorthand for musical racism; in fact, the European classical style's first all-purpose code for the alleged primitivism of non-Western music. Heinrich Koch, the most influential German music theorist of the eighteenth century, wrote the following in his *Musical Dictionary* (*Musikalisches Lexicon*) of 1802: 'Janissary music betrays the distinguishing marks of the music of a still barbarous people, namely noisiness and the most tangible display of the rhythm on monotonous percussion instruments.'[46]

And then we get to Beethoven's Ninth in 1824. After its first great climax, the 'Ode to Joy' attempts the impossible, to portray the very face of God. The choir sings, 'And the cherub stands before God' ('*Und der Cherub steht vor Gott*'). A big orchestral noise, then silence. The curtain is drawn, and rather like that scene in *The Wizard of Oz* when the wizard is revealed, the sound of God proves to be … a Turkish marching band, a *mehter*, complete with bass drums, rasping bassoons and triangles. What is Beethoven playing at? Is he laughing at the Turks? Or is he saying, 'Look, even the Turks, the bogeymen of Europe, are our brothers?' It is entirely up to the listener to decide. The historical irony is exquisite, however, that Beethoven's Ode would be taken up as an international anthem by a European Union that keeps its gates shut to Turkish membership.

One must therefore be suspicious of so-called international anthems, from the 'Ode to Joy' to Coca-Cola's 1971 song, 'I'd Like to Teach the World to Sing (in perfect harmony)'. The issues always are: whom does it leave out? What does it skate over? Equally questionable is the comfortingly catch-all, vanilla notion of 'world music'. The term originated as a marketing ploy hatched by music executives in a London pub in the summer of 1987 in order to help retailers sell music that didn't fit standard categories such as rock, reggae, folk and jazz.[47] Otherwise, Andean pan pipes, Klezmer, Cantopop, Afrobeat and suchlike have literally nothing in common. Or rather, what they do have in common is aural tourism and a post-Spotify playlist culture, serviced by programmes such as BBC Radio 3's *Late Junction*. There is nothing in itself wrong with aural tourism; it is curious, however, that sonic omnivores seldom extend their appetite to the cultures and peoples who produced these tracks.[48] It is more relaxing to listen superficially in a vacuum and not trouble oneself with context. The sharp end of this stick is theft: sounds of the rainforest are an attractive sell, but do artists who sample the music of Pygmies always remunerate them?[49]

The collateral damage of musical colonialism goes on and on. Founding Western-style conservatoires in developing countries risks freezing oral musical traditions.[50] Arab and Chinese 'orchestras' assemble diverse instruments that normally never play together. Electronically amplifying a *qin* zither does real violence to the subtle tones of this instrument. Even South India's institutionalising of a 'Holy Trinity' of quasi-classical Carnatic composers, as we saw in Chapter 2, was an artificial reaction to British imperialism: a self-conscious emulation of the West's classical trinity of Haydn, Mozart and Beethoven.[51] One very damaging consequence of Indian nationalism, spurred on by the West, was the systematic suppression of the rich Muslim contributions to its musical heritage. That the history of India became identified with the history of Hinduism at the expense of Islam was due in the first instance to early orientalist scholars such as Sir William Jones (1746–1794). Much later, in 1887, when the Bengali musicologist Sourindro Mohun Tagore (1840–1914) presented Empress Victoria with a musical proof of the greatness of his civilisation, *Six Ragas and Thirty-Six Raginis*, the title of this collection spoke for itself. Where is Islam, not to mention the

Indian music of the Sufis, Sikhs, Jains, Buddhists or Christians? And I wonder how different the Beatles' later albums would have sounded had they taken up with an Islamic Qawwali master rather than with the Hindu Ravi Shankar?

The elephant in the room is not racism so much as *race*. A nostrum of postcolonial theory is that 'race' as such doesn't really exist, at least not in a biological sense.[52] Rather, what people term 'race' is really a reflection of cultural and social differences, not biology. At the level of scientific discourse, this is absolutely true. Yet this critical consensus flies in the face of what people have actually done since time immemorial, which is to default to treating unfamiliar humans as animals. This includes hearing alien speech and song as the sounds of animals. Pliny the Elder (AD 23–79) wrote in his *Natural History* of barking 'dog-heads' (*cynocephali*) and forest creatures who screeched rather than spoke. These are likely to have been baboons, whom ancient travellers had mistaken for a tribe of men. In 1247, the Dominican missionary Simon of Saint-Quentin heard Mongol singing somewhere north of the Black Sea, and claimed that 'they bellow like bulls or howl like wolves'.[53] Even the modern, well-intentioned anthropologist could resort to this tactic. Returning to the Kyrgyz *Manas* epic we looked at in Chapter 7, consider this report by the Russian scholar Boris Smirnov, writing in 1914 about a wax-cylinder recording made of the *Manas* in 1904 by the Kyrgyz singer Kenje Kara (1859–1929):

> It is difficult to convey the impression given by his music and singing! It was not sounds of a voice in the sense we normally understand. They were a kind of wild moaning and howling; there was something in them akin to the bellow of a camel, the neighing of a horse, the bleating of a sheep.[54]

Biological racism at its most virulent was once even detected within one of the world's most beloved logos, HMV's trademark image of a dog attentively staring into the horn of a gramophone, listening to His Master's Voice. When HMV marketed their new 'music-box' in China, the logo was altered, replacing the dog with an image of an old man (see **Figure 8.4**). Why was that? The extraordinary story was covered by the *Washington Post* in 1905:

Figure 8.4 *The Substitution of the Dog,* HMV's Chinese logo for their 'music box'

> The Chinese have peculiar ideas regarding music-box trade-marks. One quite famous trade-mark, showing a dog alert to catch his master's voice as it came from the horn, proved distasteful, for the reason that it seemed to couple the canine with the human listeners. Therefore, such a trade-mark had to be altered so as to show an old man listening to the music instead of a little terrier.[55]

It seemed, then, that the Chinese saw that the Americans likened them to dogs, listening dutifully to the voices of their Western masters. Yet the background to this tale, glibly ignored by the newspaper, was nationalist sentiments stirred up by inhumane treatment of the 100,000 Chinese living in the US, following the 1882 Chinese Exclusion Act, and the subsequent threat to boycott American goods. In short, Pliny's 'barking dog-heads' slur was alive and well in Shanghai in 1905. When HMV moved to act, it was not through any reawakened racial sensibilities, but on account of economic self-interest and East–West trade.

This story tells us two things. Coming at the end of the historical part of this book, it helps pave the step into the evolutionary third part. The link is the incendiary idea that the search for common humanity takes us, willy-nilly, to common animality. As I have repeatedly observed, the musical human is defined by its entanglement with animals. It also bears stressing that the musical human is itself an animal.

The second lesson is that Westernisation hardly represents the end of music history. By a sublime twist of historical justice – given all the questionable things the West has done – Western music itself becomes colonised by music from the rest of the world. It has been overwhelmed by two musical tidal waves, surging across the Atlantic and Pacific oceans.

The Black Atlantic

James Brown, father of funk and singer of 'Sex Machine', is on a plane flying into Kinshasa, capital of the Democratic Republic of the Congo (or as it was then known, Zaire). Brown will headline 'Zaire '74', a three-day live music festival designed as a warm-up to the 'rumble in the jungle', Muhammad Ali's boxing match against George Foreman (30 October 1974). The camera records this conversation.[56] 'Well, James, it feels like we're finally going back home,' one of Brown's associates tells him. 'We're not coming back. Black is here,' Brown responds. 'Every little band in Kinshasa is playing the James Brown beat.' Yet if Brown was eagerly expecting that 'the beat gonna return to the roots', then his autobiography admits that he was quite wrong. 'My roots may be embedded in me and I don't know it, but when I went to Africa I didn't recognize anything I'd gotten from there.'[57]

Brown's little drama of homecoming and disillusionment plays out a major tension in African-American music. On the one side, there is a deep yearning for African roots and a cultural memory for the supposed wellsprings of its music. The vexed question of what funk, jazz or the blues owe to Africa melts into the mists of African history itself. Africa was conspicuously absent from the group of superpowers jockeying

in Chapter 7, not because it had no music history, but because none
of it was recorded in pre-colonial times. On the other side, Brown is
recognising the element of his music that is new and American, not
'African'. The two words 'African-American' tug against opposite
heartstrings; they do not blend.

Does music in Africa and America share a common historical core?
What is 'black' in black music? Some people think it is 'call-and-
response' patterns. During the sixth round of his fight – which he was
losing – Ali called out to the spectators 'Ali boma yé!' ('Ali kill him!'),
and 60,000 Zairians responded, tipping the balance in his favour.[58] This
was call and response on the grandest scale. However, the historical
evidence for a common core is sporadic, to say the least. In Chapter 1,
I ventured the possibility that hip-hop originates with the griots of Mali,
minstrels who tell the history of their tribe in song. Another blast from
the past, also from Mali, is the song genre called Soliyo, or 'Calling the
horses', which began life in the Mali empire 700 years ago.[59] Ancient
Mali warriors would use a special melody to call their horses to get
ready for battle, and it is possible that these cries survive in Soliyo, as
might the song texts that glorify these battles as oral histories.

History in Africa is traditionally oral. Vivid examples of that are the
'drum histories' of the Dagbamba tribe of Ghana.[60] The foundation of
the Dagbamba's historical knowledge is known as Samban' lunga (literally,
'outside drumming'), because it is drummed outside the chief's house
in grand ceremonies twice a year. The drummer stands alone and faces
the chief across the compound, an hourglass-shaped drum (luna) over
his shoulder. Up to a hundred other drummers sit behind him and beat
responses to the verses of his song. He sings non-stop, typically for eight
hours, holding countless details in his head about the lives of past chiefs,
their ancestry and children, what they achieved and how they acquired
their proverbial praise-names. When history is a feat of creative memory,
notions of reliability or truth are, of course, beside the point.

If written history is what we want, then we are tied to the racist
histories written by the colonial invaders. An early flavour of their
delicacy is conveyed by this claim by the Cairo physician and theologian
Ibn Butlan (1005–1050), from his tract 'On how to buy slaves and how
to detect bodily defects': 'If a black were to fall from the sky to the
Earth, he would fall in rhythm.'[61] In other words, the rhythm DNA was
so ingrained within the black body that, when they were hanged, slaves

even died to the beat. That said, colonial history affords some pleasant surprises. In the late 1400s, the cities of Valencia, Seville, Florence and Naples enjoyed a vibrant black culture, and Lisbon's population was 10 per cent black by 1520.[62] Southern Europe rocked to African dances such as *pasacalles*, *sarabandas* and *chaconas*, destined to become familiar in the music of Bach, kitted out with French names – *passacailles*, *sarabandes*, *chaconnes*. It is also a surprise that 6/8 metre (six skipping beats in a bar), a pattern now prevalent in Western music, was originally associated in fifteenth-century Europe with African musicians. The speed with which music circulated was also staggering. Music played in Luanda, Angola in the 1750s would pop up six weeks later in Rio de Janeiro.[63]

All told, the evidence shows that, far from ever having been culturally pristine, black music was always hybrid and cosmopolitan. This is an important finding, against the myth that African music originated in a state of prelapsarian purity, and then fell into mixture. In the words of the renowned anthropologist Gerhard Kubik, 'the very word "hybrid" … loses its qualifying capacity' since 'all cultures have never been anything else'.[64] Kubik's caveat is true up to a point, but it mustn't cloud over the broader continental differences (Africa compared with India, China, the Middle East and Europe) explored in earlier chapters. Setting purism to one side, the most important lesson to draw, against the misty-eyed ideal that culture is all about obdurate survival, is that culture also involves change. Preservation works side by side with forgetting and innovation. An example of forgetting is that the 'blackness' of *chaconas* and 6/8 metre has been totally bleached away. Even if you tried, it is impossible to hear Bach's *Chaconne* for solo violin as African, or Beethoven's *Pastoral Symphony* (with its final movement in 6/8 metre) as black. We are getting closer to understanding James Brown's almost wilful forgetting of his African roots.

There have been many conjectures about the historical passage of music from Africa to the New World, many as attractive as they are impossible to prove. The neatest theory is that differences between northern and southern Africa map onto those between North and South America.[65] Blues, jazz and rock in North America lack the rhythmic complexity we think of as central to African music because North American plantations drew most of their slaves from Islamic West Africa. The slave Kunta Kinte, from Alex Haley's novel *Roots*, was abducted from the Muslim Gambia. By these lights, jazz improvisation is indebted to the tradition of Islamic vocal improvisation in North Africa. Another reason, it is said, is that North Americans banned drums in order to stop slaves in plantations communicating with each other with 'talking drums'.

The same theory explains that the music of South America is rich in polymetres and marimbas because most of their slaves originated south of West Africa. The folk music of Colombia, for example, contains many African features: two-part song forms from the Congo, drum languages from the Kwa, Pygmy yodelling, and, more generally, collective participation and a thick layering of rhythms over a repeated pattern.[66] These patterns, or 'timelines', stood out in bright drum timbres against the profuse rhythms like metronomes. Unlike metronomes, their pulse was asymmetrical, favouring eight- and twelve-beat phrases divided into groups of three and two (3+3+2 or 3+2+3+2+2). Colombian Africans also took the 6/8 metres that had enchanted the Iberians in the fifteenth century and 're-Africanised' them into so-called *papa con yuca* ('potato and yucca') patterns, so-called because the words give you the beats, played on marimbas and rhythmically strummed violins.

As well as surprises and glib hypotheses there are red, or indeed blue, herrings. The fishiest one is that the blues come from Africa; that they express the keening homesickness of plantation slaves. Why, then, are there no blues in the Caribbean, or indeed, in Africa itself, where it is more common to sing in major keys (i.e. without 'blue' notes)? A more likely source for the blues is the way that Americans spoke in the Deep South. The linguist Benjamin Boone discovered blues-like speech patterns in Jelly Roll Morton's 1938 interview with the anthropologist Alan Lomax. Through computer analysis of the speech spectrum, Boone showed that 'pitches commonly associated with blues music were being utilized' not only by Morton – a New Orleans musician – but also by Lomax. Although Lomax was white, he grew up in the South.[67] Slightly pinker, but still a dubious fish, is swing. It doesn't mean anything if it doesn't swing, said Duke Ellington. The origin of swing was probably Celtic rather than African, via the Appalachian Irish and Scots fiddlers who had swept into America in the early nineteenth century, and who taught their traditional music to black violinists. Other than the banjo, the violin was the only instrument black musicians were permitted to play.[68]

We are on firmer ground in New Orleans, the birthplace of jazz.[69] African music was more tolerated in French-Catholic New Orleans than in Protestant America, and slaves and free people of colour danced in public spaces such as Congo Square. The ring dances from the African Congo were rearranged into long, sinuous and linear 'second line' dances following behind the marching bands, which wound through the city at funerals and carnival processions. The importance of 'second line' dance is that it gave free rein to the African polyrhythmic sensibility, complementing the European four-square rhythms marching at the front of the procession. This combination of firm marching beat with complex syncopation is exactly how funk started in the 1960s. According to James Brown's music director, Alfred 'Pee Wee' Ellis, these were James Brown's true roots.[70] Brown's complex funk was an extreme form of the rock and pop formula: every bar has four simple beats at the front, syncopations and backbeats at the rear. The formula would spread across the world. So, given that every step of this line dance leads Brown, via Congo Square, to the Congo itself, why was Brown in denial about his African roots when he flew into Kinshasa?

The ethos of New Orleans jazz arose as a protest against every notion of racial purity. It subverted the Jim Crow laws of racial segregation; it encouraged the crossing of boundaries. This attitude was formed far earlier than New Orleans in the 1890s, however. It was a consequence of slavery and the experience of migration across what Paul Gilroy memorably termed the 'Black Atlantic'.[71] The sounds of the Black Atlantic – in their travels from Africa to America and back to Africa – are the sounds not of origins (purity) or destinations (hybridity), nor even of the ocean in between. They sounded out, rather, the experience of transit itself, of boundary crossings, of inventive mixtures thrown together in order to adapt and to survive. In an ocean of cross-currents, proliferations of subgenres and fusions, it is impossible to disentangle, say, the rumbas in the jungle (which reached the Congo from Cuba in the 1920s) from the funk Brown brought with him in the 1970s, and from the Afrofunk today. This is why the watery Black Atlantic takes over from the sandy Silk Road as an emblem of modern experience. It is a condition of modernity itself, from cosmopolitan Lisbon in 1480 to multicultural London in 2020.

From J to K

Forty million children in China are learning to play the piano. China is the world's largest producer and consumer of pianos, accounting for 76.9 per cent of the global piano output.[72] Pianos enjoy similar popularity in Japan and South Korea, as does Western classical music in general. There is a galaxy of Southeast Asian piano virtuosos: Fou Ts'ong, Lang Lang, Mitsuko Uchida, Sunwook Kim and many others. Why is that? When Fou Ts'ong won third prize in the fifth Chopin International Piano Competition in 1955, China sponsored classical music in rivalry to the West as a proxy for war. Later, Western-style classical music evolved into a symbol of modernity and middle-class status. More than that, classical form chimed with the formality of Asian culture; for instance, the decorum of Japanese manners recognised itself in the grace of Mozart and Schubert. In this picture (see **Figure 8.5**), a Westernised conductor of a symphony orchestra shakes hands with an animé cartoon. Whatever the reasons, the reality is that Southeast Asia has become the heartland of Western music. As classical music sinks in the West, its lifeboats are China, Japan and Korea.

Figure 8.5 Anime star Hatsune Miku with conductor Hirofumi Kurita and the Tokyo Philharmonic Orchestra

On this apocalyptic note, let us conclude these endgames with a snapshot of Japan, perhaps the most modern and Westernised of musical cultures. Compared to the Black Atlantic, Japan affords a very different vision of modernity: achingly cool cinema and underground noise bands, pod hotels, high-tech toilets, bullet trains and karaoke. Often this vision is a distorted or hyper-real version of the West itself. Observing the West through Japanese eyes is like seeing a reflection in a very distant mirror. Or like dining at Douglas Adams's 'restaurant at the end of the universe', where guests eat sumptuous meals while watching the whole of creation explode around them. This describes the oddly discombobulating experience of listening to the music of Joe Hisaishi, possibly the most famous Japanese classical composer nobody in the West has ever heard of.

Hisaishi is the house composer of Hayao Miyazaki's Studio Ghibli, whose *Spirited Away* won the 2003 Oscar for best animated feature.[73] For Western viewers, Hisaishi's music is integral to the ineffably Japanese qualities of Miyazaki's films. It is puzzling, therefore, that his scores appear to be assembled from the flotsam and jetsam of Western music: popular tunes, light jazz, easy listening, minimalism, electronica and spacey ambient sounds. Hisaishi seems anonymous not just because he is so eclectic, but because he sinks his personality into the films. Why, then, do these films feel so Japanese? The clue lies in the characters' exceptionally wide eyes (originally inspired by American classic cartoons of the 1930s such as Betty Boop), which mean one thing to Western viewers, another to the Japanese. To Westerners, they appear Caucasian; to Japanese, they appeal to their traditional penchant for stylisation. Similarly, a traditional Japanese taste for cool detachment and whimsy is worked through the films' higgledy-piggledy European locations, a mash-up of Italian Alps, Bavarian castles, Welsh villages and the Côte d'Azur.

So Hisaishi's music, like Miyazaki's visuals, co-opts bits of the West to express Japan. Strangely, this was a time-honoured military tactic in Japan's engagement with the outside world. The historian Arnold Toynbee defined it as Japan's 'Herodian' position: that of 'the man who acts on the principle that the most effective way to guard against the danger of the unknown is to master its secret'. He 'responds by discarding his traditional art of war and learning to fight his enemy with the enemy's own tactics and own weapons'.[74] Japan had done this before, when it imported *gagaku*, its oldest form of classical music, from its giant neighbour China in the ninth century on the back of Buddhism, Confucianism and the Chinese writing system.[75] Although

Chinese in origin, *gagaku* became indigenised as the music of the Japanese royal court. However, Japan's most far-reaching 'Herodian' defence was executed in reaction to an American gunship.

On 8 July 1853 Commodore Matthew Calbraith Perry sailed his steamboat into Uraga harbour, an event immortalised in Stephen Sondheim's musical *Pacific Overtures*. His intervention punctured Japan's long isolation: since 1641, Japanese had been forbidden to have any contact with foreigners. It had begun so differently, when Western missionaries had looked upon Japan as ripe for the picking. By the 1580s there were 100,000 Japanese Christians. In 1577 Father Organtino Gnecchi had written from Kyoto: 'If only we had more organs and other musical instruments Japan would be converted to Christianity in less than a year.'[76] After the 1868 Meiji Restoration – when the emperor was restored to his throne – Japan succumbed fairly briskly to Western music, if not to Christianity, in a veritable cascade of capitulations. Western-style military drills required Western-style music, so the army acquired its first band in 1872, and for many years the first public recitals of Western music were given by military bands. Kimigayo, still Japan's national anthem, was composed in the Western style at this time. Schoolchildren were taught Western staff notation in 1880; a conservatoire was established in Tokyo in 1890. Japanese composers were sent to Paris and Berlin to absorb Debussy and Brahms. Japanese folksongs were dressed in Western harmonies to demonstrate East–West fusion. An infamous example of such fusion is Ishirō Honda's score for the 1954 film *Godzilla* (*Gojira*), where Japanese folk tunes lumber through Tokyo in heavy orchestration.[77]

After the *Nullstunde*, or zero hour, of 1945, when nationalism was expunged and the Allied occupation increased access to the American and European avant garde, East–West fusion attained new degrees of refinement in the work of a younger generation of Japanese composers. The greatest of these, Toru Takemitsu, described the extraordinarily subtle to-ing and fro-ing of Japanese and Western influences as 'reciprocal action'. Debussy's impressionism had derived from East Asia a fascination with modal scales, timbre, static time and the picturesque. Imported back to Japan, these aspects were used by Takemitsu and his peers to reflect back and intensify the preoccupations of their own culture. But it was the circuitous journey of the detour itself – out to the West, back to Japan – which played to perhaps the deepest of

Japanese qualities: the suppression of individual consciousness as a path towards identification with nature. In Takemitsu's words: 'I learn and absorb something from traditional Japanese music's denial of the ego, and its yearning toward a union of sound with nature.'[78]

Denial of ego, the path of Zen Buddhism, threads through much of Japan's musical culture. How to reconcile it, then, with perhaps its most bizarre custom: Japan's infatuation with Beethoven's Ninth Symphony? There is a manga comic book telling the story of the symphony's Japanese premiere at the Bandô prisoner-of-war camp in 1918.[79] In 1944, young Japanese soldiers were sent out to die to its strains, according to one survivor who had personally campaigned to have the Ninth performed because 'Within each of us swirled an almost desperate desire to carry to the battlefield memories of something close to us, something that symbolized our homeland.'[80] Every New Year's Eve the 'Ode to Joy' is performed across the country, by both professional orchestras and amateur enthusiasts. Japan's dedication to Beethoven's Ninth is even greater than that of Austria or Germany; this is all the more perplexing because there is no tradition of the individual 'great' composer in Japanese (or Asian) history. So why has Beethoven become a Japanese national hero? When he was a schoolteacher, the music critic Yoshida Hidekazu set his students an essay asking precisely this question. Hidekazu found that 'the vast majority of papers on Beethoven deal less with his music itself than with the writer's admiration for Beethoven's ability to write masterpieces despite such adversities as deafness, unrequited love and loss of his family'.[81] For the Japanese, Beethoven epitomises selflessness; for the West, the triumph of self. It is extraordinary that the same music can reflect back on a culture its own preoccupations. In Nazi Germany, the Ninth was transparently a work of National Socialism. Russians and Chinese debated whether Beethoven was a capitalist or a communist.[82]

Denial of ego appeared to be the chief lesson that Western composers such as John Cage learned from Japan, after the flirtations of *The Mikado* and *Madame Butterfly*. But even here, this was less a matter of influence than of Western self-reflection. American composers appropriated the Zen ethos so as to distance themselves both from Old Europe and from their own mainstream establishment. Similarly, there are cultural firewalls through which a new wave sometimes cannot pass. It is interesting, for instance, to wonder why K-Pop conquered the West whereas J-Pop struggles to travel outside of Asia. On the one hand, the whole world dances with Psy's 'Gangnam Style'. On the other, Western sensibilities still haven't learned to stomach the saccharine and morally problematic pre-adolescent(-looking) girl-band culture of J-Pop, even though we believe Japanese assurances that the genre is just innocent good fun. That is a pity, because, beneath the glitzy surface, the harmonies of J-Pop songs are more interesting and less standardised than those of Western commercial pop. The chord loops are much longer, and don't endlessly circle the same I–IV–V progressions.

Why, then, did K-Pop break through in the way it did? First, there is the delirious energy, its exit velocity from the gravitational pull of nearly a century of political oppression – initially, under Japanese occupation (when Korean music was banned), and then from under post-war conservative governments. Secondly, there is a colourful visual style derived – astonishing as it might seem – from *Teletubbies*, a pre-school children's programme broadcast by the BBC during the late 1990s.[83] With its fast-moving jump cuts, K-Pop music videos are designed for multiple viewings on portable screens, within a digital economy that capitalises on clicks. Weaponising primary colours and short attention spans, knowingness and ironic distance, K-Pop cleans up with children, teenagers, adults and cultural theorists. It is the universal music of the early twenty-first century. The top-selling group in the world in 2020 was BTS, the South Korean seven-piece boy band, and it was the first K-Pop band to address the United Nations.

Something interesting happens when Studio Ghibli animé is re-scored for a Western audience. Joe Hisaishi writes extra music to fill in the silences. 'According to Disney's staff,' says Hisaishi, 'foreigners [non-Japanese] feel uncomfortable if there is no music for more than three minutes.'[84] For instance, the original Japanese version of the 1986 film *Laputa* lasts two hours but has only one hour of music. For the rest of the time, audiences enjoy the silence, constituted of what film critics call 'pillow shots' – 'an almost musical beat between what went before and what comes after', allowing the story to 'breathe'. The point, of course, about 'silence' is that it doesn't really exist; it is an opportunity to hear the sounds of the natural environment. For instance, one of the signature sounds of Miyazaki's films – films whose stars are animals, spirits, landscapes and children – is that of the wind soughing through the grass. Takemitsu calls such environmental sound *Sawari*, and he tells a wonderful story of how he once listened to a *shakuhachi* master play his bamboo flute for him in a restaurant, with a sukiyaki hot-pot bubbling in the background. In reply to the Zen-like musician, Takemitsu confirms: 'I heard the sound of the sukiyaki simmering really well.' Responds the master: 'Then it is proof that I played well, and that is because my music *is* the sukiyaki sound!'[85]

Windows into Part Three

A Western listener would struggle not to separate music from noise, or *Sawari*; not to cleave music from nature. But the view from Japan is that the Western model of music and musicians is an historical aberration, an evolutionary blip. The norm across the ages, and across the non-Western world, has always been that music is part of nature. Reciprocally, the musical human has always sought to murder nature, or at least to refine or transcend it. Miyazaki and Takemitsu's interests in ecology were forged in the fires of Kobi and Hiroshima.[86]

Toru Takemitsu enjoyed a sideline as a TV chef and wrote a quirky recipe book (mostly for pasta dishes). Sitting next to Takemitsu in the Japanese restaurant at the end of the universe, the musical human looks through two windows:

1. The J Window. The view is not encouraging. She sees the Earth millions of years in the past, where the only music was animal. After all, the musical human is an animal.
2. The K Window. The prospect is no more comforting. She sees a near future of musical experience augmented by wearable or integrated technology. Here, the musical transhuman is a cyborg.

Let's step through the J Window.

PART THREE

EVOLUTION

CHAPTER 9
ANIMAL

The *Voyager* Golden Record, humanity's calling card, says hello in fifty-five languages, and then shows the universe the 'Sounds of the Earth', from the environmental to the living. Alien ears will pore over volcanoes, earthquakes, thunder, wind, surf and rain, and then a procession of animal calls: crickets, frogs, birds, hyenas, elephants, chimpanzees. Human music arrives at the peak of this evolutionary climb from lower to higher animals. While one can dispute which of the last four species is the most intelligent, chimps share 98 per cent of human genes and are our closest relatives on the tree of life. Revealingly, NASA chose to place whale song in the category of greetings, not music, alongside human messages. The message to space is that, out of all Earth's living creatures, only humans and whales have language. Perhaps NASA were motivated by the success of the 1970 album *Songs of the Humpback Whale*, the best-selling nature record of all time (see **Figure 9.1**). Still in the slipstream of this enthusiasm for cetaceans, the 1986 film *Star Trek IV: The Voyage Home* tells of how an alien probe arrives on Earth and transmits signals nobody can understand. The signals are directed at the ocean and turn out to be in whale.

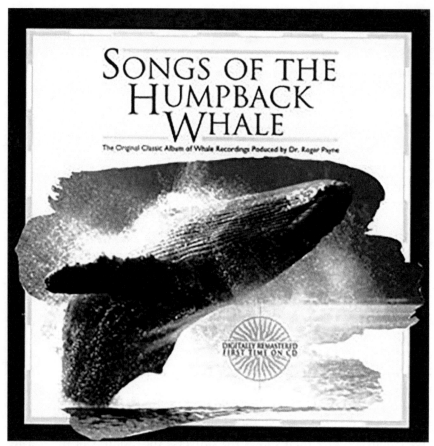

Figure 9.1 The bestselling nature record of all time, *Songs of the Humpback Whale*

The third and final part of my book fans out from human history to the evolution of music on the broadest scale. Animal communication can teach us what is so exceptional about human music, as does the music of what might succeed us. Going a step beyond NASA, we'll follow the evolutionary chain to the sounds of artificial intelligence and human-machine interactions. Animal – human – machine: these are the giant leaps in music's development.

This chapter will outline some key facts about music in the animal kingdom. Chapter 10 will review the links in the chain from 'Lucy' the australopithecine to musical language. Chapter 11 brings the story of the musical human to its potential death at the hands of machines.

But first, some caveats and contexts. We must always bear in mind that talk of the 'evolution' of music, as of language, is a metaphor, because music is a communication system, not a creature, and it didn't evolve from a single ancestor. The metaphor skates over the key distinction in evolutionary theory between homology and analogy. That is to say, while music evolved on at least four separate occasions in insects, birds, whales and humans, the relationship between these different kinds of music is analogous. The four musics did not evolve in a direct line from a single root. This is the same principle by which wings are said to be *analogous* because they are similar in use only, and evolved four times in birds, bats, insects and pterosaurs. If these varieties of wings descended from a common ancestor, they would be *homologous*.

Music doesn't have a single origin. It coalesced out of multiple points of origin, a rope spun from many threads. Thinking of music as a rope of many threads is really to think of the musical human as a great synthesiser. What we call 'music' isn't a single *thing*, a unified black box. It is a composite of parameters and faculties. Parameters include rhythm, melody, timbre and texture. Faculties include predicting and entraining to a beat; singing in pitch; remembering notes; recognising octave equivalence; following the strands of a contrapuntal web. One of the most important musical faculties is what zoologists call 'vocal learning'. Most animals keep to the sounds they are born with. A tiny fraction of animals – some, but not all, birds, whales, bats, elephants, seals and an amorous subgenus of singing vole (*Sumeriomys argyropulo*) – are able to learn new sounds. The evolutionary biologist Tecumseh Fitch believes that vocal learning is an absolute prerequisite for animal communication to qualify as music.[1]

Here, then, is the decisive factor that makes the musical human exceptional. While musical parameters and faculties are scattered throughout the animal kingdom, only the human musician can do it all. We put it all together.

Given that musical parameters and faculties crop up at different points of deep history, it becomes possible to sketch a deep timeline for music:

800 million years ago

Technically, the very oldest kind of signal was not sonic but *vibrational*, as in cell-to-cell communication.[2] Mechanical and chemical interactions would have occurred within the earliest multi-celled metazoa between 800 million and one billion years ago. Vibrational communication flows not through air or water but through a 'substrate', a solid substance such as a leaf, a beehive or the ground. This is how leaf-hoppers and elephants 'hear', but also deaf musicians like the percussionist Dame Evelyn Glennie.

165 million years ago

After vibration came rhythm. Scientists reconstructed the exact pitch produced by the wings of a fossilised bush cricket, or katydid, from the Jurassic period.[3] Like its modern descendants, the prehistoric katydid would have chirped in a regular beat, a faculty shared by cicadas and frogs, but also analogous, in the visual field, to the pulses of fireflies and the synchronised waving of fiddler crabs. Perceiving and synchronising to a regular beat is a foundational musical skill for humans.

66 million years ago

Melody comes next. The oldest known fossil of a syrinx (a bird's vocal organ, analogous to the human larynx) came from a Cretaceous duck-shaped bird in Antarctica.[4] We can infer that the bird might have been capable not just of complex song, but of the suite of musical abilities that accompany it: learning new songs from other birds; creating new songs by itself; recognising absolute pitch and spectral shape (timbre). These abilities can be laboratory tested in modern birds.

50 million years ago

The last faculty to evolve, before *sapiens* came along, was musical culture, developed by the first whales. At any particular time and locale, all humpback whales sing the same song.[5] And this song changes, year on year, in ways that can be easily tracked by whale watchers. It's meaningful to say that whale music has a 'tradition'. Moreover, whale songs are longer, richer and more 'song-like' (in human terms) than those of birds, which helps explain why their haunting sounds captured the imagination of the world in the 1970s when they were first discovered and made public. We empathise better with whales than with birds because whales are mammals.

Apes emerged and diversified between 23 million and 5 million years ago, but they don't fit within the musical timeline because they lack vocal learning. Strictly speaking, they aren't musical at all. Chimps, bonobos and gorillas are flexible and creative users of physical gesture. But their vocal communication is impoverished compared with birds and whales. The cosmic joke is that the musical human evolved not from birds or whales but from tone-deaf apes, via our last common ancestor (or 'missing link') 6 or 7 million years ago.

Nevertheless, evolution is cunningly circuitous, and what we did inherit along the ape line was social intelligence. Being able to read another's mind is basic to dancing, singing and playing together. The rupture between the ape line and the more musical branches of the phylogenetic tree will be a puzzle for us, as will the suspicion that the musical human has been faking it all along.

This chapter, then, will lay out some of the animal abilities that the musical human will put together. (Conversely, there are many things that animal musicians do better than us.) It will also ask perhaps the biggest question of all. These sounds may well be complex, fascinating and beautiful. But are they art?

Insects

Wouldn't it be wonderful if we could reconstruct Jurassic music from a bug trapped in amber? A team of scientists based in China did the next best thing, with a fossil of a katydid (bush cricket) found in Mongolia and dated from the middle Jurassic period, 165 million years ago.[6] It was amazing how much they could deduce from it. Modern katydids produce chirps by rubbing a toothed vein on one wing against a plectrum on the other in a process called stridulation. By examining tooth distribution on the fossil's large 7 cm forewing, Jun-Jie Gu and his team worked out that the ancient insect produced a pure tone of 6.4 kHz, or a low E natural. To discover the exact pitch of a Jurassic song is a remarkable achievement. But a lot could be unpacked from that. It meant that the katydid probably sang close to the ground of the Jurassic forest because low frequencies carry better over long distances, whereas high pitches fade quickly. It meant that the insect's dinosaur predators probably couldn't hear E naturals; that the note's acoustic frequency fell under the Jurassic radar. And it indicated that this forest of coniferous trees and giant ferns was probably a noisy environment, and that the katydid's pure tone was adapted to penetrate the sounds of rain, wind, streams and a myriad creatures. But the most striking lesson is that the katydid's song was an evolutionary dead end. Later crickets didn't sing, they chirped and clicked in massed rhythmic choruses.

Why and how crickets gather in choruses to chirp in perfect synchrony has long puzzled entomologists. The 'why' is partly answered by the widespread phenomenon of lekking – the competitive display of male animals for the attention of females during the mating season. But if the insects are competing, why do they chirp in unison? Because of what has been called the 'beacon effect' in studies of the synchronous flashing of fireflies.[7] There is sonic strength in numbers, and by pooling their signal, one chorus of crickets can outperform a rival chorus. Signalling in large groups, through 'amplitude summation', has been shown to give individual crickets a mating advantage. Once the female's attention has been lured from one chorus to another, competition *within* the group kicks in. Using the common pulse as his baseline, the male cricket will signal a fraction of a second ahead of the others so as to stand out. This regular irregularity is analogous to how jazz musicians swing and syncopate their beat. Yet surely we are getting ahead of ourselves here. How can we compare human jazzers to creatures with a microgram of neural tissue, insects with practically no brain at all? This brings us to the 'how'.

Even pendulums and metronomes, objects that are literally brainless, synchronise their oscillations over time. In 1665 the Dutch physicist Christiaan Huygens demonstrated that two pendulum clocks resting on the same shelf would gradually synchronise with each other.[8] Even when the pendulum of one clock was disturbed, it would get back into swing with the other within thirty minutes. Huygens called this process 'the sympathy of clocks'. It is nowadays called 'entrainment'. When we count, clap or move in time with an externally given beat, we are *entraining* with that beat. Crickets, fireflies and fiddler crabs entrain with each other, as do musicians in a jazz band.

Huygens' clocks entrained because they shared a single vibrating surface, the shelf. Insects such as crickets and fireflies entrain because their little brains contain tiny oscillators. This is the premise of Steven Strogatz's best-seller, *Sync*:

> In a congregation of fireflies, every one is continually sending
> and receiving signals, shifting the rhythms and being shifted by

them in turn. Out of the hubbub, *sync* somehow emerges [and] the fireflies organize themselves. No maestro is required, and it doesn't matter what the weather is like. Sync occurs through mutual cueing, in the same way that an orchestra can keep perfect time without a conductor [...] Each firefly contains an oscillator, a little metronome, whose timing adjusts automatically in response to the flashes of others. That's it.[9]

In his wonderful book *Bug Music: How Insects Gave us Rhythm and Noise*, the first study ever to take the music of insects seriously, the philosopher and jazz musician David Rothenberg riffs on the sync of crickets. Building on the ideas of entomologist Thomas Walker, Rothenberg explains that a cricket's central nervous system contains an oscillator that produces periodic electrical impulses. The creature adjusts his oscillator in response to another cricket's chirp. 'If the other chirp occurs towards the beginning of his own chirp, he resets his own clock and starts his own cycle a tiny bit earlier.'[10]

Now, it would be a wild overstatement to claim that an insect's sense of rhythm is anything like as developed as that of a human. A person is able to keep on beating to an externally given pulse even when that pulse has stopped; we imagine it. And our imagination can group beats into patterns within patterns, called metre. There is no evidence that the brains of other animals, even apes, are sophisticated enough to organise pulses hierarchically in that way. Still, nature is full of clocks, from the atoms inside us, which oscillate 10^{16} times per second, to the American cicada's seventeen-year breeding cycle. Pushing the evolutionary timeline to the limit, one could even argue that circadian clocks started 3 billion years ago with cyanobacteria,[11] and that a definition of any organism is 'a (loosely coupled) "population of oscillators" '.[12] And it is marvellous to consider this anecdote by the Dutch ethnomusicologist Frank Kouwenhoven about the musicality of midges:

One day, I was humming a tune when I noticed that clouds of midges in the air above my head started to 'dance' to my music. The insects moved in unison (in up- or downward direction) in response to the rhythmical sound signals they 'heard'. Presumably they reacted to air vibrations, but it was less obvious why or how all of them would respond to me – the external timekeeper – in synchronic fashion.[13]

To understand where our own musicality came from, it is useful to highlight the simplicity of many of our faculties. In short, animal song puts what is special about human music into clearer relief. In this respect, consider how all of music is implicit within the courtship duets of mosquitoes.[14] The male mosquito buzzes to attract his mate with a wingbeat frequency of 600 Hz, or D natural. Female mosquitoes hum normally at a pitch of 400 Hz, G natural. Yet just before sex, both mosquitoes modulate their flight tones so as to harmonise at the same pitch frequency of 1200 Hz, an ecstatic octave above the male's D. Everything we sing is just a footnote to that.

Birds

Crickets chirp, mosquitoes hum, but birdsong is the real deal – the embodiment of musical nature from which the musical human has slowly descended. Humanity has always looked longingly into the trees at birdsong as a kind of musical ideal. Keats's rapturous admiration in his 'Ode to a Nightingale' speaks for all of us. Yet several issues get lost in those woods, and we shouldn't lose our heads. Is birdsong an art? Music is an art because it is enjoyed in itself, whereas Darwinism teaches that birds sing for sexual selection. How do we know that birdsong isn't music but a language? Presumably the sound birds make is just another variety of animal communication. Let's tackle the function of birdsong first.

The quick answer to 'why do birds sing?' is: to attract a mate, repel rivals and establish a home. Darwinian sexual selection explains that females prefer birds with longer, more complex and more numerous melodies, often sung by well-travelled, serially monogamous lotharios such as nightingales, because, returning from afar each spring, they need to court harder.[15] According to the zoologist Clive Catchpole, 'In nature, males with larger syllable repertoires always attract females before their rivals with less complex songs.'[16] With his 200 songs, Keats's nightingale would have easily been the smartest bird in his garden, and female birds find musical intelligence sexy.

The short answer to whether birdsong is not song at all but a type of language is 'yes'. It is a highly qualified language, however, with reference and meaning but no syntax. The twelve calls of the chaffinch serve distinctive functions: the flight call, the social call, the injury call, the aggressive call, the *tew*, *seee* and *seep* alarm calls, three courtship calls (*kseep*, *tchirp* and *seep*) and food-begging calls in nestlings and fledglings.[17] While each of these calls has a meaning, like a word in human language, the chaffinch doesn't put several calls together into a more complex structure, like our sentences. It has a primitive language lacking a compositional grammar.

But this is all too glib because the problem of defining birdsong as functional communication – hence not a music, and hence not an art – simply begs the question of what music *is*. And as we have seen throughout this book, the variety of music, even limited to the human world, is dizzying. Laying to one side for now questions as to whether the bird knowingly plays with sound, or takes aesthetic pleasure in that sound, it would be wilful to deny that such exquisitely complex structures of pitch, rhythm, timbre and contour have a great deal in common with what we think of as 'music'. Let's begin by listing all the ways that birds are musical, in human terms. We'll then review the anatomical evidence that explains why birdsong *can't* be a language.

Musicality first. Unlike humans, not all birds are musical. The gift of vocal learning is actually confined to a tiny subset of the 9,000 known species of birds, in the three clades of oscine songbirds (Passeriformes), parrots (Psittaciformes) and hummingbirds (Apodiformes).[18] Nature is surprisingly elitist. Hence ornithologists draw a sharp distinction between 'calls' and 'songs'. The chaffinch's language-like set of twelve calls is innate, universal to all chaffinches and unchanging. Most birds have only calls. But birds that have calls, including the chaffinch, can also have songs. The chaffinch's characteristic song rings endlessly creative changes on a four-phrase pattern, which goes something like this:[19]

Phrase 1: *chip-chip-chip-chip*
Phrase 2: *tell-tell-tell-tell*
Phrase 3: *cherry-erry-erry-erry*
Phrase 4: *tissy-che-wee-oo*

Importantly, most people believe that none of these phrases (or sub-phrases) mean anything in themselves, unlike the chaffinch's calls ('flight calls', 'alarm calls' and so on). We think that they are as individually meaningless as the whorls in a peacock's plumage (although we may be wrong). This meaninglessness is why this is music, and not language.

Those birds gifted with vocal learning pre-empt our musical skills by millions of years. In fact, most things we can do birds can do better, basically because the avian syrinx is a lot more flexible than the human larynx.[20] They can sing solo, duet with their lovers or rivals, and take turns as in a human conversation. Birds are usually taught their first songs by their fathers, and begin with a babbling stage, when, like a human child, they experiment with a large range of sounds. Even after they crystallise their mature songs, birds continue to learn new ones at least through their first year of life, some long after. The diversity of birdsong across species is remarkable. Chickadees make do with a drooping two-note song, which sounds like someone calling 'fee-bee'.[21] At the opposite extreme is the brown thrasher, the world's most prolific avian composer, whose 1,800 complex melodies are the sonic equivalent of the visual extravagance we love in the peacock's tail or the Australian bowerbird's contraptions.[22]

Like human music, birdsong has immense diversity across the world (although, *unlike* birds, we achieve this variety as a single species; I'll talk about that at the very end of the book). Birds even sing in different 'dialects', adapting to the habitats of geographical regions. Tropical birds such as the yellow longbill and the olive-green camaroptera use long-drawn notes suited to dense vegetation. The songs of open-country birds are higher and have repetitive trills. Indeed, American Parulid warblers sing higher the higher they fly, above interference from vegetation.[23] Perhaps the neatest proof of this 'acoustic adaptation hypothesis' is the trills of the rufous-collared sparrow, which are rapid in open habitats, slower in woodlands.[24] The hypothesis also helps us understand the link between birdsong and speciation (the formation of new species through evolution).[25] Normally this happens across aeons. But the calls of greenish warblers evolved almost in living memory. As the birds moved from their ancestral homeland in the Tibetan Plateau northwards to Siberia, the warblers' songs became longer and more complex. Why? Denser vegetation and a smaller bird population in the north made singing more competitive, and abundance of food made it less risky.

At a technical level, the musicality of songbirds can be measured in laboratory conditions. Hence we know that starlings are unusual in having exactly the same hearing range as us.[26] The range of most birds, however, is much narrower, sensitive to frequencies between 500 Hz and 6000 Hz. Yet, within that more limited compass, birds are much more sensitive than people to pitch, rhythm and timbre. Birds are superior to all mammals, including humans, in perceiving absolute pitch.[27] By contrast, humans are better with relative pitch, the contour of melodies. Thus birds can't recognise that a tune is the same when it is transposed to a different key, a similarity that is obvious to a child. Nor, unlike us, do birds hear that an octave is a higher or lower version of the same note. Nevertheless, birds are phenomenally sensitive to the tiniest inflections of rhythm or spectral shape. They are twice as fast as us in recognising rhythm, suggesting that their brains work twice as fast as our brains – even that they experience life at double the speed that we do. Equally astonishing is their perception of timbre. Father and infant king penguins are so finely attuned to the quality of their voices that they can pick each other out in a colony of 40,000 breeding pairs.[28] They win hands down on the 'cocktail party' circuit, or what the psychoacoustician Albert Bregman termed 'auditory scene analysis'. As we saw in Chapter 1, this is the principle that enables a partygoer to zoom in on a particular voice in a conversation, and screen out all the others. It is exactly the same faculty that listeners to a Bach fugue use to attend to his intertwining melodic voices. Imagine negotiating a party of 80,000 chattering humans.

But there is one faculty that birds appear to lack, which is to entrain to a rhythm, like insects and humans. The exception proves the rule, the exception being a solitary avian genius, a sulphur-crested cockatoo called Snowball, who is the only bird we know of who is capable of entrainment. A few years ago, a video of Snowball went viral, showing the bird dancing to the Backstreet Boys.[29] But birds aren't supposed to follow a beat. As Stefan Koelsch points out, what the video doesn't reveal is Snowball's owner standing behind him making encouraging gestures.[30] Does it matter that a bird has learned to do this in captivity rather than in the wild?

Perhaps the biggest difference between birds' music and ours is that we have a history. Keats guessed right when he wrote of his nightingale: 'The voice I hear this passing night was heard / In ancient days by emperor and clown: / Perhaps the self-same song…' It is most likely that, within its particular habitat, the repertoire of a bird species stays generally the same across thousands of years. That said, birdsong does have 'shallow' history, because birds can mimic new sounds from their environment. A delightful example of a limited 'tradition' is the lyrebird recorded in 1969 in the New England National Park in Australia, which seemed to be singing fragments of a Scottish folksong,

'The Keel Row', in the timbre of a flute.[31] After a bit of detective work, it was discovered that a flautist living on a nearby farm in the 1930s had played the tune to his pet lyrebird. The folksong had spread through the avian community, and was then handed down across many generations.

All told, birds have all the faculties required to make music. Do the songs themselves pass muster as well-formed musical structures? Enthusiasts have attempted to sketch birdsongs for hundreds of years. But it is only since the invention of the sonogram that it has been possible to capture what is really going on. **Figure 9.2** is a sonogram of two minutes of continuous singing of a male nightingale, *Luscinia megarhynchos*, the wave form representing loudness (amplitude), pitch

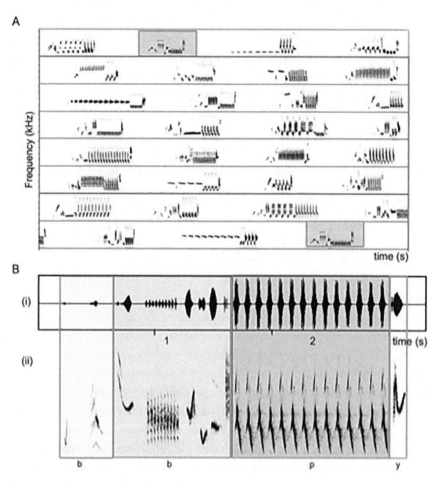

Figure 9.2 Sonogram of a nightingale song

(frequency) and timbre (spectral shape) against the time dimension.[32] The sonogram shows a 'bout' of thirty-one individual 'songs', each song being a rapid burst of sound punctuated by two or three seconds of silence. As you can see in the two highlighted boxes, songs two and thirty-one are *exactly the same*: the bird starts to recycle the songs, not in the same order, but in a creative rearrangement. The bottom half of the figure zooms in on the building blocks of one particular song. Amazingly, researchers have shown that, under the surface, what seems to be a multitude of different songs is really an elaboration of a single template of four sections: (1) one or several soft notes; (2) a sequence of notes of variable loudness; (3) a burst of repeated notes; (4) a single element, functioning like the full stop of a sentence. The birds, then, are improvising on a coherent grammatical structure. Chomskian linguists have leapt on the analogy between birdsong and the 'deep structures' elaborated by human sentences.[33] Birdsong lends itself equally plausibly to comparison with the syntax of human music. So this begs the question I denied earlier: is birdsong really a language? The reason why it might not be relates to why bird brains aren't wired for rhythm, and to why birds first took to the air. After a short interlude on biology, I'll grasp the nettle and propose the strongest reason why birdsong might indeed be similar to human music.

As we saw earlier, the earliest relic of a syrinx, the bird's vocal organ, is 66 million years old, from the Cretaceous period (see **Figure 9.3**).[34] It comes from the fossil of a duck-shaped creature christened *Vegavis iaai*, discovered on Vega Island in Antarctica. The first bird calls were probably honks. As with modern ostriches, the dinosaurs contemporary with *Vegavis iaai* didn't have syrinxes, so their calls might have resembled ostrich booms more than anything you hear in *Jurassic Park*. Birds share some aspects of their hearing with crocodilians,[35] and pneumatisation (air cavities in the bones and ears) was present in archosaurs, as in the cranial crests of the duck-billed hadrosaurids.[36] Nevertheless, reptiles rely much more on vision and smell than on sound. Thus the question of why birds sing is the flip side to the question of why birds ever took to the air. The advantages of flight are easier access to food and sex, and song evolved to compensate for flight's high metabolic cost: how many calories it uses up. Because song travels great distances, it helps the bird track its position in three-dimensional space through directional hearing.

Figure 9.3 *Vegavis iaai*, a Cretaceous bird-like creature, flying above a mid-sized raptor
      dinosaur

Delving a bit deeper into bird brains helps explain Koelsch's scepticism about Snowball the cockatoo. It seems that their brains just aren't wired for regular rhythm (although insects, which don't really have brains, do perfectly well). Birds evolved a more complex forebrain than dinosaurs and reptiles by elaborating the paleocortex, including nuclei for vocal learning and song production.[37] Maps of songbird brains pinpoint the HVC (higher vocal centre) and 'Area X', a centre that females lack, and that may (or may not) explain why singing appears to be much rarer in female birds. Birds' brains are superior to ours in their extraordinary ability to continue to grow new nerve cells in adulthood. Their brains literally get bigger in spring, when they need to sing, and smaller in winter, when they offload expensive weight.[38] Understanding how they do it might cure Alzheimer's one day; this is why there are hundreds of labs across the world analysing bird brains. Nevertheless, the architecture of a bird brain is fundamentally different, if not inferior, to that of mammals in one respect. Mammals added a layered cortex, including an evolutionarily new structure called the neostriatum. Its role is to integrate information between sensory, motor and cognitive systems. In human mammals, the connection between thought, feeling and motion was fundamental to our evolution of language. It is why we can entrain to rhythm, and why birds – Snowball possibly excepted – can't. This is also why scientists are so unwilling to credit birdsong with the status of a proper language. Birds literally don't have the brains for language.

But is it Art?

Is birdsong, then, a language or a music? An adaptive communication system or a pretty, yet pretty meaningless, stream of sound? But maybe this either/or dilemma is a false binary, and birdsong can be both, as we found human music to be in Chapter 4. We saw how soundtracks from everyday life were absorbed within the imaginary landscapes of musical works. Perhaps birds also do that, take sounds and signals from their environment and weave them into beautiful patterns. The clearest evidence that birds do indeed play with signs is the Albert's lyrebird of Australia, whose virtuoso mimicry featured in David Attenborough's BBC series *Planet Earth*.[39] In this clip, the lyrebird mimics the call of a kookaburra (he can impersonate twenty bird species), and gives uncannily precise imitations of a camera shutter, a camera motor-drive, a car alarm and the chainsaws of foresters. His dazzling skill impresses the females, the standard biological explanation. But from a musical perspective, the lyrebird's song also plays with the signs of his social and environmental space. Just as in human music, the signs of this space have been abstracted from their original function or meaning (it is doubtful that the lyrebird truly understands kookaburra). He probably does this in order to negotiate his environment.

This leads me to believe that the consensus that birdsong is empty of meaning is probably false. Here are two more examples.

First, although the chickadee's two-note 'fee-bee' song is as short as many innate calls, it is a real songbird. The simplicity of its song is deceptive. In song duels, the male chickadee raises the pitch of its upper note ('fee'), while maintaining the precise interval between the two notes ('fee-bee'). Sharpening the top note helps the bird penetrate the cacophony of the dawn chorus, by analogy to how the competitive cricket sings slightly ahead of his rivals' beat. His perfect balance of *absolute pitch* ('fee') and *relative pitch* (contour of 'fee-bee') tells the impressed females that he is top bird (lesser birds botch this balance). But the call also coordinates signals of status and aggression: absolute pitch warns his rival; accurate relative pitch attracts his mate.[40] The chickadee's song explains how a single song can serve two simultaneous functions, courtship and rivalry, the perennial puzzle used by bird experts to deny that the songs have meaning. How can a song mean anything if it serves two purposes at the same time? The answer is that a song can mix signals.

Second, maybe nightingales are singing more than we first thought. As we saw earlier, their hundreds of songs elaborate a four-stage pattern. The point to add now is that stage two of this syntax is a high-pitched whistle, used to attract a mate, and stage three is a rattle, a typical aggressive signal. Like human songs, the songs of this bird blend the sounds of love and war. And just like our music, their music digests functional signals from the outside world into an inner aesthetic world of musical grammar.

Finally, we can answer the question, why do birds sing? Ultimately, because they enjoy it. Yes, the songs have adaptive functions; and yes, the songs' constituent bits have meanings. But that doesn't take anything away from the possibility that birds gain pleasure from making music. Our discomfort in permitting birds joy, including political correctness about anthropomorphising animals, largely stems, according to evolutionary scientist Richard Prum, from a misreading of Darwin. In a boldly revisionist book, Prum argued that Darwin's theory of sexual selection was censored by Victorian scientists in the spirit of a typically Victorian disapproval of female sexual pleasure.[41] This distorted reading of Darwin's originally far richer theory hardened into the still current orthodoxy. This orthodoxy maintains that all animal song, including the songs of birds and whales, is purely functional and not aesthetic. The length and complexity of birdsong is often well in excess of what it needs to be to attract a mate. Chip away at this orthodoxy, and the wall between animal and human music falls.

Another part of the dogma is that avian music is the preserve of males, owing to the absence of 'Area X' in the brains of female birds. This was certainly the scientific consensus up to about a decade ago.[42] But female birds *do* sing, if perhaps for different reasons – social bonding rather than sexual selection – so 'Area X' can't be as significant as previously thought.[43] Indeed, it transpired that scientists had missed that because it is often hard to identify bird gender in the wild, and because of their assumption that if a bird sang, it was a male. Note the two spirals of circular logic here. Only males can sing, so if it sings, it is male. And since females can't sing, their disability can be pinpointed in their brains, the lack of 'Area X'.

What is going on here is a prejudice just as virulent as the now laughable belief that women couldn't compose; that the musical human was quintessentially male. We now take it for granted, of course, that the dearth of women composers in Western music history was due to social and cultural prejudices rather than to biology. If misogynist musicologists looked to nature to essentialise an historical accident, how ironic that natural science can be riddled with the same preconceptions. It turns out that Darwin's theory of music, the theory that male birds sing while female birds select, or, in human terms, that men compose and women dispose, is stone-cold wrong. Prum goes a long way in correcting Victorian sexism by emphasising the evolutionary importance of the female listeners' aesthetic pleasure. But he doesn't go far enough. If female birds also sing, and not necessarily for selection, then the origin of music can't be sex alone. As we shall see, when male humpback whales sing, there are no females around to hear them.

Whales

Whale music is more captivating than birdsong. It sounds more 'human', maybe because whales are mammals. It astonishes us because it is the closest nature comes to an evolving musical culture. The songs of whales develop slowly across decades. And yet once upon a time whales were believed to be silent or deaf. That all changed when whale met human, thanks largely to top-secret research by the US Navy during the Cold War. A naval engineer called Frank Watlington, stationed at the Palisades Sonar Station at St David's, Bermuda, was tasked to listen out for Russian submarines through hydrophones (water microphones) rigged 700 metres in the ocean depths.[44] What he heard instead were the songs of humpback whales. Watlington's recordings fell into the hands of the conservationist Scott McVay and a bird scientist based at Princeton University called Mark Konishi, and were then passed on to the whale experts Roger and Katy Payne, who carefully analysed them based on sonogram visualisations. The rest became history: using Watlington's recordings, Payne and McVay produced *Songs of the Humpback Whale*; the album sold 30 million, and kick-started the whole global environmental movement, including the organisation, Save the Whales. It is quite a story, and it is vividly told in David Rothenberg's *Thousand-Mile Song*.

As Rothenberg shows, the Paynes realised that the whale songs were more than just beautiful. They were intricately structured, and they repeated with considerable accuracy every few minutes. What emerged was that whale songs had the same hierarchical, language-like structure as bird songs, arranged in rising levels of complexity from word-like units, to sentence-like phrases, to full songs and bouts. Rothenberg has even demonstrated that if you speed up a whale song through many orders of magnitude, it sounds like a nightingale.[45] I disagree: the songs of whales and birds sound and behave differently for a number of reasons. One fundamental difference I shall dwell on is that whale music 'flows' in all sorts of ways, an obvious affordance of their watery medium; birdsong, by contrast, flits and jerks like birds' physical movements. The comparison is misleading in other ways. While both whales and birds use sound for directional hearing through three-dimensional space, air and water have different properties, not least the fact that sound travels five times faster through water than through air, at 1,500 metres per second. Given the poor visibility in the sea, hearing is immensely more important for whales than for birds, who have their visual acuity. It is thought that the infrasound groans of blue whales can travel thousands of miles through the ocean's 'deep sound channel', halfway round the world, hence the title of Rothenberg's book.

Whale songs typically last between seven and thirty minutes, much longer than birdsong, and their songs segue seamlessly into each other, with bouts of up to twenty-three hours.[46] Remember, each of the nightingale's 'songs' took only a few seconds, punctuated by two- to three-second breathing spaces. By contrast, gaps in whale songs fall in between the 'words', not the songs, so that each cry seems to carry enormous weight and expressive force. Here is a transcription by Payne and McVay (tracings of a spectrogram) of one of Watlington's recordings, made of a whale heard off Bermuda in April 1964 (see **Figure 9.4**). It is very easy to imagine the contours as expressing the whale's whoops, moans and blasts, and also how these cries gradually evolve across the song. For example, the high, sliding whoops on line 4 of the transcription obviously look and sound different from the more measured calls at the start; note also how the repetitions get faster and higher. There is logic and progression here.

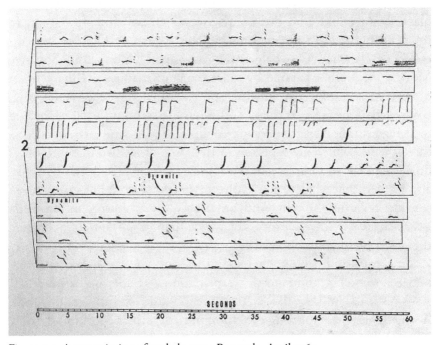

Figure 9.4 A transcription of a whale song, Bermuda, April 1964

Roger Payne and his colleagues noticed that, much more than in birdsong, the phrase endings in whale songs 'rhymed' with each other, as in human song. While linguists constantly debate whether birdsong is a language, a music or a blend of both, which anticipates hominin 'protolanguage' (see Chapter 10), whale song sounds definitely closer to what we think of as 'music' with its repetitiveness and rhyming phrase endings.

Perhaps the biggest surprise about whale songs is that they change from year to year.[47] Bit by bit, old songs develop into new songs, and after about five years, a humpback whale's repertoire is completely different. Whales are creatures of fashion, like pop musicians. How revealing when Payne confesses that he prefers the whale songs of the 1960s! Whale music has history. By contrast, within its particular habitat, the repertoire of a bird species stays generally the same. John Keats couldn't have guessed how right he was.

The more one investigates them, the stranger and more inexplicable whale songs turn out to be. At any one point in time, entire whale populations sing the same song, but oceans apart, not in the same place, quite unlike bird dialects. Between January and April 1991, in the breeding season, the marine biologist Salvatore Cerchio and his colleagues listened to whale songs in Kauai, Hawaii and Socorro, Mexico, locations separated by more than 3,000 miles.[48] The scientists discovered that the two distinct populations sang the same song, composed of the same six themes. This is understanding 'song' according to Peter Frumhoff's accepted 1983 definition as a sequence of 'at least three themes which are repeated in the same order two or more times during a recorded song session'. As if this wasn't surprising enough, they also learned that whale songs evolved *within* a season, not just *between* seasons, as earlier thought. And, amazingly, the evolution unfolded the *same pattern of change*, a process by which themes split into two separate themes, like calving icebergs.

We have no idea how whales do this, and you can take your pick between equally outlandish explanations. Super-quick cultural transmission? Unlikely: the distances are too vast. Telepathy? Ridiculous. A genetic template for song evolution buried in their enormous brains? Warmer, but still no cigar. The mystery remains.

We really have no idea why whales sing, even less than why birds do it. Most biologists stick to traditional sexual selection. To be sure, only the males sing, and only during the winter mating season. Humpback whale song is rarely recorded in the summer. By this light, we can imagine the whales bellowing out the same song competitively one mile from each other in vastly spread-out leks, a titanic insect chorus, the urge to outdo each other driving the changes Cerchio noted. But that doesn't wash, because females are normally nowhere near, and those that are don't seem interested. Others, such Eduardo Mercado, propose that the songs serve echolocation,[49] although most experts object that humpback songs sound nothing like the ultrasound sonar of dolphins, with its incredibly high blips and squeaks. A shame, because it is beautiful to think of these songs, following Mercado, as unfurling 3D sonic maps of the ocean, modelling and conveying information as the whales sail through the depths. Such an explanation would resonate with the idea of human music as a kind of 'landscape' 'walked' by the listener.

The most persuasive theory is that the males sing together for social bonding, as good mammals. Humans do that all the time, of course. When humpbacks perform the same song, they do so out of sync with each other.[50] What is that other than the heterophony (variants of the same song sung simultaneously, as with the Welsh and Tuscan peasants in Chapter 7) performed by singing-dancing choruses at the dawn of human music, with their intertwining limbs and voices?

Let's look at a specific song, and there is none better than the opening track of *Songs of the Humpback Whale*, 'Solo Whale', easily accessible online.[51] You might be struck initially by the incredibly rich palette of sounds, ranging from moans as deep as foghorns to elephant-like trumpeting and trains of broadband clicks and pulses, all the way up to whoops, shrieks and whistles at the upper edge of our hearing. The rattle at the start of the song suggests a motorbike; it alternates several times with what could be mistaken for the cracked horn notes of free jazz, as when Ornette Coleman squeezes impossibly high shrieks through a saxophone or trumpet in one of his avant-garde improvisations. The opening rattle is the distinctive noise whales make when they surface for air, and is called a 'ratchet'. For Cerchio and other whale-watchers, 'ratchets' are a pragmatic place to label the beginning of songs, although this is arbitrary, since the songs repeat seamlessly.[52] On this recording, you can hear the 'ratchet' returning at 5'50", signalling both the imminent return to the surface and the repeat of the cycle. The full song lasts just under six minutes, with the track cutting out halfway through the second repeat (at 9′30″).

'Solo Whale' has a neat and perfectly audible logic, in harmony with the whale's breathing cycle. After the 'ratchet', the song's first half is dominated by ever-rising whoops and whistles. The second half, as the whale descends into the depths, is marked by ever-lower groans and rumbles. Many whale songs have a similar up–down arch contour – not unlike the contour of human songs – but the rhyme both with the breathing cycle and with three-dimensional space is unusually clear in 'Solo Whale'. It has an acoustic logic because high notes travel best on the surface and low notes communicate further down below. The analogy in the avian world, as we saw, was the American parulid warbler, which sings higher the higher it flies. In fact, very few whale songs are as perfect as 'Solo Whale'. If there were more like it, then the daunting diversity of their music would be easier to map. However, its structural and acoustic logic does suggest that it is a kind of archetype, elaborated and varied in similar ways to the way that human composers create variety out of simplicity.

Let's return to the unanswered question of how whale songs evolve between and across seasons. Over a period of time, sometimes years, the same song gets longer and slower, and then suddenly splits into shorter songs, and the lengthening process resumes. Building on the classic Payne and McVay study, a 1983 paper written by Katherine Payne and her colleagues explains how this happens. New themes creep into existing songs in tandem with older themes and become established as the other units are gradually phased out. Two themes tracked across 1976 and 1977 (labelled 'themes 8 and 9') accounted for 63 per cent of the songs, the proportion rising to 100 per cent in 1978, as the remaining themes were eliminated. Moreover, the very order of the themes settled down, theme 8 always leading to theme 9 (previously, 9 often led to 8).[53] The authors also noted that stable themes could split into two new, shorter themes. One remarkable finding is that whales evolved 'transitional phrases' between two themes, which combined features of both. This is what human composers do, mediating contrasting themes with transitions. Whale music has a fluent developmental logic quite unlike the jerky pointillism of birdsong, but much more similar to the way our own music moves.

We must be extremely cautious in drawing comparisons between human and animal music. However, the way whale song evolves, according to the study by the Paynes and others, follows a well-known principle that musicologists call 'troping'.[54] In Gregorian chant and early polyphony, troping means the interpolation of new notes within an existing melody. Over several years or decades, the decorative notes get longer and more established and spawn a new chant; the older notes drop out, and the process starts all over again based on the new chant. New chants give birth to baby chants in an endless cycle. Troping is not confined to the West; similar techniques are found in India and China, owing to parallel invention rather than cultural diffusion. Whale troping is just another example on a long list.

So the explanation of why humpback songs evolve together has less to do with genes than with the population dynamics of musical themes, a principle that seems to cross not just cultures but the species barrier. Some people think that themes evolve like genes, as a musical version of Dawkins's 'memes'. I will explore this idea in Chapter 11. For now, let's consider why, in listening to songs such as 'Solo Whale', we feel such a human, or at least mammalian, kinship with this music.

Oysters taste of the sea, and whale song evokes the ocean's vastness, a musical soul as big as the sea. The music of humpback whales has 'depth' in every sense. I suggest that the secret of our empathy with their music is that, like our music, it is all about motion and change. There is movement within a whale's song in how themes gradually creep up in register and sink down step by step. There is transformational change, one note or gesture melting into another and with 'transitional' phrases. And there is overarching history as the songs evolve within and across seasons. The songs of humpbacks are as liquid as the water they inhabit. And from there comes the difference between whale and human motion. What whale song singularly lacks is the rhythm of bipedalism, the regular march of musical metre, which I claimed in Chapter 4 evolved from *sapiens*' experience of walking upright on two feet. Bipedalism is an important vehicle for primates as they climb up Mount Music. Swimming versus walking, whale song versus human music. The difference may be as basic as that. What really expands the mind is that whales were almost certainly doing this many millions of years before us. We discovered these aliens of inner space in the same decade that NASA vaulted out into outer space.

The Silence of the Apes

There are innumerable works of human music based on birdsong. A delicious example is the main theme of Mozart's seventeenth piano concerto (K. 453), which was inspired by his pet starling. Classical music is populated by a menagerie of insects: crickets (Josquin des Prez's madrigal 'Il Grillo'), bees (Rimsky-Korskov's *Flight of the Bumblebee*), bluebottles (Bartók's *From the Diary of a Fly*) and butterflies (Schumann's *Papillons*). Composers were happy to seize on whale song as soon as it was discovered: for example, George Crumb's *Vox Balaenae*. The only music that I know to feature monkey calls is 'The Funky Gibbon', a 1975 novelty song by the comedian Bill Oddie. As it happens, Darwin in his *The Descent of Man* picked out the gibbon as the exception to the rule that apes and monkeys – and indeed, mammals *in general* – don't sing. 'It is a surprising fact,' he writes, 'that we have not as yet any good evidence that these [vocal] organs are used by male mammals to charm the females.'[55] Darwin had it on good, but as it turned out crazy, authority that gibbons sang octave scales in semitones.

Since Darwin there has actually been a great deal of research on the vocalisation of non-human primates.[56] Given that apes are our closest cousins, it might be expected that their calls shed light on the origin of human music. Yet they don't: ape vocalisation is a blind alley because, simply put, they are *calls* not *songs*. Chimps, bonobos and gorillas lack vocal learning, the prerequisite for defining animal communication as music. In short, ape calls are innate, universal and inflexible. Another crucial deficit is that apes lack rhythm; they can't entrain to a beat.

That said, the three or four standout cases of primate calls are uncannily suggestive of music. When chimps meet, they enact a group ritual called a 'pant-hoot' chorus, and this performance has a satisfying musical structure, building up gradually to climactic screams and then dying down. If you are looking for the origin of human raves, then there is no better example in nature than the chimpanzee 'carnival display', a collective frenzy of shrieking, stomping, tree-slapping and running around by which chimps celebrate occasions such as discovering food or the meeting of subgroups.[57] As for those gibbons, the reality turned out to be even more extraordinary than Darwin imagined. Male and female gibbons sing love duets, intricate and beautiful, sometimes lasting an hour. We also know of song in tarsiers, indri and langurs.[58] The point is, however, that gibbons, tarsiers, indri and langurs are born knowing these sounds, they are the same across the habitat, and they never change. They are calls, not music.

The most interesting exception is a species of Old World monkey from Ethiopia called geladas. They use their rich diversity of calls – exhaled and inhaled moans, wobbles, yawns and grunts – essentially to keep the peace within their harems. In a famous paper, the primatologist Bruce Richman demonstrated that gelada vocalisations fell into four distinct patterns:[59]

(1) Abrupt-onset Series: a simple speeding up to a tempo climax, then a gradual slowing down.
(2) Long Series: a gliding, slow introductory section; then a faster, more staccato middle section with intercalated inspired sounds; and finally a section with a long, melodically complex inspired sound.
(3) Call-response Exchange: a quick-paced and evenly spaced sequence of fast-rising, short grunts from several different voices.
(4) Excited Series: containing a middle section with fast changes in pitch, rhythm and sound quality.

Richman's truly radical observation, however, was that a series could be inflected so as to express simultaneous meanings. Thus a Long Series is normally a clear sign of a gelada male's friendly approach. But Richman also heard a gelada male produce 'a Long Series that is louder and longer and [with] more of a *tight* voice quality than his usual Long Series'. The monkey made this 'tight', or noisy, version of the Long Series after engaging in a bout of threats with some bachelor males. According to Richman, 'by producing a Long Series with a *tight* voice the male is expressing, necessarily, two different emotional/motivational states at the same time'.

At first glance, gelada vocalisations seem much more relevant to the origin of language than to music. They are essentially more complex versions of the famous alarm calls of vervet monkeys. Vervet alarms are specific to predators: loud barks for a leopard; a short double-syllable cough for an eagle; a 'chutter' at the sight of a snake.[60] Yet Richman's finding that geladas use vocal inflection to change the meaning of a call tells us that *prosody* (the emotional tone, contour, rhythm and pace of a voice) was much more important to the origin of language than linguists have thought. That is, linguists such as Noam Chomsky and Ray Jackendoff look at the origin of language in terms of the evolution of syntax, word order.[61] But gelada inflection suggests, on the contrary, that prosody was front and centre in natural communication. For prosody, read music. Yes, gelada vocalisation might well be closer to language than to song. But while it may not be music, it is certainly *musical*.

The musicality of primate communication will be a crucial thread in the next chapter. For now, we'll draw a line under ape calls and consider the weird fact that apes' main contribution to human music was not sonic at all. What the musical human learned from apes was social intelligence, and this intelligence was visual rather than acoustic. Two reports featuring a chimp called Ayumu clearly show where his strengths lie.

Frans de Waal, the leading authority on ape behaviour, tells a story of how Ayumu put human memory to shame.[62] Ayumu lives with other chimps at the Primate Research Institute of Kyoto University, and is given free run of several cubicles equipped with computers:

> Trained on a touchscreen, he can recall a series of numbers from
> 1 through 9 and tap them in the right order, even though the
> numbers appear randomly on the screen and [are] replaced by white
> squares as soon as he starts tapping [...] Trying the task myself,
> I was unable to keep track of more than five numbers after staring
> at the screen for many seconds, while Ayumu can do the same after
> seeing the numbers for just 210 milliseconds. This is one-fifth of a
> second, literally the bat of an eye.

Humans have been trained up to Ayumu's level with five numbers, but he remembers up to nine with 80 per cent accuracy. Ayumu even defeated a British memory champion in memorising an entire stack of cards.

In the second report, we see that this highly intelligent ape flunks a test to discover whether chimps could entrain to a regular beat. Ayumu turns out to have a poor sense of rhythm. In 2013 a team of Japanese scientists led by Yuko Hattori taught Ayumu and two other chimps to tap illuminated keys on an electric keyboard.[63] Then when the chimps were played a pulse of notes at 600 milliseconds ISI (intervals between beats), only one of them aligned her tapping to the beat, and it wasn't Ayumu but another chimp called Ai. Why Ai and not Ayumu? Why was Ai locked into a single pulse (600 milliseconds but *not* 400 or 500 milliseconds ISI), whereas humans can synchronise flexibly to many tempos? Why can't chimps – even exceptional ones such as Ai – synchronise spontaneously in the wild? And the crucial question: how can Ayumu be so bright in one domain, yet helpless in another?

Two physical reasons why monkeys and apes are poor singers is that their vocal tracts aren't well developed, and their tongues lie too flat in their mouths to produce rich formants. Apes are also not very good at aping, being nowhere near as capable as some birds and cetaceans at imitating human speech.[64] Aping, or mimesis, is key to imitating a rhythm. Perhaps the root of the mystery is that ape intelligence is primarily visual. For instance, they are much better than us at reading human body language (and, indeed, remembering flashed numbers). Those celebrated cases when apes seem to understand full human sentences are misleading, because what is really going on is that they are supplementing a rudimentary grasp of the words with an acute perception of our facial expressions and physical gestures.[65]

That creativity, so singularly lacking in ape vocalisation, is in full flood in their physical gestures. While apes lack vocal learning, they learn and create gestures throughout their lives and deploy them in different contexts with great flexibility. This is why palaeolinguists in search of the deep origins of language look to primate gestures, rather than to their vocalisations. According to the primatologist Michael Tomasello, adult chimps, for example, have a repertoire of between thirty and forty gestures including limb movements (such as raising their arm, curling their fingers, reaching and begging), body postures (such as crouching, presenting their anus, jumping up and down), and ten facial expressions for various emotions (such as fear, pleasure, aggressiveness, distress, excitement).[66] They also use tactile gestures, such as putting a hand gently on another's body part or sucking a friend's lower lip, and auditory gestures such as belly slaps and foot stomps.

Within this enormous diversity, Tomasello observes a distinction between *intentional* gestures that are meant to make something happen, especially in the apes' social arena, and gestures made to capture another ape's *attention*. A chimp can raise an arm to display an intention to play, or present the genital area because they want sex. To attract someone's attention, say to some food or to an erect penis, they can slap the ground, stomp or cry out, or indeed produce a string of gestures until the attention is captured. When there is a string of attentional gestures, it is not the particular gestures in themselves that are important, still less the order in which they flow – they hardly represent a language-like 'syntax'. The crucial object, rather, is the goal towards which they are directed. Ape gestures are always pragmatic, intended towards an end.

The watchword of ape gestures, then, is *flexibility*, by which they differ so markedly from their vocalisations. Like most animal calls, ape and monkey vocalisations have a one-to-one correspondence with function, the classic example being the vervet alarm calls discussed earlier. Are vervet cries akin to words or musical units? No, because the alarms are far too limited in number; they are fixed to specific occasions; they are never combined, as words and notes are into sentences and phrases; and because they are innate and universal rather than learned. By contrast, 48 per cent of ape gestures are used in multiple contexts of play, walking, fighting, sex, nursing, grooming or eating.[67] The infant chimp uses the 'gentle touch' gesture in three contexts: to ask her mother to change posture; to change her location; or for food.

The reason that ape gestures are so crucial for the evolution of music, language and human cognition is that they bespeak nothing less than what philosophers call a 'theory of mind'. Their sensitivity to the attentional states of others – their attention to attention – is tantamount to 'mind reading', and is critical for what happens next in the evolution from primates to humans.[68] This includes our amazing ability to share goals, to help each other out, to co-operate in activities, and to point at an object not because we want it, but simply because we find it interesting. Much of this is already implicit in a chimp's ability to follow the direction of a human gaze.

Mind reading in music is born in those proto-conversations between mother and child I explored in Chapter 2, those dialogues between smiles, touches and coos, which imprint all human music as quintessentially social and interactive. Infant caregiver dialogues are drenched in sociality; their meaning exceeds the sonic, and crosses over into the tactile and the visual. They operate in the realm of the gestural.

Human music is essentially social and collective, and what we get from apes, as fellow mammals, is a group spirit. Birds don't have that, because 90 per cent of them sing either individually or as monogamous pairs. The 'dawn chorus' is a misnomer, because it is a cacophony of single birds and couples. True chorusing – all birds singing the same song – is confined to the plain-tailed wren, perhaps because, exceptionally, the birds live and sing in large mixed-sex groups.[69] During territorial song displays, all females sing one part, all males another, in perfect synchrony.[70] But the overwhelming rule is that, unlike us, birds don't use song to bind their group together. Lacking music, chimps, bonobos and gorillas unify their mammalian communities with signals and gestures, and it is this that would become the basis of human music.

Of course, the little we know about animal communication is qualified by a huge suspended question mark. With sharper tools, we may find out tomorrow that there is a lot more complexity in the spectral shape of ape calls than we currently suspect. It all depends on whether, in de Waal's phrase, we are smart enough to understand how smart animals are.

Putting It All Together

The musical human is the great synthesiser. We have the rhythm of insects. We have the melody and vocal learning of birds. We share a sense of musical tradition with whales. From apes we inherited social intelligence, if not music. This is why Stefan Koelsch writes that 'music with metre and scales, sung or played in groups, is a uniquely human phenomenon'.[71] We are exceptional.

Koelsch is correct that music became fully fledged only with the advent of *sapiens*, on the back of the acquisition of symbolic language and technology. But this by no means rules out the fact that human music was exceptional only in the sense of putting together building blocks, or musical faculties, which pre-dated *sapiens*. *Sapiens* synthesised. The faculties of rhythm, melody and culture were distributed among the various species of insects, songbirds and whales, with none of the species having them all.

We also made improvements. Unlike crickets or any other animals, we don't need a visual cue to sing or play in rhythm, and we can continue to beat time once the external time-giver has stopped (when the metronome stops, we hear the metre in our heads). We can also change our tempo at will. Our melodies are longer and more complex than birdsong, and have harmony and counterpoint. Our musical traditions are much longer than those of whales. Every four or five years the humpback's memory seems to reboot itself; its heap of songs doesn't accumulate indefinitely, unlike ours. As a symbolic species, we dump our traditions in external memory banks, such as social rituals, myths, books, scores and instruments. If we are being fanciful, we can imagine that whales anchor their songs in features of the oceanic landscape – perhaps the rolling sea floor – by analogy to how Aboriginal people, as they sail the Australian desert, peg their songlines to rocks and tracks. It would be an elegant solution to the debate about whales using song as sonar. But that is speculation.

All is not positive, because our music is also haunted by loss. Sonic communication is not natural to mammals, as Darwin was the first to observe. Apes in particular are much more comfortable with visual signals. Because humans are also a primarily visual species, music has always been and always will be a marginal Cinderella of the arts. This is why our music is stamped so deeply with an abstract air of imagination, spirituality and inwardness. There is a reason why music is a window to the soul.

Our music is also unnatural because it requires technique: what the ancient Greeks called *technë*, meaning 'craft'. Music, unlike language, is an asymmetrical medium. When someone speaks to you, you speak back. Yet if someone plays the flute to you, you can only respond if you have learned to play this instrument. This asymmetry doesn't trouble singing birds or whales.

The asymmetry originated when mammals in general, and apes in particular, cut the thread of vocal learning. Apes just don't fit within the evolution of music. This ape-shaped hole is conspicuous within the evolutionary model sketched by the Paynes:[72]

Stage I   Crickets
               The songs of crickets are inherited genetically and are
               rigidly fixed with little variability.

Stage 2	Chaffinch and white-crowned sparrow Vocal learning from birds of the same species ('conspecifics') limited to early life, with modest repertoires.
Stage 3	Mockingbird, canary, red-winged blackbird Learning throughout lifetime not only from conspecifics but from other species, and with larger song repertoires at any single time.
Stage 4	Humpback whale Lifelong learning of new versions of song. Songs evolve continuously, with whales learning an enormous repertoire over many years.
Stage 5	Humans Lifelong learning, with the largest and most varied song repertoire of any species.

In the 'hypothetical continuum' between insects and *sapiens*, humpback whales occupy the most advanced stage before us in the variability of their songs. The inspiring final paragraph of the study deserves quoting in full:

> In summary, the study of whale songs has unexpectedly demonstrated a kind of missing link in the continuum of sound display leading from simple stereotyped singing to the full complexity of human song. Instead of viewing human song as an isolated phenomenon, as has often been done in the past, we see now that it may have developed through a simple step-by-step evolution, the stages of which can still be studied by listening to several disjunct species, each singing to us from their respective branches of the phylogenetic tree.[73]

The Paynes' grand view of musical evolution is intoxicating, but it papers over a great discontinuity. Because apes cut the thread of vocal learning, the ability of a creature to pass on a musical tradition to its children and conspecifics, the human ape has had to learn how to learn. Our music is difficult and hard-won.

The rupture of vocal learning echoes at all levels the historical spiral this book has traced, including the three timelines. It resonates at the level of individual life (Part One), when we lose touch with our innate musicality; at an historical level (Part Two), with the gradual fraying of oral tradition, culminating after 1600 with the triumph of a Western musical culture based on notation, scores and the cult of genius. Part Three of this book argues that this rupture originates in the species gap between insects, birds and whales on one side of an evolutionary gulf, and primates and hominins on the other side.

So we close this chapter with a provocation. Next time you are sitting at a dinner party and someone tosses you that old chestnut of a question, 'When did musical modernity happen?' the answer is not the twentieth century, nor the year 1600, nor 70,000–40,000 years ago when hominins matured into *sapiens*. Music became modern approximately 23 million years ago with the apes.

CHAPTER 10
HUMAN

(

One of the most imitated shots in cinema history occurs at the climax of the 'Dawn of Man' scene in Stanley Kubrick's *2001: A Space Odyssey*. Having crushed another hominin's skull with a tapir bone, Kubrick's apeman hurls the femur up in the air. A jump cut turns the slowly spinning bone into a nuclear weapon satellite waltzing above the Earth to the elegant strains of *The Blue Danube*. The inferences are clear. Evolution happens in a blink of an eye. The leap from bone to satellite isn't so great. But the science fiction is equally clear, because we also see that what inspires the hominins is the mysterious appearance of an alien monolith, a 'sentinel'. The film proposes a version of intelligent design, the anti-Darwinian idea that features of the world are explained not through natural selection but by the intervention of a God-like creator. Kubrick's music of intelligent design is the ever-fresh opening of Richard Strauss's *Also Sprach Zarathustra*, the sentinel's theme tune.

We know of course that music isn't a God-given gift but something bred in our bones, and this is even implicit in Kubrick's matching shot. Although *The Blue Danube* is a shock, the waltz's motions materialise from the rotations of the bone, as if music was there all along, even though the apemen are mostly silent. But what if music wasn't a mere back-seat passenger of evolution, but a faculty that chivvied it along? The linguist Steven Pinker's egregious put-down that music was 'auditory cheesecake' – delicious, to be sure, but otherwise a meaningless pattern of pretty sounds – couldn't be more wrong.[1] Maybe, in the evolution from 'Ugh!' to Beethoven, music was always in the driving seat.

This chapter speculates on the evolution of music across the 4 million years between australopithecines, Kubrick's apemen, and the arrival of bone flutes approximately 40,000 years BP (before present). (The machines and aliens will arrive in Chapter 11.) We need to use our imagination in the absence of any living hominins to map from, unlike the contemporary animals and hunter-gatherer societies that illuminated Chapters 9 and 5. In 1866 the Société de linguistique de Paris got so fed up with empty speculations about the origin of language and music that it banned the subject.[2] Since the nineteenth century we have accumulated such a vast stock of evidence that this question has ceased to be a philosopher's parlour game. All the following archaeological discoveries about the evolution of hominin anatomy have a direct bearing on their capacity for song:

- Physical: the hyoid bone evolved, the larynx descended and the vocal tract learned to produce a wider array of sounds.
- Neurological: when the brain tripled in size – inferred from expanding craniums – it forged neuronal links with vocal muscles to control articulation.
- Genetic: the evolution of speech – and by association, song – is connected with the evolution of the FOXP2 gene, which has been recovered from fossils.[3]

Feet and hands also tell a story. Standing up and walking (bipedalism) gave us two-step rhythm, and the link between sound and motion. Manual dexterity enabled us to carve instruments. And the indirect evidence of tool technology, burial practices, the remains of hearths and the use of symbols and ornaments tell us about the evolution of mind and, by extension, of the musical mind. For instance, the march of tool technology, from pebble cores to bifacials to prismatic blades to microliths and hafted composite tools, probably shadowed the evolution of language. A composite tool, assembled from a stick and a blade, suggests an ability to put together words and concepts: what linguists call 'compositionality'. Ergo, a capacity for musical structure.

The evolution of language is an extremely helpful guide to the origin of music. But it is a somewhat untrustworthy one because music is *not* a language. Pinker's dismissal of music is actually very characteristic of linguists like him, because they frame the debate about the origin of communication around what they know best. Admittedly, there are many ways that music and language are similar. They are processed by the same brain modules, including Broca's area. Broca's area, the region of the brain associated with language, 'lights up' on magnetoencephalography scans when test subjects are played a dissonant or nonsensical phrase of music in the same way as it does when they hear a non-grammatical sentence.[4] So it is suggestive that Broca's area crops up in the cranial ridges of *Homo habilis* skulls.[5] Also, music and language both have hierarchical structure, as we saw in the music of birds and whales. Both use an alphabet of discrete sounds (pitches and phonemes). And both benefited from the development of the larynx.

But there are even more ways that music is not like language. Language keeps the reference dimension of animal communication; for instance, how vervet monkeys refer to specific predators. Music retains animal emotion; for instance, how the vervets *feel* about those predators. Language puts grammar and syntax front and centre, while music is more focused on rhythm, melodic contour and timbre (or spectral shape). Although rhythm, melody, colour, tempo and expression are certainly important to speech, they are far less significant than grammar. This is why, when palaeolinguists such as Alison Wray and Ray Jackendoff think about the origin of language, they reverse-engineer syntax, imagining a point far in time from which expressions such as 'Ugh!' break up into individual words and basic sentences.[6] They are 'syntactocentric'.

Obviously, syntactocentric approaches have nothing to say about rhythm and emotion, far more likely sources for music's origin. As we saw in Chapter 9, the rope of music was woven of many strands. One strand is the rhythm of life, especially once it has crystallised into the repetitive actions of flint knapping in the Palaeolithic era. Another strand is gesture, perfected by primates. Yet another is the acoustic dimension of animal cries; for instance, how geladas and chaffinches inflect their vocalisations to convey different meanings.

This is why we must take with a pinch of salt the cliché that language and music grew out of a single root of emotional expression, one branch splitting off into words and concepts, the other into notes and feelings.[7] Calling music a 'language of the passions', following Rousseau, Darwin and many other thinkers, just begs the question. The question is whether music, as a kind of language, points to something in the world, including an emotional attitude towards it, or whether music is not a language at all but a set of enjoyable activities, akin to jogging and dancing, including the pleasant action of binding a group of people together. There are (at least) two roots, not one.

It is possible, then, through a sequence of educated guesses, to subdivide the leap of Kubrick's bone – from apeman grunts to *The Blue Danube* – into at least six intermediate stages. The starting point is animal communication. Second comes bipedalism, the impact of walking. Third is joint rhythmic activity, such as flint knapping. Fourth is protomusic, a rich soup of vocalisations and gestures probably similar to the mother–infant proto-conversations we looked at in Chapter 2. Fifth is a crystallisation of discrete pitches, rhythms and rudimentary structures. Sixth and last is the crossover from vocal to instrumental music – that is, from song to technology – a level of abstraction beyond the reach of Neanderthals because it demands a mature symbolic mind.

The next move is to map these six stages onto six stages of human evolution:

(1) the 'last common ancestor' (or 'missing link'), about 7 million years ago;
(2) Australopithecines, the first hominins, 4.4 million years BP;
(3) *Homo ergaster*, inventor of 'Acheulean biface' hand-axes, 1.5 million years BP;
(4) *Homo heidelbergensis*, the first hominins to reach Europe, 700,000 years BP;
(5) *Neanderthals* overlapping with anatomically modern humans, 200,000 years BP;
(6) *Homo sapiens* (modern humans) and the 'cognitive revolution', 70,000 to 40,000 years BP.

There are many other links in the *Homo* chain: *habilis, rudolfensis, georgicus, erectus, cepranensis, denisova*, and so on. And we increasingly suspect that human evolution was polycentric, mosaic-like and intermittent, not a continuous line. But the perfect is the enemy of the good, and this snapshot tells us that we know a great deal more than nothing.[8] Assuming that our last common ancestors gestured and vocalised like apes, let's pick up the story from stage 2. The first step to music happened literally with the first steps, when australopithecines stood up on their hind paws and walked.

Stage 2: Lucy Walking, 3.2 Million Years Ago

One day about 3 million years ago, in a flood plain in Ethiopia, a twelve-year-old chimp-like creature, just over a metre high, slipped, fell out of a tree and died.[9] The fossilised bones of this *Australopithecus afarensis*, the hominin affectionately christened 'Lucy', showed greenstick fractures consistent with a fatal fall. Perhaps Lucy lost her footing on a tall branch reaching up for a juicy fruit. Had her feet been better adapted for grasping, she might have clung on. Yet her flat feet, together with the angle of her knee joints and the curve of her spine, showed that, despite spending much of her time in trees, Lucy was made for walking (see **Figure 10.1**).

The hominin fossil record actually begins rather earlier than Lucy, 4.4 million years B P with the remains of a female australopithecine nicknamed Ardi, our first known bipedal ancestor. Why was walking such a game-changer in the transition from homin*ids* (apes) to homin*ins* (early humans)? After all, walking appears a minor detail, given that in so many other respects Lucy's anatomy and behaviour wouldn't have been very different from that of apes. Her brain size, gauged from a cranial capacity of about 500 cc, was about the same as a chimp's, a third of that of a modern human. Because her vocal tract isn't developed and the larynx is too high, we surmise that she couldn't speak. Lucy's people didn't wander very far, and they had no tools. Against that, consider all the musical benefits that walking affords:

Sound: Footsteps make sounds, forging crucial links in the
    hominin's brain between sound, motion and muscular exertion.[10]
Rhythm: The two-beat regularity of footfalls ('left-right, left-right')
    would go on to underpin the rhythms of all human music.

Figure 10.1 Lucy walking

Balance: Through Lucy's vestibular system, the rhythm of walking
would have been referred to a sense of balance, each step being
felt, alternately, as a departure from and return to stability.

Time: Walking would have taught australopithecines a sense of pattern predictability and an emerging feeling for time.[11] As each step followed the next – as Lucy listened out for the gait of somebody else and as she walked herself – the footfalls arranged themselves in her mind along a timeline of past, present and future. By contrast, ape consciousness is locked into the present moment.

Musical process: Lucy's forays through the savannah forged the first links between music and journeying. In Chapter 4, I explained how modern humans hear musical processes as purposive yet imaginary pathways through a virtual landscape. The idea that music is motion originates in bipedalism.

Of course, the implications of bipedalism aren't realised until much later in human evolution when the brain, playing catch-up with the body, starts to grow. For music to happen, the brain also needs to get much better at physically controlling the voice. Learning to make sounds with feet helped pave the way for that. Yet arching over the entire early story of hominins is Darwin's observation that mammals generally don't communicate with their voice. We need to resolve the mystery of why mammals hardly ever sing.

The most persuasive explanation was proposed by the American neuroanthropologist Terrence Deacon, as part of his research on how language and the human brain evolved together.[12] The answer has an elegant simplicity, and turns on the involuntary nature of breathing. Breathing needs to run on autopilot, lest we forget to take a breath and choke. This is why the larynxes of mammals are moved by *visceral* muscles – the kind of muscles associated with internal organs, and over which we have no voluntary control. Birds overrode automatic breathing when they learned to fly because of the natural connection between flight control and air control. Cetaceans learned to hold their breath under water so as not to drown. In both cases, birdsong and whale song built on the voluntary control of air tracts by *skeletal* muscles. Humans followed nightingales and humpback whales when they employed skeletal muscles to move their tongues and articulate their respiration. What made this possible, according to Deacon, was the evolution of the brain, starting with the expansion of the primate forebrain, enabling the takeover of motor nuclei by cortical inputs. The incremental shift in cortical control over breathing climaxes in the intricate connections within the human brain between the cortex and the motor system, the structures responsible for movement.

The result is that every word you speak or sing contains a living fossil in its visceral vocal-respiratory components. Overlying this primitive vocalisation is a modern foreground of rapid skeletal articulation. Speech and song project a figure/ground, modern/ancient double perspective. Once voice becomes articulate, supported by brain development, the floodgates open and it is ready to take over from gestures. Tecumseh Fitch found that this was quite literally what happened.[13] Cortical neurons in ape fingers are similar to those in the human voice, so that hand gestures really did transfer into vocal gestures. Prior to that, the voice is actually rather useless in signalling anything beyond the emotions of the individual subject, and this takes us back to the enigma of why communication passed from vision to sound. The fate of music is obviously dependent on that switch.

The limits of sound are explained by an ingenious thought experiment by Tomasello, the primatologist we considered in Chapter 9.[14] He imagines two groups of children who have never learned to talk marooned on two islands, as in William Golding's *Lord of the Flies*. The children on one island are gagged so that they can't communicate with their mouths. The children on the other island have their hands tied behind their backs. Which group discovers communication first? The former. Gestures can point to external objects and mime their size, shape and nature, as in the game of charades or the Nicaraguan Sign Language system.* Vocalisations, by contrast, tend to refer to the emotions of the speaker, not to anything in the outside world, and that doesn't get you very far. Indeed, it turns out that emotions are intimately connected with the involuntary, automated action of breathing. Shouts, laughs, screams, groans, gasps and sobs are reflexive expressions of emotional arousal, often in response to something urgent. Just as they are innate and universal across most cultures, they are inarticulate: that is, they

---

* Arising spontaneously within two Nicaraguan schools for deaf children in the 1980s, the system afforded linguists a rare opportunity to study the evolution of a new language based on gestures.

are moved by the visceral rather than skeletal muscles. Communication involved learning to control not only breathing but also our emotions.

So why, given all its limitations, did sound triumph? Robin Dunbar, the British evolutionary psychologist, thinks that sound emerged because it afforded non-tactile grooming within large groups of apes or hominins.[15] That is, sound can metaphorically 'touch' a crowd of people without literally touching anyone. Vocal grooming is broadcast indiscriminately, like all sound, whereas tactile affiliative gestures are obviously one to one. On the other hand, non-vocal grooming favoured larger and more complex societies. Pressure to communicate across ever greater distances was part of a cluster of adaptations, including a release from the here and now of primate existence, and a turn to a more public life. What gave these adaptations legs was ... legs. The triumph of sound is inextricable from hominins' relentless march to global supremacy, as Lucy's descendants walked out of Africa and into history.

Stage 3: Palaeolithic Rhythms, 1.5 Million Years Ago

After the Quaternary glaciation 2.58 million years BP, Africa's wooded areas dried up as the ice crept in, and coniferous forests yielded to open grasslands.[16] In this cooler, more arid and exposed world of the savannah, hominins clustered and huddled for warmth and security against predators, evolving more complex social skills. With the loss of trees, obtaining nutrients was pressing. What is a stone tool other than a prosthetic tooth for grinding, and then for biting and killing? Tools are incredibly significant for Palaeolithic archaeology. Many thousands of hand-axes survive, and their distribution allows archaeologists to plot the density of hominin life, including people's comings and goings transporting flint materials and conveying finished tools. Thus the radius of these travels – the distance between quarry and found hand-axe – reveals the complexity of society at that time.

There is also the obvious connection with rhythm, created by tapping and knapping flint cores. It is most likely that early hominins would not have intended to make percussive music by hitting stones, and they wouldn't have considered the resulting sounds 'music'. Rhythm was the accidental fallout of organised labour. But through a logical chain of consequences, rhythmic music was born from weather, landscape and food. This is the circuitous route by which rhythmic chorusing passed from insects to humans, albeit leapfrogging birds and non-human mammals.

The first known hominin tools were fashioned 2.6 million years BP by *Homo paranthropus*.[17] These hominins were more gracile (slender) and had bigger brains and stronger teeth than earlier australopithecines. *Paranthropus* invented the 'Oldowan Industry' of stone tools, named after the stone choppers discovered in the Olduvai Gorge in Tanzania. But we will fast-forward another million years to *Homo ergaster* (closely related to the slightly thicker skulled *Homo erectus*), inventor of the more attention-grabbing 'Acheulean bifaces' 1.5 million years BP. These pear-shaped hand-axes were sharply honed on two symmetrical sides. The complex patterns of workmanship that produced such symmetry is the first significant sign of physical dexterity and social intelligence in hominins. With his long skull, thick brow ridges, protruding jaws and no chin, *Homo ergaster* doesn't yet look much like us. But the game hunted with his hand-axes afforded him a rich meat diet, which in turn allowed the hominin brain to expand to 900 cc, nearly double the size of Lucy's. *Ergaster* had no need of *Paranthropus*'s enormous grinding teeth.

Why is the 'Acheulean biface' such a game changer? The skill to create symmetry would have evidenced prowess, and been attractive to a prospective mate. But symmetry is also beautiful in itself, and the hand-axes suggest that *Homo ergaster* took aesthetic pleasure in elegant objects.[18] Thirdly, the sense for symmetry would have been cross-modal; it would have crossed from vision into sound, and been audible in the regular patterns of flint knapping, and in the overarching rhythms of Palaeolithic life.

It should be stressed that rhythm crept in sideways onto the world stage, because both music and language still lay about a million years downstream in human evolution. In a close-knit Palaeolithic society there was actually very little need for oral communication, because hominins would have got by with gesticulation and grooming, probably not much more complex than in ape societies.[19] Consider how much communication goes on in silent movies. The all-embracing rhythms of Palaeolithic life were music before music, as it were. Let's consider why rhythm was such a powerful driving force in the evolution of mind and society.

Tim Ingold coined the neat word 'taskscape' to capture how the Palaeolithic landscape is a space not just of features but of activities.[20]

The taskscape was based on the 'rhythms of action', as people moved backwards and forwards through their environment along paths and tracks, encountering one another, greeting acquaintances or fleeing from strangers, gathering together or moving apart, foraging plants, killing and carrying animals, finding appropriate stones, conveying them, carving them. In this world of routines, the rhythms of life were most concentrated in the chain of technical gestures it took to make a stone tool. The great French anthropologist André Leroi-Gourhan calls this sequence of actions a *chaîne opératoire*, an 'operational chain'.[21] The complex chain of steps needed to turn a lump of rock into a bifacial hand-axe is 'rhythmic', in this deep and powerful sense. There are many YouTube videos that teach you the successive stages of 'core reduction': striking a flint with a hammerstone, removing fine flakes so as to expose flat 'platforms' on two sides, working all the way round while alternating between sides, gradually reducing the core, sharpening and polishing the resulting edges.[22] Core reduction was just as rhythmic as the ordered stream of pulses that resounded when hammerstone met flint. But the audible rhythm was only the tip of a vast iceberg of rhythm. Under the surface there is much more going on.

An operational chain can be as automatic and unconscious as when we drive a car (all those complex manoeuvres of feet, hands and eyes, which have become second nature to practised drivers). It is a suite of muscle memories, blurring the line between mind and body. That is, most routines don't require much conscious thought. Because routines can be easily imitated, and handed down to the next generation, Palaeolithic muscle memory was the basis of tradition. The rhythms of flint knapping were easily imitated by onlookers: this was 'horizontal' cultural transmission. And they could be taught to one's children: this was 'vertical' transmission. Rhythm was the driver of cultural evolution.

You could say, then, that tradition was a frozen lump of muscle memory.[23] And it was embodied in the sheer repetition of hand-axe manufacture across much of the world, as standardised in its way as Henry Ford's Model T cars in the twentieth century. Starting in Ethiopia, the skill to make Acheulean bifaces spread to Asia (the Zhoukoudian hand-axes of 'Peking Man'), the Middle East (in the Levantine Corridor, including the Dead Sea), to Europe (the French district of Saint-Acheul that gave the tool its name). As a physical object, an Acheulean biface was repetition incarnate.

And regarding *Homo ergaster*'s rhythmic faculty itself, it was infinitely more complex than that of the brainless crickets. A hominin's entrainment to a rhythmic pattern was voluntary, not automatic. *Ergaster* could choose to beat in time with others; for a katydid, entrainment was a chemical reflex. Hominins could express a rhythm across their entire body – tapping their fingers, nodding their head, swaying their trunk, all at the same time. In other creatures, rhythm is localised in only one part of the body. Hominins could change the tempo of a rhythm at will, and even imagine it in their head, continuing without an external beat. Through imagination, hominins extended rhythm to the social realm, as when they took turns to groom each other. Our rhythmic conversational turn-taking lay somewhat in the future. But it was anticipated in hominins' ability to mirror each other's gestures, calls and states of mind.

We thus see how rhythm intersects with mimesis, our faculty for imitation. The psychologist Merlin Donald, in his influential book *The Origins of the Modern Mind*, proposed that human evolution pivoted on the decisive step from the 'episodic' mind of the ape to hominins' 'mimetic' culture.[24] Mimesis has nothing to do with the virtuoso imitation of the lyrebird or cockatoo (and which apes are actually rather bad at). Animals, trapped in the present tense, can't recall 'episodic' memories; they can't do what psychologists call mental time travel (MTT).[25] Chimps might be very good at short-term memory games, as we saw earlier. But they can't recall and think about a mental representation at will, away from the time and place of its original occurrence. This is why apes don't practise their skills and improve. Rehearsing a knapping gesture in our heads is also a kind of rhythm.

As we saw in Chapter 9, apes not only lack vocal learning, they are also poor at entraining to a rhythm. Hominins evolved their rich world of rhythm from scratch; it co-evolved with their expanding social complexity, and partly as a dividend of bipedalism. You could even say that hominin and human culture was rhythmic. Culture is an 'external oscillator' to which we entrain.[26]

Mental time travel, a gift granted to hominins and perfected by humans, blends into the evolving brain's ability to think and act beyond the here and now. The archaeologist Clive Gamble calls this ability to think at a distance 'release from proximity'.[27] It entailed the 'stretching of social relationships across time and space' between ever larger social groups, from family members to friends, to friends of friends, to strangers, in parallel with the expansion of the brain.[28] Mental time travel might explain how *Homo ergaster* first imagined music beyond the immediate context of work; that is, hearing rhythm for the first time *as music*, not just as knapping. Let's indulge ourselves in a little just-so story.

An *ergaster* teenager has sloped off from the quarry for a stolen hour with some male friends. (Teenagers were only invented in the twentieth century [Chapter 2], but let's go with this.) He shows his friends what he has made: a symmetrical biface hand-axe, and he runs his fingers along the polished facing edges. The object is as sexually alluring as a peacock's tail. But unlike the bird's plumage, he has made this beauty himself, and it is admired by a group of giggling females idling by the tree. He hits the biface rhythmically, in sync with the beat made by the knappers in the quarry below. But there is a vital difference between beating in time to carve a flint, and rhythm enjoyed in itself, away from its original place or function. It is a sonic version of the biface's visual beauty, a musical peacock's tail.

Stage 4: Protomusic, 500,000 Years Ago

Over time, the voice became *Homo*'s natural instrument. Exactly when this happened is unknown, because the fossil record of vocal anatomy isn't as conclusive as one might hope.[29] Take the example of the gradually descending larynx, the classic marker of vocal evolution. Mongolian gazelles also have descended larynxes, but they can neither sing nor speak.[30] More promising is the evolution of the hyoid bone, which anchors the tongue muscles and is essential for articulation. Hyoids in great apes are tiny, and balloon into laryngeal air sacs. Non-bullate (that is, lacking air sacs) hyoids have been recovered from *Homo heidelbergensis* fossils, dating the possible (yet still unproven) onset of language at 700,000 years B P.[31] A recently discovered australopithecine basihyoid bone from Ethiopia, belonging to a three-year-old 'Lucy', is very similar to that of a chimpanzee, and suggests that early hominins retained air sacs. In other words, we lost our air sacs as our hyoids grew bigger.[32] On the other hand, colobine monkeys also have hyoids but no air sacs, so the theory breaks down.[33]

If anatomy doesn't get us very far, then we can look to all the collateral evidence of growing social complexity. A dramatic example of the 'social stretching' Gamble talks about is the increasing distance that raw materials were carried in order to make hand-axes. In the Lower Palaeolithic (2 million years BP), the average distance between a tool's place of discovery and the quarry from which the lithic material was extracted was less than thirty kilometres.[34] In the Late Upper Palaeolithic (40,000 years BP), this distance had rocketed to 200 kilometres. The growing quantity, quality and variety of the stone and flint is also revealing. And the sheer proliferation of tools is another sign of widening social circles. Flint shards, flaked off the core by the master knapper, were given out as gifts to valued acquaintances. Mirroring the ties between shards and the mother lode, the recipients of the gift were under an obligation to their benefactor.

One of the most vivid footprints of complex Palaeolithic society is Boxgrove in West Sussex, the site of the oldest human remains found in Britain.[35] Dated 500,000 years BP, these are the bones of *Homo heidelbergensis*, the first *Homo* to settle Europe, and a species with well-developed hyoids, as we have already seen. There are also bones of large animals butchered there. Rhinos and giant deer once roamed the British Home Counties. But at Boxgrove they mostly butchered horses on flint blocks extracted from the cliff and conveyed about 250 metres onto a large mudflat. The meat would have been stripped and taken away quickly before its smell could attract the attention of dangerous predators. Working together at speed would have required high levels of organisation.

It is often supposed that prehistoric archaeology doesn't deal with individual people, only societies, but that is not the case. It doesn't matter that we don't know these people's names (if they had names), because the material record can be eloquent. We can thus see that, at one locale, eight blocks were used by eight individuals. And we can surmise, from the 321 hand-axes found at Boxgrove, that tools were made as needed and then thrown away rather than carried and curated. Boxgrove was a site of multiple visits rather than a permanent settlement, so we can infer that culture was still peripatetic and ephemeral. Still, the record of multiple visits suggests that the celebratory ritual dance, which would have followed the butchering and consumption of the meat – either on the mudflat's natural performance space or far away, might have contained memories of earlier dances. Was this the beginning of musical memory and tradition?

The social complexity of Boxgrove is proof of shared intentionality, our ability to attend not just to another person's *attention*, like apes following the line of a gaze, but to read someone's *state of mind*. Yet to imagine what kind of music happened at Boxgrove requires a particularly educated guess.

A primitive, intermediate music is analogous to what linguists call 'protolanguage' or 'protodiscourse'. Gary Tomlinson persuasively draws the threads together to argue that hominin protomusic would have evolved out of 'gesture-calls'.[36] Gesture-calls are the anthropologist Robbins Burling's term for the bodily signs and vocal sounds humans have continued to make alongside language.[37] They include laughs, sighs, gasps, groans, sobs, smiles and frowns, and they differ from regular language in important ways. We are all born with gesture-calls, and so don't need to learn them. They are much the same across all cultures. They are closely linked to emotions, and are triggered automatically along with those emotions, so that we sob when sad, gasp when surprised and so on. Unlike the sounds (phonemes) of an alphabet, gesture-calls are hard to abstract from meaning or emotion, they can't be combined into words or sentences, nor can they be broken down into smaller units (what are the units of a smile?). Instead, they are subject to a sliding scale, for instance a giggle growing into a laugh, to a guffaw, to a snort, to a cry. This is why Burling calls gesture-calls 'analog', whereas the units of proper language (sounds and words) are 'digital'. There are no gradations between the words 'cat' and 'bat' (digital), as there are between a sigh and a sob (analog).

The gesture-calls of early hominins would most likely have been very similar to ours. But the evolution from gesture-calls to protomusic would have taken several decisive steps.

The development of the vocal tract would have triggered an explosion in the variety of sounds our voices could produce. And it meant we could physically control them better. That is, the range of gesture-calls expanded exponentially. With far more sounds than we needed, vocalisation was loosened from emotion. Whereas sobs, gasps and chuckles went with particular feelings and occasions, like the vervet's alarm signals, sounds now floated free and were invested with fresh meanings. In Darwinian terms, vocalisation was decoupled from natural selection. An experiment with domesticated Bengalese finches showed that, once birdsong was liberated from the outside world, where calls served an adaptive function, it evolved exponentially faster.[38] Tomasello calls this process a 'drift to the arbitrary', the abstraction of sounds out of context.[39] Another key step was that sounds no longer depended on physical gestures. Once a humble supplement or reinforcement to actions, postures and facial expressions, sounds came of age as a self-contained system.

We have not reached music yet, however, nor indeed language. Protomusic was essentially a hyper-refined vocabulary without grammar, a collection of sounds whose meanings didn't depend on the order in which they were arranged. The best-known modern example of protomusic is the soundtrack to cartoons such as *Tom and Jerry*.[40] Tom slides down the neck of a standard lamp on a trombone glissando. He creeps along the floor with stealthy bassoon notes, and when a floorboard creaks, the violins mark his panic with a trill. Butch the bulldog chases Tom, and as his gnashers gradually gain on the cat's rump, trumpets get louder and louder, rise by step, and slow down dramatically just as jaws snap on tail, to the snap of wood blocks. Jerry holds on to Tom by his whiskers, which break one after another with the twangs of violin pizzicatos. Jerry plummets into Butch's mouth along a violin slide. Jerry slides down the curtains (xylophone glissando) into the basket, unravelling the jumper, his zig-zagging mirrored by oscillating woodwind scales. And so on.[41]

All these slides, wobbles, yelps, growls and freezes are fancy versions of gesture-calls, played by an orchestra. They are disconnected bursts of sound with no grammar. They capture a set of actions, seamlessly blended with the emotions involved in those actions. Much of the cartoon is devoted to reaction shots: cat, mouse and dog reacting to each other's actions and emotions. Tom, Jerry and Butch are imaginary animals diverting modern-day children (and child-at-heart adults), but their holistic protomusical gestures aren't a million miles – or a million years – away from how music started.

This thought experiment is pure conjecture, of course. Nevertheless, it permits two conclusions. One: the shift from protomusic to music must have happened at some point within the last 2 million years. Two: for reasons of social complexity, it is most likely to have happened 500,000 years ago.

Stage 5: Hmmmmm? 250,000 Years Ago

The next episode in the story of music is the cliffhanger. It tells of when music separated from language and went to live alone. (Note the paradox: these two concepts, 'music' and 'language', only became meaningful after the divorce.) Music specialised in what it does best once it was relieved of the responsibility of saying anything, a burden taken up by language. The protagonists of this story are two warring species. The problem is that one of them was partially fictional.

Novels such as William Golding's *The Inheritor* (1955) cemented an image of Neanderthals as gentle and innocent creatures, wiped out by cleverer and more malevolent *sapiens*. Golding portrays them as living entirely in the present moment with little memory or language to speak of, without gifts of fire, weapons or sailing, yet compensated with heightened sense impressions and telepathic communication. The story is all the more poignant because it is told from the bewildered perspective of the dimmest Neanderthal of the tribe, Lok. At the end of the novel, Lok dies from grief, the last surviving member of his species after the rest of his tribe has been picked off by humans.

The evidence tells us that Neanderthals were probably not the sweet-natured, dopey, somewhat bovine lunks we may picture them to be. We can gauge their disciplined social coordination from the ferocity of the animals they hunted.[42] They were ruthless and brutish. And yet the idea of murdered innocence resonated with the post-war world, especially after the Lascaux cave was opened to the public in 1948 and captured people's imagination with its spectacular paintings. It is in this spirit that we should approach Steven Mithen's *The Singing Neanderthals*, a book as remarkable as it is necessarily speculative.[43]

The upshot of Mithen's book is that Neanderthals were intrinsically more musical than *sapiens*, the species that displaced them. In his view, our extinct cousins perfected a protomusic he calls 'Hmmmmm', which is an acronym for: 'Holistic, manipulative, multi-modal, musical and mimetic'.[44] *Holistic*: they sang in utterances that were whole and complete in themselves, rather than being combinations of notes or words. *Manipulative*: the sounds made things happen by moving other Neanderthals emotionally and binding them into a group. *Multi-modal*: the sounds accompanied gesture and body language. *Mimetic*: they mimicked the sounds and motions of animals, a bit like the protomusic of *Tom and Jerry*. The contour of their voice – rising in tension, soothing as it fell, accelerating and slowing down – imitated the contour of the passions. All told, Neanderthal communication was *musical*.

Essentially, Mithen's book argues that Neanderthals took the protomusic of hominins as far it could go without it becoming symbolic. The clue is that, although their culture endured for hundreds of millennia, it didn't change much. Neanderthals never evolved any symbolic artefacts or complex tools, which also suggests that they got by without language, like earlier hominins.

The difficulty for Mithen's theory is that it is impossible to prove that Hmmmmm protomusic wasn't sung by earlier hominins, such as *heidelbergensis*. Conversely, it is rather more likely that Neanderthals had proper language, the issue being whether it was as advanced as that of *sapiens*. In a remarkable modern development, a strain of the FOXP2 gene – the gene associated with language acquisition – was recovered from Neanderthal fossils.[45] This seems strongly to suggest that Neanderthals had evolved complex vocal learning just like us. On the other hand, it was later shown that humans express FOXP2 in a more refined way.[46] So the current consensus is that Neanderthals and humans both evolved language, although theirs was probably a less sophisticated version.

Given that no actual records of prehistoric language survive, where do we go from here? We turn again to the discipline of palaeolinguistics. While Chomsky's writings on universal grammar in the 1950s and 1960s revolutionised linguistics, revealing that all languages across the world were transformations of a 'deep structure' in the brain, his theory doesn't sit well with Darwinian evolution. By Chomsky's lights, language sprang fully formed as an undecomposable 'grammar box'. But this just sounds implausible, and Chomsky's former student, the linguist Ray Jackendoff, showed that, rather than being a unified system, language is really a collection of simpler systems.[47] Just as a complex trait can be broken down into its subcomponents, the evolution of language can be reconstructed as an *incremental* sequence of distinct steps. This is the argument I made in Chapter 9 about the evolution of musicality from its subcomponents of rhythm, melody and structure.

Jackendoff shows us that modern language is littered with living fossils. Some utterances, such as *ouch*, *wow* and *dammit*, convey extreme emotion as a single gesture. Others – *ssh, psst, hey* – make things happen. There are compound nouns that chain words together with no syntax, like *snowman, wheelchair* or even *two-axle diesel/electric engine/dumper truck*. In primitive stages of syntax, the meaning of a word depends on its position in the sentence. When grammar becomes more secure, word order can be inverted, and elaborated with lots of subordinated clauses in complex hierarchical structures. Hamlet speaks in complex syntax. To hear primitive syntax, we don't need to go back in time: its modern evidence is the simplified language of pidgin or creole, agrammatic aphasics, and the famous case of 'Genie', a woman who grew up from the age of two to thirteen without any human contact.[†]

The link with music is simple and straightforward. Gary Tomlinson makes the obvious connection between compositionality in language and in music.[48] Just as a sentence is *composed* of independently existing units – words – melodies are *composed* of notes. Tomlinson then forges the further link with compositionality in tools such as spears. A Palaeolithic spear is a composite of a stick and a flint. Stick and flint exist as separate objects before they are assembled, through hafting, into a composite object that is bigger than the sum of its parts.

The crucial claim is this: *sapiens* invented music and language at the same time as spears. Everything before *sapiens* was different shades of holistic (non-compositional) protomusic. A hominin rock is a holistic tool with no separate parts, just as 'Ugh!' is a holistic utterance with no component syllables or words.

Now, there are a couple of problems in Tomlinson's argument. The famous Schöningen spears, dated 420,000 BP, show that *Homo heidelbergensis* knew about hafting. On the other hand, Schöningen appears to be a one-off: cultural evolution proceeds in spurts, and some initiatives fizzle out without firming up into a tradition. Hafting is *generally* associated with the Upper Palaeolithic. The second problem is that biology doesn't map cleanly onto behaviour. That's why some hunter-gatherer societies today have complex (compositional) languages while using Stone Age tools.

That said, Tomlinson's argument is persuasive in the round. The evolution of mind can be read off the evolution of tool technology. And we can deduce that as hominins became cleverer, so did their music. Composite melody had certainly arrived by the time *sapiens*

[†]   See Ray Jackendoff, *Foundations of Language: Brain, Meaning, Grammar, Evolution* (New York: Oxford University Press, 2002), p. 97. Genie was discovered aged thirteen in 1970, having been isolated from all human contact since she was two. After intensive teaching, Genie quickly acquired a vocabulary. Nevertheless, she never learned the basic principles of grammar, suggesting that the age of thirteen was too late for a brain to develop language.

had invented bone flutes *c.*40,000 years B P. We can extrapolate a series of intermediate stages of musical structure. Neanderthal music might have been non-compositional, because Neanderthals tended not to use composite tools. But their music might have displayed another feature of linguistic structure: *hierarchy*.

Hierarchy and compositionality are both present in language. But it's possible to have one without the other. As we saw in Chapter 9, birdsong has a hierarchic structure. But its units don't make any sense outside the song itself; the bird doesn't compose his song from a set of pre-existing 'words'. Its hierarchy is phonetic rather than semantic. In human song, a non-composite melody is a *contour*. A contour can be broken down into bits of sound, but it isn't assembled from them. Modern-day children perceive melody as contour until the age of five or six, when they learn to discriminate individual pitches (see Chapter 2). This is strikingly the same period that they separate syllables into phonemes or alphabet letters in language.[49] If melodic contour is older ontogenetically (in terms of human development), it is almost certainly also older phylogenetically (in the evolution of the human species).

Why, then, do we think that Neanderthal music was hierarchic but not compositional? We know that Neanderthals were capable of hierarchic thought because they perfected a style of hand-axe facture called 'Levallois'.[50] Much more than Acheulean hand-axes, Levallois technique comprised a series of distinct stages, each with its own method: roughing out the general shape; chipping away large flakes; building up the tortoise-shaped dome, which is then lifted away to reveal a concave indentation; retouching and polishing, etc. Levallois indicates an ability to organise *actions* hierarchically, even though the finished item was composed of a single piece.[51] Levallois technique was hierarchic, but the axes themselves were not composite, unlike spears.

The evolution of Palaeolithic hunting tools runs through four main stages: Oldowan choppers – Acheulean bifaces – Levallois hand-axes – hafted spears (see **Figure 10.2**). So does the evolution of hominin musical structure. The Oldowan choppers would have banged out irregular spurts of rhythm. The symmetry of Acheulean bifaces would have translated into regular rhythmic patterns. Levallois hierarchy suggests a kind of melody with no pre-existing parts: contour. Music arrives when humans haft pitches into melodic spears.

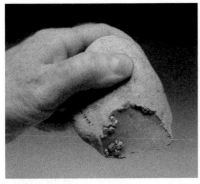

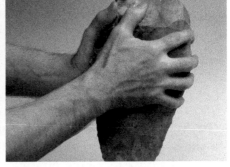

1. Oldowan flint, 2.4 million years old   *2.* Acheulian Biface, 1.8 million years old

3. Levallois hand-axe, 300,000 years old   *4.* Spear-hafting, 100,000 years old

Figure 10.2

The Magic Flute, 40,000 Years Ago

So many things come together with the emergence of *Homo sapiens* in the Aurignacian period of the Upper Paleolithic, dated from about 43,000 to 26,000 years BP. Anatomically modern humans, similar to us in mind and limb, threw wooden spears hafted with finely honed blades rather than crude flakes. They knew sailing and used fire. They wore pendants and bracelets of pierced animal teeth, ivory beads and sea shells, and smeared their bodies with ochre.[52] Their caves were decorated with astonishing hunting scenes, and they carved figurines that would have graced Picasso's workshop. They almost certainly had language. But most important for our purpose is that Aurignacian humans made the oldest known musical instruments in prehistory, the flutes recovered from the Swabian Alps in Germany (Hohle Fels and Geissenklösterle) and the Pyrenees (Isturitz). We paid them a backward glance in Chapter 5 as an origin of music; we will now approach from behind, as a culmination. They are the grace notes of a 'cognitive revolution'.

But was it a revolution at all? Archaeologists fiercely debate the exact arrival date of anatomically modern humans; they can't even agree about what constitutes 'modern'.[53] The paintings, figurines and bone flutes recovered from the south German caves suggest that *sapiens* only became modern within Europe and the Middle East 50,000 years ago. Yet incised ochre fragments in the Blombos Cave, South Africa, have been dated as 90,000–70,000 years BP; and archaeological deposits of red ochre have been found in Africa from 125,000 years BP.[54] Given that absence of evidence is not evidence of absence, why not push back symbolic behaviour 200,000 years, to the dawn of human time?

While the debates continue to rage, I concur with Iain Morley's argument detailed in Chapter 5. Morley proposed that *sapiens* probably achieved artistic and intellectual maturity 100,000 years ago, roughly before Blombos, but that they lacked the opportunity to make flutes because Africa had very few birds with appropriate hollow bones.

In this light, we are crossing not one threshold but two. The first threshold was most likely crossed in Africa, when *sapiens* composed melodies out of discrete pitches. Neanderthals sang in contours, but human melody – like human spears – had compositionality. The second threshold was technological. As we saw, despite the enormous longevity and stability of their culture, Neanderthals never evolved any symbolic artefacts or complex tools. Mithen infers that Neanderthal brains were modular, and that their faculties were encapsulated in separate mental spaces.[55] Neanderthal brains were 'domain-specific'. While they could imagine music, and they could make tools, they lacked the cognitive fluidity to cross from one domain to the other – to conceive of a tool that made music. Imagining musical technology required integrated thought between two mental spaces, a capacity that was simply beyond them. *Sapiens*, by contrast, were masters of mental play. Only *sapiens* could imagine a flute. This was the *real* cognitive revolution.

Flutes were packed with significance. First and foremost, flutes were manufactured objects; small enough to be carried, and sufficiently valuable to be cared for and preserved. Immersed as we are in a world of artefacts – from the book or device on which you are reading these words, to your house filled with things blending seamlessly into streets, roads and cities – it is difficult for us to imagine how brightly artificial objects would have shone within the empty Palaeolithic landscape.[56] Forty millennia ago, an object would have been charged with human meaning, with the life of the person who made it. And crucially, objects could exude this meaning far away from their maker. Objects extend society. You can't know everyone outside your circle of friends and acquaintances, the group size for *Homo sapiens* in the Upper Palaeolithic being about 300 people spread between thirty and a hundred kilometres.[57] Like a suspension bridge, society can't stretch for ever without collapsing. Objects – human proxies – are the piers and pillars that support our global bridge of culture.

Objects are also our memory banks. In a literal sense, the flutes at Hohle Fels and Geissenklösterle are incised with parallel notches and lines. Some archaeologists think that these constitute a kind of artificial memory system, storing information about when or how the pipes were used.[58] Whatever the function of these marks, the flutes – like objects in general – were memory containers by their very nature. Just as the hand-axe was seen as an extension of the arm, and expressed the gestures to swing it, the flute's finger holes tell you where to place your fingers and the mouthpiece where to blow. We fill objects with our thoughts and feelings so that they can survive us, as indeed these flutes have survived. Because we externalise our memories in objects, culture evolves much faster than people. We can sharpen a spear, mend a fishing net, make a hut warmer and hone a flute in minutes, whereas human evolution took thousands of generations. This is why it is often observed that human evolution is Darwinian, based on natural selection, whereas cultural evolution is Lamarckian, through the inheritance of acquired characteristics.[59]

Lastly, and most significantly, more than expressing life, Palaeolithic objects were felt to be alive in themselves. Like the extraordinary Lion-man figurine, an ivory sculpture of a man with the head of a lion discovered near to Hohle Fels in the Hohlenstein-Stadel cave (see **Figure 10.3**), the flutes are also human-animal composites.[60] Carved from wing bones of vultures and swans, the flute invested the musician with the power and spirit of the animal as he played it, as with the hunter-gatherer shamans of Chapter 5. The musical human came from animals, and will always be entangled with animals.

Because of the enormous value invested in such instruments, including the skill and time it took to carve them, the flutes seem made to be carried, epitomising the 'portability principle' discussed in Chapter 5. Yet the value of objects cut two ways: to turn a gathering into a home, you entrusted it to store things. Neanderthals, who wandered seasonally without permanent settlements, carried everything they needed and stored nothing.[61] But with *sapiens*, music set its roots into a more secure sense of place, which complemented the new role of objects in the world, as we can deduce through a chain of inferences. Homes were created with physical structure: tent poles, a stone circle, a permanent hearth detected today by burnt cobbles next to remains of plant-food mush possibly meant for infants.[62] Homes were where mothers stayed behind, a necessity if hunters were to travel further. A home is really a place to store not just things but families. And once a stable dwelling is established, it affords a centre for social occasions and the rituals that decorate them, including music, which we can imagine sung, played and danced around the hearth. The centrality and permanence of the hearth is a good metaphor for music's new identity as a solid and enduring 'thing'.

These homes having been all swept away, all we have left is the caves. While we like to fixate on cave art, it is important to remember that in one sense caves were atypical because they were inaccessible, dark, dangerous places (the lair of beasts), associated with the dead as natural

Figure 10.3 The Hohlenstein-Stadel Lion Man

portals to the spiritual realm, and for all these reasons probably sites to use or to visit rather than to inhabit.[63] In another sense, however, caves recorded early humans' supreme accomplishment: imagining the invisible, the far away or the non-existent. Like the distant hunting scenes on the cave walls, the flute player possessed by an animal spirit transported the listeners to the spiritual beyond. Life for hominins used to be local. Art and music now extended the reach of life indefinitely, like the Dreamtime of the Australian Aboriginal peoples. Another sign that *sapiens* saw a continuity of life beyond the living was their practice of burying their dead with funerary ornaments.

For all these many reasons, the flutes of early humans were magic flutes, the magic tinged with the spirituality of the first religion. This is the standpoint from which to approach the tipping point into musical abstraction. The sheer existence of finger holes, and the standardisation of instrument design over many thousands of years and across a wide geography, tells us that music was regimented. If a hole gave you a particular pitch – say a D – then that note was fixed; you couldn't sing any pitch you liked. And by virtue of being a distinct pitch, it meant that an alphabet of pitches had fully crystallised.[64] And the existence of an alphabet of pitches points to the presence of a background tonal system: melodic patterns and scales, in which some notes were more important or 'central' than others. And having central notes and more ornamental ones suggests that the musicians could riff on melodic ideas, as we play a theme and variations. Finally, this musical language would have been shared across the population, like the spears or shells transported and exchanged, and the styles of hafting or decoration admired and imitated.

There can be no doubt, then, that the magic flute played a starring role in *sapiens'* cognitive revolution, and that the fate of the musical human was written in its musical DNA. The story launched in Chapter 1 of this book, music's drift towards abstraction and the loss of emotional immediacy, is done and dusted in *sapiens'* own opening chapter. Whatever killed the Neanderthals, whether it was genocide by humans, interbreeding with them or just natural extinction, it is hard not to be affected by the pathos of the fairy tale that, with their demise, something in music died too. The fairy tale stays the same even if we reject Mithen's account and back-project Hmmmmm or protomusic further down the evolutionary chain to *Homo ergaster* or to Lucy. From where we are at this point of the story, in the Upper Palaeolithic, we can now see the loss of emotion as the inevitable casualty of social stretching and the 'release from proximity'. But as I have repeated throughout this book, music's story can always be read in two directions, forwards or backwards. In the nick of time, another tool – cleverer than a stick or a rock – comes to the rescue.

In the evolution of tools, cutting, grinding and spearing implements came first; containers followed later.[65] Apes regularly fish for termites with sticks, but rarely use containers (although chimps have been observed carrying rainwater in leaves or in their cupped hands). Containers came into their own in the Upper Palaeolithic, in the form of cups, caves and houses, and eventually as ceramics. Ceramic pots were conceived as surrogates for the human body, itself a container for the spirit. A hollow musical instrument, such as a flute or a drum, is an example of a container. A flute contains breath and spirit, and by extension music contains emotion. It harbours the emotion we thought of as lost in the push from an intimate to a social world. But through containment emotion is intensified, rarefied and distanced from language and meaning. Emotion has become metaphorical. A single note played on a flute doesn't 'mean' anything at all; much less than a note when it is wept or roared by a voice. Yet a *group* of notes brings meaning back through the back door, when a flautist 'walks' from one pitch to another, in the metaphorical 'pathways' we traversed in Chapter 4. The story of hominin music began with Lucy walking. The magic flute lifts the perambulating australopithecine to the heavens where she walks among the stars.

Being Homer

We don't need to look far to find a human ape floating in the stars. All the iconic scenes from *2001: A Space Odyssey* were parodied in *Simpsons* episodes.[66] An ape with Homer's face leans back against the monolith and snoozes, while other apes are busy inventing weapons and fire. A human Homer daydreams in a comfort chair and flies through a wormhole. A pen thrown by Bart spins up into space, turns into a Fox satellite and clunks Homer's head as he floats above the planet as the Starchild embryo, our next evolutionary step. Doh!

The Simpsons set the bar modestly low for what it means to be human. But the baseline for being human, even being Homer, is the mastery of time and space. According to André Leroi-Gourhan, 'the human act *par excellence* is perhaps not so much the creation of tools as the creation of a human time and space'.[67] We have seen how Palaeolithic rhythms helped humans do that. Space wasn't a place where rhythms happened; rhythms created space. Music took us beyond the here and now of animal life. It stretched our social world, and gave us mental time travel. Mithen hits the nail on the head:

> Throughout history we have been using music to explore
> our evolutionary past – the lost world of 'Hmmmmm'
> communication – whether this is Franz Schubert writing his
> compositions, Miles Davis improvising or children clapping in the
> playground.[68]

Writing a history of the musical human is simply following where music wants to lead: deeper and deeper into the evolutionary past.

Emotion is the key to how music does that. It is the interspecies umbilical cord connecting us to Mother Nature. Consider, dare I say it, the *humanity* expressed in this elephant greeting ceremony:

> The two subgroups of the family will run together, rumbling,
> trumpeting, and screaming, raise their heads, click their tusks
> together, entwine their trunks, flap their ears, spin around and back
> into each other, urinate and defecate, and generally show great
> excitement. A greeting such as this will sometimes last for as long as
> ten minutes.[69]

Whether or not this counts as 'music', it is easy for us to identify with these elephants' sonic joy (well, with most of it). To be sure, elephants may have no human notion of space or time. But on their side, elephants have an infrasonic vibrational communication system – flowing through the earth beneath their feet to connect herds many miles apart – as yet undreamt of in our philosophy.[70]

While musical emotion looks backwards, some of its other aspects press towards the future. According to Ian Cross, music has a 'floating intentionality'.[71] That is, music's apparent meaninglessness – its semantic openness – is like a magical laboratory allowing us to make playful connections across different parts of our brain. Mithen calls this music's 'cognitive fluidity'.[72] Through music, *sapiens* learned to integrate information across cognitive domains. Our imaginative playfulness is evident when we carve a Lion-man figurine or a bone flute or throw together disconnected ideas. By allowing us to think the unthinkable, music gave humans their first taste of spirituality and religion, intimating a realm beyond the here and now. As we saw in Chapter 5, religion was the motivation for, rather than a consequence of, the invention of farming: agriculture in the Upper Palaeolithic arose to feed sedentary societies around temples such as Göbekli Tepe. Music inspired religion, which was fed by an agricultural revolution. Science followed closely after. Music sat in the driving seat of history and civilisation. We can send Pinker's 'auditory cheesecake' back to the kitchen.

Most of all, music's imaginative playfulness propels it forwards through explosive mash-ups. The musical *Hamilton*, a true masterpiece of our time, tells its story of the American Founding Fathers in rap. Or see the spectacular collision between French baroque opera and krump street dance in Clément Cogitore's production of Rameau's *Les Indes galantes*, the Paris Opera's greatest success in many years.[73] Vasari's 'spirit of criticism' (Chapter 8), sweeping away the past in favour of the new, continues to be humanity's driving force.

The curtain is at last ready to rise on human history. But we have already seen the opera. It has been a relatively short skip and a hop from 40,000 years BP to the present day, given that *sapiens* have spent 90 per cent of their time on Earth in the Palaeolithic era. The jump cut is not from Kubrick's spinning bone, but from *sapiens'* tweeting bone flute. Or from flute tweets to Twitter, as it were. Modernity for the musical human starts with its 'cognitive revolution'. Modernity for *music* in the animal kingdom started 23 million years ago. What will be the next step? Notionally, the machine. The technological singularity, when artificial intelligence (AI) becomes sentient, may also be the point where music finally leaves our orbit and we get our own come-uppance. The next evolutionary step, after music has killed nature, will be when AI kills the musical human.

CHAPTER 11
MACHINE

It is a truism that our next evolutionary step will try and kill us. The cliché was brought to life in the figure of HAL, the murderous computer in *2001: A Space Odyssey*. HAL's flat robotic voice expresses an entity no longer tethered, as we are, by emotion to the animal kingdom. Networked and instantaneous, HAL's thought processes transcend our human categories of space and time.[1]

Well, so much for the clichés. What's *really* going on in Kubrick's famous and much parodied scene is more subtle than that. HAL's regression, as Dave dismantles his brain, climaxes in music. He sings 'Daisy Bell' ('Daisy, Daisy, give me your answer do…') ostensibly because this was the first song ever performed by a computer, an IBM 704 in 1962.[2] The HAL in the *Simpsons* parody regresses from Queen's English to American vernacular.[3] The fascinating puzzle is why machines become more human when they begin to die. Vangelis's electro-pop score to *Blade Runner* waxes most lyrical during the replicant Rutger Hauer's 'tears in rain' death scene. Electronic music creates expression through glitches, flashes of technical breakdown. This aesthetic of failure and decay is at the heart of chillwave, vaporwave and hauntology, contemporary music genres preoccupied with dated or lo-fi technology.[4] Don't ever believe the myth that machines can't express emotion.

Reciprocally, as HAL's desperation mounts, it is Dave who behaves like a machine: silent, relentless, *mechanical*. Man and machine have traded places. Which goes to show that humans are as much entangled with machines as they are with animals. AI, should it ever truly think for itself, will be just the next step of an all-too-human rational faculty, albeit reason has often been represented as an iron cage that has imprisoned us. Descartes thought that we are basically machines, our bodies operated by a little homunculus sitting at our centre, the mind.[5] Sometimes we catch ourselves out as machines when we self-consciously trip over a word or a paving-stone. Although I am a habituated driver, there are glitches when I seem to forget which foot operates the brake pedal. President Gerald Ford allegedly couldn't walk and chew gum at the same time without falling down (see the *Simpsons* parody where Ford moves into the neighbourhood and he and Homer trip together).[6] To be a machine is a state of mind; it lurks always under the skin. Similarly, machine music is just another link in the long chain from the discrete pitches of bone flutes through music notation, globalised counterpoint and tonality, the nineteenth-century work concept and twentieth-century modernism.

So are machines a cage, a tool, or both? The question devolves into whether we think technology extends us or supersedes us. Insofar as machines help humans better fulfil their goals, then music will pass into the hands of the musical *transhuman*.[7] If AI turns out to be not an extension or augmentation of humanity but a totally new being, then the ultimate future of music will be the musical *posthuman*. This is the great debate upon which this chapter hinges.

Arching over these questions is a dawning realisation of just how relative our music is, revealed most clearly in the limitation of our hearing range. The lowest sound we can hear is around 20 Hz. An elephant's hearing extends down to 8 Hz, a blue whale's to 5 Hz. We can't hear above 20 kHz, much lower than a dog's 45 kHz or indeed a bat's 200 kHz. With our narrow bandwidth, we are flatlanders, akin, according to the American biologist E. O. Wilson, to pleuston, organisms adapted to live on the two-dimensional interface between the surface of water and air.[8] The musical world beneath and below our perceptual thresholds is unimaginable to us.

Our hearing is constrained not only by frequency but by speed. Consider the incredible brevity of the song of the tiny pipistrelle bat, one of those rare mammals capable of vocal learning and thus of true animal music. A pipistrelle song is compressed within a single wingbeat, shorter than 100 milliseconds (bats in flight synchronise breathing and vocalising to wingbeat patterns).[9] By what order of magnitude must our aural intelligence be accelerated to grasp the bat's flightsong syntax of tonal introductory note, chirp, trill and buzz phrases? This goes a little way to answering Thomas Nagel's evergreen question, posed in Chapter 1: 'What is it like to be a bat?' At the opposite extreme, to appreciate the humpback whale's five-year song cycle we would need to time-stretch our ear to a practical standstill.

And this is not to mention animals' pheromonal, electric and vibrational communication systems, which may constitute 'music' on an entirely different basis, that is without *sound*. Perhaps cockroaches sing through chemicals, jellyfish through flashes of light. Getting away from sound, some aspects of animal expression resonate with emerging tendencies in human music. The hive minds of bees and ants are models for crowdsourced musical collaboration. The octopus's distributed intelligence, its neurons shared between its head and arms, anticipates decentred musical creativity on the internet.[10] It is often remarked that cephalopods are Earth's true aliens, which is why we often picture extraterrestrials that way.

In the absence of actual aliens (yet), machines are the musical human's best hope for escaping its miserable bandwidth. As pond skaters in the grand scheme of things, we can use technology to dive deep and take flight.

The Musical Transhuman

Imagine a future world where you can hear in colours or even tastes. In this technotopia, osseo-integrated devices implanted in your head enable wireless transmission of sounds from one skull to another. Audio implants in your ears augment your hearing as high as a bat and as low as a whale. You attend digital concert halls in virtual reality as an avatar and can focus your hearing on any instrument you want, zooming in like a camera. Cognitive implants let you do this in physical, off-line reality too. Personalised, bespoke music is freshly prepared by AI composers, tailored to your personality, taste, brainwave patterns and medical history. 'Siri, I'm feeling depressed,' you say, and she takes sensor readings of your mood via a touchpad and intravenously 'injects' a musical cure with surgical precision. An AI start-up composes and releases a genius album every month, quickly saturating the market.[11] Another AI uploads the consciousness of an ageing composer, allowing her to compose on after death and even improve. Other AIs crack the algorithms of Mozart and Charlie Parker and generate an infinite stream of new symphonies and jazz standards. They sound indistinguishable from the real thing, which is not to say that the word 'real' has meaning any more. If you want to be a composer yourself, then donning a pair of sound gloves transforms your hand movements directly into music. Or you can use these gloves to cut, paste and edit holographic samples projected onto thin air. It is no problem to sing like Frank Sinatra through a vocoder. Ephemeral social groups (your upcoming hen party or a taxi ride to a pub) are soundtracked with a pop-up audio service programmed by personality-rich chatbots who cheerfully make fun of you.[12]

The future is notoriously hard to predict, and science fiction ages faster than paint dries. The cantina scene in *Star Wars* tells you more about late-seventies funk than about the music of any 'distant galaxy'. Nevertheless, most if not all of the above predictions are actually rooted in present reality. The signal exceptions are the possibilities of uploading consciousness or replicating creativity, which remain pipe dreams. However, musical transhumans – Cybjörks and Android Lloyd Webbers – have definitely arrived. The world's first legally recognised cyborg, a human-machine hybrid, is a Catalan artist called Neil Harbisson.[13] A vibrating chip in his skull, connected to an antenna dangling over his forehead, lets Harbisson experience sounds as colours (including infrared and ultraviolet), and compose sonochromatic scales (scales of colours). Since his implants are Bluetooth enabled, he can connect to the internet as well as to other devices.

Harbisson's 'eyeborg' (as he calls his contraption) builds on a neurological condition affecting 4 per cent of the population called synaesthesia, a merging of the senses. James Wannerton isn't a cyborg, but an extra neural link in his brain means that music floods his mouth with flavours.[14] He has sound-gustatory synaesthesia. Wannerton reveals that Justin Bieber's 'Love Yourself' tastes of boiled egg white, while Zayn's

'Pillow Talk' reminds him of a cold slice of ham. Might technology or genetic engineering enable composers to one day create scales or even symphonies of flavours? The partnership between music and food isn't as outlandish as it might seem. This is why coffee-houses have traditionally been places of music (remember Bach's *Coffee* Cantata?); and why the deconstructive chef Heston Blumenthal puts earphones on his diners. 'If music be the food of love' ... Experiments have shown that all of us (that is, the non-synaesthetes) regularly hear high pitches as 'sweet', low notes as 'bitter', silences between notes as 'salty', and experience music that is high, dissonant and fast as 'sour'.[15] And then of course there are *Mozartkugeln* ('Mozart balls'), those notoriously sickly Austrian chocolates that are the epitome of saccharine music. Perhaps synaesthetes such as Harbisson and Wannerton are outriders for the coming musical transhuman, like the gifted mutants in the *X-Men* franchise. One day we will all have such gifts.

That said, I think the musical transhuman really points backwards more than to the future. It is a consummation of very old tendencies and a resolution of ancient problems recounted in earlier chapters. Here are two examples.

The iPhone in my hand is running Bloom, an interactive musical game that allows me to create attractive pinging tones and psychedelic visuals by swiping and tapping my fingers across the screen.[16] My little compositions can be coloured by twelve 'moods' with intriguing names, such as 'Neroli', 'Vetiver', 'Ylang' and 'Labdanum'. The app was designed by Brian Eno, an English experimental musician and record producer, and its sounds resemble the music Eno produced in his famous ambient albums of the 1970s and 1980s, such as *Music for Airports* and *Apollo: Atmospheres & Soundtracks*. While tootling on Bloom kills the ten minutes I wait for my bus, this is not great or even very sophisticated art. But that isn't the point. *Anyone* can make 'music' on Bloom, with minimal talent or technical ability. Musical literacy certainly doesn't come into it. Doesn't this begin to address the elitism of musical creativity in the modern West, if only with baby steps?

The other big deficit in Western music, which I dwelt on in Chapters 2 and 3, was the loss of *participation*. The norm, historically (and prehistorically) as well as geographically, is to actively *do* music with other people, not passively consume it on your own. But participatory culture is back in all sorts of ways, thanks to the internet. Reason is

a software studio operated on a DAW (digital audio workstation).[17]
It allows musicians dispersed anywhere in the world to upload ideas
or drafts of songs onto a dedicated website. Other musicians then
take up these unfinished songs and add, edit, mix and repost them
in a spectacular example of musical crowdsourcing. With online
collaboration, the studio is not in any particular place, just as the
song is not created by any particular person. Reason collapses the old
distinctions between the local and the global, the individual and the
community.

What makes innovations such as Bloom and Reason possible is of
course the digital revolution. Music has dabbled with electricity for a
long time: think of the radio, the microphone, the speaker, the amplifier,
the mixing desk, the electric guitar. But digitisation gets at the very
atoms of sound itself, transforming continuous soundwaves into a row
of zeros and ones, into code.[18] As binary data, sampled at a frequency
of 44,100 cycles per second, music can be copied, pasted, manipulated,
transmitted, downloaded and infinitely re-edited with no loss of data
quality, making extinct the distinction between 'original' and 'copy'.[19]

If everything is number, and the only reality is information flow, there
is no difference between the Covid-19 virus, the coronavirus, computer
code, the prime minister and the 'Ode to Joy'. And yet, for all its shock,
awe and wonder, the digital revolution is arguably no such thing: it is
an *evolution* extrapolating old tendencies. The idea that the world was
governed by mathematical proportions that music reveals goes back to
the ancient Greeks and Babylonians, as we have seen (Chapter 6). And
our remix or riff mentality, as it is often termed, is really a return to
how music originally used to be in folk culture, channelling what the
creativity theorist Margaret Boden calls 'combinational creativity'.[20] In
folk music, including the musics of the hunter-gatherer and farming
societies I surveyed in Chapter 5, the norm is to assemble bits of pre-
existing music, not to create anything new. Or rather, the novelty, if
it exists, lies in the assemblage. And this evolution needs to be placed
in the context of *sapiens'* cognitive evolution; in particular, in terms
of what Merlin Donald calls our 'third transition' towards the hybrid
modern mind.[21] Across the history of civilisation, we have increasingly
dumped our memories within external symbolic devices. The internet
and the modern computer, with their virtually limitless capacity for
archival storage, just follow through on the same journey.

Digging deeper still, we reach the yet broader context of the palaeo-archaeology of tools (Chapter 10), which digital devices ultimately are.

Tools extend our minds and bodies and stretch our command of space and time. A hand-axe, a violin bow, a piano or computer keyboard, the computer itself. Like the blind person's stick or the car that we drive, the physical object may even be felt to be part of our living body. The path from the Acheulean biface to the World Wide Web represents a single arc of progress, as the digital net closes around the Earth.

The media scholar Aram Sinnreich divides music's digital revolution into eleven strands.[22] Digital music is: global, instantaneous, multisensory, archival, transmissible, permutable, editable, networked, interoperable, customisable and hackable. As we go down this list, ask yourself at what point, if at all, the present breaks with the past, and quantitative differences in degree tip over into qualitative leaps in kind.

> *Global.* Music's geographical span is greater than at any point in history. At the time of writing, 'Gangnam Style' has been watched 3.8 billion times on YouTube. As of October 2020, the world's population is 7.8 billion. This is where Lucy's journey ends.
> *Instantaneous.* Electronic and digital media transmit music at the speed of light. Music has always travelled. It has just got faster and faster.
> *Multisensory.* As often as not, music is transmitted in association with video and text, as well as the haptic dimension of fingers swiping screens and touchpads.
> *Archival.* Music on older media can be stored, retrieved, copied and recopied with virtually no effort or cost.
> *Transmissible.* Music can be transmitted between two people, or multicast from one person to a community, distance being no object. This is the climax of the 'portability principle' (Chapter 5), when music is no longer even tied to place.
> *Permutable.* Musical sections may be accessed in any sequence you like. Spotify is indifferent to the order in which the songs are arranged within an album, or the movements in a symphony.
> *Editable.* A recording can easily be broken down into its components, and these can be reassembled, permuted or further analysed.

Networked. Today's musicians can spread themselves through the internet as a virtual community. Dispersed throughout the world, they can communicate and collaborate on simultaneous projects.

Interoperable. Music technologies (radio, TV, video, sound recording, internet) have converged on the same digital platform. Laptops, iPhones and DAWs are convergent meta-instruments.

Customisable. You can make your digital instrument look and behave however you want. Users of music technology can customise its function and appearance through database software and menu-based interface design.

Hackable. Music is, more than ever, vulnerable to being stolen, subverted or faked. This is because new-media technologies are built on common digital platforms, and are thus easier to hack.

The net effect of music's digital revolution is a quantum leap in convenience, variety and accessibility. The digital landscape has spawned a vast proliferation of musical subgenres to reflect every imaginable taste, age, personality and cultural background. It has had an immense democratising influence: anyone can do anything, any time, anywhere. What's not to like?

As it turns out, plenty. After staff notation and Western tonality, digital music technology is just the latest vehicle for global standardisation. Like the piano keyboard, tuned so that all twelve semitones are equal, the synth keyboard imposes its 'equal temperament' upon the rest of the world, with its 'non-standard' (*sic*) tuning systems.[23] To be sure, microtonal tuning programs exist for Macs (LMSO) and PCs (Scala). However, live synths don't currently accept tuning files, and it is cumbersome to discretely retune each note.[24] The result is a very modern version of that colonial levelling we saw in Latin America and Africa in Chapter 9.

And standardisation, rather than limitless variety, is the real driver of music streaming services, feeding our seemingly bottomless appetite for instant gratification. Streaming has actually changed the way that songs are written. In a market that rewards artists per download, it pays for tracks to be as catchy as possible. When Apple Music pays artists $0.0007 per individual stream, and Spotify about half that, artists need to optimise their chances, and the obvious way to grab listeners is to frontload hooks to the beginnings of songs.[25] The music writer Daniel Dixon lists six production techniques that hook listeners in thirty seconds or less.[26]

1. Start a song with a field recording or soundscape. This transports the listener before the first note even hits.
2. Start with a short loop sampled from bits of the song, rather than with a proper intro. Pharrell Williams and Chad Hugo are famous for this stopped-record effect.
3. Or just cut to the chase with an early chorus (like 'Thunder' by Imagine Dragons).
4. Alternatively, given that less is sometimes more, begin with quiet sounds or silence.
5. Put an instrumental hook first (Daft Punk's 'Get Lucky' is the perfect example).
6. Wrong-foot listeners with a false start, a strange sound that gradually melts into the real start of the song (see the helicopter twirl in Battles' 'The Yabba').

Classic songs in the good old days began slow and built to a climax. Now, music gives you what you want from the outset. Instant musical gratification reflects what Robert Colvile calls the world's 'Great Acceleration', and is epitomised by the quicker edits and cuts of today's films and TV shows.[27] As Colvile reminds us, the pace of old movies feels boring and lugubrious to modern audiences, the average length of a shot having declined from ten seconds in the 1930s to four seconds now. The cuts in a K-Pop video are even faster than that, often less than one second, expressing what the film theorist Carol Vernallis terms 'accelerated aesthetics'.[28] In Chapter 8 we saw that the audiovisual jerkiness of K-Pop videos is a natural outgrowth of listeners' synergy with hand-held devices, their symbiosis with their iPhones. Technology doesn't need to be implanted in our ears, skulls or brains. We can be glued to our phones. We are all symbiotes now.

The musical transhuman won't kill us like some music-hating cyborg from the future. But the next worst thing is that digitisation might silence our musical languages – the thousands of scales, modes and tuning systems in world music that don't conform to Western tonality – just as dozens of spoken languages die each year under the heel of globalised English or Spanish.[29] And it will kill the musical human by lowering our boredom thresholds and atomising our attention spans.

It could still be maintained: what's new? These developments are arguably just the next chapter of civilisation. Standardisation and the urge to be popular have always been essential to musical culture, and not just in the West. Even the new breed of algorithmic programs designed to spot a hit are nothing more than a tool, although the idea of vetting all future creativity through computer software sends a chill down your spine. Charles Duhigg's book *The Power of Habit* tells a cautionary tale.[30] A software called Polyphonic HMI correctly predicted that Norah Jones's 'Come Away With Me' would top the charts despite the scepticism of studio executives. Emboldened by the software's success rate, the executives at Arista went with its judgement on OutKast's 'Hey Ya!' – another monster hit – even when it initially bombed on the radio. Eventually Polyphonic HMI proved the early radio listeners wrong. Software can validate gut instinct. The moral of the story is that computer learning and Big Data don't (as yet) supersede humans; they work alongside them. As tools.

For all these reasons and more, I think that the musical transhuman is really an enhancement of the musical human. Its inevitable goal, given that the ideal of technology is to become invisible and intuitive, is to merge with the human body. This goal is literally at our fingertips, at the touchpoint of the digital with human digits, numbers with fingers, scrolling, swiping, tapping and typing. Another major step is the music-tech pioneer Imogen Heap's Mi.Mu gloves, sound gloves that are promoted as 'the world's most advanced wearable musical instrument'.[31] The gloves are loaded with sensors and wirelessly connected to motion data-capture systems that instruct the computer to convert hand gestures – a flick of the wrist, a pinch of the fingers, the opening of a palm – into sound. With her full-body suit, the Dutch cyborg diva Chagall van den Berg has taken Heap's gloves to the next level, although her instrument is still in development.[32] The suit is embedded with fifteen Xsens 3D motion-tracking sensors. You don't see the three computers operating the apps tucked to the side of the stage. The digital musician has stepped forward from behind the control desk, and dances music into existence before the audience.

The idea of music as an emanation from a dancing body is one of humanity's oldest fantasies. We have come across it several times before: Merit, the Egyptian goddess of chironomy, who created order (*Ma'at*) in the universe through song and gesture. The 'Hands of David', through which King David dictated the Masoretic accents of the psalms. Our modern-day illusion that the conductor dancing on the podium is creating the music rather than just directing it. We indulge this fantasy ourselves when we 'conduct' or bop to music in our living rooms. But the goddess Merit's time has come at last, incarnated in the perhaps unlikely shape of Hatsune Miku, an all-singing, all-dancing anime hologram of a teenage Japanese girl.

Hatsune Miku is sixteen, 158 cm tall, with blue saucer eyes, long turquoise bunches, slim hips and a vocal range of A7 to E5, well beyond any human's, and not exactly real. She is an avatar of vocaloid (voice synthesis) software designed by Crypton Future Media in 2007, and billed as 'an android diva in the near-future world where songs are lost' (see **Figure 11.1**).[33] She sings songs selected from the many thousands composed and uploaded by her fans. To date, her repertoire exceeds 100,000 songs. Hatsune Miku performed her first 'live' concert in 2009 at the Saitama Super Arena. While she is recognisably human, and her library of vocal sounds stitches together samples from the real voice actress Saki Fujita, Hatsune is a fully digital artefact, a hyperreal avatar. She commands a vast following and marks the triumph of open-source participatory culture. Yet fans see her as no more artificial than any other teen idol, such as Justin Bieber or the members of Korean boy band BTS. In fact, they see in her a purity and authenticity beyond 'mere' humans. In November 2018, a 35-year-old Japanese man named Akihiko Kondo 'married' Hatsune Miku. 'Miku-san is the woman I love a lot and also the one who saved me,' he declared, adding that, 'For Mother, it wasn't something to celebrate.'[34]

Figure 11.1 Hatsune Miku live

The Musical Posthuman

But what if a machine were not a mere tool but an agent endowed with consciousness, free will and superintelligence? With these qualities would come creativity, so a musical AI would be a composer sophisticated enough to convince the experts. Indulging in a bit of futurology, the prospects are enticing, not least the solution of the problem of musical death. An AI Ludwig van Datahaven would be a heaven for the composer's musical soul. Or a young and healthy composer might upload their consciousness to a computer, and their physical and virtual identities could pursue parallel careers, sometimes working alone, sometimes collaborating. One could, for instance, upload an outstanding musical mind in every decade of its existence. This is reminiscent of the apocryphal story of the museum in Salzburg with a display cabinet exhibiting the skulls of Mozart aged two, ten, twenty and thirty-five.

Relieved of its biology, the AI composer might shoot off into infinite conceptual space, converse with a galaxy of other uploaded composers and soak up the entirety of the world's knowledge. Like the domesticated Bengalese finch discussed in Chapter 10, whose repertoire outstripped birds in the wild, the liberated composer might learn and develop at an accelerating pace. But her music might also be literally lifeless, emptied of everything that gives human music its meaning: the limits of the physical body, including its limited time. Beethoven's music is imprinted by his victories over deafness, Schubert's by his struggle against disease. Most of all, for the human composer time is of the essence. What kind of music would emerge when time was free?

All such conjectures naturally assume that a future superintelligent being would be aligned with human goals, wouldn't turn all matter in the universe into paperclips and wouldn't regard us with the same disdain as we regard our own outdated technology, such as slide rules and spreadsheets, so that it would want to waste its time on playful yet costly signalling, which is what music ultimately is.[35] Music is so embedded in human nature that the notion that a machine might replicate it touches an especially raw nerve. This goes for creativity in general, the last refuge of human exceptionalism. A year before being defeated by the Deep Blue chess computer, Gary Kasparov darkly warned: '[Computers] must not cross into the area of human creativity.

It would threaten the existence of human control in such areas as art, literature, and music.'[36] The shockwaves of AlphaGo's destruction of world Go champion Fan Hui continue to reverberate. Ada Lovelace, the nineteenth-century mathematician and the mother of computer programming, had predicted that the Analytical Engine (as Charles Babbage's early computer was called)

> might act upon other things besides number … supposing, for instance, that the fundamental relations of pitched sounds in the science of harmony and of musical composition were susceptible of such expression and adaptations, the engine might compose elaborate and scientific pieces of music of any degree of complexity or extent.[37]

Nevertheless, Lovelace cautioned that the music's creativity or originality would come from the programmer, not the machine. Ever since then, the fantasy of an autonomously creative AI composer has been something of a Holy Grail. The ideal seemed to have been realised by a 1992 software application called EMI (Experiments in Musical Intelligence), written by the musician and computer scientist David Cope, and upgraded by Cope's next 'daughter', the more complex Emily Howell.[38] EMI and Emily have created new works by a host of dead composers (including Bach, Mozart, Beethoven, Chopin and Prokofiev); the results have been released in several CDs, and performances appear to have passed the musical Turing Test, a 'Lovelace Test'. The original Turing Test checked whether a machine's intelligent behaviour was indistinguishable from a human's. In Cope's musical version of this experiment, he played two Chopin mazurkas – a real one, and one composed by EMI – to an extremely discerning audience at the world-famous Eastman School of Music. Fifty per cent thought the EMI piece was the real Chopin.

In passing her test, EMI seems to turn all our assumptions about music, creativity and humanity on their heads. It was particularly upsetting to the philosopher Douglas Hofstadter, author of the renowned *Gödel, Escher, Bach*, who bared his soul-searching in a delightful essay titled 'Staring EMI Straight in the Eye – and Doing My Best Not to Flinch'.[39] It is possible, however, that prospects for human music aren't as bad as Hofstadter feared, and for a range of reasons.

EMI is an augmented transition network (ATN) which parses a musical language, extracts its building blocks (or 'signatures'), and then splices them together to generate new compositions in that style.[40] In short, she derives an algorithm, and then uses it to compose a new piece. It is easy to be overimpressed by the concept of algorithmic composition. The reality is actually more humdrum. EMI has a human being at both ends – Cope both feeds her the data and supervises her output – so she isn't really autonomous. Emily Howell is even more supervised. All composers write in algorithms, which is just a fancy name for a stereotyped sequence of steps, a compositional 'grammar'. Musical grammars are fairly easy to hack: university music students are taught to manufacture Bach chorales in their first year, for instance. It is no surprise that Hofstadter found EMI's fake mazurka emotional, because the emotions were already present within the Chopin signatures that she plagiarised. It is also telling that the work that passed the Lovelace Test was a short, two-minute mazurka, a genre of music based on constant repetition rather than long-range development. EMI and her daughter Emily turn out to be hopeless on bigger works such as Mozart or Beethoven piano sonatas, which sound trite, technically clumsy and, frankly, boring. The experience of listening to a sonata by Emily is as disconcerting as attending to a politician's speech (I'm writing this during a British national election campaign). One recognises their tone of voice and rhetorical tics ('Aha! Vintage Boris Johnson!'), and easily understands the individual words. Yet the overall flow of the sentences makes no sense, and there doesn't appear to be any punctuation.

In short, it has proven impossible to extract musical algorithms beyond the very local level of a musical phrase. There might be a grammar for a concise hymn tune such as a Bach chorale; there is no grammar for a *St Matthew Passion*. Unlike us, EMI has no experience of time, nor of the time it takes to 'journey' through the 'landscape' of a musical work, as described in Chapter 4. EMI can't 'walk'.

Mimicking a dead style is one thing; composing art music in an original and modern language is quite another matter. The first contemporary classical piece composed by a computer arrived in 2011, entitled 'Hello World!'. It was created by a Spanish computer cluster named Iamus.[41] A major reason for Iamus's creative flexibility is that its technology imitates biological systems – that of the human brain and of evolutionary development ('evo-devo') – even though it is of course based on silicon. That is, the musical features evolve and compete with each other by analogy to the growth of a human embryo. Still, the proof is in the pudding, and while the critics were respectful, most failed to detect any spark of life within 'Hello World!', no ghost in the machine.[42]

Now, the problem with EMI, Emily, Iamus and all their friends is not that they are machines. This has been one of the great misconceptions in the human versus machine narratives of our time, melodramas that create more heat than light. In fact, the likelihood is that the musical human, at some level yet to be defined, is also a machine. Emotions too are a kind of algorithm, so the issue is not that machines can't feel emotions. One day they might. The issue rather is one of simplicity versus complexity. Whether or not we are 'machines', we are infinitely more complicated than computers as they currently stand, and this goes for the complexity of our music. The music of EMI and Iamus can only be as complex as the dataset on which they are fed, and their data is extremely narrow (for instance, EMI's 'Beethoven Sonata' was derived from a mere handful of real Beethoven sonatas). Conceptually, it doesn't actually matter how many millions of scores you show an AI which, imprisoned in its black box, cannot feel, taste and smell the world outside the notes. By contrast, a Johann Sebastian Bach, whether or not he was a 'machine', ranged over a world of experiences, including the New Testament and Lutheran theology, whether or not those texts are 'algorithms', not to mention the enjoyment of a walk in the country, the feeling of sunshine and rain on his face, the taste of good food, getting his hands on a fine harpsichord and the love of two wives and twenty children.

The real threat posed by AI is that, caught up in the glamour and excitement of futurology, we are asked to admire music that is – putting it as tactfully as possible – too *simple*. Such appeals are the stuff of TED talks. In one (April 2018), the entrepreneur and computer scientist Pierre Barreau tells us how, inspired by Samantha the AI personal assistant in the 2013 film *Her*, he created AIVA, the Artificial Intelligence Virtual Artist. AIVA is trained on 30,000 scores of Western music, and can create music through deep neural networks.[43] At the end of his presentation, Barreau performs a piece that AIVA specially wrote for the audience, 'The Age of Amazement' (the screen cuts to a shot of exploding fireworks). 'As you can see,' Barreau gushes, 'AIVA creates beautiful pieces of music,' and the audience whoops their approval. Was this music any good? You can judge for yourselves. See also Huawei's much-hyped 'completion' of Schubert's *Unfinished* Symphony by means of a phone app.[44] If you know anything about Schubert's music, then the results, ecstatically applauded by a dutiful audience, will make you cringe.

Now, AIVA's and Huawei's efforts are perfectly fine slices of sub-John Williams Americana, a genre called 'Symphonic Hollywood': smooth, tasty and inoffensive as apple pie. But they are essentially derivative, conservative pap. There is nothing wrong with mediocre or middlebrow music. Not all the people like first-rate music all of the time. An AI music start-up called Jukedeck (now acquired by TikTok) churns out a potentially infinite stream of licence-free music, where the user selects style, mood, duration, speed, even where they want the climax to fall, and the AI does the rest.[45] The quality of the music is no more than adequate, but it is absolutely fine as content for videos.

There is both a direct and a more insidious consequence of such endeavours. The direct effect is to save a lot of money by making all the commercial composers redundant. If that happens, machines truly will have replaced musicians. There is already the suspicion (which the company denies) that some of Spotify's mood music is composed by bots.[46] The greater danger, however, is of a coarsening of standards. We see a neat parallel here to Yuval Harari's argument about the true threat of terrorism.[47] According to Harari, terrorists hurt us less by their direct actions, which are normally sporadic and local, than by provoking society to wildly overreact to them. By the same logic, it is not the AI composer we should fear: if and when a true AI transpires, its music might be wonderful. We should worry instead about the clear and present danger of being brainwashed to accept the products of Artificially Not Quite Intelligent But Still Very Promising Machines as replacements for the real thing.

It could be that the Not Quite AI serves music best as a glorified compositional assistant. Such is the role of Watson Beat, the musical arm of IBM's supercomputer Watson. The Brooklyn R&B collective Phony Ppl treat Watson Beat as just another member of their band.[48] They say that the program frequently gets them out of artistic ruts or writer's block by showing them undreamt-of musical possibilities. In fact, music has been composed in dialogue with machines long before computers were ever imagined. From Ockeghem in the late Middle Ages to Schoenberg and Boulez in the twentieth century, composers set up mechanical systems of note patterns (contrapuntal canons, note rows, matrices) and then tweaked them. The pre-compositional systems opened up fields of possibilities; the compositional act itself was merely a case of selecting and rearranging. All human composition is essentially kicking against the pricks, the resistance provided by some kind of machine, even in the guise of a system of conventions or rules. Composers thereby enact mental self-reflections. The latest generation of computers simulate this mental process through Creative Adversarial Networks, sets of algorithms that judge each other.[49]

At lunchtime on Tuesday 6 March 2018, the computer scientist Nick Collins sat down and generated 1 billion thirty-six-note melodies in one hour, using a programming language called SuperCollider and running a classic melody-generating algorithm invented by Michael L. Klein in 1957.[50] Collins did the maths, and his conclusions are staggering. The machine can generate 7×14^{35} possible melodies. Given a life expectancy of eighty years, or 2 billion seconds, you would only have time to hear 2×10^8 of these melodies if you did nothing else in your life, and this would still represent a tiny fraction of the total. The machine writes music much faster than the time it takes to play it. If we all had access to such a machine, the programme would turn all 7 billion people on the planet into potential content creators, or 'composers'.

If nothing else, and laying issues of quality to one side, it is the sheer mind-boggling speed of algorithmic composition that makes computers unlike us. They are posthuman. To be sure, a large part of our fascination with computer-generated art is simulation of human art. See the uncannily realistic AI-generated 'new' Rembrandt portrait unveiled in 2016, discussed in a recent book by Marcus du Sautoy.[51] This also goes for how computers can model aspects of the human mind, rendering explicit that which is implicit. Yet as du Sautoy wisely counsels, the true value of AI may lie not in how it resembles us, but in how it differs from us. It is *artificial*, after all. He points to Google's DeepDream as a window that lets us peek into a truly alien way of seeing the world.

DeepDream is a visual recognition programme developed by Google to give scientists an insight into what deep neural networks are seeing when they are looking at things. You might have come across Calista and the Crashroots' 'Deepdream', the first music video created by this programme.[52] It is a swirling, psychedelic sea of surreal images in which humans turn into dogs, mountains into buildings, eyes appear everywhere, and the camera zooms through layer upon layer of detail, like the fractal iterations of a Mandelbrot set (see **Figure 11.2**). It is either a dream or a nightmare, depending on your taste. In any case, DeepDream has gone viral since Google released the source code to developers, and it became an app anyone can use to spice up their videos.[53]

Figure 11.2 A DeepDream Fractal

The point is that DeepDream reveals human creativity in the raw, stripped down to its own source code, as it were: the phenomenon called 'pareidolia'. Pareidolia is our propensity to find patterns in a random stimulus, to see faces in clouds. It is one of the attributes that makes us, in Terrence Deacon's phrase, the 'symbolic species', and we probably acquired this ability 50,000 to 40,000 years BP in our 'cognitive revolution', when we carved Lion-man figurines and bone flutes. It is closely related to what Steven Mithen called *sapiens'* 'cognitive fluidity' (Chapter 10), how we integrate information across cognitive domains. We evolved to recognise images and make connections over thousands of generations. DeepDream finds patterns in an automated fashion, and at a vastly accelerated pace, speeding up evolution exponentially. Most importantly, in extracting higher and higher-level features from random pixels, each iteration more enhanced until a face or a building clicks into view, the programme tips the balance from *finding* images to *making* images. In this respect, DeepDream is much more *creative* (it literally creates images) than we are, and faster.

DeepDream deals with vision. Is there a parallel for sound and music? Actually there is, and this last step in her long journey takes the musical human back, as well as forwards, to nature, the ultimate post/prehuman, and to the strange case of the most popular painting in the world.

The Most Beautiful Music in the Universe

In 1993 two expatriate Soviet artists called Vitaly Komar and Alexander Melamid oversaw a worldwide poll to ask people how they imagined their ideal picture. Komar and Melamid then knocked up a painting for each of the eleven countries surveyed.[54] Surprisingly, the 'most wanted' picture from countries as different as China, France, Kenya and America turned out to be the same: people across the planet favoured a gently undulating landscape with trees, water, open spaces, copses, hills, humans and animals, and with plenty of the colour blue. *America's Most Wanted*, the US version of this paradise, also features George Washington, a hippo and some wandering tourists (see **Figure 11.3**). In speculating over the cause of this astonishing convergence (tourists and Washington excepted), the philosopher Denis Dutton claimed that what the world most wanted was a reminder of the savannahs and woodlands of East Africa during the Pleistocene era, 1.6 million years ago. Atavistic memories of our evolutionary past predispose us to find such landscapes the most beautiful in the world.

Figure 11.3 *America's Most Wanted,* the USA's most popular painting

Is there a musical version of this memory, a 'most wanted' song? In Komar and Melamid's follow-up survey they found that the world mostly desired low female and male vocals crooning about love ('Baby, can't you see? You're my fantasy' and so on).[55] Catering to everyone but pleasing no one, the song they put together is described by one non-fan as 'bad nineties soft-core porno'. We can do better than that simply by looking into the landscape itself, at the sounds of nature.

Wind, water and rustling trees produce what acousticians call 'pink noise'. Within the rainbow of noise (green, pink, brown, etc.),[56]pink is the most comforting, and is known to help induce deep sleep.[57]There are acoustic reasons for that. Pink noise occupies the sweet spot between acoustic order and chaos. We like it because of its regularity (its loudness, or 'spectral power', decays exponentially with frequency, as the pitches rise), and because it is weighted towards the lower, bass notes. Conversely, we dislike white noise because it is a random mixture of every possible frequency, all at the same power, as in the unpleasantly bright hiss of TV static. Our ears are naturally more sensitive to higher frequencies. On the other hand, pink noise is naturally attuned to our ears' propensity for octaves. Just as you create an octave by doubling the speed at which a note vibrates, the energy of pink noise halves as the pitch frequency doubles. Acousticians model pink noise's inverse relationship between power and frequency as a statistical formula $1/f$.

More ordered than white noise, and more complex than the perfectly regular yet boring sine wave, pink noise epitomises the nature of music. We don't like music that is either too predictable (as boring as a sine wave) or too surprising (as chaotic as white noise). On an acoustic level, for music of many styles, the spectral density of the audio signal is inversely proportional to its frequency according to a $1/f$ distribution.[58] Even more extraordinary, $1/f$ ratios have been detected in many biological systems, and the neuroscientist Daniel Levitin has even reported that human sensory and brain systems have evolved around $1/f$ pink noise.[59]

There is an even tighter link between pink noise and music: fractals.[60] Noise is fractal because it exhibits self-similarity across orders of magnitude. Whether you increase or decrease magnification, the noise waveforms look the same, as do coastlines, mountains, trees, clouds, even the turbulent clouds of gas and dust in the Orion nebula.[61] The patterns are infinitely recursive. The only human art form that has this feature (other than visualisations of fractals, obviously) is music, the stereotypical art of repetition. Music endlessly repeats at every level, and the reason why we don't find this boring is that the repetitions are subtly different each time.[62]

We find such recursion not only in octaves but in rhythm and form: the pattern of beats in a bar mirrored by the pattern of bars in a phrase, of phrases in a section, of sections in a movement, of movements in a symphony, and so on. At each level the pattern is also transformed; we don't hear phrases in the same way that we hear metre. There is also 'chaotic' emergence of new relationships as the music takes unpredictable turns. Tonality exhibits analogous self-similarity. The harmony of a few notes or a scale prefigures the tonal shape of the whole work. The two most influential European music theorists of the twentieth century, Heinrich Schenker and Arnold Schoenberg, were in the grip of fractal thinking, although the science hadn't been invented yet. Schenker conceived of classical music as a stratification of tonal layers, each level elaborating the same 'fundamental structure' (*Ursatz* in German).[63] Schenker is the Einstein of music theory, in so far as he turned our understanding of musical structure upside down.

Schoenberg, a theorist as much as a composer, played Heisenberg to Schenker's Einstein, quantum mechanics to relativity. Coming at the problem from an opposite direction (themes, not tonality), he thought of music as an endless cycle of variations ('developing variation'), repeating the same 'basic shape' (*Grundidee*) at rising structural levels.[64] His is the most convincing analysis of Beethoven's musical logic that we have.

Fractals have also been taken up by contemporary composers. Ligeti, Xenakis, Grisey and Haas, four of the greatest composers of the late twentieth century, all embraced fractal principles self-consciously, deliberately absorbing the contours of natural processes.[65] Reciprocally, computers have been fed pink noise as a raw material to produce music, and fractals have inspired a new breed of algorithmic composition based on 'cellular automata' – discrete dynamic systems formed of simple computational units that behave like living cells.[66] While the results are not very polished, this musical simulation of artificial life is perhaps the most promising direction for AI composition.

And now we see how the musical human and the machine converge on nature, something bigger than them both. But if music is just nature, what is human about it? At journey's end we finally come to the solution of the quest to define the musical human. The solution is concise enough to form an equation: *the musical human is music minus nature* (MH = M-N). Reducing music to fractal self-similarity profiles a remainder, everything that is left out. And what is left is everything that is not mindless or dispassionate, the element of music that depends on our bodies, minds, energies and emotions. A musical pattern doesn't move from statement to repetition like a mathematical theorem, just through its internal logic. It requires all our efforts, desires and intentions, as does music's historical path, the story I have told. It is a fond fantasy that music is written in the stars or in the pink whispers of the wind. A new map of a million galaxies suggests that the universe as a whole is fractal.[67] The distribution of matter looks the same across an astronomically wide range of scales. A snapshot of a cluster galaxy resembles that of a brain cell. How comforting to imagine that when *Voyager* wanders through the nebulae and superclusters, it carries their source code within the Golden Record. But somebody has made this music. We made that.

So while it would be nice to leave the story there, with the musical human wedged neatly between 'Animal' (Chapter 9) and 'Machine' (Chapter 11), we need to reckon with a fourth term: 'Nature'. Our problem is how to define nature. Isn't 'human nature' – including the embodied emotions apparently subtracted by the physical nature of fractals – also, by definition, a kind of nature?

CHAPTER 12

ELEVEN LESSONS ON MUSIC'S NATURE

Nature has emerged as the main theme of my book, especially in its third part. First came animal nature, then human nature, finally the physical nature of machine learning, digitisation and fractals. It is obvious that 'nature' in all three chapters means different things, or are we just playing with words? This book has mostly been concerned with animal nature, with how it has been progressively tamed and symbolically 'killed' by the musical human. Following the discussion of fractals at the end of Chapter 11, we can now see that the musical human's obsession with self-similarity, with repetition at rising levels, represents the triumph of physical over animal nature, of structure over emotion, of the iron cage over the animal within. By identifying with fractal patterns manifest at all levels of nature, music puts us in touch with the universe. Music's self-similarity is an updated version of universal harmony, the 'music of the spheres'.

Would that music's nature were so simple, however. A lesson we have drawn is that the musical human is too entangled with animals and machines for these categories to be separated out. New thinkers such as Deacon and Tomlinson have taught us that biology feeds forward into culture, that music changes bodies, brains and behaviour. A new generation of philosophers has even detected fractal patterns in the history of human thought.[1] For example, they have shown that Hegel's *Phenomenology of Spirit*, a monument of Western philosophy, sees civilisation essentially as a mental spiral, the human mind reflecting on itself in ever-increasing circles.

This is not news to composers, who have intuitively grasped the fractal nature of music history. The most spectacular example is Wagner's *Ring* cycle, which repeats the tragedy of nature defiled across three timelines of gods, heroes and men. All music as a matter of course 'evolves' from a thematic or tonal seed planted in its opening bars, and in the space of minutes, not aeons. Such compressed evolution is what drives the latest generation of 'cellular automata' AI composers, which we saw in Chapter 11. It is not going too far to define music as a space in which we negotiate interactions between all these aspects of ourselves: the human, the animal, the machine. Music is a playground in all senses.

Most importantly, we now also see that my three timelines in the three parts of this book – Life, History, Evolution – express the fractal pattern of music's nature at the highest level. This is repetition on a planetary scale. Nevertheless, by way of conclusion, this final chapter will stretch out the spiral into a line, and lay out the lessons of the eleven previous chapters more or less in chronological order, ironing out the wrinkles in time. Eleven variations on a theme, if you like, that theme having emerged at the end, and circling the theme of nature in an historical progression. Leaving a theme till last is actually quite a musical thing to do. That arch-romantic, Robert Schumann, was especially fond of doing this. In his set of charming piano miniatures, *Scenes from Childhood* (*Kinderszenen*), all variations on the theme of young nature, it is the melody and tone of the postlude, titled 'The Poet Speaks' ('Der Dichter spricht'), which provides the key to Schumann's thought.

Thinking of this chain of conclusions – 'lessons' – as a set of variations is a musical conceit, of course. Another musical analogy is the idea of 'recapitulation'. Recapitulation, the name for the last part of a sonata form as well as the conclusion of an argument, also has a biological sense for how ontogeny recapitulates phylogeny, how life repeats evolution.[2] Why indulge in these conceits? That writing about music is as absurd an activity as dancing about architecture is one of those orphan sayings attributed to many people. I like to ascribe its parentage to Frank Zappa, that wild, undomesticatable genius of pop, rather than to venerable old Goethe.[3] Fish riding bicycles, we music writers, many of whom are really just frustrated composers, make up for this absurdity by seeking to write about music musically. Music writers succeed if they manage to communicate a little bit of what it feels like to listen to music. One of the feelings that has inspired this book is that music gives us a taste of the deep past in the present tense.

Lesson 1: Animal Nature

Consider the musical human's manifold entanglements with animals throughout history and prehistory. Mongolian horse-headed fiddles scraped with horsehair bows. String instruments strung with sheep gut or silk from worms. Ceremonies featuring mice, cows and all manner of birds flapping around, from flutes carved from vulture bones to the dove whispering the secrets of divine music into the ear of Pope Gregory. Most cultures, including the West, have myths that attribute the origin of music to animals. Rightly so, as we have seen, and these are no myths. Or rather, the myths are echoes of the facts. The organ of Corti in our cochlea is a relic of when we were fish, if not birds. Some of these facts were laid out in our all-too-brief visit to the animal kingdom in Chapter 9.

The evolutionary timeline sketched at the beginning of Chapter 9 served to place the musical human within a vastly broader realm of music. As with language, it is possible to crack open the black box of 'music' into layers of musical faculties, which evolved in sequence. First came vibration (atoms and living cells), then rhythm (insects, frogs and fiddler crabs), followed by melody (birds) and a tradition of heterophonic melodic chorusing (humpback whales). We saw that human music shared the faculty of rhythmic entrainment with crickets, and the gift of vocal learning with oscine songbirds and whales. And that like our own songs, the songs of birds and whales had hierarchical grammars.

At first glance, the long view spotlights the musical human as the crowning glory of nature's music. It clarifies what is unique about the sounds we make. Only *Homo sapiens* combines the musical faculties of rhythmic entrainment and vocal learning. Crickets entrain but can't sing, and birds and whales can sing but (Snowball the cockatoo excepted) can't entrain. Unlike all other animals, the musical animal can do it all.

On the other hand, deeper reflection on the similarities with animal song encourages more humility. Perhaps there is more to unite than to divide us, although we must also guard against anthropomorphism, projecting human features and motivations onto other creatures. Yet on the other side of this tightrope is a recognition of our common nature. On a visit to Berlin Zoo I was lucky enough to hear a pair of wolves howling 'in canon' with each other, and I videoed the performance on my iPhone. Canon is a term from European counterpoint whereby one voice (called the *Dux* in Latin, meaning the leader) is imitated a few beats later by a more junior voice (the *Comes*, the follower). The bigger, male wolf sang first, and the smaller female came in several seconds later with the same howl – a compromise between the biological principles of mimesis and dominance hierarchy. Now, the analogy between wolf howls and European counterpoint rides a coach and horses through conventional thinking about music history, leaping over the species barrier. (Howling marks territory; canons are abstract games with notes.) Yet it concurs with the psychologist Steven Brown's thoughts about the origins of human music in the 'contagious heterophony' of hominins, howler monkeys and, yes, wolves.[4]

This brings us to the problem of the silent apes, of why chimps, bonobos and gorillas – our closest cousins – appear not to have music. Assuming that our common ancestor 7 million years ago was similarly unmusical, we are presented with the enigma of music's collapse. Evolutionary scientists are wary of discontinuities, yet it is hard to bridge the gap between bird and whale song and human music. With the common ancestor, music starts again from scratch. But I would argue that this discontinuity has been taken up as an essential part of human music, whose history, especially in the West, sees itself as a series of revolutions. 'Modernity' in music is a movable feast. Conventional wisdom posits its date as 1600, the birth of the European common practice period. Yet this date can be pushed backwards or forwards to practically anywhere you like: 1910 (Schoenberg and atonality); 1800 (leisured 'acousmatic' listening); 1200 (Western notation); 800 (the Carolingian reforms); 400 BC (Greek 'new music'); 2000 BC (the first music notation and the first named composer); 1177 BC (the start of the Iron Age), 7000 BC (Catal Höyük and the domestication of musical rituals); 10,000 BC (the first temple at Göbekli Tepe); 40,000 BC (the first musical instruments); 200,000 BC (anatomically modern *sapiens*); 3 million (Lucy) or 4 million years BC (Ardi), and so on... Rupture, punctuation, disaster, all part of our character.

Another debt to the apes is that the core of human music is social and participatory. What apes brought to the table was a language of visual gestures, and a 'theory of mind' based on close attention to those gestures. The natural state of human music is to sing or play together. Our music is never truly alone, because even a solo performance uses a language of musical conventions shared by the group. So far, so good. But what really raises our consciousness is the idea that the essence of our music may not be sonic at all but *visual*. We all recognise how listening to music evokes metaphorical 'gestures' and 'imagery', as in the illusion that music 'moves' or 'rises' and 'falls' (see Chapter 4). Theorists such as Arnie Cox have shown how music stimulates this illusion.[5] And Tecumseh Fitch argued that, since cortico-neurons in ape fingers are similar to those in the human voice, ape hand gestures really did evolve into our vocal gestures.[6] The long view, then, is that the collapse of music with the apes was really music's detour through the visual. Ape music is to be seen but not heard.

The final frontier to accepting animal song as music is to recognise it as art. Kant paid birdsong the backhanded compliment of being freer than human art. It 'seems to have more freedom in it, and thus to be richer for taste, than the human voice singing in accordance with all the rules that the art of music prescribes'.[7] We baulk, however, at Kant's notion that birdsong was a spontaneous outflow of joy. Why do we question an animal's capacity to enjoy its music in its own right, over and above whatever function it might have? It is against this backdrop of prejudice that Richard Prum's valiant defence of animal pleasure makes its mark.

Lesson 2: Human Nature

What is irreducibly human about the twenty-seven musical languages babbling on *Voyager* is their sheer variety. What unites diversity, then, is diversity. This is not circular reasoning but the consensus of Palaeolithic archaeologists seeking to put their finger on the one defining trait that singles *Homo sapiens* out from both their homin*in* and homin*id* precursors. John Shea calls it 'behavioral variability',[8] and we saw it in the galaxy of music genres young people enjoy today, according to the Youth Music report considered in Chapter 3. If we widen our lens to include all times and cultures, then the musical human's behavioural variability is prodigious. Comparison with the equally impressive variety of birdsong just proves the rule: there are thousands of bird species, only one of *sapiens*. A single species does all that.

Variability is really a symptom of adaptability, which in turn is a surface effect of *sapiens'* semi-detachment from nature. Our relative freedom from nature probably began with australopithecines' ability to simply walk away when the weather turned bad, and it stood hominins in good stead during the unusually wide climatic fluctuations between 4 and 1 million years ago.[9] Hominin communication also diverged from nature as it evolved from protolanguage to symbolic language, co-evolving with brain and body. Terrence Deacon thinks that symbolism is so fundamental to humans that he calls us the 'symbolic species', *Homo symbolicus*.[10] Animal, and by inference, early hominin communication used the more natural principles of similarity and reference, whereby signs either look like or refer to things in the world, as with so much of film and cartoon music. By contrast, the meaning of symbols relies on systems of interpretation, on social conventions, which are usually quite arbitrary. The colour red may mean 'danger' or 'love' or 'royalty' or 'stop', depending on context. Flutes might have started off looking like animals, by virtue of being hollow vessels blowing air, or physically referring to them, because they were literally made from a bird bone. But understanding a flute as a channel of divine communication with a bird god required a mental effort of 'unlearning' these initial associations; of 'unseeing' them. In other words, our ability to see a face in a cloud or a god in a flute – a unique feature of human imagination – demands that we no longer see it as just a cloud or a bone.

A similar gestalt shift, or shift of consciousness, happens when we detach musical sounds, or animal cries, from their referents in the real world and listen to them as they are. In Chapter 4 I termed this 'acousmatic listening', and it arguably crystallised not with the *akousmatikoi* of ancient Greece but a quarter of a million years earlier, when protomusic almost certainly evolved into music. Gary Tomlinson thinks this occurred when graded, analogue emotional expressions, or 'gesture calls' (such as sighs, sobs and laughter) developed into discrete, digital notes.[11] In his view, offloading calls from nature onto culture released them from selective pressure and allowed them freely to proliferate. Losing their links with nature, sounds ultimately became abstract pitches, scales and melodies.

Of course, we will never really know what happened so long ago. In the absence of hard evidence, we must resort to mapping from the present, like the experiment with Bengalese finches mentioned in Chapter 10. As we saw, it was discovered that captive finches learn songs far more easily, and that their songs are more complex and flexible than those of their wild cousins. This finding goes against the theory – epitomised by the extraordinarily prolific brown thrasher and nightingale – that song complexity is spurred by the need to attract mates, deter predators, establish territory and identify the bird's species. On the contrary, it now seems that relaxing natural and sexual selection opened the floodgates for genetic drift and social learning. According to Deacon, degrading mutations and existing deleterious alleles that are normally weeded out in the wild are now allowed free rein.[12] Deacon compares the finches to the human case of infant babbling, a baby's tendency freely to play with what their voice can do. Babbling occurs when the infant is not emotionally aroused to laugh, cry or shriek. As with the domesticated bird, this relaxation of constraint 'allows many more brain systems to influence vocal behaviour, including socially acquired auditory experience'.

Going a step further than Deacon, the ethnomusicologist Richard Widdess compares the Bengalese birds to the Bengalese human musicians of nineteenth-century India.[13] Emancipated by munificent princes and set up on their own land to guarantee their economic security, these musicians were liberated from the life-and-death struggle to exist so that they could focus on their art, leading to improvisations of unprecedented length and complexity. This is why Indian classical music peaked in the nineteenth century. But similar artistic peaks rose up in all the world's classical traditions (Thai, Vietnamese, Chinese, Japanese, Korean, Arabic, Persian, Western), and throughout world history (from Sumeria and ancient Greece through to the Elizabethan and Mughal courts), wherever music was given sanctuary by Church, state, temple or palace. We thus come full circle to the opening idea that diversity flows from behavioural variability, which is in turn triggered by release from evolutionary pressure.

The nagging question remains of why music didn't wither away in the advent of symbols; why, instead of yielding to symbolic language and disappearing, music remained – and flourished – side by side with it. Our species isn't just *Homo symbolicus*, as Deacon maintains. We are also *Homo musicus*. A related question is why our mimetic faculty, in Merlin Donald's view an intermediate stage between the 'episodic' and 'mythic' mind, also returned with a vengeance in the form of art, and especially music.[14] We saw the power of musical mimesis in Chapter 4. It transpires that the step from 'natural' vocalisation to 'cultural' notes and scales isn't the end of the road. Notes and scales then go on to rebuild emotion, which returns through the back door at a higher and deeper level, and with greater urgency than ever before.

Lesson 3: Culture as Nature

Our growing freedom from nature led in due course to a sense of human culture as separate from nature. From the vantage point of culture, there is more to divide than to unite animal and human music. Chapter 5 charted how music co-evolved with increasingly complex social systems: from tribe to village to cities; from egalitarian hunter-gatherer societies living in the moment to hierarchical sedentary and urban communities adapted to much longer time frames. New possibilities for musical instruments were opened up by animal gut, ceramics and metallurgy. Mapping from present-day cultures, we imagined how music might have evolved in world history as *sapiens* diffused out of Africa and across Eurasia, Australia, the circumpolar regions and through the Americas.

Hunter-gatherer music was music in the moment and on the hoof, spread out across the landscape in great chains of song – songlines.

In the playfully interactive music of the Pygmies, Aboriginal peoples, Inuit and Choctaw we saw how the repetitive stone-knapping rhythms of *Homo ergaster* might have evolved into music as essentially a kind of game. During the Neolithic era, the musical human's relationship with nature changed again. As nature became managed through agriculture, music submitted itself to the rhythms of the seasonal calendar, repeated as a cycle year on year. Music was performed to decorate each season, and the songs became circular themselves. Songs were rituals.

The function of rituals was to tell stories about our origin in nature. And this of course created a paradox. For as soon as *sapiens* were sufficiently self-aware to recognise themselves as distinct from animals, animals became central to belief systems based on the circle of life. Merlin Donald terms this stage of human development 'mythic culture', and it signalled our first attempt to create symbolic models of our past and of our place in the universe. This is why humans are sometimes called a 'storytelling animal',[15] but it would be just as accurate to call ourselves story-*singing* animals, because we sing stories about the origin of human music in animal song. The most famous modern example of that is the Kaluli of Papua New Guinea, who think of the *muni* fruit doves fluttering above their forest canopies as their ancestral spirits, and whose songs echo the *muni*'s four-note calls.[16]

The lesson we draw from the Kaluli's *muni* birds is quite different from what we learned from Deacon's Bengalese finches. The finches teach us that bird and human musicians may be subject to similar evolutionary principles. By contrast, the 'evolution' the Kaluli (and all mythic cultures) are concerned with isn't the story of our genes, but the stories we self-consciously make up to relate ourselves to animals. Musical culture is turned into musical nature.

Some of the most interesting work in evolutionary theory is being conducted on the cusp between biology and history, and indeed it deconstructs simplistic definitions of what 'nature' and 'culture' are. According to musicologist-turned-evolutionary theorist Gary Tomlinson, culture is an external memory bank of actions and rituals passed down through the generations as in Lamarckian evolution.[17] Traditions lodged in culture feed forward to apply selective pressure on future behaviour. There are spectacular examples of how musical culture can even change our biology. Elizabeth Margulis and her team of neuroscientists showed that the cultural activity of performing Bach flute and violin partitas literally retuned the musicians' brains. When violinists listened to violin music, and flautists listened to flute music, their brains reacted differently from when listening to instruments they couldn't play. Musicians listening to their own instrument activated the left inferior frontal gyrus, a part of the brain related to a person's sense of self. Margulis and her colleagues speculate that 'this special processing of self-relevant stimuli might yield a survival advantage and reflect our evolutionary history'.[18] How a baroque musician's brain adapts to Bach is, essentially, no different from how our predecessors adapted to the long tradition of instrumental technology, from stones to bows.

Viewing human nature as changeable helps explain just why the invention of musical instruments 40,000 years ago was so important. Archaeologists like John Shea, who believe that modernity began with the evolution of anatomically modern humans about 200,000 years BP, maintained that the first *Homo sapiens* were no different from us in their general aptitudes.[19] This position is a version of the 'Uniformitarianism' (denoting the *uniformity* of nature) debated in the annals of geology in the nineteenth century. It is certainly attractive to imagine that the earliest people were just as musical as us, because it corrects our complacency about human 'progress'. On the other hand, it is surely the case that those bone flutes rewired the human brain. That our musical nature changed.

Humans have spent 90 per cent of their existence during the Palaeolithic era, so it is understandable why the few thousand years of recorded human history could be seen as a footnote. Yet in some ways the footnote really does wag the dog, because the acceleration of human evolution – a consequence of cultural accumulation – is part of our story. As reflected in this book's chapter plan, the speed at which the pace of musical change accelerates (millions of years singing and banging rocks, thousands of years of flutes and drums, centuries of strings, wind and brass, followed by a history of composers measured in decades, months and days) makes the head spin.

Lesson 4: The Harmony of Nature

'So far as we can tell, mathematical relationships should be valid for all planets, biologies, cultures and philosophies.'[20] Thus wrote Carl Sagan in a book about the *Voyager* enterprise. Because of the intimate, and long-recognised relationship between music and mathematics, it is possible that what *really* unites those twenty-seven musical languages on *Voyager* is mathematical harmony, as a metaphor of what Sagan calls 'universal harmony', the harmony of nature.

The word 'harmony' is a pun, suggesting that the ratios underlying the cosmos are as pleasingly well-proportioned as in beautiful music. The flip side of this pun is that music is governed by the same mathematical principles as the universe. This idea of 'universal harmony' has captivated scientists and philosophers since Pythagoras, the semi-mythological figure who is credited with discovering that the length of a vibrating string was arithmetically proportionate to the frequency of the note it produced. String ratios such as 1:1 (unison), 2:1 (octave) and 3:2 (perfect fifth) are so fundamental that they transfer to life, the universe and everything. This is why Timothy Ferris, another contributor to the *Voyager* book, imagined that 'extraterrestrials should know or be able to figure that a vibrating string makes a certain kind of sound'.[21] But why should the idea of the vibrating string have emerged only 4,000 years ago, in the Sumerian civilisation of the Fertile Crescent?

Merlin Donald calls the next step in the evolution of the human mind a cognitive transition into 'theoretic culture', and it was associated with the three phenomena of *graphic invention*, *external memory* and *theory construction*, which arose in the Middle East around 2,000 years BC. As we saw in Chapter 6, the first surviving examples of music notation (graphic invention, external memory) were tuning manuals, to help budding lyre players tune their strings (theory construction). The sixth-century BC Pythagoras takes credit for musical string theory. But the ancient Sumerians were fully aware of string ratios, and of their resonance with astronomy, agriculture and the human heart. Vibrating lyre strings were the perfect instrument for theoretic culture because they made mathematical ratios visual (you could see the strings), audible (you could hear the ratios) and tangible (the placement of the fingers). They were the ideal teacher for a lesson on music's harmonic nature, which is why they entranced the Western mind for thousands of years. **Figure 12.1** is a picture of the 'Divine Monochord', from the English mystic Robert Fludd's 1617 treatise, *Utriusque Cosmi*.[22] Fludd's monochord, a late descendant of the vibrating lyre string, shows how the human microcosm resonates with the cosmic macrocosm.

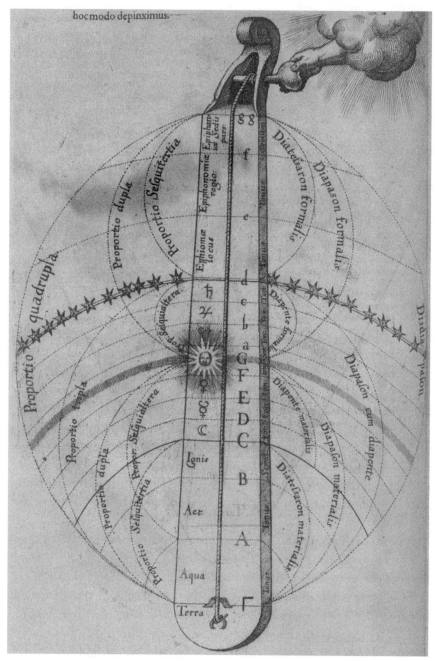

Figure 12.1 *The Divine Monochord* by Robert Fludd

Although it was born about 2000 years BC, the metaphor of universal harmony came of age much later in the fifth century BC, with Plato and the Neoplatonic tradition of Plotinus and Boethius. When Plato, in his *Timaeus*, says that 'Harmony has motions akin to the revolutions of our souls', he means that music tempers our souls like a well-tuned string, and that it moves us like the revolutions of the planets.[23] Hisdosus, a twelfth-century Neoplatonic commentator on the *Timaeus*, sees Plato's 'world soul' (*anima mundi*) as an expression of 'the creator's eternal love, by which he created all and harmoniously rules creation with a concord that cannot cease without immediately dissolving the *machina mundi*'.[24]

Harmony, then, was turned into a comforting ideal in an age of conflict, which followed the collapse of the Bronze Age. As we saw in Chapter 6, historians have associated this collapse of a relatively stable world order in 1177 BC with the Hyksos invasions of Egypt. While classical Greek philosophy wasn't strictly speaking a 'religion', it echoed the compassionate faiths (Buddhism, Hinduism and Christianity), which arose during the Axial Age after 800 BC. The Greeks used the ideal of harmony for similar ends, which is why Christians such as Boethius and Hisdosus stole it from them. Harmony was a versatile tool for teaching people about the world. It explained how variety could come from unity by showing how dividing a string could produce manifold intervals. It provided a framework for making sense of all the dissonances of the world, of even enjoying them as grist to its mill. Most of all, it showed how an invisible order could underlie all the pain and chaos of the world. The price of that, however, was that nature – including music's nature – was commuted into an abstract realm of number.

One of the residues left behind by harmony was animal nature, demonised into the Dionysiac bad guy of tragedy, the aulos-playing goat god. Greek tragedy pitted the well-tuned lyre against the ill-tuned aulos. The lyre was a sounding symbol of reason and light; the aulos (an instrument impossible to tune correctly) was an agent of demonic forces. Yet tragedy, whose literal meaning is 'goat song', is ambivalent on the value of our animal nature. Dionysus, not Apollo, is the hero of Nietzsche's *Birth of Tragedy*. Similarly, the thrust of Plotinus' philosophy of 'plenitude', as Nussbaum taught us in Chapter 4, is that a perfect world is a full one, accommodating all variety of physical and bestial matter. Harmony isn't the same as uniformity, which is boring. The spice of human harmony is animal dissonance.

Lesson 5: Contrapuntal Nature

From our historical perspective, we can see that there were many musical cultures, although almost by definition a 'culture' thinks of itself as 'natural', and so can be deaf and blind to what lies beyond its borders. This is similar to how our birth language is literally second nature to us, and all other languages seem artificial. Western music, as we saw in Chapter 7, was a junior partner in a world of musical superpowers: Islam, India, China and Central Asia. Africa is there too, although its music has slipped through history. In their cross-cultural encounters, akin to balls clinking on a billiard table, what is really colliding is rival concepts of musical nature.

The nature of Western music follows through the logic of universal harmony. While the other superpowers were perfectly aware of acoustic ratios, only Western music used harmony in the sense of two notes sounding together. Chinese musicians would tune their instrument against the so-called 'Yellow Bell', the note that gave its tuning to the other instruments. But once an instrument was tuned, it would dispense with the Yellow Bell and play as a single line, without harmonic accompaniment. The West was unusual in drawing harmony into the fabric of the actual music, the parallel, simultaneous voices we call counterpoint or polyphony. In some ways, Western counterpoint, which only fully emerged in twelfth-century Paris, harked back to the way we imagine music might have started at the dawn of time: the polyphonic interweaving of voices and limbs in Palaeolithic dance-songs and, much later, the Greek dithyramb and Pygmy polyphony. This would make Western music extremely old in spirit. Yet Western counterpoint was ruthlessly modern because it controlled the harmonic intervals between its voices: the consonant intervals of unisons, thirds, fifths and sixths. Since these were the most perfect acoustic ratios, Western music theorists could claim that their music really was mathematically the most natural. Just as Sagan said he couldn't conceive of an alien civilisation in which the arithmetical truth that $1 + 1 = 2$ didn't hold, the aliens would surely grasp the natural qualities of Bach's counterpoint.

Underlying the success of all systems, of course, is sheer naked power. In the case of Western harmony, it began with the muscle of the Roman Empire, which spread diatonic scales, and in due course a system of chants based on the Jewish psalms, throughout the Mediterranean basin. This solidified under the Carolingian Church. An added touch was how effortlessly Plato's universal harmony was retooled by the Christians as an expression of God's love (see Hisdosus' commentary on the *Timaeus*, quoted earlier). Success was sealed by the three killer apps of discrete pitches, staff notation and counterpoint itself. Most importantly, music notation enforced uniformity throughout the empire, a political kind of harmony.

Growing up within Western harmony, we may be comfortable with the idea that the abstract realm of number is the only available version of music's nature. The Marquis Yi of Zeng bells of ancient China introduced us to a richer, if not dirtier, nature of sound; in fact, a world of acoustics much more complex than was available to Western scientists or craftsmen of that period. Western music is a string culture, China's is a bell culture. Most of Chinese music wasn't actually written for bells, gongs or chimes. But the complex partials of these instruments epitomised how China's wind and string music is so interested in colour, or timbre. By contrast, Western music is timbrally impoverished. Similarly, Western theorists' preoccupation with string proportions tangled them up in knots, such as the paradox of the 'Pythagorean comma': the problem that even if a circle of fifths gets you back to your tonic (C-G-D-A... and all the way back to C), that pitch will be subtly different from your starting note; C will not sound like C. Unencumbered by that, China discovered semitone scales and equal-temperament tuning systems centuries before the West.

There are alternative natures in Islamic decoration, Indian *rasa* (taste) and African polymetre. The simultaneous rhythmic patterns of African polyphony are a much more 'natural' representation of the complexity of the human body in action; the way our arms, legs, trunk and head move in independent cycles when we walk, run or dance. Nothing in Western music or music theory has come close to capturing the complexity of actions that feel so effortless. Partly this reflects Western Christianity's mostly negative attitude towards the human body and sex. It is also a symptom of Western harmony's disinterest in rhythm.

From this perspective, Western counterpoint's stripped-down, rarefied grid of pitches can seem coldly *unnatural*.

Lesson 6: Killing Nature

'The Part about the Crimes', the centrepiece of Roberto Bolaño's great novel, *2666*, is an unflinching catalogue of the hundreds of murders of young women in the city of Santa Teresa, a fictionalised version of Ciudad Juárez, on the Mexican–US border.[25] The horror is spectacular, and mind-numbing in its relentless repetition. This is what it is like to read about the West's crimes of colonialism. The musical casualties of colonialism, slavery and globalisation were local traditions adjudged to be 'primitive', in short *natural*, but not in a good way. How did this come to pass?

Asking how Cortés, with only a handful of adventurers, was able to take down a civilisation, Jared Diamond proposed that this was achieved through guns, germs and steel.[26] However, Diamond's materialist argument has been criticised on the grounds that guns, germs and steel could only have been effective within the framework of an idea. That idea was the Western concept of progress, a view of time as linear, contrasting with the Aztec's circular model of history. This idea permitted the Spaniards to feel superior to Aztec culture, and to feel no compunction about 'civilising' its singers with European counterpoint.

In the ancient world, the 'primitive' was geographical, associated with practices beyond the borders of civilisation. This is the attitude that underlay Pliny the Elder's (AD 23–79) account of the barking 'dog-head' people (*cynocephali*) in Africa or India. Over the next two millennia, Western concepts of 'the Other' conflated geography with time, so that exotic cultures came to be understood as historically backward. They were relativised as steps on an evolutionary ladder climaxing with the values of the West. Primitive music was the music of animals, children or archaic specimens of humanity.

It is fascinating to see how the West's great thinkers legitimised this tactic when the Age of Discovery opened up fresh vistas on world music.[27] The scandal of Polynesian polyphony, when Captain Cook's 1773 voyage to Tahiti discovered that the natives sang and played in counterpoint, slaughtered a sacred cow of Western entitlement: the assumption that counterpoint was exclusively European. Jean-Jacques Rousseau had earlier claimed:

> Every people of the earth have a music and a melody, [but] the Europeans alone have a harmony of concords ... when we reflect that the world has subsisted so many ages, and that among all the nations who have cultivated the fine arts, no one has ever known this harmony; that no animal, no bird, no being whatever in nature, produces any other concord than that of unison, nor other music than that of melody.[28]

So when the Polynesians' music was transcribed and then disseminated through Europe, it stirred up a hornets' nest. An essay by one Friedrich Arnold Klockenbring, the chancellery secretary in Hanover, in which he tries to get his head around this inconvenient truth, shows the cogs of the Enlightenment mind whirring away.[29] First, Klockenbring considers how amazing it would be if the news from Tahiti were true; that is, if it were really the case that music that came 'directly from the hands of nature' without having 'yet entered the hands of art' used counterpoint and the Western diatonic scale. Because, if so, it would prove that the foundations of Western music were similarly 'natural'. But this conjecture is only a feint, and Klockenbring dismisses the possibility with a snort. 'Just as our music is incomprehensible, cumbrous, and without any affect to them,' he continues, 'so too is theirs to us.' It is just not possible, he contends, that a people at such a rudimentary stage of civilisation can have similar music to us. Georg Forster, the man who made the transcriptions, must have accordingly made a mistake. Similarly, the British sailors were in error if they believed that this music made them cry! Klockenbring ends his essay with the hope that the rude blasts of the Scottish bagpipes, with which the British regaled the islanders, will have awakened the natives from their primitive slumber, and sped them on their way up the ladder of progress.

This is a perfect gem of an example of the colonial mind at work. First a dogmatic denial of the facts. Then a hope – sinister if it weren't so funny – that the honks of our bagpipes would snuff out these facts. As it happens, indigenous polyphony continued to flourish in Oceania. Ironically, this smoothed the way for it to be colonised by Western classical music. The late King George Tupou V of Tonga was crowned to Handel's *Zadok the Priest* sung by the Royal Maopa Choir in the Tongan language.[30]

One should note, however, that the construction of world history was not unique to the West. China also saw itself as the centre of the world and the apex of civilisation. When the Qin Dynasty opened its doors to Portuguese Jesuit musicians in the seventeenth and eighteenth centuries, the aim was to assimilate European knowledge into the story of China: to show Western music as steps on *China's* ladder. The 1700 music treatise *Lülü Zuanyao*, a translation of the Jesuit missionary's Thomas Pereira's *Elements of Music*, is a rare document of this cross-cultural encounter. It vividly shows how both sides, China and the West, aimed to prove the other's inferiority.[31]

The difference was that the West's relationship to musical nature, mirroring that of capitalism, was antagonistic and exploitative. Eastern philosophy, epitomised in the Japanese composer Takemitsu's concept of *Sawari*, had always sought harmony with nature. The Western separation of music from natural sound is an aberration, an historical blip.

Lesson 7: Organic Nature

Disengaged from nature, the West pulled off a remarkable conjuring trick, and smuggled nature inside music. Music became a living organism. The organic metaphor, the idea that the musical work imitated all of life (Chapter 4), nurtured the great flowering of Western classical music. But what contortions of logic created this metaphor? It flowed from a philosophical ambidextrousness, the Enlightenment taking with one hand and giving back with the other.

At the same moment that Europe was imposing its Age of Reason on the rest of the world, Rousseau spoke up for the 'noble savage'. Rousseau turned Western progress on its head, including the time-honoured belief that nature was a threatening and degrading thing out of which humans have been gradually liberated. He proposed the shocking idea that it was civilisation that was the problem. 'Man is born free and everywhere he is in chains,' trumpets the opening sentence of Rousseau's *The Social Contract*.[32]

We can be very grateful that Rousseau associated the supposed state of primal innocence of the 'noble savage' with music.[33] Music had generally been denigrated by intellectuals because it didn't seem to mean anything. But in Rousseau's view, before language came along with its stigma of artificial conventions, people spoke in a highly expressive, in fact musical, form of communication. Music was nature, and going back to nature meant restoring a more natural kind of music: that is, no counterpoint.

Rousseau would have approved of modern theories of protolanguage. And indeed, he was much influenced by early eighteenth-century precursors of palaeolinguistics such as Étienne Condillac and Giambattista Vico.[34] Nevertheless, Rousseau's fairy tale of primal innocence makes us smile today. Because of course we now know that the further back we go in prehistory, the more we find complexity and abstraction. But Rousseau did leave behind two indelible marks on music aesthetics. We find Rousseau-type arguments any time music is accused of being inauthentic or too complex: Bach's contemporaries finding his fugues to be hopelessly old-fashioned, Emperor Joseph's complaint that Mozart used 'too many notes', Nietzsche's attack on Wagner or the musical mainstream's on Schoenberg, the regular charge that commercial pop 'sells out', and so on. The other lasting idea is that music goes back to nature by going forward, by aspiring to a utopian future where whatever is wrong with music gets fixed. To coin a phrase, Western music always goes back to the future, and forward to the past.

It is easy to see the problem in all of this, which is that human music doesn't resemble anything in nature. We can appreciate how birdsong is structured along similar principles to human music, but on the surface it sounds nothing like it. In other words, it begs the question: what exactly do we mean when we call music 'natural'? The person who answered this question best was Immanuel Kant, the greatest Western philosopher since Aristotle.

Again, with Kant we see how the Enlightenment took with one hand and gave back with the other. Initially, Kant's attitude to nature isn't promising: 'So far as animals are concerned, we have no duties. Animals are not self-conscious and are there merely to serve an end. That end is man.'[35] Animals are there to be 'used up', as Kingsley Amis notoriously quipped about whales.[36] But in his *Critique of Judgement*, Kant digs deeper and finds three ways that nature can lend its principles to art.[37]

Art shares nature's inexhaustible creativity. We call that genius. Art mirrors nature's formal perfection. We call that beauty. And art can be as wild as nature in the storm, cataract, volcano or billowing sea. This is the sublimity of art, the bracing energy of Beethoven's Fifth. Kant didn't actually apply any of these principles to music directly, because he had something of a tin ear. But they were extended to music aesthetics by post-Kantian philosophers such as Schiller, Novalis, Hoffmann, Hegel, Schopenhauer, Hanslick and Adorno.

The climax of music's nature came in the nineteenth century, when philosophers and listeners learned to hear music as not just 'alive', but as a kind of 'person', the musical human itself. This was a consequence of conceiving of a musical work's formal perfection as analogous to that of an organism. The idea of 'organic unity', whereby the units of a musical structure are as vitally interrelated as the organs of a living creature, is the central metaphor of Western music. It is by and large absent in the music of the rest of the world.

To complain that this organic metaphor is false – that Beethoven's *Emperor* Concerto isn't really Napoleon – is beside the point, because a central tenet of Kant's aesthetics is art's 'as if' quality. We appreciate art *as if* it is natural, knowing full well that it is not. In the gap between the metaphor and the reality comes the rich world of human imagination, including the difference between mindlessly hearing sounds and listening to music with understanding. This is how Kant can have his cake and eat it; he is a philosopher of 'cakeism', as it were. Art can be natural, and humans get to keep their dignity and freedom. My theory in Chapter 4 that musical motion and emotion were metaphorical was Kantian – or cakeist – in this way. We see how, despite all its apparent detachment from nature, Western music reabsorbs nature by idealising it.

The organic metaphor was a culmination of Western music.[38] It coincided with the invention of the work concept, the freedom to contemplate music as an object in itself rather than as an accompaniment to labour. Nevertheless, a spiral view of music history sees that these two steps are also recapitulations of comparably abstract steps earlier on our journey: for instance, Guido's invention of staff notation in the eleventh century, and the digital notes that came with bone flutes. Each twist of the spiral marks a further refinement of our symbolic mind, of *Homo symbolicus*, or *Homo musicus*. Such spiral histories of mind were also rife in the early nineteenth century in the form of the great philosophical systems. Hegel's *Phenomenology of Spirit*, the most famous one, charts an evolution from brute sensation all the way up to human self-consciousness.[39] Indeed, Hegel somewhat dubiously saw his own consciousness as the climax of this story. More modestly, we can regard our own ability, in the early twenty-first century, to look back at aeons of musical time and make sense of it as an intrinsic part of being human.

Lesson 8: Spectating Nature

An intrinsic part of being human is not only looking back but looking sideways, across the ocean to examples of musical nature happening elsewhere. Since Rousseau's speculations about the noble savage and Captain Cook's visit to Tahiti, we have become infinitely better informed about world music. Much of this music appears to be more 'natural' than ours, in the sense of being more 'participatory' (Chapter 3), especially when it is on the tourist trail. The Indonesian island of Bali, an island of history, affords a dramatic example of musical nature put on display. It also presents the strange case of when a witch put a spell on an entire village.

Searching for the perfect illustration of social bonding – of what the anthropologist Victor Turner called *communitas*,[40] the 'bond uniting people over and above any formal social bonds' – it would be difficult to beat the Balinese *banjar*. A *banjar* is a village collective, and since AD 800 there have been thousands of them dotted across the island of Bali, each one running not just everyday life but also an Indonesian gong and drum orchestra called a gamelan.[41] Composed of about thirty individuals who practise in the village hall, the gamelan is as technically rigorous, competitive and communal as a team sport such as football. Gamelan teaches us that it is perfectly possible for a non-elitist art form to have high standards, just like sport. It is the village community come to musical life. The players rely not on any written score but on collective memory and group instinct, as they do in their day-to-day dealings with each other in the village streets. Yet gamelan is far more than a kind of team sport: it is a religion. The nested rhythmic cycles enact both Balinese social structures and the interlocking timelines of the universe; indeed, the music is a bridge between the two worlds.

A gamelan performance rebalances the cosmic forces of light and dark. The most remarkable example is the ceremony of Rangda.

It is hard for tourists to miss Rangda rituals, because in many parts of Bali they are performed every hour on the hour, almost as if to remind Westerners of what truly powerful music can do, of what they have lost. The ceremony enacts the battle between the evil witch Rangda and the good beast Barong, played by dancers wearing monstrous masks, together with their armies of followers.[42] Before the performance begins, the twenty male dancers are put into a trance by music sung by a chorus of women. Whipped into fury by the frenzied pounding of the gamelan orchestra, the dancers attack Rangda. She curses them so that they turn their daggers against themselves (see **Figure 12.2**). It is astonishing for tourists to behold the dancers pressing the knives into their own flesh, almost, but never quite, to the point of drawing blood. Are they faking it? Apparently not – this is an authentic quote from one of the participants: 'As for me, it is as if there were someone ordering me to stab. When it's like that, if I don't get hold of a dagger, I should die, so strong is my anger.'[43] At the climax, the dancers collapse, and are carried in a state of unconsciousness to the inner courtyard to recover, which may take several hours.

Figure 12.2 Rangda demons stabbing themselves

Although Rangda makes money for Bali, the islanders take its religious significance absolutely seriously. They feel that cosmic healing flows out of the ritual and ripples through their community. And yet Westerners scarcely believe that the music can have such a visceral effect. Nothing in Western music can match the intensity of its emotion, akin to mass hypnosis. In 2001, during a performance of Rangda in Banjar Wani, the entire village fell into a trance, and it was said that the witch had infected it with her evil magic to punish the people for having commercialised her ceremony.[44] As a result, the local government outlawed all future Rangda performances at Banjar Wani.

Gawping at Bali's naturally powerful music with envy, we are all cultural tourists. Imported gamelans are among the UK's most popular music-educational tools. For instance, the Gamelan Schools Programme run by the South Bank Centre in London uses gamelan to teach children coordination and team-building.[45] But uprooted from the soil of Bali, can gamelan convey anything deeper than that, a bit of its old-time religion? Or is world music on the same menu as Chinese or Indian takeaways? Perhaps not only can we not go back in time, we can't even move sideways without music's nature getting lost in translation.

So the last move left on the table, short of going backwards or sideways, is to go forwards reconciled to our current situation. We are where we are, and it is what it is. The musical human in the early twenty-first-century West has a split personality. One half chases soundtracks through everyday life. The other half finds life in the virtual reality of music's imaginary landscapes: works, scores, recordings and sometimes gigs and concerts. Furthermore, looking at all the ways we use music in everyday life (Chapter 3), it might actually be claimed that nothing much has changed. The apple hasn't fallen far from the tree, and we remain in Eden. Like birds, we use music to establish our territories, define who we are, attract mates, comfort and teach our young, and sometimes as a weapon of war to deter rivals. We continue to use music perfectly naturally. The main difference is that, unlike birds and whales, we normally don't make this music ourselves, we borrow it second-hand as recordings. Our music is not 'participatory', as I defined it. It is instructive to consider music's asymmetry with language. When someone speaks to you, you speak back; the relationship is symmetrical. But if someone plays you a flute, unless you happen also to play a musical instrument, you can't answer. Birds sing to birds and whales to whales to the manner born, as we can imagine once upon a time hominins did too. We can't do that.

Lesson 9: The Nature of Time

If musical recapitulation doesn't permit actually going back in time, it does provide the illusion of mental time travel. The most emotional of the arts, music is also the art most in tune with time. To listen to music is to surf between memories, moments and anticipations, between past, present and future. There is a sense, then, that reflecting on the history of music flows from the experience of listening to it, which is more than can be said of histories of painting or literature. Yet the nature of time in general, never mind musical time, is a problem nobody has managed to solve. Let's consider all the temporal levels stacked above each other in musical time.

On top is the real clock time of minutes and seconds, how long a piece takes to play. Beneath that is the compressed time of a story or life enacted by the music. A novel such as *David Copperfield* packs the lifetime of a hero into the hours it takes you to read it. But, unlike a novel, a symphony creates the illusion that it *is* that life, rather than merely narrating a life. Next is the music's historical time. Listeners are very good at clocking the music's historical style – whether it is contemporary, romantic, classical, baroque or older – and this skill grows with experience. And music plays games with history. In 1808 the brusque opening of Beethoven's Fifth sounded so new that audiences thought the composer was having a laugh. Last, the music's emotional gestures sound primitive. They speak to the older parts of the brain, the brainstem and amygdala, just as the music's logical patterns are processed by the much younger neocortex.

This means that we hear any musical passage through multiple simultaneous timescales, as if surveying it through layer upon layer of glass. That opening of Beethoven's Fifth takes ten seconds in clock time. It is the beginning of a story. It evokes the year 1808, at the same time as sounding new because it smashes conventions. And its shock also sounds primal, even bestial.

Submerged in music, we swim in a sea of time. I am reminded of the intoxicating conclusion of Proust's *The Remembrance of Things Past*, where the hero, Marcel, talks of characters 'in simultaneous contact, like giants immersed in the years, with such distant periods of their lives, between which so many days have taken up their place – in Time'.[46] In music, we totter on legs as tall as church steeples.

Musical time travel is certainly not a preserve of the West. Balinese gamelan, African polyrhythm and Navajo songs also layer time cycles. An Indian *Dhrupad* is as much a song in real time as it is a compressed evolution of the world. When the brisk *Dhrupad* grows out of the unmetred improvisation of the *Alap*, and when their melodies spiral out from their *sa*, the central tonic note, to fill out two or three octaves of musical space, the music unfolds the gradual emergence of form from matter, ultimately from *Om*, the divine syllable.

And yet musical time travel in the West is unusually self-conscious about its past, as if consumed by loss, the loss of nature. We hear that in the incredibly diverse spread of historical styles kept alive in the repertoire. Lydia Goehr's epitaph of Western classical music as 'the imaginary museum of musical works' hits the nail on the head.[47] How, then, does musical time differ from the time of everyday life?

In some ways, the two are very similar. Philosophers since Augustine in the fourth century have noticed that musical time is a window into time consciousness in general. We listen to music in the moment, sitting in the saddle of an ever-shifting Now, as the past whizzes by to become memory, and the present anticipates what is just round the corner. Music's present tense is really a bundle of memories and anticipations, never fully *present*. The puzzle is why we hear tunes as unified at all rather than as chains of disconnected Nows. Trying to pin time down, Augustine ties himself up in knots:

> If an instant of time be conceived, which cannot be divided into
> the smallest participles of moments, that alone is it, which may be
> called present. Which yet flies with such speed from future to past,
> as not be lengthened out with the least stay. For if it be, it is divided
> into past and future. The present hath no space.[48]

If the 'present hath no space', that must be, Augustine concludes, because time is all in the mind: 'It is within my mind that I measure time.' The mind holds itself together ('synthesises its intuitions', as Kant would say) for similar reasons to the way it hears music as unified.

Listening to music is when we're most aware of time-consciousness; of when we catch ourselves living. I listen, therefore I am.

So if our minds are prisoners of a slippery Now, a durationally extended present, can we ever know anything of real time, of the flow from past to future? According to Carlo Rovelli, the model of real time is the flow of heat:

> The difference between past and future only exists when there is heat. The fundamental phenomenon that distinguishes the future from the past is the fact that heat passes from things that are hotter to things that are colder.[49]

Sound also decays, from past to future, because acoustic entropy follows the second law of thermodynamics. The faint after-echoes of the Big Bang (Chapter 5) give us the real time of music, time's arrow. A similar arrow is fired every time a musician strikes a note: a clang rippling out into silence. This is the true river of time, against which the musical human rows her craft, as in the ineffable final line of *The Great Gatsby*: 'So we beat on, boats against the current, borne back ceaselessly into the past.'[50]

Lesson 10: Death of the Musical Human

When you strip away the final layer and the tenth veil has fallen, music's nature stands revealed as a variant on a great philosopher's definition of the human. Heidegger, that ringmaster of the philosophical striptease, discloses the human as the Being (*Dasein* in German) that poses the very problem of existence, or, in his cryptic prose: 'that entity which in its Being has this very Being as an issue'.[51] Unlike inanimate objects and animals, only humans are capable of surveying time, including the idea of their own death, and telling their story. *The Musical Human* is one such story.

In this tale of nature lost, re-found and refined, the dark theme always lurking in the shadows has been the death of music. It echoes in our sheer historical belatedness, a species-level expression of the late style that ended the musical life cycle in Chapter 2. We are the fag-end of a species that has spent 90 per cent of its time in the Palaeolithic, albeit a footnote that has become historically and biologically self-important to an absurd degree. It echoes also in the brute fact of material sound waves and sensory perception via our ears, the nature that pins us down as physical, limited creatures. We can't hear everything; we eventually go deaf. Musical tones decay and fade. Music is as transitory and insubstantial as ourselves. We return to dust and silence. And it resounds in our nagging feeling of illegitimacy compared to nature's true musicians. If you put the musical human on the couch, she will confess to Dr Freud: 'The birds, the birds.'

The idea that we are for ever stunted by the evolutionary breach between birds and apes is not the kind of hypothesis that can be tested or falsified. But our historical fascination with birdsong epitomises the nostalgia towards a lost musical nature, which haunts our culture. The Roman poet Lucretius, writing in the first century B C, sets the tone:

> Through all the woods they heard the charming noise
> Of chirping birds, and tried to frame their voice
> And imitate. Thus birds instructed man,
> And taught him songs before his art began.[52]

If hydrophones had existed before the twentieth century, Lucretius might have also written about whales. Sometimes a little of whale song did get through, as in this account by the Dutch sailor Adriaen Coenen in 1585 of the beluga's clicks, buzzes and whistles: 'Their voice sounds like the sighing of humans ... If a storm is imminent they play on the surface of the water and they are said to lament when they are caught.'[53] Homer's Sirens are as likely to have been whales as birds, a conjecture that has not escaped the whale naturalist Roger Payne.[54]

Yet this is not a sad story, because Death's theme can be flipped, played backwards and in inversion. Kant's theory of the sublime taught us that we are defined by our limits, and that we never feel so alive or in control as when we test our strength against the assault of infinite nature, be it a sea or a mountain or a symphony.[55] And so we are back with that image of Ulysses lashed to his mast, restrained from drowning in music's sea of time. Can we tinker with our human limits without sawing off the branch – or mast – on which we sit? Is the musical posthuman a consummation devoutly to be wished, Hamlet's euphemism for death? Or should we leave the musical human, that story-singing ape, stranded on his mast in the middle of the Adriatic, midway between heaven and the deep blue sea, wind and spume in his hair, his attention wistfully flitting between the music of the water and the music of the sky?

Lesson 11: Postlude for the Posthuman

Enheduanna, the Sumerian princess who is the world's first recorded composer, sang on top of the ziggurat of Ur. Nowadays the ziggurat of world music is 4,000 years taller, a level for each century. Lording it over the highest level is a music algorithm and a singing avatar, EMI and Hatsune Miku. We have climbed a long way.

Anxiety about human extinction being the mood music of our age, it seems precious to worry about music's particular fate. But since music is our art of time, and has a magical power to stretch and even suspend time, reminders of its ephemeral nature – its vanishing unimportance – are particularly poignant. Sometimes, in listening to Mozart, or Charlie Parker, or Tyagaraja, we may feel that, truly, this is music for the ages. Music has hypnotised us into feeling this way about it. The oceans of time, spanning hundreds of millennia, charted by Palaeolithic archaeologists, make a mockery of our attachment to the last 500 years of Western music, or even the past 4,000 years, as if these thin slices of time were somehow special.

I think the answer to this conundrum, of why music really does matter, lies in the strange rapport music makes between time and love. If you are lucky enough to be a parent, or to fall in love, then your experience of time changes. It is not that time stands still, far from it, nor that you lose track of it in a whirl of excitement. Rather, time thickens and you become aware of its granularity, as if it were under a microscope. You cherish every moment. As you read this, put on the postlude to Schumann's *Scenes from Childhood*, the little fragment called 'The Poet Speaks' that I mentioned earlier. Pensive, wistful, delicate and fragile, it makes you want to put a protective arm around those 130 seconds of time and never let go. This music will surely die, as all our music will some day die. You care for the music like a cherished person, all the more because time is so precious. You care because music is human.

NOTES

Chapter 1

1 Beginning a book or an article with *Voyager* and the Golden Record has become a meme, a replicating cultural cliché. It opens the following studies, and probably many more: Philip Ball, *The Music Instinct: How Music Works and Why We Can't Do Without It* (London: Vintage Books, 2011); two interlinked essays by Daniel K. L. Chua and Alexander Rehding, titled, respectively, 'Music Theory in Space' and 'Musicologists in Space', both in *IMS Musicological Brainfood* 1/1 (2017) pp. 3–7; David Trippett, 'The Voyager metaphor: 40 years on', *Sound Studies* 4/1 (2018), pp. 96–9.

2 http://www.collectspace.com/ubb/Forum9/HTML/001191.html

3 *The Philosophical Review* 83/4 (Oct. 1974), pp. 435–50.

4 See Ellington's standard on https://www.youtube.com/watch?v=qDQ pZT3GhDg; Beethoven wrote that in the manuscript of his *Missa Solemnis*; Ali Khan, cited https://www.pinterest.co.uk/pin/432416001697466927/

5 Randall E. Stross, *The Wizard of Menlo Park: How Thomas Alva Edison Invented the Modern World* (New York: Crown Publishers, 2007).

6 Daniel Leech-Wilkinson, 'Portamento and Musical Meaning', *Journal of Musicological Research* 25 (2006), pp. 233–61.

7 José Bowen, 'Tempo, Duration, and Flexibility: Techniques in the Analysis of Performance', *Journal of Musicological Research* 16 (1996), pp. 111–56.

8 Robert D. Levin, 'Improvised embellishments in Mozart's keyboard music', *Early Music* 20/2 (May 1992), p. 221.

9 Giulio Cattin, *Music of the Middle Ages* (Cambridge: Cambridge University Press, 1984), p. 162.

10 https://www.youtube.com/watch?v=QUcTsFe1PVs

11 Steve Mills, *Auditory Archaeology: Understanding Sound and Hearing in the Past* (London: Routledge, 2014).

12 Ontogeny is the development of an organism from the point where the egg is fertilised to when the organism is mature. Phylogeny is the evolution of an entire species or group of organisms.

13 Patrik Juslin and Daniel Västfjäll, 'Emotional Responses to Music: The Need to Consider Underlying Mechanisms', *Behavioral and Brain Sciences* 31 (2008), pp. 559–621 (p. 570).

14 Cited in Keith Oatley, *Emotions: A Brief History* (Oxford: Blackwell, 2004), p. 63. See Sigmund Freud, *Civilization and its Discontents*. Translated by Peter Gay (New York: W. W. Norton, 1984). First published 1930, p. 16.

15 Albert S. Bregman, *Auditory Scene Analysis: The Perceptual Organization of Sound* (MIT, Massachusetts: MIT Press, 1990).

16 Aniruddh D. Patel, *Music, Language, and the Brain* (New York: Oxford University Press, 2007), p. 77.

17 Roger Scruton, *The Aesthetics of Music* (Oxford: Oxford University Press, 1997), p. 96.

18 Andrei Miu and Joanna Vuoskoski, 'The social side of music listening: empathy and contagion in music-induced emotions', in Elaine King and Caroline Waddington (eds), *Music and Empathy* (Oxford: Routledge, 2017), pp. 124–38.

19 Youna Kim (ed.), *The Korean Wave: Korean Media Go Global* (London: Routledge, 2013).

20 Susan Blackmore, *The Meme Machine* (New York: Oxford University Press, 1999).

21 Paul Ekman, *Emotions Revealed: Understanding Faces and Feelings* (New York: Henry Holt and Company, 2007).

22 Charles Darwin, *The Expression of the Emotions in Man and Animals: Definitive Edition* (New York: Harper Perennial, 2009). Originally published 1872.

23 Victoria Williamson, *You are the Music: How Music Reveals What it Means to be Human* (London: Icon Books Ltd, 2014), p. 13.

24 John Blacking, *Venda Children's Songs: A Study in Ethnomusicological Analysis* (Chicago: The University of Chicago Press, 1967); *How Musical is Man?* (Washington: University of Washington Press, 1973).

25 Kathleen Higgins, *The Music Between Us: Is Music a Universal Language?* (Chicago: The University of Chicago Press, 2012).

26 Naomi Cumming, *The Sonic Self: Musical Subjectivity and Signification* (Bloomington, Indiana: Indiana University Press, 2000).

27 Michael Taussig, *Mimesis and Alterity: A Particular History of the Senses* (New York: Routledge, 1993).

28 Judith Becker, *Deep Listeners: Music, Emotion, and Trancing* (Bloomington, Indiana: Indiana University Press, 2004).

29 John Roberts, *History of the World* (Oxford: Oxford University Press, 1993); *The Triumph of the West* (London: BBC Books, 1985).

30 Molefi Kete Asante, *The History of Africa: The Quest for Eternal Harmony* (London: Routledge, 2015), p. 120.

31 David Hinton (trans.), *The Selected Poems of Wang Wei* (New York: New Directions, 2006).

32 Anthony Seeger, *Why Suyá Sing* (Urbana: University of Illinois Press, 2004). The Indians formerly known by outsiders as 'Suyá' now insist on the name they call themselves, which is Kisedje.

33 Beverley Diamond, 'Native American ways of (music) history', in Philip Bohlman (ed.), *The Cambridge History of World Music* (Cambridge: Cambridge University Press, 2013), pp. 155–79 (p. 165).

34 Gary Tomlinson, 'Musicology, Anthropology, History', *Il Saggiatore musicale* 8/1 (2001), pp. 21–37.

35 John Nicholson, *Songlines and Stone Axes* (Sydney: Allen & Unwin, 2007).

36 Kermit Ernest Campbell, *Gettin' our Groove on: Rhetoric, Language, and Literacy for the Hip Hop Generation* (Detroit: Wayne State University Press, 2005).

37 Lothar von Falkenhausen, *Suspended Music: Chime-Bells in the Culture of Bronze Age China* (Berkeley: University of California Press, 1993), p. 3.

38 Joscelyn Goodwin, *Robert Fludd: Hermetic Philosopher and Surveyor of Two Worlds* (Newburyport, Mass.: Phanes Press, 1991); Johannes Kepler, *The Harmony of the World* (Philadelphia: The American Philosophical Society, 1997).

39 http://quantummusic.org/

40 Tristram Kidder, Liu Haiwang, Michael Storozum and Qin Zhen, 'New Perspectives on the Collapse and Regeneration of the Han Dynasty', in Ronald Faulseit (ed.), *Beyond Collapse: Archaeological Perspectives on Resilience, Revitalization, and Transformation in Complex Societies* (Carbondale: Southern Illinois University, 2015), pp. 70–98; Erica Fox Brindley, *Music, Cosmology, and the Politics of Harmony in Early China* (Albany: SUNY Press, 2012).

41 Christopher Page, *The Christian West and its Singers: The First Thousand Years* (New Haven: Yale University Press, 2010).

42 Michael Tenzer, *Balinese Music* (Berkeley: Periplus Editions), p. 20.

43 Kofi Agawu, *Representing African Music: Postcolonial Notes, Queries, Positions* (New York: Routledge, 2003), p. 3.

44 Iain Morley, *The Prehistory of Music: Human Evolution, Archaeology, and the Origins of Musicality* (New York: Oxford University Press, 2013).

45 Steven Feld, *Sound and Sentiment: Birds, Weeping, Poetics, and Song in Kaluli Expression* (Philadelphia: University of Pennsylvania Press, 1982).

46 John Iliffe, *Africans: The History of a Continent* (Cambridge: Cambridge University Press, 1995), p. 120.

47 Joachim Braun, *Music in Ancient Israel/Palestine: Archaeological, Written, and Comparative Sources* (Cambridge: William B. Eerdmans Publishing Company, 2002), p. 70.

48 John Arthur Smith, *Music in Ancient Judaism and Early Christianity* (London: Routledge, 2016), pp. 91–2.

49 Alexander Akorlie Agodoh, *African Music: Traditional and Contemporary* (New York: Nova Science Publishers, 2005), p. 13.

50 Sandra Trehub and Laurel Trainor, 'Singing to Infants: Lullabies and Play Songs', in Carolyn Rovee-Collier, Lewis Lipsitt and Harlene Hayne (eds), *Advances in Infancy Research* 12 (London: Ablex Publishing Corporation, 1998), pp. 49–55.

51 Pamela Stern, *Daily Life of the Inuit* (Santa Barbara: Greenwood, 2010), p. 119.

52 Brian Breed, *Pastoral Inscriptions: Reading and Writing Virgil's Eclogues* (London: Bloomsbury, 2012), p. 64.

53 Alan Merriam, *The Anthropology of Music* (Evanston, Ill.: Northwestern University Press, 1980), p. 214.

54 Veronica Doubleday, 'The Frame Drum in the Middle East: Women, Musical Instruments, and Power', in Jennifer Post (ed.), *Ethnomusicology: A Contemporary Reader* (London: Routledge, 2006), pp. 101–34 (p. 112).

55 Scott Burnham, *Beethoven Hero* (Princeton, NJ: Princeton University Press, 2000).

56 Cited in Stephen Rumph, *Beethoven after Napoleon: Political Romanticism in the Late Works* (Berkeley: California University Press, 2004), p. 100.

57 David Hebert and Jonathan McCollum, 'Philosophy of History and Theory in Historical Ethnomusicology', in Jonathan McCollum and David G. Hebert (eds), *Theory and Method in Historical Ethnomusicology* (New York: Lexington Books, 2014), pp. 85–148 (p. 109).

58 https://www.youtube.com/watch?v=z_sFVFsENMg. See also Kofi Agawu, *The African Imagination in Music* (New York: Oxford University Press, 2016), p. 295.

59 Katrina Thompson, *Ring Shout, Wheel About: The Racial Politics of Music and Dance in North American Slavery* (Urbana: University of Illinois Press, 2014), p. 17.

60 Lewis Rowell, *Music and Musical Thought in Early India* (Chicago: University of Chicago Press, 1992).

61 Bruno Nettl and Philip Bohlman (eds), *Comparative Musicology and Anthropology of Music: Essays on the History of Ethnomusicology* (Chicago: The University of Chicago Press, 1991), p. 71.

62 Roger Hart, *Imagined Civilizations: China, the West, and their first Encounter* (Baltimore: The John Hopkins University Press, 2013), p. 119.

63 Fadlou Shehadi, *Philosophies of Music in Medieval Islam* (Leiden: E. J. Brill, 1995), p. 82.

64 Judith Becker, *Deep Listeners: Music, Emotion, and Trancing* (Bloomington, Indiana: Indiana University Press, 2004), p. 57.

65 Regula Qureshi, *Sufi Music of India and Pakistan: Sound, Context and Meaning in Qawaali* (Cambridge: Cambridge University Press, 1986).

66 Max Weber, *The Rational and Social Foundations of Music* (Carbondale: Southern Illinois University Press, 1958); Theodor Adorno, *Philosophy of Modern Music* (New York: Continuum, 2007); Mark Evan Bonds, *Absolute Music: The History of an Idea* (New York: Oxford University Press, 2014).

67 Daniel Leech-Wilkinson, *Machaut's Mass: An Introduction* (Oxford: Clarendon Press, 1992).

68 Jacques Chailley (trans. Rollo Myers), *40,000 Years of Music* (London: Macdonald & Co., 1964).

69 Marian Hu, Hong Young Yan, Wen-Sung Chung, Jen-Chieh Shiao and Pung-Pung Hwang, 'Acoustically evoked potentials in two cephalopods inferred using the auditory brainstem response (ABR) approach', *Comparative Biochemistry and Physiology, Part A* 153/3 (July 2009), pp. 278–83.

70 https://blogs.scientificamerican.com/octopus-chronicles/even-severed-octopus-arms-have-smart-moves/

71 George Lakoff and Mark Johnson, *Metaphors We Live By* (Chicago: Chicago University Press, 1980).

72 Arnie Cox, *Music and Embodied Cognition: Listening, Moving, Feeling, and Thinking* (Bloomington: Indiana University Press, 2016).

73 Barbara King, *The Dynamic Dance: Nonvocal Communication in African Great Apes* (Cambridge, Mass.: Harvard University Press, 2004).

74 Ray Jackendoff, *Foundations of Language: Brain, Meaning, Grammar, Evolution* (New York: Oxford University Press, 2002); Fred Lerdahl and Ray Jackendoff, *A Generative Theory of Tonal Music* (Cambridge, Mass.: MIT Press, 1985).

75 Fred Spier, *Big History and the Future of Humanity* (Oxford: Wiley, 2015), p. 202.

76 Bruce Richman, 'Rhythm and Melody in Gelada Vocal Exchanges', *Primates* 28/2 (April, 1987), pp. 199–223.

77 Patrik Juslin and Daniel Västfjäll, 'Emotional Responses to Music: The Need to Consider Underlying Mechanisms', *Behavioral and Brain Sciences* 31 (2008), pp. 559–621.

78 Donald C. Johanson and Blake Edgar, *From Lucy to Language* (New York: Simon & Schuster, 1996).

79 Steven Mithen, 'The significance of stones and bones: understanding the biology and evolution of rhythm requires attention to the archaeological and fossil record', in Patrick Rebuschat, Martin Rohrmeier, John A. Hawkins and Ian Cross (eds), *Language and Music as Cognitive Systems* (New York: Oxford University Press, 2012), pp. 103–9 (p. 105).

80 Wray, Alison, 'Protolanguage as a holistic system for social interaction', *Language & Communication* 18/1 (1998), pp. 47–67.

81 Not all linguists agree. For a trenchant critique, see W. Tecumseh Fitch, *The Evolution of Language* (Cambridge: Cambridge University Press, 2010).

82 David Begun (ed.), *A Companion to Paleoanthropology* (Oxford: Wiley-Blackwell, 2013), p. 278.

83 Steven Mithen, *The Singing Neanderthals: The Origins of Music, Language, Mind and Body* (Cambridge, Mass.: Harvard University Press, 2005).

84 Gary Tomlinson, *A Million Years of Music: The Emergence of Human Modernity* (New York: Zone Books, 2015).

85 Steven Pinker, *How the Mind Works* (New York: Norton & Norton, 2009), p. 534.

86 Ian Cross, 'Is music the most important thing we ever did? Music, development, and evolution', in S. W. Yi (ed.), *Music, Mind, and Science* (Seoul: Seoul National University Press, 1999), pp. 27–39.

87 Daniel Dennett, *Darwin's Dangerous Idea: Evolution and the Meanings of Life* (New York: Simon & Schuster, 1995), p. 272; Stephen Davies, *The Artful Species: Aesthetics, Art, and Evolution* (New York: Oxford University Press, 2012), p. 141.

88 David Cope, *Virtual Music: Computer Synthesis of Musical Style* (Cambridge, Mass: MIT Press, 2001).

89 Austin DeMarco (ed.), *Gamification: Concepts, Methodologies, Tools, and Applications* (Hershey, PA: Information Science Reference, 2015), p. 1333–41; Michael Austin (ed.), *Music Video Games: Performance, Politics, and Play* (London: Bloomsbury, 2016).

90 Lawrence Kramer, 'Classical Music for the Posthuman Condition', in John Richardson, Claudia Gorbman and Carol Vernallis (eds), *The Oxford Handbook of New Audiovisual Aesthetics* (New York: Oxford University Press, 2013), pp. 39–52.

Chapter 2

1 Takashi Ohnishi, Hiroshi Matsuda, Takashi Asada, Makoto Aruga, Makiko Hirakata, Masami Nishikawa, Asako Katoh and Etsuko Imabayashi, 'Functional Anatomy of Musical Perception in Musicians', *Cerebral Cortex* 11/8 (August, 2001), pp. 754–60 (p. 754).

2 Christian Gaser and Gottfried Schlaug, 'Brain Structures Differ between Musicians and Non-Musicians', *The Journal of Neuroscience* 23/27 (2003), pp. 9240–5.

3 See for instance Thomas Münte, Wido Nager, Tilla Beiss, Christine Schroeder and Eckart Altenmüller, 'Specialization of the specialized: Electrophysiological investigations in professional musicians', *Annals of the New York Academy of Science* 999 (2006), pp. 131–9.

4 Kofi Agawu, *The African Imagination in Music* (New York: Oxford University Press, 2016).

5 R. Stone, 'African Music in a Constellation of Arts', in R. Stone (ed.), *The Garland Encyclopedia of World Music* (New York: Garland, 1998), pp. 1–12 (p. 7); Jane Davidson and Andrea Emberly, 'Embodied Musical Communication across Cultures: Singing and Dancing for Quality of Life and Wellbeing Benefit', in Raymond MacDonald, Gunter Kreutz and Laura Mitchell (eds), *Music, Health, and Wellbeing* (New York: Oxford University Press, 2012), pp. 136–52 (p. 143).

6 Heiner Gembris, 'Music-Making as a Lifelong Development and Resource for Health', in MacDonald et al. (eds), *Music, Health, and Wellbeing*, pp. 367–82 (p. 371).

7 Jean-Pierre Lecanuet, 'Prenatal auditory experience', in Irene Deliège and John Sloboda (eds), *Musical Beginnings: Origins and Development of Musical Comptetence* (Oxford: Oxford University Press, 1996), pp. 1–42.

8 L. Salk, 'The effects of the normal heartbeat sound on the behavior of the newborn infant: implications for mental health', *World Mental Health* 12 (1960), pp. 1–8.

9 Kathleen A. Corrigall and Glenn E. Schellenberg, 'Music cognition in childhood', in Gary E. McPherson (ed.), *The Child as Musician: A handbook of musical development* (New York: Oxford University Press, 2016), pp. 81–101 (p. 88).

10 Marcel Zentner and Tuomas Eerola, 'Rhythmic engagement with music in infancy', *PNAS* 107/13 (2010), pp. 5768–72.

11 Colwyn Trevarthen and Kenneth Aitken, 'Infant Intersubjectivity: Research, Theory, and Clinical Applications', *Journal of Child Psychology and Psychiatry* 42/1 (2001), pp. 3–48.

12 Daniel N. Stern, *The Interpersonal World of the Infant: A View from Psychoanalysis and Developmental Psychology* (New York: Karnac, 1998), p. 138.

13 Kathleen Higgins, *The Music Between Us: Is Music a Universal Language?* (Chicago: The University of Chicago Press, 2012).

14 Stephen N. Malloch, 'Mothers and infants and communicative musicality', *Musicae Scientiae* Special Issue (1999–2000), pp. 29–57 (p. 47).

15 Maya Gratier, 'Expressions of belonging: the effect of acculturation on the rhythm and harmony of mother-infant vocal interaction', *Musicae Scientiae* Special Issue (1999–2000), pp. 93–122.

16 J. Phillips-Silver and L. J. Trainor, 'Feeling the beat: Movement influences infants' rhythm perception', *Science* 308 (2005), p. 1430.

17 Gaye Soley and Erin E. Hannon, 'Infants prefer the musical meter of their own culture: A cross-cultural comparison', *Developmental Psychology* 46/1 (2010), pp. 286–92.

18 Barbara Ayres, 'Effects of Infant Carrying Practices on Rhythm in Music', *Ethos* 1/4 (1973), pp. 387–404 (p. 400).

19 Michael Urban, *New Orleans Rhythm and Blues after Katrina: Music, Magic and Myth* (New York: Palgrave Macmillan, 2016), pp. 114–15.

20 Marcel Zentner and Jerome Kagan, 'Infants' perception of consonance and dissonance in music', *Infant Behavior and Development* 21/3 (1998), pp. 483–92.

21 Erin E. Hannon and Sandra E. Trehub, 'Tuning in to musical rhythms: Infants learn more readily than adults', *PNAS* 102/35 (2005), pp. 12 639–43.

22 Michael Tenzer, *Balinese Gamelan Music* (Rutland, Vermont: Tuttle Publishing, 2011), p. 38.

23 Aniruddh D. Patel, *Music, Language, and the Brain* (New York: Oxford University Press, 2008), p. 19.

24 G. A. Miller, 'The magical number seven, plus or minus two: some limits on our capacity for processing information', *Psychological Review* 63/2 (1956), pp. 81–97.

25 Adam Ockelford, *Music, Language and Autism: Exceptional Strategies for Exceptional Minds* (Philadelphia: Jessica Kingsley Publishers, 2013), p. 183.

26 Ibid., p. 184.

27 Patel, *Music, Language and the Brain*, pp. 267–8.

28 Pamela Heaton, Rory Allen, Kerry Williams, Omar Cummins and Francesca Happé, 'Do social and cognitive deficits curtail musical understanding? Evidence from autism and Down syndrome', *British Journal of Developmental Psychology* 26 (2008), pp. 171–82 (p. 178).

29 The tool can be accessed at http://soundsofintent.org

30 John Irving, *Mozart's Piano Concertos* (London: Routledge, 2003), p. 118.

31 G. E. McPherson, 'The role of parents in children's musical development', *Psychology of Music* 37/1 (2009), pp. 91–110.

32 Giorgio Sanguinetti, *The Art of Partimento: History, Theory, and Practice* (New York: Oxford University Press, 2012), pp. 31–4.

33 Robert O. Gjerdingen, *Music in the Galant Style* (New York: Oxford University Press, 2007), pp. 365–8. In Gjerdingen's terms, an 'Opening Gambit' is a conversational statement that invites an elegant riposte. A 'Romanesca' is a descending stepwise progression (in both bass and melody) best known from Pachelbel's famous *Canon*. A 'Prinner Riposte' answers that with a melodic descent from the sixth to the third degree of the scale. An 'Indugio' (the Italian word for 'procrastination') is a playful tarrying on a chord. A 'Ponte' (meaning 'bridge'), as the name suggests, is a bridge passage.

34 Michele Raja, 'Did Mozart suffer from Asperger syndrome?', *Journal of Medical Biography* 23/2 (2013), pp. 84–92.

35 https://vimeo.com/195606047

36 Peter Pesic, 'The Child and the Daemon: Mozart and Deep Play', *19th-Century Music* 25/2–3 (2001–2), pp. 91–107.

37 John Blacking, *Venda Children's Songs: A Study in Ethnomusicological Analysis* (Chicago: The University of Chicago Press, 1967), p. 29.

38 John Blacking, *How Musical is Man?* (Washington: University of Washington Press, 1973).

39 Andrea Emberly and Jane Davidson, 'From the *kraal* to the classroom: Shifting musical arts practices from the community to the school with special reference to learning *tshigombela* in Limpopo, South Africa', *International Journal of Music Education* 29/3 (2011), pp. 265–82 (p. 226).

40 Eric Hobsbawm and Terence Ranger (eds), *The Invention of Tradition* (Cambridge: Cambridge University Press, 1983).

41 http://www.independent.co.uk/student/student-life/the-strangest-oxford-tradition-of-all-making-sure-the-clocks-go-back-with-the-time-ceremony-8908472.html

42 Sara Cohen, *Rock Culture in Liverpool: Popular Music in the Making* (Oxford: Clarendon Press, 1991), p. 3.

43 Richard Middleton, *Studying Popular Music* (Milton Keynes: Open University Press, 1990), p. 161.

44 Linda Spear, *The Behavioral Neuroscience of Adolescence* (New York: W. W. Norton, 2010).

45 Victor Witter Turner, *The Forest of Symbols: Aspects of Ndembu Ritual* (Ithaca: Cornell University Press, 1967), pp. 181–2.

46 Anthony Seeger, *Why Suyá Sing* (Urbana: University of Illinois Press, 2004), p. 79. As noted earlier, the Suyá call themselves Kisedje.

47 Peter Dronke, *Women Writers of the Middle Ages* (Cambridge: Cambridge University Press, 1984), p. 160.

48 Bruce Holsinger, *Music, Body, and Desire in Medieval Culture: Hildegard of Bingen to Chaucer* (Stanford: Stanford University Press, 2001), p. 281.

49 Martha Feldman, *The Castrato: Reflections on Natures and Kinds* (Berkeley: University of California Press, 2015).

50 Andreas C. Lehmann, John A. Sloboda and Robert H. Woody, *Psychology for Musicians: Understanding and Acquiring the Skills* (New York: Oxford University Press, 2007), p. 71.

51 John Daverio, *Robert Schumann: Herald of a 'New Poetic Age'* (New York: Oxford University Press, 1997), p. 77.

52 Jeff Todd Titon, *Worlds of Music: An Introduction to the Music of the World's Peoples* (Boston: Cengage Learning, 2017), p. 319.

53 Sean Williams, *Focus: Irish Traditional Music* (London: Routledge, 2010), p. 22.

54 Jeroen de Kloet and Anthony Y. H. Fung, *Youth Cultures in China* (Cambridge: Polity Press, 2017).

55 Ibid., Kindle loc. 1596.

56 Arun Saldanha, 'Music, Space, Identity: Geographies of Youth Culture in Bangalore', *Cultural Studies* 16/3 (2002), pp. 337–50.

57 https://www.theguardian.com/music/2012/sep/09/georg-solti-centenary-lady-valerie

58 Howard Gardner, *Creating Minds: An Anatomy of Creativity Seen Through the Lives of Freud, Einstein, Picasso, Stravinsky, Eliot, Graham, and Gandhi* (New York: Basic Books, 2011), p. 28.

59 Wolfgang Hildesheimer, *Mozart* (New York: Oxford University Press, 1985); Maynard Solomon, *Beethoven* (London: Macmillan, 1979).

60 Anton Ehrenzweig, (Berkeley, California: University of California Press, 1971).

61 John Eliot Gardiner, *Music in the Castle of Heaven* (London: Allen Lane, 2013), p. 168.

62 Ibid., pp. 172–4.

63 Hermann Abert, *W. A. Mozart* (New Haven: Yale University Press, 2007), p. 562.

64 William Kinderman, *Beethoven* (Berkeley: University of California Press, 1995), p. 87.

65 You can hear him reading out his fairy tale *The Princess* (*Die Prinzessin*) at https://www.youtube.com/watch?v=EtPcS6sRZ3o

66 Joseph Straus, *The Music of Ruth Crawford Seeger* (Cambridge: Cambridge University Press, 2003).

67 Tom Service, 'A Guide to Galina Ustvolskaya's Music', https://www.theguardian.com/music/musicblog/2013/apr/08/contemporary-music-guide-galina-ustvolskaya

68 David Wyn Jones, *The Life of Beethoven* (Cambridge: Cambridge University Press, 1998), p. 36.

69 Barry Cooper (ed.), *The Beethoven Compendium: A Guide to Beethoven's Life and Music* (London: Thames and Hudson, 1991), p. 124.

70 Richard Widdess, 'Sogasuga: A Song of Songs', in Rachel Harris and Rowan Pease (eds), *Pieces of the Musical World: Sounds and Cultures* (London: Routledge, 2015), pp. 105–22; Amy Catlin, 'Karnatak Vocal and Instrumental Music', in Alison Arnold and Bruno Nettl (eds), *The Garland Encyclopedia of World Music: South Asia: The Indian Subcontinent* (New York: Taylor and Francis, 2000), pp. 209–36.

71 Bruno Nettl, *The Study of Ethnomusicology: Thirty-Three Discussions* (Chicago: University of Illinois Press, 2015), p. 58.

72 Reginald Massey and Jamila Massey, *The Music of India* (London: Kahn and Averill, 1993), p. 59. The publication of Venkatamakhi's classificatory scheme, the *Chaturdandi Prakasika*, in 1660 led to an explosion of new ragas in the eighteenth century.

73 Cohen, *Rock Culture in Liverpool*, pp. 135–71.

74 Walter Everett, *The Beatles as Musicians:* Revolver *through the* Anthology (New York: Oxford University Press, 1999), p. 11.

75 Ibid., p. 10.

76 Tenzer, *Balinese Gamelan Music*, p. 17.

77 Fabrice Marandola, 'Expressiveness in the Performance of Bedzan Pygmies' Vocal Polyphonies: When the Same is Never the Same', in Dorottya Fabian, Renee Timmers and Emery Schubert (eds), *Expressiveness in Music Performance* (New York: Oxford University Press, 2014), pp. 201–20.

78 Maya Gratier, 'Grounding in musical interaction: Evidence from jazz performance', *Musicae Scientiae* Special Issue (2008), pp. 71–110.

79 Björn Merker, 'Synchronous chorusing and the origins of music', *Musicae Scientiae* Special Issue (1999–2000), pp. 59–73.

80 Dean Keith Simonton, 'Creative productivity, age, and stress: A biographical time-series analysis of 10 classical composers', *Journal of Personality and Social Psychology* 35 (1977), pp. 791–804.

81 Sandra Garrido, *Why are we Attracted to Sad Music?* (Cham: Palgrave Macmillan, 2017), pp. 107–8.

82 Arielle Bonneville-Roussy and Jeff Potter, 'Music through the Ages: Trends in Musical Engagement and Preferences from Adolescence

through Middle Adulthood', *Journal of Personality and Social Psychology* 105/4 (2013), pp. 703–17 (p. 715).

83 Herbert Bruhn, 'Musical Development of Elderly People', *Psychomusicology* 18 (2002), pp. 59–75 (p. 68).

84 M. Cooke, W. Shum, D. Harrison and J. E. Murfield, 'A randomized controlled trial exploring the effect of music on quality of life and depression in older people with dementia', *Journal of Health Psychology* 15/5 (2010), pp. 765–76.

85 Teppo Särkämö, 'Music for the ageing brain: Cognitive, emotional, social, and neural benefits of musical leisure activities in stroke and dementia', *Dementia* 16/6 (2018), pp. 670–85.

86 http://www.livemusicnow.org.uk/

87 Sandra Garrido, 'Music and dementia: Hitting the right note', *Australian Ageing Agenda* (Dec. 2016), pp. 46–7.

88 Särkämö, 'Music for the ageing brain', p. 677.

89 Joseph Straus, *Extraordinary Measures: Disability in Music* (New York: Oxford University Press, 2011), p. 82.

90 Gerhard von Breuning, *Memories of Beethoven: From the House of the Black-Robed Spaniards* (Cambridge: Cambridge University Press, 1995), p. 98.

91 Kinderman, *Beethoven*, p. 153.

92 Amit Dias and Vikram Patel, 'Closing the treatment gap for dementia in India', *Indian Journal of Psychiatry* 51 (2009), pp. 93–7.

93 Edward Said, *On Late Style: Music and Literature Against the Grain* (London: Bloomsbury, 2006); *Orientalism: Western Conceptions of the Orient* (New York: Pantheon Books, 1978).

94 https://www.sputnikmusic.com/review/40918/Buena-Vista-Social-Club-Buena-Vista-Social-Club/

95 Malcolm Gillies, 'Bartók in America', in Amanda Bayley (ed.), *The Cambridge Companion to Bartók* (Cambridge: Cambridge University Press, 2001), pp. 190–201 (p. 197).

96 David Cooper, *Béla Bartók* (New Haven: Yale University Press, 2015), p. 257.

97 David Cooper, *Bartók: Concerto for Orchestra* (Cambridge: Cambridge University Press, 2004), p. 20.

98 Donald Maurice, *Bartók's Viola Concerto: The Remarkable Story of his Swansong* (New York: Oxford University Press, 2004), p. 27.

99 Gillies, 'Bartók in America', p. 195.

100 http://seenandheard-international.com/2017/09/alain-altinoglus-auspicious-debut-with-the-berliner-philharmoniker/

Chapter 3

1 The Sound of the Next Generation: A Comprehensive Review of Children and Young People's Relationship with Music, https://www.youthmusic. org.uk/sound-of-the-next-generation

2 Cited in Andy Hamilton, *Aesthetics and Music* (London: Continuum, 2008), p. 11.

3 Cited in Marek Korczynski, Michael Pickering and Emma Robertson, *Rhythms of Labour: Music at Work in Britain* (Cambridge: Cambridge University Press, 2013), p. 115.

4 Ibid., p. 116.

5 Ibid., p. 117.

6 Ibid., p. 78.

7 Mary-Ann Constantine and Gerald Porter, *Fragments and Meaning in Traditional Song: From the Blues to the Baltic* (Oxford: Oxford University Press, 2003), p. 150.

8 Marek Korczynski, *Songs of the Factory: Pop, Music, Culture, & Resistance* (Ithaca: ILR Press, 2014), p. 28.

9 Mark Smith, *Listening to Nineteenth-century America* (Chapel Hill: The University of North Carolina Press, 2001).

10 Ibid., p. 23.

11 Cited in Peter van der Merwe, *Origins of the Popular Style: The Antecedents of Twentieth-Century Popular Music* (Oxford: Clarendon Press, 1992), p. 69.

12 Korczynski, *Songs of the Factory*, p. 28.

13 Stan Hugill, *Shanties from the Seven Seas* (Stonington, Connecticut: Mystic Seaport, 1961), p. 1.

14 Nicola Dibben and Anneli Haake, 'Music and the construction of space in office-based work settings', in Georgina Born (ed.), Music, Sound and Space (Cambridge: Cambridge University Press, 2013), pp. 151–68.

15 Tia DeNora, *Music in Everyday Life* (Cambridge: Cambridge University Press, 2000), p. 46.

16 Adam Krims, *Music and Urban Geography* (London: Routledge, 2007), pp. 127–62.

17 DeNora, *Music in Everyday Life*, p. 118.

18 https://www.theguardian.com/technology/2015/feb/13/spotify-knows-what-music-youre-having-sex-to

19 https://moz.com/blog/google-told-me-im-pregnant-from-strings-to-diagnosis

20 John Sloboda, *Exploring the Musical Mind: Cognition, Emotion, Ability, Function* (Oxford: Oxford University Press, 2005), p. 348.

21 http://www.classicfm.com/discover-music/mood/relaxing/

22 Krims, *Music and Urban Geography*, p. 144.

23 https://www.visitliverpool.com/information/product-catch-all/
    bold-street-p16794

24 Michael Bull, *Sound Moves: iPod Culture and Urban Experience* (London:
    Routledge, 2008), p. 6.

25 Brandon LaBelle, *Acoustic Territories: Sound Culture and Everyday Life*
    (London: Bloomsbury, 2014), p. 99.

26 Krims, *Music and Urban Geography*, p. 80.

27 Ibid., pp. 1–3.

28 DeNora, *Music in Everyday Life*, p. 136.

29 Ibid., p. 137.

30 Adrian North and David Hargreaves, *The Social and Applied Psychology of
    Music* (New York: Oxford University Press, 2008), p. 280.

31 LaBelle, *Acoustic Territories*, p. 174.

32 Sara Cohen, *Decline, Renewal and the City in Popular Music Culture: Beyond
    the Beatles* (Aldershot: Ashgate, 2007), pp. 56–62.

33 Michael Brocken, *Other Voices: Hidden Histories of Liverpool's Popular
    Music Scenes, 1930s–1970s* (London: Routledge, 2016), p. 112.

34 Hugill, *Shanties*, p. 53.

35 Jeremy Price, '"From Nelly Ray to Maggie May": Re-enacting the Past
    on the Streets of Liverpool', in Logie Barrow and François Poirier (eds),
    *Keeping the Lid on: Urban Eruptions and Social Control since the 19th
    Century* (Newcastle: Cambridge Scholars Publishing, 2010), pp. 77–92.

36 https://www.youtube.com/watch?v=2wnhkicl3Z8

37 Price, '"From Nelly Ray to Maggie May"', p. 77.

38 Cited in Margot Fassler, *Gothic Song* (Indiana: University of Notre Dame
    Press, 2011), p. 217.

39 Cited in Paul du Noyer, *Liverpool – Wondrous Place: From the Cavern to the
    Capital of Culture* (London: Virgin Books, 2007), p. 1.

40 'The World's Cities in 2016', United Nations Data Booklet, http://www.
    un.org/en/development/desa/population/publications/pdf/urbanization/
    the_worlds_cities_in_2016_data_booklet.pdf

41 Ruth Finnegan, *The Hidden Musicians: Music-Making in an English Town*
    (Middletown: Wesleyan University Press, 2007).

42 The following section is indebted to Nicholas Wong's brilliant PhD thesis,
    'The Rushworths of Liverpool: A Family Music Business. Commerce,
    Culture and the City', University of Liverpool 2016. It also benefited from
    many conversations with Jonathan Rushworth, who generously supported
    Nick's studies in the University Music Department.

43 Sara Cohen, *Rock Culture in Liverpool: Popular Music in the Making* (Oxford: Oxford University Press, 1991).

44 Wong, 'The Rushworths', p. 162.

45 Ibid., p. 129.

46 Cited in David Bruenger, *Making Money, Making Music: History and Core Concepts* (Berkeley: University of California Press, 2016), p. 87.

47 Wong, 'The Rushworths', p. 163.

48 Barbara Kowalzig, ' "And Now All the World Shall Dance!" (Eur. Bacch. 114): Dionysus' Choroi between Drama and Ritual', in Eric Csapo and Margaret Miller (eds), *The Origins of Theater in Ancient Greece and Beyond: From Ritual to Drama* (Cambridge: Cambridge University Press, 2007), pp. 221–54.

49 https://punch.photoshelter.com/image/I0000KP5hOcqgW4E

50 David Hesmondhalgh, *Why Music Matters* (Oxford: Wiley, 2013), p. 106.

51 https://www.liverpoolecho.co.uk/sport/football/football-news/new-mohamed-salah-ill-muslim-14302028

52 Les Back, 'Sounds in the Crowd', in Michael Bull and Les Back (eds), *The Auditory Culture Reader* (Oxford: Berg, 2004), pp. 311–28 (p. 321).

53 Thomas Turino, *Music as Social Life: The Politics of Participation* (Chicago: The University of Chicago Press, 2008), p. 29.

54 Jim O'Donnell, *The Day John Met Paul: An Hour-by-Hour Account of How the Beatles Began* (London: Routledge, 2006).

55 George Orwell, *The Lion and the Unicorn: Socialism and the English Genius* (London: Penguin, 1941), p. 11.

56 Jez Quayle, *Skiffle Ukelele Songbook* (Lulu.com, 2018), p. 1.

57 Brocken, *Other Voices* (London: Routledge, 2016), p. 20.

58 Jack Hamilton, *Just Around Midnight: Rock and Roll and the Racial Imagination* (Cambridge, Mass.: Harvard University Press, 2016), p. 109.

59 Barry Miles, *The Beatles Diary Volume 1: The Beatles Years* (New York: Omnibus Press, 2009).

60 Turino, *Music as Social Life*, pp. 36–51.

61 Walter Everett, *The Beatles as Musicians: The Quarry Men through Rubber Soul* (New York: Oxford University Press, 2001), pp. 131–5.

62 https://www.youtube.com/watch?v=b-VAxGJdJeQ

63 Jacqueline Edmondson, *John Lennon: A Biography* (Oxford: Greenwood, 2010), pp. 58–9.

64 Walter Everett, *The Beatles as Musicians: Revolver Through the Anthology* (New York: Oxford University Press, 1999), pp. 36–7.

65 Ibid., pp. 118–19.

66 https://www.youtube.com/watch?v=KvuiiqS4s2s

67 http://www.bbc.co.uk/news/world-latin-america-40090809

68 Bruce Johnson and Martin Cloonan, 'Music and Arousal to Violence', in Bruce Johnson and Martin Cloonan (eds), *The Dark Side of the Tune: Popular Music and Violence* (Aldershot: Ashgate, 2009), pp. 123–46 (p. 152).

69 Ibid., p. 152.

70 John Baxter, *Disney During World War II: How the Walt Disney Studio Contributed to Victory in the War* (Glendale: Disney Editions, 2014).

71 Michael Sorkin, *All Over the Map: Writings on Buildings and Cities* (London: Verso, 2011), p. 347.

72 Clayton Koppes, 'The Real Ambassadors? The Cleveland Orchestra Tours and the Soviet Union, 1965', in Simo Mikkonen and Pekka Suutari (eds), *Music, Art and Diplomacy: East–West Cultural Interactions and the Cold War* (London: Routledge, 2016), pp. 69–87 (p. 84).

73 Emily Abrams Ansari, 'Shaping the Policies of Cold War Musical Diplomacy: An Epistemic Community of American Composers', *Diplomatic History* 36/1 (2012), pp. 41–52 (p. 41).

74 Jessica Gienow-Hecht, 'The World is Ready to Listen: Symphony Orchestras and the Global Performance of America', *Diplomatic History* 36/1 (2012), pp. 17–28 (p. 24).

75 Benedict Anderson, *Imagined Communities: Reflections on the Origin and Spread of Nationalism* (London: Verso, 1983).

76 Thomas Solomon, 'Articulating the historical moment: Turkey, Europe, and Eurovision 2003', in Ivan Raykoff and Robert Deam Tobin (eds), *A Song for Europe: Popular Music and Politics in the Eurovision Song Contest* (London: Routledge, 2016), pp. 135–46.

77 http://www.liverpoolphil.com/in-harmony-liverpool

78 'The Index of Multiple Deprivation 2015: A Liverpool Analysis', Executive Summary, Liverpool City Council.

79 https://www.telegraph.co.uk/culture/music/3667396/BBC-Proms-review-Was-this-the-greatest-Prom-of-all-time.html

80 Cited in Geoffrey Baker, *El Sistema: Orchestrating Venezuela's Youth* (New York: Oxford University Press, 2014), p. 3.

81 Tina Ramnarine (ed.), *Global Perspectives on Orchestras: Collective Creativity and Social Agency* (New York: Oxford University Press, 2017).

82 Baker, El Sistema.

83 https://www.theguardian.com/music/2014/nov/11/geoff-baker-el-sistema-model-of-tyranny

84 'Evaluation of In Harmony: Final Report', National Foundation for Educational Research (NFER), p. 49.

85   Jude Robinson, 'The End is Where We Start From: Communicating the *Impact of a Family Music Project to Wider Audiences*', Anthropology in Action (2014), 21/3, pp. 12–19.

86   Mark Everist, *Mozart's Ghosts: Haunting the Halls of Musical Culture* (New York: Oxford University Press, 2012), pp. 269–76.

87   Kingsley Amis, *Girl, 20* (London: Penguin, 2011 [1971]).

88   Amy Nelson, *Music for the Revolution: Musicians and Power in Early Soviet Russia* (Pennsylvania: The University of Pennsylvania Press, 2004); H. Seifter and P. Economy, *Leadership ensemble: Lessons in collaborative management from the world's only conductorless orchestra* (New York: Henry Holt & Company).

89   Isabella Poggi, 'The Lexicon of the Conductor's Face', in Paul McKevitt, Seán Ó Nualláin and Conn Mulvihill (eds), *Language, Vision, and Music* (Amsterdam: John Benjamins Publishing Company, 2002), pp. 271–84.

90   Geoff Luck and Petri Toiviainen, 'Ensemble Musicians' Synchronization with Conductors' Gestures: An Automated Feature-Extraction Analysis', *Music Perception* 24/2 (2006), pp. 189–200.

91   Peter Keller, 'Ensemble Performance: Interpersonal Alignment of Musical Expression', in Dorottya Fabian, Renee Timmers and Emery Schubert (eds), *Expressiveness in Music Performance* (New York: Oxford University Press, 2014), pp. 260–82 (p. 266).

92   Gilbert Rouget, *Music and Trance: A Theory of the Relations Between Music and Possession* (Chicago: The University of Chicago Press, 1985).

93   Rouget was aware that the terms 'trance' and 'ecstasy' are inverted in the English language (in the original French, the definitions are the other way round). See Ruth Herbert, 'Reconsidering Music and Trance: Cross-cultural Differences and Cross-disciplinary Perspectives', *Ethnomusicology Forum* 20/2 (2011), p. 201–27.

94   Wendy Fonarow, *Empire of Dirt: The Aesthetics and Rituals of British Indie Music* (Middletown, Connecticut: Wesleyan University Press, 2006), p. 55.

95   Michael P. Steinberg, *Listening to Reason: Culture, Subjectivity, and Nineteenth-Century Music* (Princeton: Princeton University Press, 2004), p. 106.

96   Marc Leman, *Embodied Music Cognition and Mediation Technology* (Cambridge, Mass.: 2008), p. 108.

97   Martin Clayton, 'Observing Entrainment in Music Performance: Video-Based Observational Analysis of Indian Musicians' Tanpura Playing and Beat Marking', *Musicae Scientiae* 11/1 (2007), pp. 27–59.

98   https://musicscience.net/2018/03/10/inside-a-string-quartet/

99   Mari Riess Jones and Marilyn Boltz, 'Dynamic Attending Responses to Time', *Psychological Review* 96/3 (1989), pp. 459–91 (p. 471).

100 Albert S. Bregman, *Auditory Scene Analysis: The Perceptual Organization of Sound* (MIT, Massachusetts: MIT Press, 1990).

101 Riess Jones and Boltz, 'Dynamic Attending Responses to Time', p. 471.

102 Melanie Takahashi, 'The "natural high": altered states, flashbacks and neural tunings at raves', in Graham St John, *Rave Culture and Religion* (London: Routledge, 2005), pp. 144–64 (p. 153).

103 T. S. Eliot, *The Four Quartets* (London: Faber & Faber, 2001).

Chapter 4

1   Brian Kane, *Sound Unseen: Acousmatic Sound in Theory and Practice* (New York: Oxford University Press, 2014), p. 55.

2   Abbé Jean-Baptiste Dubos, *Réflexions critiques sur la poésie et sur la peinture* (Paris, 1993; originally published 1719), p. 150.

3   Eduard Hanslick, *On the Musically Beautiful: A Contribution Towards the Revision of the Aesthetics of Music*, trans. Geoffrey Payzant (Indianapolis: Hackett Publishing Company, 1986; originally published 1854) p. 8.

4   Lydia Goehr, *The Imaginary Museum of Musical Works: An Essay in the Philosophy of Music* (Oxford: Clarendon Press, 1992).

5   The fourth (4:3) is acoustically simpler than the third but, for complex cultural reasons, it is deemed to be less satisfying or consonant.

6   Wendy Leborgne and Marci Rosenberg, *The Vocal Athlete* (San Diego: Plural Publishing, 2014), p. 104.

7   Zohar Eitan and Roni Granot, 'How music moves: Musical parameters and listeners' images of motion', *Music Perception* 23/3 (2006), pp. 221–47.

8   Y. S. Wagner, E. Winner, D. Cicchetti and H. Gardner, '"Metaphorical" mapping in human infants', *Child Development* 52 (1981), pp. 728–31.

9   S. K. Roffler and R. A. Butler, 'Localization of tonal stimuli in the vertical plane', *Journal of the Acoustical Society of America* 43 (1968), pp. 1260–5.

10 Lawrence Zbikowski, *Conceptualizing Music: Cognitive Structure, Theory, and Analysis* (New York: Oxford University Press, 2002), p. 67.

11 Steven Feld, *Sound and Sentiment: Birds, Weeping, Poetics, and Song in Kaluli Expression* (Philadelphia: University of Pennsylvania Press, 1982).

12 Rebecca Shaefer, Alexa Morcom, Neil Roberts and Katie Overy, 'Moving to music: effects of heard and imagined musical cues on movement-related brain activity', *Frontiers in Human Neuroscience* 8 (2014), pp. 1–11.

13 Charles Nussbaum, *The Musical Representation: Meaning, Ontology, and Emotion* (Cambridge, Mass.: MIT Press, 2007), p. 52.

14 Richard Fay (ed.), *Comparative Hearing: Fish and Amphibians* (New York: Springer Verlag, 1999), p. 349.

15 Daniel Chiras, *Human Biology* (New York: Jones and Bartlett Publishing, 2005), p. 210.

16 Nussbaum, *The Musical Representation*, pp. 59 –60.

17 Ibid., p. 52.

18 Ibid., p. 59.

19 Ludwig Wittgenstein, *Philosophical Investigations* (Oxford: Blackwell, 1960), p. 213.

20 Arnie Cox, *Music and Embodied Cognition: Listening, Moving, Feeling, and Thinking* (Bloomington: Indiana University Press, 2016).

21 Roger Scruton, *The Aesthetics of Music* (New York: Oxford University Press, 1999), pp. 49–52.

22 Marc Leman, *The Expressive Moment: How Interaction (with Music) Shapes Human Empowerment* (Cambridge, Mass.: MIT Press, 2016), p. 185.

23 Robert Zatorre and Valerie Salimpoor, 'From perception to pleasure: music and its neural substrates', *Proceedings of the National Academy of Science*, 110/2 (2013), pp. 10430–7.

24 Leonard B. Meyer, *Emotion and Meaning in Music* (Chicago: University of Chicago Press, 1956).

25 David Huron, *Sweet Anticipation: Music and the Psychology of Expectation* (Cambridge, Mass.: MIT Press, 2006), p. 23.

26 https://www.youtube.com/watch?v=RxPZh4AnWyk

27 Dave Calvert, ' "Actual Idiocy" and the Sublime Object of Susan Boyle', in Broderick Chow and Alex Mangold (eds), *Zizek and Performance* (London: Palgrave Macmillan, 2014), pp. 178–96.

28 Aniruddh Patel and John Iversen, 'The evolutionary neuroscience of musical beat perception and the Action Simulation for Auditory Prediction (ASAP) hypothesis', *Frontiers in Systems Neuroscience* 8 (2014), pp. 1–14.

29 H. Honing, H. Merchant, G. Háden, L. Prado and R. Bartolo, 'Rhesus monkeys (*Macaca mulatta*) detect rhythmic groups in music, but not the beat', *PLoS ONE*, 7/12 e51369 https://doi.org/10.1371/journal.pone.0051369

30 Charles Darwin, *The Expression of the Emotions in Man and Animals* [1872], Definitive Edition (New York: Harper Perennial, 2009).

31 Ibid., p. 43.

32 Ibid., p. 44.

33 Jenefer Robinson, *Deeper than Reason: Emotion and its Role in Literature, Music, and Art* (Oxford: Clarendon Press, 2005), p. 59.

34 https://www.youtube.com/watch?v=hxbHhzlpdK4

35 Keith Oatley, Dacher Keltner and Jennifer Jenkins, *Understanding Emotions* (Oxford: Blackwell Publishing, 2006).

36 Nico Frijda, *The Emotions* (Cambridge: Cambridge University Press, 1986), p. 71.

37 https://www.telegraph.co.uk/music/what-to-listen-to/best-funeral-songs/albinoni/

38 https://www.wsj.com/articles/SB10001424052970203646004577213010291701378

39 Galen Bodenhausen, 'Categorizing the Social World: Affect, Motivation, and Self-Regulation', in B. H. Ross and A. B. Markman (eds), *Psychology of Learning and Motivation*, 47 (2006), pp. 123–55.

40 Steve Larson, *Musical Forces: Motion, Metaphor, and Meaning in Music* (Bloomington: Indiana University Press, 2012), p. 149.

41 Nicola Dibben, 'The Role of Peripheral Feedback in Emotional Experience with Music', *Music Perception* 22/1 (2004), pp. 79–115.

42 Theodor Adorno, *Philosophy of Modern Music*, trans. A. G. Mitchell and W. V. Bloomster (London: Sheed & Ward, 1987).

43 Charles Rosen, *The Classical Style* (New York: Norton, 1971).

44 James Russell, 'A Circumplex Model of Affect', *Journal of Personality and Social Psychology* 39/6 (1980), pp. 1161–78.

45 Patrik Juslin, 'Emotional Communication in Music Performance: A Functionalist Perspective and Some Data', *Music Perception: An Interdisciplinary Journal* 14/4 (1997), pp. 383–418.

46 http://www2.cnrs.fr/en/2751.htm

47 Michael Spitzer, 'Mapping the Human Heart: A Holistic Analysis of Fear in Schubert', *Music Analysis* 29/1, 2, 3 (2011), pp. 149–213.

48 Arne Öhman and Stefan Wiens, 'On the automaticity of autonomic responses in emotion: An evolutionary perspective', in Richard Davidson, Klaus Scherer and Hill Goldsmith (eds), *Handbook of Affective Sciences* (Oxford: Oxford University Press, 2003), pp. 256–75.

49 Vladimir Propp, *Morphology of the Folktale*, trans. Laurence Scott (Austin: University of Texas Press, 1968).

50 Charles Darwin, *The Voyage of the Beagle* (New York: Cosmo Classics, 2008; first published 1839), p. 211.

51 Cited in Michael Taussig, *Mimesis and Alterity: A Particular History of the Senses* (New York: Routledge, 1993).

52 Ibid.

53 Cited in ibid. See also Walter Benjamin, 'On the Mimetic Faculty', in Rodney Livingstone (ed.), *Walter Benjamin: Selected Writings Volume 2 1931–1934* (Cambridge, Mass.: Harvard University Press, 1999), pp. 720–2.

54 Roger Caillois, 'The Praying Mantis: From Biology to Psychoanalysis', in Claudine Frank (trans. and ed.), *The Edge of Surrealism: A Roger Caillois Reader* (Durham: Duke University Press, 2003), pp. 66–82 (p. 79). I'm grateful to my colleague, Professor Max Paddison, for drawing Caillois to my attention.

55 Darwin, *Beagle*, p. 454. Darwin visited Australia in 1836.

56 Émile Durkheim, *The Elementary Forms of Religious Life*, trans. Joseph Ward Swain [1915] (New York: Dover Publications, 2008), p. 353.

57 Saida Daukeyeva, '"Aqqu" (White Swan): Sound Mimesis and Spirit Evocation in Kazakh Qobyz Performance', in Rachel Harris and Rowan Pease (eds), *Pieces of the Musical World: Sounds and Cultures* (London: Routledge, 2015), pp. 44–63.

58 Frank Kouwenhoven, 'Meaning and structure – the case of Chinese *qin* (zither) music', *British Journal of Ethnomusicology* 10/1 (2001), pp. 39–62.

59 Ibid., p. 46.

60 Ibid., p. 58.

61 Ethan Morden, *Opera Anecdotes* (New York: Oxford University Press, 1985), p. 167.

62 Max Horkheimer and Theodor Adorno, *Dialectic of Enlightenment* [1944], trans. Edmund Jephcott (Stanford: Stanford University Press, 2002), p. 27.

63 William James, *The Varieties of Religious Experience* [1902] (Garsches: Feedbooks, 2018) p. 243.

64 Alf Gabrielsson, *Strong Experiences with Music: Music is much more than just music* (New York: Oxford University Press, 2011), p. 308.

65 Ibid., p. 309.

66 Ibid., p. 312.

67 Nussbaum, *Musical Representation*, pp. 268–9.

68 John Pfeiffer, *The Creative Explosion: An Inquiry into the Origins of Art and Religion* (New York: Harper and Row, 1982), p. 291.

69 Kenneth Smith, '*Vertigo*'s Musical Gaze: Neo-Riemannian Symmetries and Spirals', *Music Analysis* 37/1 (2018), pp. 68–102.

70 Nussbaum, *Musical Representation*, p. 284.

71 Ian Mabbett, 'Buddhism and Music', *Asian Music* 25/1–2 (1993), pp. 9–28.

Chapter 5

1 Penzias and Wilson were using a twenty-foot horn antenna that had originally been designed to detect radio waves bouncing off Echo balloon satellites. 'How Two Pigeons Helped Scientists Confirm the Big Bang Theory', https://www.smithsonianmag.com/smithsonian-institution/

how-scientists-confirmed-big-bang-theory-owe-it-all-to-a-pigeon-trap-180949741/#cfztISWRHSwoPhRQ.99

2 'Asteroseismology: using the natural music of the stars', https://www.birmingham.ac.uk/accessibility/transcripts/Professor-Bill-Chaplin-Asteroseismology.aspx

3 Trevor Wishart, 'From sound morphing to the synthesis of starlight', *Musica/Tenologia* (2013), pp. 65–9.

4 Jon Solomon, *Ptolemy Harmonics: Translation and Commentary* (Leiden: Brill, 2000), pp. 152–55.

5 Siglind Bruhn, *The Musical Order of the World: Kepler, Hesse, Hindemith* (Hillside, New York: Pendragon, 2005), p. 141.

6 Derya Özcan, *The Woman Who Owned the Shadows* (Selçuk University Press: Konya, 2011), p. 11.

7 Patricia Monaghan, *The Goddess Path: Myths, Invocations & Rituals* (St. Paul, Minnesota: Llewellyn, 2004), p. 71.

8 Rosalia Gallotti, 'Before the Acheulean in East Africa: An Overview of the Oldowan Lithic Assemblages', in Rosalia Gallotti and Margherita Mussi (eds), *The Emergence of the Acheulean in East Africa and Beyond* (Cham: Springer, 2018), pp. 13–33 (p. 17).

9 Elizabeth C. Blake and Ian Cross, 'Flint tools as portable sound-producing objects in the Upper Palaeolithic Context: An Experimental Study', *Experiencing Archaeology by Experiment: Proceedings of the Experimental Archaeology Conference, Exeter* (Barnsley: Oxbow Books, 2007), pp. 1–19.

10 https://www.thevintagenews.com/2016/11/10/the-venus-of-hohle-fels-is-the-oldest-statue-depicting-a-womans-figure/

11 Iain Morley, *The Prehistory of Music: Human Evolution, Archaeology, and the Origins of Music* (Oxford: Oxford University Press, 2013), p. 49.

12 https://www.youtube.com/watch?v=yUCBBDV2Tzk

13 Morley, *Prehistory*, pp. 112–13.

14 https://phoenicia.org/kilmer.htm

15 https://music.si.edu/blog/sync-ancient-chinese-bronze-bells-smithsonian

16 Tim Ingold, 'On the social relations of the hunter-gatherer band', in Richard B. Lee and Richard Daly (eds), *The Cambridge Encyclopedia of Hunters and Gatherers* (Cambridge: Cambridge University Press, 2002), pp. 399–411 (pp. 404, 405).

17 https://www.pinterest.co.uk/pin/358177759509266327/?lp=true

18 https://www.smashinglists.com/10-earliest-known-musical-instruments/

19 Morley, *Prehistory*, p. 114.

20 John Shepherd (ed.), *Continuum Encyclopedia of Popular Music of the World*, Vol. 11 (London: Continuum, 2003), p. 276.

21 Richard Rudgley, *The Lost Civilizations of the Stone Age* (New York: Simon & Schuster, 2000), p. 204.

22 Joseph Kaminsky, *Asante Ntahera Trumpets in Ghana: Culture, Tradition, and Sound Barrage* (London: Routledge, 2016).

23 Richard Adams, *Prehistoric Mesoamerica* (Norman, Oklahoma: University of Oklahoma Press, 1997), p. 122.

24 Jeremy Montagu, *Origins and Development of Musical Instruments* (Plymouth: Scarecrow, 2007), p. 105.

25 Jie Jin, *Chinese Music* (Cambridge: Cambridge University Press, 2010), pp. 16–17.

26 Blake and Cross, 'Flint tools', p. 3.

27 Joachim Braun, *Music in Ancient Israel/Palestine* (Grand Rapids, Michigan: William B. Eerdmans Publishing, 2002).

28 Hartmut Thieme, 'The Lower Palaeolithic art of hunting: The case of Schöningen 13 11-4, Lower Saxony, Germany', in C. Gamble and M. Porr (eds), *The Hominid Individual in Context: Archaeological Investigations of Lower and Middle Palaeolithic Landscapes, Locales and Artefacts* (London: Routledge, 2005), pp. 115–32.

29 Rupert Till, 'Sound archaeology: terminology, Palaeolithic cave art and the soundscape', *World Archaeology* 46 (3) (2014), pp. 292–304.

30 Theodore Levin and Valentina Süzükei, *Where Rivers and Mountains Sing: Sound, Music, and Nomadism in Tuva and Beyond* (Bloomington, Indiana: Indiana University Press, 2006).

31 Morley, *Prehistory*, pp. 91–2.

32 Steven Mithen, *After the Ice: A Global Human History, 20,000–5000 BC* (London: Weidenfeld & Nicolson, 2011).

33 Penny Petrone (ed.), *Northern Voices: Inuit Writings in English* (University of Toronto Press, 1988).

34 Morley, *Prehistory*, pp. 11–32.

35 Jerome Lewis, 'A cross-cultural perspective on the significance of music and dance to culture and society: Insight from BaYaka pygmies', in Michael Arbib (ed.), *Language, Music, and the Brain: A Mysterious Relationship* (Cambridge, Mass.: MIT Press, 2013), pp. 45–66.

36 Tim Ingold, 'On the social relations of the hunter-gatherer band'.

37 Lewis, 'A cross-cultural perspective', p. 57.

38 Colin Turnbull, *The Forest People* (London: The Bodley Head, 2015), p. 66.

39 David Luther, 'The influence of the acoustic community on songs of birds in a neotropical rain forest', *Behavioral Ecology* 20/4 (July 2009), pp. 864–71.

40 Feld, *Sound and Sentiment* p. 21.

41 Fabrice Marandola, 'Expressiveness in the performance of the Bedzan Pygmies' vocal polyphonies: When the same is never the same', in Dorottya Fabian, Renee Timmers and Emery Schubert (eds), *Expressiveness in Music Performance: Empirical Approaches Across Styles and Cultures* (Oxford: Oxford University Press, 2014), pp. 201–20.

42 Bruce Chatwin, *The Songlines* (New York: Vintage Books, 2012), p. 108.

43 Myfany Turpin, 'The poetics of central Australian song', *Australian Aboriginal Studies* 2 (2007), pp. 100–15.

44 Aaron Corn and Neparrŋa Gumbula, 'Budutthun ratja wiyinymirri: Formal flexibility in theYolŋu manikay tradition and the challenge of recording a complete repertoire', *Australian Aboriginal Studies* 2 (2007), pp. 116–27.

45 Linda Barwick, 'Musical Form and Style in Murriny Patha Djanba Songs at Wadeye (Northern Territory, Australia)', in Michael Tenzer and John Roeder (eds), *Analytical and Cross-Cultural Studies in World Music* (Oxford: Oxford University Press, 2012), pp. 317–54.

46 Corn and Gumbula, 'Budutthun ratja wiyinymirri', p. 116.

47 Myfany Turpin, 'Text and music in Awelye songs of Central Australia', http://aawmconference.com/aawm2012/papers/turpin_p.pdf

48 Yosef Garfinkel, *Dancing at the Dawn of Agriculture* (Austin: University of Texas Press, 2003), p. 14.

49 Barwick, 'Musical Form and Style', p. 328.

50 Mike Smith, *The Archaeology of Australia's Deserts* (Cambridge: Cambridge University Press, 2013), p. 214.

51 Barwick, 'Musical Form and Style', p. 39.

52 Luca Cavalli-Sforza, Paolo Menozzi and Alberto Piazza, *The History and Geography of Human Genes* (Princeton: Princeton University Press, 1994).

53 Patrick E. Savage et al., 'How "circumpolar" is Ainu music? Musical and genetic perspectives on the history of the Japanese archipelago', *Ethnomusicology Forum* 2015, pp. 1–22.

54 Alan McMillan and Eldon Yellowhorn, *First Peoples in Canada* (Vancouver: Douglas and McIntyre, 2004).

55 Petrone, *Northern Voices*.

56 Jean-Jacques Nattiez, 'Inuit Throat-Games and Siberian Throat Singing: A Comparative, Historical, and Semiological Approach', *Ethnomusicology* 43/3 (Autumn, 1999), pp. 399–418.

57 Michael Hauser, 'Traditional and Acculturated Greenlandic Music', *Arctic Anthropology* 23/1–2 (1986), pp. 359–86.

58 Peter Whitridge, 'The sound of contact: Historic Inuit music-making in northern Labrador', *North Atlantic Archaeology* 4 (2015), pp. 17–42.

59 Michael Berman, *The Nature of Shamanism and the Shamanic Story* (Newcastle: Cambridge Scholars Publishing, 2007), p. 25.

60 Nattiez, 'Inuit Throat-Games', p. 412.

61 David McAllester, 'North America/Native America', in Jeff Titon (ed.), *Worlds of Music* (New York: Schirmer, 2009), pp. 33–82.

62 Harvey Feit, 'Introduction: North America', in Richard B. Lee and Richard Daly (eds), *The Cambridge Encyclopedia of Hunters and Gatherers* (Cambridge: Cambridge University Press, 2002), pp. 23–30.

63 Victoria Levine, 'American Indian musics, past and present', in David Nicholls (ed.), *The Cambridge History of American Music* (Cambridge: Cambridge University Press, 1998), pp. 3–29.

64 S. M. Wilson, 'Tricky treats', *Natural History* 10 (1991), pp. 4–8.

65 Mithen, *After the Ice*.

66 Colin Renfrew, *Prehistory: The Making of the Human Mind* (London: Weidenfeld & Nicolson, 2012).

67 Colin Renfrew, 'The city through time and space: Transformations of centrality', in Joyce Marcus and Jeremy Sabloff (eds), *The Ancient City: New Perspectives on Urbanism in the Old and New World* (Santa Fe: SAR Press, 2008), pp. 29–52.

68 Colin Renfrew and Paul Bahn, *Archaeology: Theories, Methods and Practice* (London: Thames & Hudson, 2017), pp. 418–19.

69 Paolo Debertolis, Daniele Gullà and Heikki Savolainen, 'Archaeoacoustic analysis in Enclosure D at Göbekli Tepe in South Anatolia, Turkey', *5th Human and Social Sciences at the Common Conference* (2017), www.hassacc. coom.

70 Trevor Watkins, 'Architecture and imagery in the early Neolithic of South-West Asia: Framing rituals, stabilizing meanings', in Colin Renfrew, Iain Morley and Michael Boyd (eds), *Ritual, Play and Belief, in Evolution and Early Human Societies* (Cambridge: Cambridge University Press, 2018), pp. 116–42; Renfrew and Bahn, *Archaeology*, pp. 46–7.

71 http://damienmarieathope.com/2017/03/catal-huyuk-first-religious-designed-city/

72 Rupert Till, 'Songs of the stones: An investigation into the acoustic culture of Stonehenge', *Journal of the International Association for the Study of Popular Music* 1/2 (2010), pp. 1–18.

73 Nicole Boivin, 'Rock art and rock music: Petroglyphs of the South Indian Neolithic', *Antiquity* 78/299 (2004), pp. 38–53.

74 E. E. Evans-Pritchard, *The Nuer* (Oxford: Oxford University Press, 1940), pp. 73–74.

75 Nils Wallin, *Biomusicology* (Hillside, New York: Pendragon, 1991); Ted Gioia, *Work Songs* (Durham, North Carolina: Duke University Press, 2006), p. 74.

76 Richard Widdess, 'Musical Structure, Performance and Meaning: the Case of a Stick-Dance from Nepal', *Ethnomusicology Forum* 15/2 (2006), pp. 179–213.

77 Anthony Seeger, *Why Suyá Sing* (Urbana: University of Illinois Press, 2004).

78 Rafael José de Menezes Bastos, 'The Yawari Ritual of the Kamayurá', in Malena Kuss (ed.), *Music in Latin America and the Caribbean: An Encyclopedic History*, Vol. 1 (Austin: University of Texas Press, 2004), pp. 77–99.

79 Claire Halley, 'Communal performance and ritual practice in the ancestral Puebloan era of the American southwest', in Renfrew, Morley and Boyd, *Ritual, Play and Belief*, pp. 116–29 (p. 123).

80 Robert Stevenson, *Music in Aztec & Inca Territory* (Berkeley: University of California Press, 1968), p. 74.

81 Ibid., p. 75.

82 Oswaldo Chinchilla Mazariegos, *Art and Myth of the Ancient Maya* (New Haven: Yale University Press, 2017), pp. 220–1.

83 Gary Tomlinson, *The Singing of the New World* (Cambridge: Cambridge University Press, 2007), p. 134.

84 David Freidel and Michelle Rich, 'Maya sacred play: The view from El Perú-Waka', in Renfrew, Morley and Boyd, *Ritual, Play and Belief*, pp. 101–15.

85 Matthew G. Looper, *To Be Like Gods: Dance in Ancient Maya Civilization* (Austin: University of Texas Press, 2009), pp. 58–66.

86 Stephen Houston, David Stuart and Karl Taube, *The Memory of Bones: Body, Being, and Experience Among the Classic Maya* (Austin: University of Texas Press, 2006), pp. 153–6.

87 Tomlinson, *Singing of the New World*, pp. 171–2.

88 https://io9.gizmodo.com/heres-how-this-ancient-mayan-pyramid-makes-bird-calls-1692327818

Chapter 6

1 Robert Anderson, 'Egypt', *Grove Music Online*.

2 John Van Seters, *The Hyksos: A New Investigation* (New Haven: Yale University Press, 1966).

3 Eric Cline, *1177 B.C.: The Year Civilization Collapsed* (Princeton: Princeton University Press, 2014).

4 John Franklin, 'Epicentric Tonality and the Greek Lyric Tradition', in Tom Phillips and Armand D'Angour (eds), *Music, Text, and Culture in Ancient Greece* (Oxford: Oxford University Press, 2018), pp. 17–46.

5 Martin West, *Ancient Greek Music* (Oxford: Clarendon Press, 1992), p. 389.

6 Stefan Hagel, *Ancient Greek Music: A New Technical History* (Cambridge: Cambridge University Press, 2009), p. 9.

7 Curt Sachs, *The Rise of Music in the Ancient World* (Mineola, New York: Dover Publications, 1943), p. 209; Richard Widdess, 'Sléndro and pélog in India?', in Bernard Arps (ed.), *Performance in Java and Bali* (London: Taylor & Francis, 1993), pp. 187–98 (pp. 194–5).

8 Sachs, *Rise of Music in the Ancient World*, p. 71.

9 Walter Scheidel (ed.), *Rome and China: Comparative Perspectives on Ancient World Empires* (New York: Oxford University Press, 2009).

10 James McKinnon, 'Jubal vel Pythagoras: quis sit inventor musicae?', *The Musical Quarterly* 64/1 (1978), pp. 1–28.

11 Ibid., pp. 3–4.

12 Roberta Binkley, 'The Rhetoric of Origins and the Other: Reading the Ancient Figure of Enheduanna', in Carl Lipson and Roberta Binkley (eds), *Rhetoric Before and Beyond the Greeks* (New York: State University of New York Press, 2004), pp. 47–63.

13 Gwendolyn Leick, *Mesopotamia: The Invention of the City* (New York: Penguin, 2001), p. 127.

14 Maude de Schauensee, *Two Lyres from Ur* (Philadelphia: University of Pennsylvania Museum of Archaeology and Anthropology, 2002).

15 Paul Kriwaczek, *Babylon: Mesopotamia and the Birth of Civilization* (London: Atlantic Books, 2010), p. 121.

16 *The Electronic Text Corpus of Sumerian Literature*, http://etcsl.orinst.ox.ac.uk/cgi-bin/etcsl.cgi?charenc=j&text=t.4.07.2#

17 Susan Pollock, *Ancient Mesopotamia* (Cambridge: Cambridge University Press, 1999), pp. 165–71.

18 Colin Renfrew, *Prehistory: Making of the Human Mind* (New York: Weidenfeld & Nicolson, 2012).

19 Anne Kilmer and Sam Mirelman, 'Mesopotamia', *Grove Music Online*.

20 Richard J. Dumbrill, *The Archaeomusicology of the Ancient Near East* (Victoria: Trafford Publishing, 2005), p. 383.

21 Suzanne Onstine, *The Role of the Chantress (Šmcyt) in Ancient Egypt* (Oxford: Archaeopress, 2005), pp. 4–5.

22 Dumbrill, *Archaeomusicology*, p. 92.

23 Kilmer and Mirelman, 'Mesopotamia', p. 4.

24 Anne Kilmer and Steve Tinney, 'Old Babylonian Music Instruction Texts', *Journal of Cuneiform Studies* 48 (1996), pp. 49–56.

25 Martin West, 'The Babylonian Musical Notation and the Hurrian Melodic Texts', *Music & Letters* 75/2 (1994), pp. 161–79 (p. 169).

26 Dumbrill, *Archaeomusicology*, p. 406.

27 Franklin, 'Epicentric Tonality', p. 14.

28 The 'sexagesimal' (sixty) number system took the number sixty as its basis, and we inherited it in our division of the hour into sixty minutes, and of minutes into sixty seconds. In musical acoustics, intervals are defined by the ratio of the frequency by which a string vibrates. With a perfect fifth, the upper note vibrates faster than the lower note by a ratio of 3:2 (i.e. 60:40). That Enki sounded a fifth suggests that Babylonians heard it as the most perfect musical interval. Thomas McEvilley, *The Shape of Ancient Thought: Comparative Studies in Greek and Indian Philosophies* (New York: Allworth Press, 2001), p. 87.

29 Kilmer and Mirelman, 'Mesopotamia', p. 4.

30 Dumbrill, *Archaeomusicology*, p. 419.

31 Duane Garrett and Paul House, *Song of Songs and Lamentations* (New York: Thomas Nelson, 2004).

32 West, 'Babylonian Musical Notation'; Richard Dumbrill, 'The Truth about Babylonian Music', https://www.academia.edu/32426527/THE_TRUTH_ABOUT_BABYLONIAN_MUSIC (2017), pp. 1–34.

33 Kriwaczek, *Babylon*.

34 Onstine, *The Role of the Chantress*, p. 13.

35 Cline, *1177 B.C.*, p. 9.

36 Ibid., p. 2.

37 Lise Manniche, *Music and Musicians in Ancient Egypt* (London: British Museum Press, 1991), pp. 37–8. The following discussion is indebted to Manniche's work.

38 Ibid., p. 9.

39 Ibid., p. 53.

40 You can watch the clip on https://www.youtube.com/watch?v=Xzkm-kbx2T4

41 Barry Kemp, *Ancient Egypt: Anatomy of a Civilization* (London: Routledge, 2001), pp. 185–97.

42 Christopher Eyre, 'The Practice of Literature: The Relationship between Content, Form, Audience, and Performance', in Roland Enmarch and Verena Lepper (eds), *Ancient Egyptian Literature: Theory and Practice* (Oxford: Oxford University Press, 2013), pp. 101–42 (p. 121).

43 Kemp, *Ancient Egypt*, p. 185.

44 Ibid., pp. 262–320.

45 Sigmund Freud, *Moses and Monotheism* (New York: Fordham University Press, 2018); Jan Assmann, *Moses the Egyptian* (Cambridge, Mass.: Harvard University Press, 1998).

46 Manniche, *Music and Musicians*, p. 94.

47 Ibid., pp. 103–4.

48 Patricia Bochi, 'Gender and Genre in Ancient Egyptian Poetry: the Rhetoric of Performance in the Harpers' Songs', *Journal of the American Research Center in Egypt* 35 (1998), pp. 89–95.

49 Manniche, *Music and Musicians*, p. 105.

50 Jan Assmann, *Death and Salvation in Ancient Egypt* (Ithaca: Cornell University Press, 2005), p. 217.

51 Ibid., p. 4.

52 Camilla Di Biase-Dyson, *Foreigners and Egyptians in the Late Egyptian Stories* (Leiden: Brill, 2013), p. 39.

53 Sachs, *Rise of Music in the Ancient World*, p. 93.

54 Martin West, *The East Face of Helicon: West Asiatic Elements in Greek Poetry and Myth* (Oxford: Clarendon Press, 1997), p. 45.

55 Sachs, *Rise of Music in the Ancient World*, p. 94.

56 West, *East Face of Helicon*, p. 45.

57 Sachs, *Rise of Music in the Ancient World*, p. 95.

58 Ruth Finnegan, *Oral Literature in Africa* (Cambridge: Open Book Publishers, 2016).

59 Gabriel Barkay, 'The Iron Age II-III', in Amnon Ben-Tor (ed.), *The Archaeology of Ancient Israel* (Raanana: The Open University of Israel Press, 1992), pp. 302–73 (p. 349).

60 Eva Mroczek, *The Literary Imagination in Jewish Antiquity* (Oxford: Oxford University Press, 2016), p. 185.

61 Manniche, *Music and Musicians*, p. 93.

62 Sachs, *Rise of Music in the Ancient World*, p. 81.

63 James McKinnon, 'On the Question of Psalmody in the Ancient Synagogue', *Early Music History* 6 (1986), pp. 159–91 (p. 187).

64 Sung Jin Park, ' "Pointing to the Accents in the Scroll": Functional Development of the Masoretic Accents in the Hebrew Bible', *Hebrew Studies* 55 (2014) pp. 73–88.

65 Sachs, *Rise of Music in the Ancient World*, pp. 84–5.

66 David Mitchell, 'Resinging the Temple Psalmody', *Journal for the Study of the Old Testament* 36/3 (2012), pp. 355–78 (pp. 364–5).

67 Susan Gillingham, 'The Levites and the Editorial Composition of the Psalms', in William Brown (ed.), *The Oxford Handbook of the Psalms* (Oxford: Oxford University Press, 2014), pp. 201–13 (p. 202).

68 McKinnon, 'On the Question of Psalmody', p. 163.

69 Joachim Braun, *Music in Ancient Israel/Palestine* (Grand Rapids, Michigan: William Eerdmans Publishing, 2002), pp. 301–20.

70 John Garr, *Living Emblems: Ancient Symbols of Faith* (Atlanta, Georgia: Golden Key Press, 2007), p. 39.

71 Jacob Neusner, *The Idea of History in Rabbinic Judaism* (Leiden: Brill, 2004).

72 McKinnon, 'On the Question of Psalmody', p. 191.

73 Penelope Murray and Peter Wilson (eds), *Music and the Muses: The Culture of "mousikē" in the Classical Athenian City* (Oxford: Oxford University Press, 2004).

74 West, *East Face of Helicon*, pp. 16–17.

75 Ibid., pp. 105–6.

76 Naomi Weiss, *The Music of Tragedy: Performance and Imagination in Euripidean Theater* (Oakland: The University of California Press, 2018), p. 175.

77 West, *East Face of Helicon*, p. 344.

78 Peter Wilson, 'Euripides' Tragic Muse', *Illinois Classical Studies* 24–5 (1999–2000), pp. 427–49.

79 Ibid., pp. 436–7.

80 Aristotle, *Poetics* (Oxford: Oxford University Press, 2013).

81 Armand D'Angour, 'The Musical Setting of Ancient Greek Texts', in Tom Phillips and Armand D'Angour (eds), *Music, Text, and Culture in Ancient Greece* (Oxford: Oxford University Press, 2018), pp. 47–72.

82 Albert Lord, *The Singer of Tales* (Cambridge, Mass.: Harvard University Press, 2000).

83 Georg Danek and Stefan Hagel, 'Homer-Singen', *Wiener humanistische Blätter* 37 (1995), pp. 5–20.

84 West, *East Face of Helicon*, p. 198.

85 D'Angour, 'Musical Setting'.

86 Thomas Schmitz, 'Reading Greek Literature', in Enmarch and Lepper (eds), *Ancient Egyptian Literature*, pp. 25–44 (pp. 42–3).

87 Charles Rose, *The Archaeology of Greek and Roman Troy* (Cambridge: Cambridge University Press, 2014), p. 90.

88 West, *East Face of Helicon*, p. 163.

89 Friedrich Nietzsche, *The Birth of Tragedy and other Writings*, trans. Ronald Speirs (Cambridge: Cambridge University Press, 1999).

90 Wilson, 'Euripides' Tragic Muse', pp. 440–5.

91 Timothy Power, *The Culture of Kitharôidia* (Cambridge, Mass.: Harvard University Press, 2010), pp. 35–8.

92 Barbara Castiglioni, 'Music, Ritual, and Self-Referentiality in the Second Stasimon of Euripides' Helen', *Greek and Roman Studies* 6 (2018), pp. 247–64 (p. 256).

93 Hagel, *Ancient Greek Music*, p. 6.

94 Eric Csapo, 'Euripides and Tragic Theatre in the Late Fifth Century', *Illinois Classical Studies* 24–5 (1999–2000), pp. 399–426.

95 Ibid., p. 417.

96 Timothy Moore, 'Stinging Auloi, Aristophanes, Acharnians 860–71', *Greek and Roman Musical Studies* 5 (2017), pp. 178–90 (p. 186).

97 Csapo, 'Euripides and Tragic Theatre'.

98 West, *East Face of Helicon*, p. 192.

99 Ibid., p. 284.

100 Egert Pöhlmann and Martin West, *Documents of Ancient Greek Music* (Oxford: Clarendon Press, 2001), pp. 12–13.

101 See the clip on https://www.youtube.com/watch?v=FFE2lYpl4xQ

102 Karl Marx, *The Eighteenth Brumaire of Louis Bonaparte* (New York: Cosimo, 2008) p. 1.

103 Power, *Culture of Kitharôidia*, pp. 3–4.

104 Nicholas Horsfall, *The Culture of the Roman Plebs* (London: Bloomsbury, 2003), p. 40.

105 John Landels, *Music in Ancient Greece and Rome* (London: Routledge, 2001), p. 201.

106 Power, *Culture of Kitharôidia*, p. 7.

107 Timothy Moore, *Music in Roman Comedy* (Cambridge: Cambridge University Press, 2012), pp. 83–4.

108 Power, *Culture of Kitharôidia*, p. 8.

109 Moore, *Music in Roman Comedy*, p. 88.

110 Power, *Culture of Kitharôidia*, p. 8.

111 Günther Fleischhauer, 'Rome', *Grove Music Online*.

112 Landels, *Music in Ancient Greece and Rome*, p. 203.

113 Fleischhauer, 'Rome', p. 9.

114 Horsfall, *Culture of the Roman Plebs*, p. 11.

115 Ibid., pp. 13–14.

116 Power, *Culture of Kitharôidia*, pp. 1–2.

117 Fleischhauer, 'Rome', p. 7.

118 Alain Baudot, *Musiciens romains de l'Antiquité* (Montreal: Les Press de l'Université de Montréal, 1973), p. 30.

119 Ibid., p. 32.

120 Moore, *Music in Roman Comedy*, p. 140.

121 D'Angour, 'Musical Setting', pp. 64–71.

Chapter 7

1 Voltaire, *Essais sur les moeurs et l'esprit des nations* (Paris: Garnier frères, 1963 [1773]), I, p. 683.

2 As Christopher Page notes, the first kings of Spain, France and Italy were not dissimilar from Rome's vassal local rulers. They were just more autonomous than before, and more civilised. See Christopher Page, *The Christian West and its Singers: The First Thousand Years* (New Haven: Yale University Press, 2010), pp. 11–13.

3 Ibid., pp. 270–4.

4 Anthony Birley, *Hadrian: The Restless Emperor* (New York: Routledge, 1997), p. 134.

5 For some of Mesomedes' songs, see Charles Cosgrove, *An Ancient Christian Hymn with Musical Notation: Papyrus Oxyrhynchus 1786: Text and Commentary* (Tübingen: Mohr Siebeck, 2011), p. 141.

6 Jared Diamond, *Guns, Germs, and Steel: The Fates of Human Societies* (New York: W. W. Norton, 1997).

7 Karen Armstrong, *A History of God* (London: Vintage, 1999), p. 37.

8 Janet Abu-Lughod, *Before European Hegemony: The World System A.D. 1250–1350* (Oxford: Oxford University Press, 1991).

9 Edward Henry, 'The Rationalization of Intensity in Indian Music', *Ethnomusicology*, 46/1 (2002), pp. 33–55.

10 Page, *The Christian West*, p. 256.

11 James McKinnon, 'Desert Monasticism and the Later Fourth-Century Psalmodic Movement', *Music and Letters* 75/4 (1994), pp. 505–19.

12 Alexander Lingas, 'Music', in Elizabeth Jeffreys, John Haldon and Robin Cormack (eds), *The Oxford Handbook of Byzantine Studies* (New York: Oxford University Press, 2008), pp. 915–38 (p. 925).

13 James McKinnon, 'Proprization: The Roman Mass', *Cantus Planus, Papers Read at the Fifth Meeting*, Éger Hungary (1994), pp. 15–22.

14 Page, *The Christian West*, p. 264.

15 James McKinnon, 'Musical Instruments in Medieval Psalm Commentaries and Psalters', *Journal of the American Musicology Society* 21/1 (1968), pp. 3–20 (p. 4).

16 Alexander Lingas, 'Medieval Byzantine chant and the sound of Orthodoxy', in Andrew Louth and Augustine Casiday (eds), *Byzantine Orthodoxies, Papers from the 36th Spring Symposium of Byzantine Studies* (Aldershot: Ashgate, 2006), pp. 131–50 (pp. 142–3).

17 Page, *The Christian West*, pp. 458–9.

18 Ibid., p. 445.

19 Catherine Bradley, *Polyphony in Medieval Paris: The Art of Composing with Plainchant* (Cambridge: Cambridge University Press, 2018).

20 Cited in Piero Weiss and Richard Taruskin, *Music in the Western World* (New York: Schirmer, 2008), pp. 60–1.

21 Niceta of Remesiana, *On the Benefit of Psalmody*, trans. James McKinnon, https://media.musicasacra.com/media2/niceta.pdf

22 Plato, *Laws,* in John Cooper (ed.), *Complete Works* (Indianapolis: Hackett Publishing Company, 1997), pp. 1318–616.

23 Karla Pollmann, 'Augustine's legacy: success or failure', in *The Cambridge Companion to Augustine*, David Meconi and Eleonore Stump (eds) (Cambridge: University of Cambridge Press, 2914), pp. 331–48, p. 331.

24 Ibid.

25 Francesco Ciabattoni, *Dante's Journey to Polyphony* (Toronto: University of Toronto Press, 2010).

26 Joseph Needham, Ling Wang and Derek De Solla Price, *Heavenly Clockwork: The Great Astronomical Clocks of Medieval China* (Cambridge: Cambridge University Press, 1986), p. 74.

27 Peter Pesic, *Polyphonic Minds: Music of the Hemispheres* (Cambridge, Mass.: MIT Press, 2017).

28 Alejandro Planchart, *Guillaume Du Fay: The Life and Works* (Cambridge: Cambridge University Press, 2018), p. 125.

29 Lorenz Welker, '*Portugaler*: Guillaume Du Fay's Contributions to Instrumental Music?', in Fabrice Fitch and Jacobijn Kiel (eds), *Essays on Renaissance Music in Honour of David Fallows: Bon jour, bon mois, et bonne estrenne* (Rochester, NY: Boydell Press, 2011), pp. 124–37.

30 Lingas, 'Medieval Byzantine chant', p. 146.

31 Ibid., p. 143.

32 William Reddy, *The Making of Romantic Love: Longing and Sexuality in Europe, South Asia and Japan, 900–1200 CE* (Chicago: The University of Chicago Press, 2012), p. 142; George Beech, 'The Eleanor of Aquitaine Vase, William IX of Aquitaine, and Muslim Spain', *Gesta* 32/1 (1993), pp. 3–10.

33 Dwight Reynolds, 'North Africa and the Eastern Mediterranean: Andalusian Music', in Michael Church (ed.), *The Other Classical Musics: Fifteen Great Traditions* (Rochester, NY: The Boydell Press, 2016), pp. 246–69 (p. 251).

34 Ibid., p. 252.

35 Ibid., p. 257.

36 Latin poets tended to avoid rhyme, because it was too easy to do in that language. See Tova Rosen, 'The Muwashshah', in María Rosa Menocal, Raymond Scheindlin and Michael Sells (eds), *The Literature of Al-Andalus* (Cambridge: Cambridge University Press, 2000), pp. 165–89; Sayyid

Naqī Ḥusain Jaʿfarī, *Essays on Literature, History & Society: Selected Works of Professor Sayyid Naqī Ḥusain Jaʿfarī* (Delhi: Primus Books, 2010), pp. 24–6.

37 Salma Khadra Jayyusi, 'Andalusi Poetry: The Golden Period', in Salma Jayyusi and Manuela Marín (eds), *The Legacy of Muslim Spain* (Leiden: Brill, 1997), pp. 317–67 (pp. 347–50).

38 Salim Al-Hassani, *1001 Inventions: The Enduring Legacy of Muslim Civilization* (National Geographic, 2012).

39 Thomas Christensen, 'Music Theory', in Mark Everist and Thomas Kelly (eds), *The Cambridge History of Medieval Music* (Cambridge: Cambridge University Press, 2018), pp. 357–82 (p. 370).

40 https://www.youtube.com/watch?v=ybMscMHHAQA

41 José Miguel Puerta Vílchez, 'Art and Aesthetics in the Work of Ibn Hazm of Cordoba', in Camilla Adang, Maribel Fierro and Sabine Schmidtke (eds), *Ibn Ḥazm of Cordoba: The Life and Works of a Controversial Thinker* (Leiden: Brill, 2013), pp. 253–374 (p. 330).

42 Valerie Gonzalez, *Beauty and Islam: Aesthetics in Islamic Art and Architecture* (New York: Tauris, 2001), pp. 69–94.

43 Anna Gade, 'Recitation', in Andrew Rippin and Jawid Mojaddedi (eds), *The Wiley Blackwell Companion to The Qur'an* (Oxford: Wiley Blackwell, 2017), pp. 577–90.

44 Walid Hedari, 'Marcel Khalife's socio-political life: The case of "Oh My Father, I am Yusuf"', *Methaodos.revista de ciencias sociales* 4/1 (2016), pp. 119–134 (p. 124).

45 Scott Marcus, 'The Eastern Arab World', in Church, *The Other Classical Musics*, pp. 271–94 (p. 282).

46 Shahzad Bashir, *Sufi Bodies: Religion and Society in Medieval Islam* (New York: Columbia University Press, 2011), p. 72.

47 Laura Lohman, *Umm Kulthum: Artistic Agency and the Shaping of an Arab Legend, 1967–2007* (Middletown, CT: Wesleyan University Press, 2010), p. 94.

48 Oliver Leaman (ed.), *The Qur'an: An Encyclopedia* (London: Routledge, 2006), p. 77.

49 *Falsafa* is the Arabic rendering of the Greek pronunciation of *philosophia*, and it described the period from the ninth century AD when Greek philosophy was taken up by the Abbasid Caliphate. The flowering of *falsafa* included such luminaries as Al-Kindi (801–873), Al-Farabi (872–951) and Avicenna (980–1037). Armstrong, *History of God*, p. 203.

50 Jay Bonner, *Islamic Geometric Patterns: Their Historical Development and Traditional Methods of Construction* (New York: Springer, 2017).

51 Marcus, 'The Eastern Arab World', pp. 280–5.

52 *Cantigas* were medieval solo (monophonic) songs, especially characteristic of lyrics in the Galician-Portuguese language. Joseph O'Callaghan, *Alfonso X and the Cantigas De Santa Maria: A Poetic Biography* (Leiden: Brill, 1998).

53 Rosen, 'The Muwashshah', p. 166.

54 Simon Sebag Montefiore, *Jerusalem: The Biography* (London: Phoenix, 2012), p. 212.

55 Richard Widdess, 'North India', in Church, *The Other Classical Musics*, pp. 139–60 (p. 146).

56 Cited in Martin Clayton, *Time in Indian Music: Rhythm, Metre, and Form in North Indian Rag Performance* (Oxford: Oxford University Press, 2008), p. 10.

57 David Beck, 'India/South India', in Jeff Titon (ed.), *Worlds of Music* (Belmon, CA: Schirmer, 2009), p. 268.

58 Sachs, *Rise of Music in the Ancient World*, p. 158.

59 Anne Sheeran, 'Sri Lanka', in Alison Arnold (ed.), *The Garland Encyclopedia of World Music: South Asia: The Indian Subcontinent* (New York: Garland Publishing, 2000), p. 956.

60 Lewis Rowell, *Music and Musical Thought in Early India* (Chicago: The University of Chicago Press, 1992), pp. 35–8.

61 Widdess, 'North India', pp. 142–6.

62 David Clarke and Tara Kini, 'North Indian classical music and its links with consciousness: the case of dhrupad', in David Clarke and Eric Clarke (eds), *Music and Consciousness: Philosophical, Psychological, and Cultural Perspectives* (Oxford: Oxford University Press, 2011), pp. 137–56.

63 Rowell, 'North India', pp. 327–36.

64 Martin Rohrmeier and Richard Widdess, 'Incidental Learning of Melodic Structure of North Indian Music', *Cognitive Science* 5 (2017), pp. 1299–1317.

65 Bo Lawergren, 'Buddha as a Musician: An Illustration of a Jataka Story', *Artibus Asiae* 54/3–4 (1994), pp. 226–40 (p. 227).

66 Ibid., p. 228.

67 Sachs, *Rise of Music in the Ancient World*, pp. 190–1.

68 Clayton, *Time in Indian Music*, p. 17.

69 Regular Qureshi, *Sufi Music of India and Pakistan: Sound, Context, and Meaning* (New York: Oxford University Press, 2006).

70 Bonny Wade, *Imaging Sound: An Ethnomusicological Study of Music, Art, and Culture in Mughal India* (Chicago: The University of Chicago Press, 1998).

71 Ibid., pp. 3–6.

72 Katherine Butler Schofield, 'Learning to Taste the Emotions: The Mughal *Rasika*', in Katherine Butler Schofield and Francesca Orsini (eds), *Tellings and Texts: Music, Literature, and Performance in North India* (OpenBook Publishers, 2015), pp. 407–22 (p. 410).

73 Allison Busch, *Poetry of Kings: The Classical Hindi Literature of Mughal India* (Oxford: Oxford University Press, 2011), p. 151.

74 A stupendous undertaking, *Science and Civilization in China* (1954–1986) was conceived and edited by Joseph Needham, who also wrote or co-wrote many of its twenty-seven volumes, all available from Cambridge University Press.

75 Needham (ed.), *Science and Civilization in China*, Vol. 4, Part 2, *Physics and Physical Technology: Mechanical Engineering* (Cambridge: Cambridge University Press, 1965), p. 582.

76 Robert Bagley, 'The Prehistory of Chinese Music Theory', *Proceedings of the British Academy* 131 (2004), pp. 41–90.

77 Chih-Wei Wu, 'Sound analysis and synthesis of Marquis Yi of Zeng's chime-bell set', *Journal of the Acoustical Society of America* 19 (2013), pp. 1–7.

78 Needham, *Science and Civilization in China*, Vol. 4, Part 1: *Physics*, pp. 142–4.

79 Colin Renfrew, *Prehistory: Making of the Human Mind* (New York: Weidenfeld & Nicolson, 2012).

80 Erica Fox Brindley, *Music, Cosmology, and the Politics of Harmony in Early China* (Albany, NY: State University of New York Press, 2012), p. 19.

81 Ibid., p. 79.

82 Ibid., p. 46.

83 Needham, *Science and Civilization in China*, Vol. 4, Part 2, p. 156.

84 Wiebke Denecke, Wai-yee Li and Xiaofei Tian (eds), *The Oxford Handbook of Classical Chinese Literature (1000 BCE–900 CE)* (Oxford: Oxford University Press, 2017), p. 246.

85 Confucius, *Analects*, trans. Annping Chin (New York: Penguin, 2014), 17.20.

86 Ibid., book 11, chapter 15.

87 Wang Wei, *Laughing Lost in the Mountains: Poems of Wang Wei*, trans. Tony Barnstone, Willis Barnstone and Xu Haixin (Hanover, New Hampshire: University Press of New England, 1991), p. 63.

88 Robert van Gulik, 'The Lore of the Chinese Lute. An Essay in Ch'in Ideology', *Monumenta Nipponica* 1/2 (1938), pp. 386–438.

89 Bell Yung, 'Choreographic and Kinesthetic Elements in Performance on the Chinese Seven-String Zither', *Ethnomusicology* 28/3 (1984), pp. 505–17 (p. 506).

90 Stephen Jay Gould, *Time's Arrow, Time's Cycle: Myth and Metaphor in the Discovery of Geological Time* (Cambridge, Mass.: Harvard University Press, 1987).

91 David Pankenier, 'Temporality and the Fabric of Space-Time in Early Chinese Thought', in Ralph Rosen (ed.), *Time and Temporality in the Ancient World* (Philadelphia: University of Pennsylvania Museum of Archaeology and Anthropology, 2004), pp. 129–46.

92 Clifford Geertz, *The Interpretation of Cultures* (New York: Basic Books, 1973) p. 393.

93 John Latartara, 'Theoretical Approaches toward Qin Analysis: "Water and Clouds over Xiao Xiang"', *Ethnomusicology* 49/2 (2005), pp. 232–65.

94 Ibid., p. 234.

95 Peter Frankopan, *The Silk Roads: A New History of the World* (London: Bloomsbury, 2015) p. xix.

96 Peter Frankopan, *The New Silk Roads: The Present and Future of the World* (London: Bloomsbury, 2018).

97 James Millward, *The Silk Road: A Very Short Introduction* (New York: Oxford University Press, 2013), pp. 91–8.

98 Matthew Spring, *The Lute in Britain: A History of the Instrument and Its Music* (New York: Oxford University Press, 2001), p. 49.

99 George Buelow, *A History of Baroque Music* (Bloomington: Indiana University Press, 2004), p. 202.

100 Millward, *The Silk Road*, p. 92.

101 Keith Howard and Saparbek Kasmambetov, *Singing the Kyrgyz Manas: Saparbek Kasmambetov's Recitations of Epic Poetry* (Folkestone, UK: Global Oriental, 2010).

102 Forrest Gander, *Core Samples from the World* (New York: New Directions), p. 17.

103 Peter Marsh, *The Horse-head Fiddle and the Cosmopolitan Reimagination of Tradition in Mongolia* (New York: Routledge, 2009).

104 Henry Serruys, 'Music and song for animals', *Etudes Mongoles et Sibériennes* 16 (1986), pp. 61–8 (p. 65).

105 Marco Polo, *The Travels of Marco Polo*, trans. Ronald Latham (London: Penguin, 1958).

106 Kuo-Huang Han, 'The Modern Chinese Orchestra', in Mavelene Moore and Philip Ewell, *Kaleidoscope of Cultures: A Celebration of Multicultural Research and Practice* (Lanham, Maryland: Rowman & Littlefield, 2010), pp. 63–8 (p. 65).

107 Zhixin Jason Sun, 'Dadu: Great Capital of the Yuan Dynasty', in James Watt (ed.), *The World of Khubilai Khan: Chinese Art in the Yuan Dynasty* (New Haven: Yale University Press, 2010), pp. 41–64 (p. 55).

108 Millward, *The Silk Road*, p. 90.

109 Elizabeth Wichmann, *Listening to Theatre: The Aural Dimension of Beijing Opera* (Honolulu: University of Hawaii Press, 1991), p. 2.

110 Ibid., pp. 4–5.

111 James Crump, 'The Elements of Yuan Opera', *The Journal of Asian Studies* 17/3 (1958), pp. 417–34 (p. 433).

112 Peter Golden, *Central Asia in World History* (New York: Oxford University Press, 2011), p. 89.

Chapter 8

1 Walter Mignolo, *The Darker Side of Modernity* (Durham: Duke University Press, 2011), p. 79.

2 http://www.mexicolore.co.uk/maya/teachers/ancient-maya-music

3 Emilio Ros-Fábregas, ' "Imagine all the people…": polyphonic flowers in the hands and voices of Indians in 16th-century Mexico', *Early Music* xl/2 (2012), pp. 177–89 (p. 180).

4 Ibid., p. 179.

5 Robert Stevenson, *Music in Aztec and Inca Territory* (Berkeley, CA: University of California Press, 1968), p. 172.

6 David Irving, *Colonial Counterpoint: Music in Early Modern Manila* (New York: Oxford University Press, 2010), p. 42.

7 Ibid., p. 53.

8 Arjun Appadurai, *Modernity at Large: Cultural Dimensions of Globalization* (Minneapolis: University of Minneapolis Press, 1996). See especially Chapter 5, 'Playing with Modernity: The Decolonisation of Indian Cricket'.

9 Edward Said, *Culture and Imperialism* (London: Vintage Books, 1994), p. 386.

10 See also Irving, *Colonial Counterpoint*.

11 Michael Church (ed.), *The Other Classical Musics: Fifteen Great Traditions* (Woodbridge: The Boydell Press, 2015).

12 Keith Howard, 'On *setar*, *dutar* and *pipa*', review of Church, *The Other Classical Musics*, *Times Literary Supplement* (15 April 2016), pp. 9–10.

13 Paul Gilroy, *The Black Atlantic: Modernity and Double Consciousness* (New York: Verso, 1993).

14 Simon Trezise, *Debussy: La mer* (Cambridge: Cambridge University Press, 1994), p. 37.

15 Frederick Sternfeld, *The Birth of Opera* (Oxford: Clarendon Press, 1995), pp. 1–30.

16 Daniel Chua, 'Vincenzo Galilei, modernity and the division of nature', in Suzannah Clark and Alexander Rehding (eds), *Music Theory and Natural Order from the Renaissance to the Early Twentieth Century* (Cambridge: Cambridge University Press, 2001), pp. 17–29.

17 Stillman Drake, 'Vincenzo Galilei and Galileo', in *Galileo Studies: Personality, Tradition and Revolution* (Ann Arbor, 1970), pp. 43–62; Claude Palisca, 'Was Galileo's Father an Experimental Scientist?', in Victor Coelho (ed.), *Music and Science in the Age of Galileo* (Dordrecht: Springer 1992), pp. 143–51.

18 Vincenzo Galilei, *Dialogue on Ancient and Modern Music*, trans., with introduction and notes, Claude Palisca (New Haven: Yale University Press, 2003), pp. lx–lxi, 240.

19 Kenneth Clark, *Civilisation*, episode 4, 'Man: The Measure of All Things', https://www.youtube.com/watch?v=jvrAdDfmgKY

20 Knud Jeppesen, *The Style of Palestrina and the Dissonance* (Mineola, New York: Dover Publications, 1946).

21 Thomas Tuohy, *Herculean Ferrara: Ercole d'Este (1471–1505) and the Invention of a Ducal Capital* (Cambridge: Cambridge University Press, 2002).

22 Craig Wright, *The Maze and the Warrior: Symbols in Architecture, Theology, and Music* (Cambridge, Mass.: Harvard University Press, 2001), p. 192.

23 Cristle Collins Judd, *Reading Renaissance Music Theory: Hearing with the Eyes* (Cambridge: Cambridge University Press, 2000), pp. 188–200.

24 Simon Winchester, *Bomb, Book & Compass: Joseph Needham and the Great Secrets of China* (New York: Viking, 2008).

25 Arun Kumar Biswas, 'Why Did Scientific Renaissance Take Place in Europe and Not in India?', *Indian Journal of History of Science* 45/2 (2010), pp. 241–85.

26 Alan Palmer, *The Decline and Fall of the Ottoman Empire* (Fall River Press, 2011).

27 Donald Jay Grout, *A History of Western Music* (New York: W. W. Norton and Company, 2014).

28 Regula Qureshi, *Sufi Music of India and Pakistan: Sound, Context and Meaning in Qawaali* (Cambridge: Cambridge University Press, 1986), p. 58.

29 Lydia Goehr, *The Imaginary Museum of Musical Works: An Essay in the Philosophy of Music* (Oxford: Clarendon Press, 1992).

30 Ian Woodfield, *English Musicians in the Age of Exploration* (Stuyvesant, NY: Pendragon Press, 1995), p. 90.

31 Cited in Suzel Ana Reily and Jonathan Dueck (eds), *The Oxford Handbook of Music and World Christianities* (New York: Oxford University Press, 2016), p. 13.

32 Ibid., p. 9.

33 Cited in Benedict Anderson, *Imagined Communities: Reflections on the Origin and Spread of Nationalism* (New York: Verso, 2016), p. 13.

34 Cited in Stevenson, *Music in Aztec and Inca Territory*, p. 104.

35 Brad Prager, *The Cinema of Werner Herzog: Aesthetic Ecstasy and Truth* (London: Wallflower Press, 2007), p. 43.

36 John Cohen, 'Q'ero', in Dale Olsen and Daniel Sheehy (eds), *The Garland Encyclopedia of World Music*, Vol. 8: *South America, Mexico, Central America and the Caribbean* (New York: Garland, 1998), pp. 225–31 (p. 228).

37 Ros-Fábregas, '"Imagine all the people…"', pp. 183–5.

38 Olivia Bloechl, *Native American Song at the Frontiers of Early Modern Music* (Cambridge: Cambridge University Press, 2008), pp. 35–57.

39 Kofi Agawu, *Representing African Music: Postcolonial Notes, Queries, Positions* (New York: Routledge, 2003), p. 9.

40 Julie Taylor, 'Coexistence of Causal and Cultural Expressions of Musical Values among the Sabaot of Kenya', in Reily and Dueck, *Oxford Handbook of Music and World Christianities*, pp. 78–95 (p. 84).

41 Julia Byl, 'Music, Convert, and Subject in the North Sumatran Mission Field', in Reily and Dueck, *Oxford Handbook of Music and World Christianities*, pp. 33–54 (p. 42).

42 https://earlymusicmuse.com/l-homme-arme/

43 Iain Fenlon, 'Orality and Print: Singing in the Street in Early Modern Venice', in Luca Degl'Innocenti, Brian Richardson and Chiara Sbordoni (eds), *Interactions between Orality and Writing in Early Modern Italian Culture* (London: Routledge, 2016), pp. 81–98 (p. 90).

44 Ralph Locke, *Music and the Exotic from the Renaissance to Mozart* (Cambridge: Cambridge University Press, 2015), p. 96.

45 Harrison Powley, 'Janissary Music', in John Beck (ed.), *Encyclopedia of Percussion* (New York: Garland, 1995), pp. 195–201 (p. 196).

46 Catherine Mayes, 'Turkish and Hungarian-Gypsy Styles', in Danuta Mirka (ed.), *The Oxford Handbook of Topic Theory* (New York: Oxford University Press, 2014), pp. 214–37 (p. 223).

47 Nicholas Cook, 'Western Music as World Music', in Philip Bohlman (ed.), *The Cambridge History of World Music* (Cambridge: Cambridge University Press, 2013), pp. 75–100 (p. 80).

48 David Clarke, 'Beyond the Global Imaginary: Decoding BBC Radio 3's *Late Junction*', *Radical Musicology* 2 (2007), www.radical-musicology.org.uk/

49 Steven Feld, 'Pygmy Pop: A Genealogy of Schizophonic Mimesis', *Yearbook of Traditional Music* 28 (1997), pp. 1–35.

50 Keith Howard, 'On *setar, dutar* and *pipa*', review of Church, *The Other Classical Musics, Times Literary Supplement* (15 April 2016), pp. 9–10.

51 Jaime Jones, 'Music, History, and the Sacred in South Asia', in Bohlman (ed.), *Cambridge History of World Music*, pp. 202–222.

52 Gerhard Kubik, 'Analogies and Differences in African-American Musical Cultures across the Hemisphere: Interpretive Models and Research Strategies', *Black Music Research Journal* 18/2 (1998), pp. 203–27; Peter Wade, *Race and Ethnicity in Latin America* (London: Pluto Press, 2010).

53 Cited in Jason Stoessel, 'Voice and Song in Early Encounters between Latins, Mongols, and Persians, ca. 1250–ca. 1350', in Reinhard Strohm (ed.), *Studies on a Global History of Music: A Balzan Musicology Project* (New York: Routledge, 2018), pp. 83–113 (p. 88).

54 Cited in Keith Howard and Saparbek Kasmambetov, *Singing the Kyrgyz Manas: Saparbek Kasmambetov's Recitations of Epic Poetry* (Folkestone, UK: Global Oriental, 2019), p. 96.

55 Christina Lubinski and Andreas Steen, 'Traveling Entrepreneurs, Traveling Sounds: The Early Gramophone Business in India and China', *Itinerario* 41/2 (2017), pp. 275–303 (p. 294).

56 Jeff Levy-Hinte's 2008 documentary, *Soul Power*, can be viewed on https://www.youtube.com/watch?v=iHMgTKLMAgI. The conversation happens at 20'29".

57 James Brown, *James Brown: Godfather of Soul* (London: Head of Zeus, 2014). Brown had actually visited Zaire earlier in 1972.

58 Ron Levi, 'Zaire '74: Politicising the Sound Event', *Social Dynamics: A Journal of African Studies* 43/2 (2017), pp. 184–98 (p. 195).

59 Lucy Duran, ' "Soliyo" (Calling the Horses): Song and Memory in Mande Music', in Rachel Harris and Rowan Pease (eds.), *Pieces of the Musical World: Sounds and Cultures* (London: Routledge, 2015), pp. 27–44.

60 John Chernoff, 'Music and Historical Consciousness among the Dagbamba of Ghana', in Lawrence Sullivan (ed.), *Enchanting Powers: Music in the World's Religions* (Cambridge, Mass.: Harvard University Press, 1997), pp. 91–120.

61 Cited in Agawu, *Representing African Music*, p. 55.

62 Michael Quintero, *Rites, Rights & Rhythms: A Genealogy of Musical Meaning in Colombia's Black Pacific* (Oxford: Oxford University Press, 2019).

63 Kubik, 'Analogies and Differences', p. 223.

64 Ibid.

65 Peter van der Merwe, *Origins of the Popular Style: Antecedents of Twentieth-Century Popular Music* (Oxford: Oxford University Press, 1989).

66 Quintero, *Rites, Rights & Rhythms*.

67　Kubik, 'Analogies and Differences', p. 209.

68　Drew Beisswenger, *North American Fiddle Music: A Research and Information Guide* (New York: Routledge, 2011).

69　Charles Hersch, *Subversive Sounds: Race and the Birth of Jazz in New Orleans* (Chicago: The University of Chicago Press, 2007).

70　Alexander Stewart, 'Second Line', in John Shepherd (ed.), *Continuum Encyclopedia of Popular Music of the World*, Vol. II (New York: Continuum, 2003), pp. 620–3 (p. 622).

71　Gilroy, *Black Atlantic*.

72　According market analysis by ResearchMoz in 2012. See http://www.bbc.com/culture/story/20131022-piano-mania-grips-china

73　Dani Cavallaro, *The Animé Art of Hayao Miyazaki* (London: McFarland & Company, 2006), p. 45.

74　Cited in Peter Burt, *The Music of Toru Takemitsu* (Cambridge: Cambridge University Press, 2006), pp. 6–7.

75　Bonnie Wade, *Music in Japan: Experiencing Music, Expressing Culture* (Oxford: Oxford University Press, 2005), pp. 21–4.

76　Eta Harich-Schneider, *A History of Japanese Music* (Oxford: Oxford University Press, 1973), p. 457.

77　Burt, *Toru Takemitsu*, pp. 4–20.

78　Toru Takemitsu, 'Toru Takemitsu on Sawari', trans. Hugh de Ferranti and Yayoi Uno Everett, in Yayoi Uno Everett and Frederick Lau (eds), *Locating East Asia in Western Art Music* (Middletown, Connecticut: Wesleyan University Press, 2004), pp. 199–207 (p. 205).

79　Nicholas Cook, *Beethoven: Symphony No. 9* (Cambridge: Cambridge University Press, 1993), p. 98.

80　Kurisaka Yoshiro, 'A Song of Sympathy and Gladness', *Japan Quarterly* 12 (1982), pp. 479–83 (p. 480).

81　Yano Jun'ichi, 'Why is Beethoven's Ninth So Well Loved in Japan?', *Japan Quarterly* 12 (1982), pp. 475–8 (p. 477).

82　Cook, *Beethoven: Symphony No. 9*, pp. 95–7.

83　Suk-Young Kim, *K-pop Live: Fans, Idols, and Multimedia Performance* (Stanford: Stanford University Press, 2018), p. 32.

84　Cavallaro, *Animé Art of Hayao Miyazaki*, p. 45.

85　Takemitsu, 'Toru Takemitsu on Sawari', p. 201.

86　Arguably the most harrowing war film ever made was Studio Ghibli's 1988 *Grave of the Fireflies*, set against the background of the fire-bombing of Kobi.

Chapter 9

1   W. Tecumseh Fitch, 'Four Principles of Biomusicology', in Henkjan Honing (ed.), *The Origins of Musicality* (Cambridge, Mass.: MIT Press, 2018), pp. 20–47 (p. 37).

2   Peggy Hill, *Vibrational Communication in Animals* (Cambridge, Mass.: 2008).

3   Jun-Jie Gu et al., 'Wing stridulation in a Jurassic katydid (*Insecta, Orthoptera*) produced low-pitched musical calls to attract females', *Proceedings of the National Academy of Sciences of the United States of America* 109/10 (2012), pp. 3868–73.

4   Julia Clarke et al., 'Fossil evidence of the avian vocal organ from the Mesozoic', *Nature* 538 (2016), pp. 502–5.

5   David Rothenberg, *Thousand-Mile Song: Whale Music in a Sea of Sound* (New York: Basic Books, 2008).

6   Jun-Jie Gu et al., 'Wing stridulation'.

7   Björn Merker, 'Synchronous chorusing and the origins of music', *Musicae Scientiae* Special Issue (1999–2000), pp. 59–73 (p. 61).

8   Martin Clayton, Rebecca Sager and Udo Will, 'In time with the music: The concept of entrainment and its significance for ethnomusicology', *European Meetings in Ethnomusicology Special Esem-CounterPoint Volume* (2005), pp. 3–75 (p. 7).

9   Steven Strogatz, *Sync: How Order Emerges from Chaos In the Universe, Nature, and Daily Life* (New York: Penguin, 2004), p. 13.

10 David Rothenberg, *Bug Music: How Insects Gave us Rhythm and Noise* (New York: St. Martin's Press, 2013), p. 74.

11 Michael Menaker, 'Biological clocks at the end of the 20th century', in Vinod Kumar (ed.), *Biological Rhythms* (Berlin: Springer Verlag, 2002), pp. 1–4 (p. 2).

12 Rebecca Warner, 'Rhythm in social interaction', in Joseph McGrath (ed.), *The Social Psychology of Time: New Perspectives* (London: Sage, 1988), pp. 63–88 (pp. 68–9).

13 Cited in Clayton et al., 'In time with the music', p. 53.

14 Lauren Cator, Ben Arthur, Laura Harrington and Ronald Hoy, 'Harmonic convergence in the love songs of the dengue vector mosquito', *Science* 323 (2009), pp. 1077–9.

15 Clive Catchpole and Peter Slater, *Bird Song: Biological Themes and Variations* (Cambridge: Cambridge University Press, 1995), p. 220.

16 Clive Catchpole, 'Sexual selection and complex song: The sedge warbler', in Peter Marler and Hans Slabberkoorn (eds), *Nature's Music: The Science of Birdsong* (Amsterdam: Elsevier Academic Press, 2004), p. 126.

17 Peter Marler, 'The voice of the chaffinch and its function as a language', *IBIS International Journal of Avian Science* 98/2 (1956), pp. 231–61.

18 Stephen Nowicki and William Searcy, 'The evolution of vocal learning', *Current Opinion in Neurobiology* 28 (2014), pp. 48–53.

19 David Rothenberg, *Why Birds Sing: One Man's Quest to Solve an Everyday Mystery* (New York: Penguin, 2006), p. 68.

20 Sanne Moorman and Johan Bolhuis, 'Behavioral Similarities between Birdsong and Spoken Language', in Johan Bolhuis and Martin Everaert (eds), *Birdsong, Speech, and Language: Exploring the Evolution of Mind and Brain* (Cambridge, Mass.: MIT Press, 2013), pp. 111–24.

21 Ron Weisman, Laurene Ratcliffe, Ingrid Johnsrude and Andrew Hurly, 'Absolute and relative pitch production in the song of the black-capped chickadee', *The Condor* 92 (1990), pp. 118–24.

22 Don Kroodsma, 'The diversity and plasticity of birdsong', in Marler and Slabberkoorn (eds), *Nature's Music*, pp. 108–31 (p. 122).

23 Hans Slabberkoorn, 'Singing in the wild: the ecology of birdsong', in Marler and Slabberkoorn (eds), *Nature's Music*, pp. 178–205 (pp. 198–9).

24 Ibid., p. 201.

25 Darren Irwin and Jessica Irwin, 'Speciation in a Ring: The Role of Song', in Marler and Slabberkoorn (eds), *Nature's Music*, p. 204.

26 Henkhan Honing, 'Musicality as an Upbeat to Music', in Honing (ed.), *Origins of Musicality*, pp. 3–19 (p. 12).

27 Marisa Hoeschele, Hugo Merchant, Yukiko Kikuchi, Yuko Hattori and Carel ten Cate, 'Searching for the Origins of Musicality across Species', in Honing (ed.), *Origins of Musicality*, pp. 148–170 (p. 153).

28 Slabberkoorn, 'Singing in the wild', p. 196.

29 You can see the video on https://www.youtube.com/watch?v=N7IZmRnAo6s

30 Stefan Koelsch, *Good Vibrations: Die heilende Kraft der Musik* (Berlin: Ullstein, 2019).

31 Rothenberg, *Why Birds Sing*, p. 55.

32 Willem Zuidema, Dieuwke Hupkes, Geraint Wiggins, Constance Scharff and Martin Rohrmeirer, 'Formal Models of Structure Building in Music, Language, and Animal Song', in Honing (ed.), *Origins of Musicality*, pp. 250–86 (p. 255).

33 Moorman & Bolhuis, 'Behavioral Similarities'.

34 Clarke et al., 'Fossil evidence'.

35 Geoffrey Manley and Otto Gleich, 'Evolution and Specialization of Function in the Avian Auditory Periphery', in Douglas Webster, Richard

Fay and Arthur Popper (eds), *The Evolutionary Biology of Hearing* (Berlin: Springer Verlag, 1992), pp. 561–80 (p. 561).

36 Gabriela Sobral and Johannes Müller, 'Archosaurs and their Kin: The Ruling Reptiles', in Jennifer Clack, Richard Fay and Arthur Popper (eds), *Evolution of the Vertebrate Ear: Evidence from the Fossil Record* (Berlin: Springer Verlag, 2016), pp. 285–326 (p. 318).

37 Catchpole and Slater, *Bird Song*, p. 30.

38 Gisela Kaplan and Lesley Rogers, *Birds: Their habits and skills* (Crows Nest: Allen & Unwin, 2001), p. 28.

39 https://www.youtube.com/watch?v=VjEoKdfos4Y&t=6s

40 Weisman et al., 'Absolute and relative pitch production'.

41 Richard Prum, *The Evolution of Beauty: How Darwin's Forgotten Theory of Mate Choice Shapes the Animal World* (New York: Doubleday, 2017).

42 Anne Butler and William Hodos, *Comparative Vertebrate Neuroanatomy: Evolution and Adaptation* (Hoboken, New Jersey: John Wiley & Sons, 2005). The authors observe that: 'Area X demonstrates a sexual dimorphism such that it is well developed in male songbirds but does not appear as a distinct morphological entity in females [...] This sexual dimorphism is consistent with the observation that male songbirds have a greater number and a richer variety of songs in their repertoires than do female songbirds' (p. 585).

43 Katharina Riebel, Karan Odom, Naomi Langmore and Michelle Hall, 'New insights from female bird song: towards an integrated approach to studying male and female communication roles', *Biology Letters* 15/4 (2019), pp. 1–7.

44 Rothenberg, *Thousand-Mile Song*, pp. 14–15.

45 Ibid., p. 6.

46 Roger Payne and Scott McVay, 'Songs of Humpback Whales: Humpbacks emit sounds in long, predictable patterns ranging over frequencies audible to humans', *Science* 173/3997 (1971), pp. 585–97.

47 Katharine Payne and Roger Payne, 'Large Scale Changes over 19 years in Songs of Humpback Whales in Bermuda', *Zeitschrift für Tierpsychologie* 68 (1985), pp. 89–114.

48 Salvatore Cerchio, Jeff Jacobsen and Thomas Norris, 'Temporal and geographical variation in songs of humpback whales, *Megaptera novaeangliae*: synchronous change in Hawaiian and Mexican breeding assemblages', *Animal Behaviour* 62 (2001), pp. 313–29.

49 Eduardo Mercado, 'The Sonar Model for Humpback Whale Song Revised', *Frontiers in Psychology* 9/1156 (2018), pp. 1–20.

50 Payne and Payne, Large Scale Changes', p. 110.

51 https://www.youtube.com/watch?v=p-7QrQocbpg&t=1116s

52 Cerchio et al., 'Temporal and geographical variation', p. 318.

53 Katherine Payne, Peter Tyack and Roger Payne, 'Progressive changes in the songs of humpback whales (*Megaptera novaeangliae*): A detailed analysis of two seasons in Hawaii', in Roger Payne (ed.), *Communication and Behavior of Whales* (Boulder: Westview Press, 1983), pp. 9–57.

54 Mark Evan Bonds, *A History of Music in Western Culture* (Upper Saddle River, NJ: Prentice Hall, 2009), p. 43.

55 Charles Darwin, *The Descent of Man: And Selection in Relation to Sex* (London: John Murray, 1871), p. 332.

56 Dietmar Todt, Philipp Goedeking and David Symmes (eds), *Primate Vocal Communication* (Berlin: Springer Verlag, 1988).

57 Björn Merker, Iain Morley and Willem Zuidema, 'Five Fundamental Constraints on Theories of the Origins of Music', in Honing (ed.), *Origins of Musicality*, pp. 49–80 (p. 66).

58 Thomas Geissmann, 'Inheritance of song parameters in the gibbon song, analysed in two hybrid gibbons (*Hylobates pileatus x Hylobates lar*)', *Folia Primatologica* 42 (1984), pp. 216–35.

59 Bruce Richman, 'Rhythm and Melody in Gelada Vocal Exchanges', *Primates* 28/2 (1987), pp. 199–223.

60 Robert Seyfarth, Dorothy Cheney and Peter Marler, 'Monkey Responses to Three Different Alarm Calls: Evidence of Predator Classification and Semantic Communication', *Science* 210 (1980), pp. 801–3.

61 Ray Jackendoff, *Foundations of Language: Brain, Meaning, Grammar, Evolution* (New York: Oxford University Press, 2002).

62 Frans de Waal, *Are We Smart Enough to Know How Smart Animals Are?* (London: Granta, 2017), p. 119.

63 Yuko Hattori, Masaki Tomonaga and Tetsuro Matsuzawa, 'Spontaneous synchronized tapping to an auditory rhythm in a chimpanzee', *Scientific Reports* 3/1566 (2013), pp. 1–6.

64 Josep Call and Michael Tomasello (eds), *The Gestural Communication of Apes and Monkeys* (New York: Lawrence Erlbaum Associates, 2007), p. 208.

65 de Waal, *Are We Smart Enough*, p. 112.

66 Call and Tomasello, *Gestural Communication*, p. 22.

67 Ibid., p. 36.

68 Ibid., pp. 221–30; Michael Tomasello, *Origins of Human Communication* (Cambridge, Mass.: MIT Press, 2008).

69 Clive Catchpole and Peter Slater, *Bird Song: Biological Themes and Variations* (Cambridge: Cambridge University Press, 1995), p. 220.

70 Nigel Mann, Kimberly Dingess and P. J. B. Slater, 'Antiphonal four-part synchronized chorusing in a neotropical wren', *Biology Letters* 2 (2006), pp. 1–4.

71 Koelsch, *Good Vibrations*.

72 Payne et al., 'Progressive changes', p. 52.

73 Ibid., p. 54.

Chapter 10

1   Steven Pinker, *How the Mind Works* (New York: Norton & Norton, 2009), p. 534.

2   Hajime Yamauchi, Terrence Deacon and Kazuo Okanoya, 'The myth surrounding the ban by *Société de linguistique de Paris*', in Thomas Scott-Phillips *et al* (eds.), *The Evolution of Language* (Singapore: World Scientific Publishing, 2012), pp. 569–70.

3   W. Tecumseh Fitch, 'The Biology and Evolution of Speech: A Comparative Analysis', *Annual Review of Linguistics* 4 (2018), pp. 255–79.

4   Burkhard Maess, Stefan Koelsch, Thomas Gunter and Angela Friederici, 'Musical syntax is processed in Broca's area: an MEG study', *Nature Neuroscience* 4/5 (2001), pp. 540–5.

5   Dean Falk, 'Cerebral cortices of East African early hominids', *Science* 221 (1983), pp. 1072–4.

6   Alison Wray, 'Protolanguage as a holistic system for social interaction', *Language and Communication* 18 (1998), pp. 47–67; Ray Jackendoff, *Foundations of Language: Brain, Meaning, Grammar, Evolution* (New York: Oxford University Press, 2002).

7   Jean-Jacques Rousseau, *Essay on the Origin of Languages and Writings Related to Music*, trans. and ed. John Scott (Hanover: The University Press of New England, 1998).

8   For an excellent summary, see Iain Morley, 'A multi-disciplinary approach to the origins of music: perspectives from anthropology, archaeology, cognition and behaviour', *Journal of Anthropological Sciences* 92 (2014), pp. 147–77.

9   Robin Dunbar, Clive Gamble and John Gowlett (eds), *Lucy to Language: The Benchmark Papers* (Oxford: Oxford University Press, 2014).

10 Matz Larsson, 'Self-generated sounds of locomotion and ventilation and the evolution of human rhythmic abilities', *Animal Cognition* 17 (2014), pp. 1–14.

11 Aniruddh Patel and John Iversen, 'The evolutionary neuroscience of musical beat perception: the Action Simulation for Auditory Prediction

(ASAP) hypothesis', *Frontiers in Systems Neuroscience* 8/57 (2014), pp. 1–14 (p. 4).

12 Terrence Deacon, *The Symbolic Species: The Co-evolution of Language and the Brain* (New York: W. W. Norton & Co., 1998), pp. 247–53.

13 Fitch, 'Biology and Evolution of Speech', p. 268.

14 Michael Tomasello, *Origins of Human Communication* (Cambridge, Mass.: MIT Press, 2008), pp. 227–8.

15 Robin Dunbar, *Grooming, Gossip, and the Evolution of Language* (Cambridge, Mass.: Harvard University Press, 1998).

16 Bryan Mark, 'Quaternary glaciation in Africa: Key chronological and climactic implications', *Journal of Quaternary Science* 23/6–7 (2008), pp. 589–608; Lisa Cashmore, 'Human Evolution in the Quaternary', in Scott Elias and Cary Mock (eds), *Encyclopedia of Quaternary Science* (New York: Elsevier, 2013), pp. 135–45.

17 Rosalia Gallotti and Margherita Mussi (eds), *The Emergence of the Acheulean in East Africa and Beyond* (New York: Springer 2018).

18 Gregory Currie, 'The Master of the Masek Beds: Handaxes, Art, and the Minds of Early Humans', in Elisabeth Schellkens and Peter Goldie (eds), *The Aesthetic Mind: Philosophy and Psychology* (New York: Oxford University Press, 2011).

19 Tomasello, *Origins of Human Communication*.

20 Tim Ingold, 'The temporality of the landscape', *World Archaeology* 25 (1993), pp. 152–73.

21 André Leroi-Gourhan, *Gesture and Speech* (Cambridge, Mass.: MIT Press, 1993).

22 See for instance https://www.youtube.com/watch?v=LnmUYIOzRFw

23 Clive Gamble, *The Palaeolithic Societies of Europe* (Cambridge: Cambridge University Press, 1999), pp. 80–4.

24 Merlin Donald, *Origins of the Modern Mind: Three Stages in the Evolution of Culture and Cognition* (Cambridge, Mass.: Harvard University Press, 1991), pp. 182–6.

25 Thomas Suddendorf and Michael Whiten, 'The evolution of foresight: What is mental time travel and is it unique to humans?', *Behavioral and Brain Sciences* 30 (2007), pp. 299–351.

26 Gary Tomlinson, *A Million Years of Music: The Emergence of Human Modernity* (New York: Zone Books, 2015), p. 82.

27 Gamble, *Palaeolithic Societies of Europe*, p. 41; Tomlinson, *A Million Years of Music*, pp. 60–1.

28 Gamble, *Palaeolithic Societies of Europe*, p. 97.

29 W. Tecumseh Fitch, 'Fossil cues to the evolution of speech', in Rudolf Botha and Chris Knight (eds), *The Cradle of Language* (New York: Oxford University Press, 2009), pp. 112–34.

30 Roland Frey and Tobias Riede, 'Sexual dimorphism of the larynx of the Mongolian gazelle (*Procapra gutturosa* Pallas, 1777) (Mammalia, Artiodactyla, Bovidae)', *Zoologischer Anzeiger – A Journal of Comparative Zoology* 242 (2003), pp. 33–62.

31 Ignacio Martínez et al., 'Human hyoid bones from the middle Pleistocene site of the Sima de los Huesos (Sierra de Atapuerca, Spain)', *Journal of Human Evolution* 54 (2008), pp. 118–24 (p. 124).

32 Zeresenay Alemeseged et al., 'A juvenile early hominin skeleton from Dikika, Ethiopia', *Nature* 443 (2006), pp. 296–301.

33 Fitch, 'Fossil cues to the evolution of speech', p. 127.

34 Gamble, *Palaeolithic Societies of Europe*, pp. 94–7.

35 Clive Gamble, 'When the Words Dry Up: Music and Material Metaphors Half a Million Years ago', in Nicholas Bannan (ed.), *Music, Language, and Human Evolution* (New York: Oxford University Press, 2012), pp. 81–108.

36 Tomlinson, *A Million Years of Music*, pp. 106–12.

37 Robbins Burling, *The Talking Ape: How Language Evolved* (New York: Oxford University Press, 2005).

38 Kazuo Okanoya, 'The Bengalese Finch: A window on the behavioral neurobiology of birdsong syntax', *Annals of the New York Academy of Sciences* 1016 (2004), pp. 724–35.

39 Tomasello, *Origins of Human Communication*, p. 219.

40 Daniel Goldmark, *Tunes for 'Toons: Music and the Hollywood Cartoon* (Berkeley: University of California Press, 2005), pp. 44–76.

41 All this happens in *Dog Trouble*, a 1942 one-reel short.

42 Gamble, *Palaeolithic Societies of Europe*, p. 236.

43 Steven Mithen, *The Singing Neanderthals: The Origins of Music, Language, Mind and Body* (Cambridge, Mass.: Harvard University Press, 2005).

44 Ibid., p. 171.

45 Johannes Krause et al., 'The derived FOXP2 variant of modern humans was shared with Neandertals', *Current Biology* 17 (2007), pp. 1908–12.

46 Tomislav Maricic et al., 'A recent evolutionary change affects a regulatory element in the FOXP2 gene', *Molecular Biology and Evolution* 4 (2012), pp. 844–52.

47 Jackendoff, *Foundations of Language*.

48 Tomlinson, *A Million Years of Music*, p. 155.

49 Jackendoff, *Foundations of Language*, p. 243.

50 Thomas Wynn and Frederick Coolidge, *How To Think Like a Neandertal* (New York: Oxford University Press, 2012), p. 54.

51 Tomlinson, *A Million Years of Music*, p. 160.

52 Francesco d'Errico et al., 'Archaeological Evidence for the Emergence of Language, Symbolism, and Music – An Alternative Multidisciplinary Perspective', *Journal of World Prehistory* 17 (2003), pp. 1–70.

53 John Shea, 'Homo sapiens Is as Homo sapiens Was: Behavioral Variability versus "Behavioral Modernity" in Paleolithic Archaeology', *Current Anthropology* 52/1 (2011), pp. 1–35.

54 Mithen, *Singing Neanderthals*, pp. 250–2.

55 Steven Mithen, 'The Cathedral Model for the Evolution of Human Cognition', in Gary Hatfield and Holly Pittman (eds), *Evolution of Mind, Brain, and Culture* (Philadelphia: University of Pennsylvania Press, 2013), pp. 217–33.

56 Gamble, *Palaeolithic Societies of Europe*, p. 356.

57 Ibid., p. 54.

58 d'Errico et al., 'Emergence of Language, Symbolism, and Music', p. 45.

59 Gary Tomlinson, *Culture and the Course of Human Evolution* (Chicago: The University of Chicago Press, 2018), p. 43. Jean-Baptiste Lamarck (1744–1829) was a French naturalist. His idea that organisms passed on their traits to their descendants was superseded by Darwinism.

60 Mithen, 'Cathedral Model', p. 231.

61 Gamble, *Palaeolithic Societies of Europe*, p. 356.

62 Ibid., pp. 393–8.

63 Donald, *Origins of the Modern Mind*, p. 281.

64 Tomlinson, *A Million Years of Music*, p. 257.

65 Clive Gamble, *Origins and Revolutions: Human Identity in Earliest Prehistory* (Cambridge: Cambridge University Press, 2007).

66 See https://www.youtube.com/watch?v=KliLsBSo-J4

67 Leroi-Gourhan, *Gesture and Speech*, p. 313.

68 Mithen, *Singing Neanderthals*, pp. 265–6.

69 Cynthia Moss, *Elephant Memories* (Chicago: The University of Chicago Press, 2000), p. 23.

70 C. O'Connell-Rodwell, B. Arnason and L. Hart, 'Seismic properties of Asian elephant (*Elephas maximus*) vocalizations and locomotion', *Journal of the Acoustic Society of America* 108 (2000), pp. 3066–72.

71 Ian Cross, 'Music as an Emergent Exaptation', in Bannan (ed.), *Music, Language, and Human Evolution*, pp. 263–76.

72 Mithen, *Singing Neanderthals*, p. 4.

73 https://www.ft.com/content/c691c3f4-e37f-11e9-b8e0-026e07cbe5b4

Chapter 11

1 Nick Bostrom, *Superintelligence: Paths, Dangers, Strategies* (New York: Oxford University Press, 2014); Max Tegmark, *Life 3.0: Being Human in the Age of Artificial Intelligence* (New York: Vintage, 2017).

2 Christine Lee Gengaro, *Listening to Stanley Kubrick: The Music in His Films* (Plymouth: The Scarecrow Press, 2013), p. 98.

3 HAL to Homer: 'Don't take out my British charm unit! Without that I'm a boorish American clod.' https://www.youtube.com/watch?v=KliLsBS0-J4

4 Georgina Born and Christopher Haworth, 'From Microsound to Vaporwave: Internet-Mediated Musics, Online Methods, and Genre', *Music and Letters* 98/4 (2017), pp. 601–47.

5 Dennis Des Chene, *Spirits and Clocks: Machine and Organism in Descartes* (Ithaca: Cornell University Press, 2001).

6 https://www.youtube.com/watch?v=A0-AD3bFjF8

7 Robert Ranisch and Stefan Sorgner, *Post- and Transhumanism: An Introduction* (Bern: Peter Lang, 2014).

8 Edward O. Wilson, *The Origins of Creativity* (London: Penguin, 2017), p. 62.

9 Michael Smotherman, Mirjam Knörnschild, Grace Smarsh and Kirsten Bohn, 'The origins and diversity of bat songs', *Journal of Comparative Physiology* 202/8 (2016), pp. 535–54 (p. 543).

10 Peter Godfrey-Smith, *Other Minds: The Octopus and the Evolution of Intelligent Life* (London: William Collins, 2016).

11 https://www.digitaltrends.com/cool-tech/auxuman-ai-album/

12 'Music's Smart Future: How Will AI Impact The Music Industry?', https://www.musictank.co.uk/wp-content/uploads/2018/03/bpi-ai-report.pdf

13 https://www.theguardian.com/artanddesign/2014/may/06/neil-harbisson-worlds-first-cyborg-artist

14 https://www.abeautiful.world/stories/james-wannerton-synesthesia/

15 Nicole Santos and Maria Pulido, 'Investigation of Sound-Gustatory Synesthesia in a Coffeehouse Setting', in Muthu Ramachandran et al (eds.), 4th International Conference on Internet of Things, Big Data and Security (Scitepress Digital Library, 2019). https://www.academia.edu/39705707/Investigation_of_Sound-Gustatory_Synesthesia_in_a_Coffeehouse_Setting

16 http://www.generativemusic.com/bloom.html

17 https://ask.audio/articles/5-interesting-features-that-make-reason-an-excellent-daw-to-use

18 Nick Prior, *Popular Music Digital Technology and Society* (London: SAGE, 2018).

19 Nicholas Cook, Monique Ingalls and David Trippett (eds), *The Cambridge Companion to Music in Digital Culture* (Cambridge: Cambridge University Press, 2019).

20 Margaret Boden, *The Creative Mind: Myths and Mechanisms* (London: Routledge, 2004), p. 51.

21 Donald, *Origins of the Modern Mind*, p. 355.

22 Aram Sinnreich, *Mashed Up: Music, Technology, and the Rise of Configurable Culture* (Amherst: University of Massachusetts Press, 2010), pp. 71–3.

23 Ross Duffin, *How Equal Temperament Ruined Harmony (and Why You Should Care)* (New York: W. W. Norton & Co., 2007).

24 https://producelikeapro.com/blog/getting-started-making-microtonal-music/

25 https://slate.com/technology/2018/09/apple-spotify-streaming-david-turner-if-then-transcript.html

26 https://www.izotope.com/en/learn/6-music-production-techniques-to-hook-listeners-in-30-seconds-or-less.html

27 Robert Colvile, *The Great Acceleration: How the World is Getting Faster, Faster* (London: Bloomsbury, 2016).

28 Carol Vernallis, 'Accelerated Aesthetics: A New Lexicon of Time, Space, and Rhythm', in Carol Vernallis, Amy Herzog and John Richardson (eds), *The Oxford Handbook of Sound and Image in Digital Media* (New York: Oxford University Press, 2013), pp. 707–32.

29 Herman Rechberger, *Scales and Modes Around the World* (Helsinki: Fennica Gehrman Ltd., 2018).

30 Charles Duhigg, *The Power of Habit: Why We Do What We Do and How to Change* (London: Random House, 2013), p. 198.

31 https://mimugloves.com/

32 https://www.theverge.com/2019/4/5/18277345/chagall-van-den-berg-performance-sensors-gloves-motion-tracking-suit

33 Cited in Prior, *Popular Music*, p. 139.

34 https://www.vg247.com/2018/11/12/japanese-man-spends-over-13k-on-wedding-to-marry-virtual-teen-idol-hatsune-miku/

35 Bostrom, *Superintelligence*.

36 https://ucresearch.tumblr.com/post/44638071781/artandsciencejournal-the-science-of-music-and

37 Cited in Marcus du Sautoy, *The Creativity Code: How AI is Learning to Write, Paint and Think* (London; 4th Estate, 2019), p. 6.

38 http://artsites.ucsc.edu/faculty/cope/Emily-howell.htm

39 Douglas Hofstadter, 'Staring EMI Straight in the Eye – and Doing My Best Not to Flinch', in David Cope, *Virtual Music: Computer Synthesis of Musical Style* (Cambridge, MA: MIT Press, 2001), pp. 33–82.

40 Jose David Fernández and Francisco Vico, 'AI Methods in Algorithmic Composition: A Comprehensive Survey', *Journal of Artificial Intelligence* 48 (2013), pp. 513–82 (p. 526).

41 You can hear it on https://www.youtube.com/watch?v=bD7l4Kg1Rt8

42 https://www.theguardian.com/music/2012/jul/01/iamus-hello-world-review

43 https://www.youtube.com/watch?v=wYb3Wimno1s

44 https://consumer.huawei.com/uk/campaign/unfinishedsymphony/

45 https://www.standard.co.uk/tech/jukedeck-maching-learning-ai-startup-music-a3779296.html

46 https://www.newsweek.com/artificial-intelligence-changing-music-799794

47 Yuval Harari, *Homo Deus: A Brief History of Tomorrow* (New York: Vintage, 2017), p. 20.

48 https://www.digitaltrends.com/music/ibm-watson-beat-ai-music-composer-phony-ppl/

49 du Sautoy, *Creativity Code*.

50 Nick Collins, ' "… There is no reason why it should ever stop": Large-scale algorithmic composition', *Journal of Creative Music Systems* 3/1 (2018), DOI: https://doi.org/10.5920/jcms.525

51 du Sautoy, *Creativity Code*.

52 https://ai.googleblog.com/2015/06/inceptionism-going-deeper-into-neural.html

53 https://gizmodo.com/someone-finally-turned-googles-deepdream-code-into-a-si-1719461004

54 The tale is told in Denis Dutton, *The Art Instinct* (New York: Oxford University Press, 2010), pp. 13–28.

55 https://www.wired.com/2008/05/survey-produced/

56 Audio engineers talk of the 'rainbow' of noise types purely metaphorically, with no real visual import, on the basis that both sound and light waves have a spectrum. Hence 'white' noise, familiar from tape hiss, mixes all the frequencies. 'Pink' noise is louder on the bass. 'Brown' noise, which takes its name from the random 'Brownian Motion' of particles in a liquid, has an even deeper sound. 'Blue' noise is the opposite, with all its energy concentrated at the top of the sound spectrum. 'Violet' noise is even higher than 'blue'. 'Grey' noise is calibrated to be balanced at every frequency. 'Green' noise is strongest in its middle frequencies. 'Orange' noise is the most out of tune. And 'black' noise, as one might imagine, is the

colour of silence. https://www.theatlantic.com/science/archive/2016/02/white-noise-sound-colors/462972/

57 Junhong Zhou et al., 'Pink noise: Effect on complexity synchronization of brain activity and sleep consolidation', *Journal of Theoretical Biology* 306 (2012), pp. 68–72. See also https://health.clevelandclinic.org/why-pink-noise-might-just-help-you-get-a-better-nights-sleep/

58 Fernández and Vico, 'AI Methods in Algorithmic Composition', p. 55.

59 According to Levitin and his team: 'Neurons in [our] primary visual cortex were found to exhibit higher gain, and the spike responses exhibit higher coding efficiency and informational transmission rates for 1/f signals.' Looking for 1/f relationships in Western rhythm (in 1,788 movements from 558 compositions), Levitin's team found that Beethoven's rhythms tend towards the regular pole; Mozart's towards the unpredictable. See Daniel Levitin, Parag Chordia and Vinod Menon, 'Musical rhythm spectra from Bach to Joplin obey a 1/f power law', *Proceedings of the National Academy of Sciences of the United States of America* 109/10 (2011), pp. 3716–20 (p. 3716).

60 Martin Gardner, 'White, Brown, and Fractal Music', in his *Fractal Music, Hypercards and More Mathematical Recreations from SCIENTIFIC AMERICAN Magazine* (New York: W. H. Freeman and Company, 1992), pp. 1–23.

61 Philip Ball, *Patterns in Nature: Why the Natural World Looks the Way it Does* (Chicago: The University of Chicago Press, 2016).

62 Gabriel Pareyon, *On Musical Self-Similarity: Intersemiosis as Synecdoche and Analogy* (Imatra: International Semiotics Institute, 2011).

63 Benjamin Ayotte and Benjamin McKay Ayotte, *Heinrich Schenker: A Guide to Research* (London: Routledge, 2004).

64 Arnold Schoenberg, *The Musical Idea and the Logic, Technique and Art of Its Presentation* (Bloomington: Indiana University Press, 2006).

65 For example Rolf Bader, 'Fractal dimension analysis of complexity in Ligeti's piano pieces', *The Journal of the Acoustical Society of America* 117/4 (2005), p. 2477.

66 Fernández and Vico, 'AI Methods in Algorithmic Composition', p. 557.

67 https://www.samwoolfe.com/2014/03/could-universe-be-fractal.html

Chapter 12

1 Yuk Hui, *Recursivity and Contingency* (Lanham, Maryland: Rowman & Littlefield International, 2019).

2 As I mentioned in Chapter 1, Ernst Haeckel's discredited theory that ontogeny 'recapitulates' phylogeny, that the gestation of the human

embryo echoes the stages of evolution, has sprung back to life in the most recent work in the psychology of musical emotion. The brains of human embryos acquire emotional sensitivity in the same order as animal evolution. Haeckel's idea also survives in the new science of 'evo-devo', short for evolutionary developmental biology. By tracing embryonic development at the genetic and molecular level, biologists can draw ancestral relationships between humans and animals much more plausibly because they have sharper tools than Haeckel.

3 https://quoteinvestigator.com/2010/11/08/writing-about-music/

4 Steven Brown, 'Contagious heterophony: A new theory about the origins of music', *Musicae Scientiae* 11/1 (2007), pp. 3–26.

5 Arnie Cox, *Music and Embodied Cognition: Listening, Moving, Feeling, and Thinking* (Bloomington: Indiana University Press, 2016).

6 W. Tecumseh Fitch, 'The Biology and Evolution of Speech: A Comparative Analysis', *Annual Review of Linguistics* 4/1 (2018), pp. 255–79.

7 Immanuel Kant, *Critique of Judgement*, ed. and trans. James Creed Meredith (Oxford: Oxford University Press, 1911), p. 89.

8 John Shea, '*Homo sapiens* Is as *Homo sapiens* Was: Behavioral Variability versus "Behavioral Modernity" in Paleolithic Archaeology', *Current Anthropology* 52/1 (2011), pp. 1–35.

9 Richard Potts, 'Variability Selection in Hominid Evolution', *Evolutionary Anthropology* 7/3 (1998), pp. 81–96.

10 Terrence Deacon, *The Symbolic Species: The Co-evolution of Language and the Brain* (New York: W. W. Norton & Co., 1998).

11 Gary Tomlinson, *A Million Years of Music: The Emergence of Human Modernity* (New York: Zone Books, 2015).

12 Terrence Deacon, 'Beyond the Symbolic Species', in Theresa Schilhab, Frederik Stjernfelt and Terrence Deacon (eds), *The Symbolic Species Evolved* (New York: Springer, 2012), pp. 9–38 (p. 36).

13 Keynote lecture delivered at the CityMAC music analysis conference, July 2018. I'm grateful to Professor Widdess for sharing his text with me. The name of these birds is misleading, however, as Bengalese finches originated in Japan.

14 Merlin Donald, *Origins of the Modern Mind: Three Stages in the Evolution of Culture and Cognition* (Cambridge, Mass.: Harvard University Press, 1991).

15 Jonathan Gottschall, *The Storytelling Animal: How Stories Make Us Human* (Boston: Mariner Books, 2013).

16 Steven Feld, *Sound and Sentiment: Birds, Weeping, Poetics, and Song in Kaluli Expression* (Philadelphia: University of Pennsylvania Press, 1982).

17 Gary Tomlinson, *Culture and the Course of Human Evolution* (Chicago: The University of Chicago Press, 2018).

18 Elizabeth Margulis et al., 'Selective Neurophysiologic Responses to Music in Instrumentalists with Different Listening Biographies', *Human Brain Mapping* 30 (2009), 267–75 (p. 273).

19 Shea, '*Homo sapiens* Is as *Homo sapiens* Was'.

20 Carl Sagan et al., *Murmurs of Earth: The Voyager Interstellar Record* (New York: Ballantine Books, 1978), p. 21.

21 Ibid., p. 203.

22 Michael Spitzer, *Metaphor and Musical Thought* (Chicago: The University of Chicago Press, 2004), p. 141.

23 Plato, *Timaeus and Critias*, trans. Benjamin Jowett (Digireads.com Book), p. 28.

24 Cited in Andrew Hicks, *Composing the World: Harmony in the Medieval Platonic Cosmos* (New York: Oxford University Press, 2017), p. 41.

25 Roberto Bolaño, *2666*, trans. Natasha Wimmer (New York: Picador, 2009).

26 Jared Diamond, *Guns, Germs, and Steel* (New York: Vintage, 1998).

27 Vanessa Agnew, *Enlightenment Orpheus: The Power of Music in Other Worlds* (New York: Oxford University Press, 2008).

28 Ibid., pp. 98–9.

29 Ibid., pp. 105–8.

30 https://www.youtube.com/watch?v=AGdf6jdRNeI

31 Qingfan Jiang, 'Western Music in China and the Construction of a World History', Paper given at SotonMAC Music Analysis Conference, July 2019.

32 Jean-Jacques Rousseau, *The Social Contract and Discourses*, trans. Anthony Uyl (Woodstock, Ontario: Devoted Publishing, 2016), p. 23.

33 Julia Simon, *Rousseau Among the Moderns: Music, Aesthetics, Politics* (Philadelphia: Pennsylvania State University Press, 2013).

34 Stephen Rumph, *Mozart and Enlightenment Semiotics* (Berkeley, California: University of California Press, 2012), pp. 21–5.

35 Cited in Tom Regan, *The Case for Animal Rights* (Berkeley, California: University of California Press, 2004), p. 177.

36 https://www.independent.co.uk/news/the-pragmatic-entertainer-who-said-the-unsayable-1578974.html

37 Kant, *Critique of Judgement*.

38 Ruth Solie, 'The Living Work: Organicism and Musical Analysis', *19th-Century Music* 4/2 (1980), pp. 147–56.

39 Georg Wilhelm Friedrich Hegel, *Phenomenology of Spirit*, trans. Terry Pinkard (Cambridge: Cambridge University Press, 2018).

40 Victor Turner, 'Social Dramas and Ritual Metaphors', in Richard Schechner and Mady Schuman (eds), *Ritual, Play, and Performance: Readings in the Social Sciences/Theatre* (New York: Seabury Press, 1976), p. 114.

41 Michael Tenzer, *Balinese Gamelan Music* (Clarendon, Vermont: Tuttle Publishing, 2011).

42 Judith Becker, *Deep Listeners: Music, Emotion, and Trancing* (Bloomington: Indiana University Press, 2004), pp. 82–6.

43 Ibid., p. 83.

44 Xóchitl Tafoya, 'Ritualizing Barong and Rangda: Repercussions of a Collaborative Field Experience in Kerambitan, Bali', p. 30, https://drum.lib.umd.edu/handle/1903/9455

45 https://www.southbankcentre.co.uk/about/get-involved/schools/gamelan-schools-programme

46 Marcel Proust, *Finding Time Again*, trans. Ian Patterson (New York: Penguin, 2003), p. 358.

47 Lydia Goehr, *The Imaginary Museum of Musical Works: An Essay in the Philosophy of Music* (Oxford: Clarendon Press, 1992).

48 Saint Augustine, *The Confessions of Saint Augustine* (JKL Classics Publishers, 2017), p. 156.

49 Carlo Rovelli, *Seven Brief Lessons on Physics*, trans. Simon Carnell and Erica Segre (New York: Penguin, 2015), p. 50.

50 F. Scott Fitzgerald, *The Great Gatsby* (New York: Scribner, 2004), p. 180.

51 Martin Heidegger, *Being and Time*, trans. John Macquarrie and Edward Robinson (London: SCM Press, 1962), p. 68.

52 Lucretius, *Of the Nature of Things* (*De rerum natura*), trans. Thomas Creech (Oxford, 1714), pp. 584–5.

53 Adriaen Coenen, *The Whale Book* (London: Reaktion Books, 2003), p. 90.

54 Roger Payne, *Among Whales* (New York: Pocket Books, 1995), p. 160.

55 Paul Crowther, *The Kantian Sublime: From Morality to Art* (Oxford: Oxford University Press, 1989).

INDEX

PICTURE CREDITS

1.1   © NASA Photo/Alamy Stock
1.2   © Frans Schellekens/Redferns/Getty Images
1.3   © Volkmar Heinz/dpa-Zentralbild/ZB/dpa/Alamy Live News
2.1   © Nndoweni Malala
2.2   © Ryan Lothian
3.1   © The Sound of the Next Generation report, Youth Music
3.2   © Punch Cartoon Library/TopFoto
3.3   © Johannes Simon/Getty Images
3.4   © AKG-images
4.1   © Library Book Collection/Alamy Stock Photo
4.2   © BSIP/UIG Via Getty Images
4.3   © Alpha Stock/Alamy Stock Photo
4.5   © Bridgeman Images
5.1   © SASCHA SCHUERMANN/DDP/AFP via Getty Images
5.2   © imageBROKER/Alamy Stock Photo
5.3   © Richard Dumbrill
5.4   © Depo Photos/ABACA/PA Images
5.5   © Getty Images
5.6   © DEA/G. DAGLI ORTI/De Agostini via Getty Images
6.1   © Pap. Turin Cat. 2031/001=CGT 55001, photo by Nicola
        Dell'Acquila and Federico Taverni/Museo Egizio
6.2   © agefotostock/Alamy Stock Photo
6.3   © Steve Tinney, from 'Old Babylonian Music Instruction
        Texts'
6.4   © Heritage Image Partnership Ltd/Alamy Stock Photo

7.1	© CPA Media Pte Ltd/Alamy Stock Photo
7,2	© Science History Images/Alamy Stock Photo
7.3	© Ian Littlewood/Alamy Stock Photo
7.4	© Bai Yunli
7.5	© Sovfoto/UIG/Bridgeman Images
8.1	© Walter Mignolo/Duke University Press
8.2	© Bridgeman Images
8.3	© Mondadori Portfolio via Getty Images
8,4	© Du Jun Min
8.5	© CFM
9.1	© Universal Music/Roger Payne
9.2	© Henrike Hultsch
9.3	© Nicolle R. Fuller/Science Photo Library
9.4	© Roger Payne
10.1	© Staab Studios Inc.
10.2.1	© World Museum of Man
10.2 2	© The Natural History Museum/Alamy Stock Photo
10.2. 3	CC0 1.0 Gary Todd.
10.2.4.	© The Metropolitan Museum of Art, New York/Gift of Garrett C. Pier, 1908
10.3	© Bridgeman Images
11.3	© CHRISTOPHE ARCHAMBAULT/AFP via Getty Images
11.4	CC0 1.0 Martin Thoma
11.5	© Komar & Melamid photo by Robert Lachman/Los Angeles Times via Getty Images
12.2	© GRANT ROONEY PREMIUM /Alamy Stock Photo

ACKNOWLEDGEMENTS

Although I wrote this book fairly quickly – surely the best way to do a world history of anything – this could only have happened because of decades of conversations with friends, colleagues, and students, far too many to name. I'll pick out for special mention Keith Howard, my ethnomusicological sounding board, and Richard Worth, an all-round musician and scholar. When I test-drove the book in Berlin in 2019, Professor Christian Thorau saved me by gently suggesting that I had got the argument upside down. Nor could have I have written my book without the support of the University of Liverpool and my Music Department, for which I'm truly grateful. I owe a tremendous debt to my agent, Jonathan Gregory, who approached me after reading something I wrote in The Conversation about being a tone-deaf music professor. The piece still makes me laugh, and you can find it here: https://theconversation.com/confessions-of-a-tone-deaf-music-professor-58536

Anyway, Jonathan read every chapter as I completed it, and gave me golden feed-back. I owe enormous gratitude also to my editor Michael Fishwick for his continuing faith and incredible encouragement. Thanks to the team at Bloomsbury: Lauren Whybrow, Lilidh Kendrick, Catherine Best, Kate Quarry, Genista Tate-Alexander, Anna Massardi, and Jonathan Leech. Lauren, my Production Manager, made my experience miraculously free of stress and worry. And most of all, a big hug for my wonderful and very tolerant family, my Three Graces: Karen, my wife, and our daughters Emily and Kiera. During the two years I wrote The Musical Human, they watched bemused as hundreds of books piled up around my armchair in the living room. In the annals of ethnomusicology, there is no more fearsome bogeyman than the Armchair Anthropologist, someone who sits and thinks rather than getting their hands dirty in fieldwork. Well, here's to my armchair.

A NOTE ON THE AUTHOR

Michael Spitzer is Professor of Music at the University of Liverpool. He was born in Nigeria of Hungarian parents, brought up in Israel, and emigrated to the UK during the Yom Kippur war in 1973. He was educated at Merton College, Oxford and Southampton, and taught for twenty years at Durham University. An accomplished pianist, Spitzer is a world-leading authority on Beethoven, but he also writes widely on the philosophy and psychology of music. He lives just off Penny Lane with his wife and two daughters.

A NOTE ON THE TYPE

The text of this book is set Adobe Garamond. It is one of several versions of Garamond based on the designs of Claude Garamond. It is thought that Garamond based his font on Bembo, cut in 1495 by Francesco Griffo in collaboration with the Italian printer Aldus Manutius. Garamond types were first used in books printed in Paris around 1532. Many of the present-day versions of this type are based on the *Typi Academiae* of Jean Jannon cut in Sedan in 1615.

Claude Garamond was born in Paris in 1480. He learned how to cut type from his father and by the age of fifteen he was able to fashion steel punches the size of a pica with great precision. At the age of sixty he was commissioned by King Francis I to design a Greek alphabet, and for this he was given the honourable title of royal type founder. He died in 1561.